P9-DGQ-080

NEW ZEALAND

www.marco-polo.com

Top Destinations

There's a lot to see at the most beautiful end of the world. But even if you have enough time, make some choices beforehand. This list of top destinations will make your choice of holiday destinations easier.

NORTH ISLAND

❶ ✶✶ Bay of Islands
More than 150 small green islands are scattered through this idyllic bay north of Auckland.
page 190

❷ ✶✶ Dargaville Kauri Coast
New Zealand's most beautiful kauri giants tell their story.
page 211

❸ ✶✶ Auckland
The former capital city has a cosmopolitan flair.
page 169

❹ ✶✶ Rotorua
The volcanic area and its geysers are nothing for sensitive noses.
page 252

❺ ✶✶ Te Kuiti Waitomo Caves
False glow worms illuminate the drip stone caves.
page 275

❻ ✶✶ Tongariro National Park
The volcanic landscape is on the World Natural Heritage list.
page 277

❼ ✶✶ Taupo Wairakei
New Zealand's largest interior body of water is a paradise for anglers.
page 265

❽ ✶✶ Napier
A one-of-a-kind Art deco city in this part of the world
page 241

❾ ✶✶ Whanganui NP
The jungle-like bush land offers great hiking.
page 308

Do You Feel Like...

... a somewhat different New Zealand? Whether it's animals, artistic Maori houses or beautiful beaches – you'll be amazed.

UNIQUE ANIMALS

* **Whales & dolphins** ▶
  In Kaikoura along with seals there are dolphins and sperm whales to see. Popular tourist attraction: swimming with dolphins.
  page 325
* **Penguins**
  Blue penguins and yellow-eyed penguins cavort along the Oamuru coast. There is a breeding station.
  page 106
* **Albatrosses**
  The only mainland breeding colony for southern royal albatrosses is located at the northern point of Otago Peninsula (Taiaroa Head).
  page 354

UNIQUE BUILDINGS

* **Napier**
  After a severe earthquake Napier was rebuilt in American Art deco style.
  page 241
* ◀ **Wellington & Auckland**
  For fans of modern architecture: government building in Wellington (ill.) and Auckland's skyline **page 290 & 169**
* **Larnach Castle**
  The only castle in New Zealand is located near Dunedin; it has an extravagant mixture of styles with Gothic and Victorian elements.
  page 353

FABULOUS BEACHES

More than 60 million sheep graze in New Zealand

TOURS

SIGHTS FROM A TO Z

PRICE CATEGORIES
Restaurants (main dish)
££££ = over NZ$25
£££ = up to NZ$50
££ = up to NZ$35
£ = up to NZ$25
Hotels (double room)
££££ = over NZ$300
£££ = up to NZ$300
££ = up to NZ$200
£ = up to NZ$100

Note
Billable service telephone numbers are marked with an asterisk: *0800...

PRACTICAL INFORMATION

Near Queenstown:
test your courage

BACKGROUND

For some a real chore, for others the thrill of anticipation: visitors reading up on facts and figures about the destination before departure find their bearings more easily, whether in politics, economy or the natural world.

Facts

Nature and Environment

Why is New Zealand's most famous animal, the kiwi, never seen during the daytime? How do the Maori respect their ancestors? Is gold still excavated in New Zealand today? And who was Abel Tasman anyway, after whom so much is named in New Zealand now?

Even though New Zealand is not a continent, but rather consists of two islands, it still has an **unusual variety of landscapes**. The two islands could not be any more different. North Island is strongly characterized by volcanic appearances of all kinds. Individual volcanos are as high as 1900m/1140ft above sea level.

Volcanic peak in the north

On South Island alpine fold mountains with several being more than 3,000m/10,000ft high as well as impressive glacial rivers dominate the scene. The climates of the two islands are also different. North Island already has a sub-tropical and also a desert-like dry climate while South Island's is colder and increasingly harsher, which of course has to do with its **proximity to Antarctica**.

Glaciers in the south

A LOOK AT GEOLOGY

The particular location of New Zealand, bordering two of the huge tectonic plates which make up the earth's crust – The Indo-Australian Plate and the Pacific Plate – gives an idea of the turbulent development of the two main islands. When the ancient supercontinent Pangaea started to break up around 200 million years ago, the result were the **large continental landmasses** of Laurasia in the North (North America, Europe, Asia) and Gondwana in the South (South America, Africa, Indian subcontinent, Antarctica, Australia).

Collision of two plates

The further disintegration of the super continents started some 150 million years ago. Gondwana broke up into the continents of South America, Africa and the Indian subcontinent. Australia, Antarctica and New Zealand were still united in one land mass. **Some 80 million years ago** New Zealand was separated from Australia and Antarctica by the formation of the Tasman Sea. So New Zealand was already isolated when Australia and Antarctica started to drift apart about 50 million years ago. A look at the globe makes clear that the edges of the Pacific Ocean are framed by mountain ranges and deep-

Divided by the Tasman Sea

World famous ever since the epic films *Lord of the Rings*: the volcanic landscape of Tongariro National Park with Mount Ruapehu

sea trenches. These are part of the unstable »circumpacific mobile belt«, a term used to describe the peripheries of the Pacific, characterised by the collision of continental and oceanic tectonic plates. Earthquakes and volcanic activity, along with the formation of mountain ranges and deep-sea trenches, are typical characteristics of this unstable belt, which is also rightly called »Ring of Fire« due to its frequent earthquakes and volcanic activity.

Earth as architect
Frequent earthquakes, numerous faultlines, volcanic activity and young fold mountains are all the result of forces born from the collision of the Indo-Australian plate with the Pacific plate. The two plates are moving both towards each other and past each other. As a consequence of these movements the Pacific plate is sliding under the Indo-Australian plate in the North Island area.

This generates **enormous differences in pressure and temperature** in the earth's crust, finding release on the surface in the form of volcanoes, geysers, thermal springs, mud pots, fumaroles (emitting volcanic gases) and solfataras (venting sulphurous gases).

Southern Alps
By contrast, in the South Island area the Pacific plate is pushing itself on top of the Indo-Australian plate. This has resulted in the continuing formation of the Southern Alps. By now, the lateral shift of the two tectonic plates along the so-called **»Alpine Fault«** line is over 450 kilometres/280 miles. The fault is clearly visible between the coeval rocks to the northwest and south of South Island.

NORTH ISLAND (TE IKA A MAUI)

Volcano Ruapehu
In the central part of North Island, visitors can hardly miss the volcanic activity. Currently standing at 2797 m/9,176-ft, the Ruapehu volcano – the highest elevation on North Island – often makes its presence known. Ruapehu forms part of a **very active volcanic zone** stretching northeast, with numerous mud holes, steam eruptions, sulphur and thermal springs. Further mighty volcanoes on North Island are the 2,287 m/7,503-ft Ngauruhoe, the 1,967 m/6,453-ft Tongariro and, pushing out to the west, the 2,518 m/8,261-ft Taranaki (Mt Egmont), an almost textbook example of a volcano.

Geysers in Rotorua
The famous **Lake Taupo crater lake** bears witness to a gigantic volcanic explosion. In the thermal area of Rotorua, bordering this lake to the north, the whole range of volcanic and post-volcanic phenomena can be studied. Alongside many smaller crater lakes, geysers and hot mud pots, there are sinter terraces dazzling with their many colours, thermal springs and steam eruptions that leave a lasting impression thanks to their **strong smell**.

Mountains, Lakes and Sea

Spring at the Mount Cook massif: while the peaks are still covered with snow, lupines bloom lower down

Hilly character North Island's central volcanic area is surrounded by **mountainous country**, lending this part of the island a rather hilly character. The area from the southern tip of North Island to the East Cape traces the extension of New Zealand's youngest range of fold mountains, which begin at the southern tip of South Island and reach their highest elevations in the Southern Alps.

Endlessly long beaches The most varied coastal formations coexist in close proximity. The »Northland« is characterised by extensive graded shorelines with miles of sandy beaches and sand dunes. Both main islands feature alluvial plains, deltas, and in some parts extremely imposing coastal cliffs.

Worthy of note are the **drowned river valleys** (»ria coasts«) to the northeast of South Island, and in particular the valleys to the southwest of South Island, which were gouged out long ago by glaciers and resemble Norwegian fjords.

The mountainous Coromandel Pensinsula to the north differs fundamentally from the other low mountain ranges on North Island. Whilst the latter mainly sit on sandstone, mudstone or limestone soils, the peninsula is **formed by volcanic material**.

Coromandel-Peninsula

Stretching north of Auckland, the so-called Northland is a subtropical and somewhat rolling **hill country**, with its highest elevations staying below 800m/2,600ft. Blessed with favourable scenery and climate, this area offers near-ideal conditions for the development of both agriculture and tourism.

Subtropical Northland

SOUTH ISLAND (TE WAHI PONAMU)

South Island is predominantly characterised by the fold mountains of the Southern Alps (Southern Alps), which are still quite young in geological terms. Rising in its centre to a height of 3,754 m/12,316ft is Aoraki/Mount Cook, **New Zealand's highest mountain**. In the immediate vicinity there are further peaks reaching 3,000m/over 10,000ft, such as Mount Tasman (3,497m/11,473ft), Mount Sefton (3,157m/10,357) and several other snow-capped mountains. The allure of this high mountain landscape is heightened by numerous glacier streams, the most spectacular being the 29 km/18-mile long Tasman Glacier, the Hooker Glacier and the Mueller Glacier. This mountainous region now enjoys special protection as »Mount Cook National Park«.

Southern Alps

Towards the west the Southern Alps drop back down to sea level within a strip measuring only 50 km/31 miles across. This kind of extreme downhill gradient across a short distance has led to the formation of the imposing glacier tongues of the Fox Glacier and the Franz Josef Glacier, reaching down to just 300 m/nearly 1,000ft in altitude. On the west coast the coastal rim along the stormy Tasman Sea, which owes its **highly varied landscape** to its cliffs, bays and coastal plains, is separated from the Southern Alps by the »Alpine Fault« geological fault zone. To the east however, the gradient of the high mountains drops more gently. Here, the many lakes lend the eastern slopes of the Southern Alps their scenic charm.

West Coast: wild seas

The north of South Island is dominated by two **low mountain landscapes**: the Tasman Mountains rising to the northwest, and what is

Marlborough Sound

Plate Tectonics

The centre of New Zealand's North Island is crossed by the so-called »Ring of Fire«, an extremely active belt characterised by earthquakes and volcanic eruption. All this geological activity is caused by the movements and collisions of the Indo-Australian and the Pacific tectonic plates. Enormous differences in pressure and temperature within the earth's crust create volcanoes, geysers, thermal springs and earthquakes.

❶ Earth's mantle

The earth's mantle, with a thickness of some 3,000km/1,860 miles, is wrapped around the hot core of the planet, forming the flexible part of the earth's outer layer. Within it, magma circulates as incandescent rock »pulp«, resulting in movements of the earth's crust, which is 5 to 35km/3 to 22 miles thick.

❷ Indo-Australian Plate

❸ Pacific Plate

»Swimming« on the earth's mantle is the hard, if relatively light, earth's crust, broken up into several oceanic and continental plates. Around New Zealand, the continental Indo-Australian plate and the oceanic Pacific plate are constantly moving towards and on top of one another. In the case of New Zealand's North Island, the Pacific plate is sliding beneath the Indo-Australian plate, while in the South the reverse is true.

❹ Subduction zone

In the area where the Pacific plate's oceanic crust dives beneath the other plate, volcanic island arcs and deep-sea trenches are created, with the mantle rock being fused on the way down. A subduction zone often experiences volcanism and earthquakes.

❺ Rising magma

The collision of the oceanic with the continental plates leads to magma rising to the earth's surface and the resultant volcanic activity.

❻ Ring of Fire

New Zealand's North Island forms part of the so-called »Ring of Fire«, which surrounds the entire Pacific Ocean and is characterised by strong volcanic activity and frequent earth or seaquakes.

❼ Mount Tongariro

Mount Tongariro counts among New Zealand's most frequently active and feared volcanoes.

❽ Lake Taupo

This lake was created in the second century AD in the wake of a whole series of volcanic eruptions. The water collected here after the collapse of the empty crater.

Situated right on Lake Rotorua, the former bathhouse in Government Gardens is a reminder of the numerous thermal springs in the volcanic area around Rotorua. Today, the curative springs are used in the setting of a modern thermal spa, while the former bathhouse shelters a museum.

The Ruahepu volcano is still feared across a wide area to this day, after 151 lives were lost following its eruption in 1953.

The volcanic chain on North Island continues into the Pacific in the shape of White Island. This small volcanic island constantly emits plumes of steam and sulphur.

©BAEDEKER

During a volcanic eruption, the rising magma pours over the terrain of the central volcanic region around Mount Tongariro in streams of lava.

in effect the hilly extension of the Southern Alps (see above) in the shape of the Marlborough region to the northeast. Worth seeing is the coast known as Marlborough Sounds, an entire system of river valleys flooded by the sea (ria coasts).

Mystical Fiordland On the other side of South Island, to the southwest, and formed under similar conditions to the Ria coasts further north, is the fascinating landscape of the so-called Fiordland. These fjords are actually **pre-glacial river valleys**, carved out and deepened by the mighty ice streams flowing down to the sea during the Ice Ages. The walls of these trough valleys are very steep. In many cases, their cross-section resembles the letter »U«. Numerous lakes, too, such as Lake Te Anau, were formed by the melting of the ice masses. Made up of granite, gneiss and shist rock, the mountain range is cleft by many valleys and reaches heights of over 1,700 m/5,577ft above sea level.

Central Otago Another region dominated by mountain ranges, reaching heights of up to 2,000 m/6,500ft, is Central Otago in the southern central interior of South Island. Broad river valleys and **a softer relief** characterise this more European landscape. One of the extensive plains stretching to the south and east of the otherwise mountainous South Island is the large Canterbury Plain to the east, with the Banks Peninsula pointing far out to sea. This peninsula is formed by an extinct volcano whose crater lake is connected to the open sea and used as a natural harbour.

FLORA AND FAUNA

Endemic richness Some 80 million years of **isolation and seclusion** from other land masses enabled the New Zealand flora and fauna a separate and independent development. So it comes as no surprise that over 70 % of the country's plants are endemic – i.e. they only occur in New Zealand. The development of the endemic fauna was primarily restricted to birds and insects, but a few species of native reptile and fresh-water fish may also be encountered.

Time for development Over millions of years, plants and animals were left to their own devices. **Volcanic eruptions and several Ice Ages** shaped the development of New Zealand's flora and fauna. The impact of the changes wreaked on New Zealand's natural world since the arrival of the Europeans cannot be overestimated. Over a time period of just 200 years, a mere blink in the earth's history, many plant and animal species have been eliminated or eradicated, while others are currently threatened with it, including the kiwi bird (▶MARCOPOLO Insight p. 26), New Zealand's national symbol.

PLANTS

Originally, all of New Zealand was covered by forest. Only smaller areas formed **different habitats**, where it was either too cold or too dry for the expansion of woodland. In particular these are the high mountain areas on South Island, as well as the low-precipitation zones to the leeward side of the New Zealand Alps. The vegetation adapted to the temperature gradient running from north to south. Consequently, the forests of the individual regions contain different types of trees.

Lush forests

Typical of New Zealand's primeval forests are **evergreen deciduous trees and conifers**. The plants are able to adapt to cold winter temperatures in such a way that – unlike many European and North American trees for instance – they do not have to shed their foliage. While in the warm season this is not so obvious, the sight of New Zealand trees sporting their winter foliage is decidedly odd at first. Those parts of New Zealand with a near-subtropical climate, Northland and the Coromandel Peninsula in particular, but also the landscape around Auckland, were originally covered by kauri forests. The kauri spruce impresses with its tremendous size.

Massive kauri pines

The undergrowth of New Zealand's forests shelters ferns, mosses, lianas, climbing plants and epiphytes, giving the scenery the feel of a tropical rainforest. An especially typical and impressive representative of New Zealand flora is the silver fern, which has now been elevated to the status of **national plant**. It can be found on both North and South Island. The most common tree species is the evergreen **southern or false beech**. Whilst on North Island this plant may grow in the company of other species such as the tall, slow-growing totara, on South Island it forms large forests, for example in Fiordland and Westland. The fairly homogeneous southern beech forests are characterised by sparse undergrowth poor in species. In contrast, the other forests are more stratified with tree ferns, shrubs and shade-loving tree species. At higher altitudes the southern beech gives way to conifer forests.

Silver fern and southern beech

> **? MARCO POLO INSIGHT**
>
> *Rata propagation*
>
> The rata tree propagates itself when the seeds are carried by the wind onto other trees and deposited there. **Aerial roots** then form and the rata proceeds to slowly kill off the host plant through its own growth.

The **rimu** (*Dacrydium cupressinum*) can be found across the whole of New Zealand. Due to its stocky growth, it is very popular as a decorative plant. In forests, examples of this type of cypress can be found

1,000-year-old trees

MARCO POLO Insight

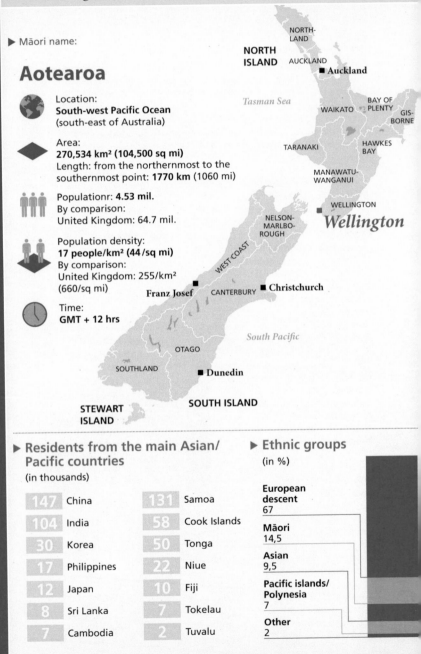

▶ Māori name:

Aotearoa

Location:
South-west Pacific Ocean
(south-east of Australia)

Area:
270,534 km² (104,500 sq mi)
Length: from the northernmost to the
southernmost point: **1770 km (1060 mi)**

Populationr: **4.53 mil.**
By comparison:
United Kingdom: 64.7 mil.

Population density:
17 people/km² (44/sq mi)
By comparison:
United Kingdom: 255/km²
(660/sq mi)

Time:
GMT + 12 hrs

NORTH-
LAND
NORTH
ISLAND AUCKLAND
■ **Auckland**

Tasman Sea
WAIKATO BAY OF
PLENTY
GIS-
BORNE

TARANAKI HAWKES
BAY

MANAWATU-
WANGANUI

WELLINGTON
Wellington

NELSON-
MARLBO-
ROUGH

WEST COAST

Franz Josef CANTERBURY ■ **Christchurch**

South Pacific

OTAGO

SOUTHLAND

■ **Dunedin**

STEWART
ISLAND

SOUTH ISLAND

▶ **Residents from the main Asian/**
Pacific countries
(in thousands)

147	China	131	Samoa
104	India	58	Cook Islands
30	Korea	50	Tonga
17	Philippines	22	Niue
12	Japan	10	Fiji
8	Sri Lanka	7	Tokelau
7	Cambodia	2	Tuvalu

▶ **Ethnic groups**
(in %)

European
descent
67

Māori
14,5

Asian
9,5

Pacific islands/
Polynesia
7

Other
2

▶ Flag

The Union Jack shows its membership in the Commonwealth. The stars represent the Southern Cross and symbolizes the location on the southern hemisphere.

▶ Languages

New Zealand English
Maori

▶ Demography

(in years)

21 % under 15
21 % 15 to 29
20 % 30 to 44
25 % 45 to 64
13 % over 65

▶ Governnment

Form of government: parliamentary democracy, at the same time a constitutional monarchy within the Commonwealth of Nations

Head of state: Queen of the United Kingdom of Great Britain and Northerrn Ireland represented by a a governor general

Executive: Prime minister and his cabinet

Parliament: House of Representatives (unicameral parliament)

▶ Administration

17 **Regional Councils** (responsible for infrastructure, water supply etc.)

74 **Territorial Authorities** (city or community administration), including:

57 **District Councils** (community administration)

16 **City Councils** (city administration)

1 **Island Council** (island administration)

5 **Unitary Authorities** (both regional and community administration)

▶ Sheep and cattle

Sheep and cattle raising is one of the major economic sectors. New Zealand is the world's largest exporter of milk, third largest exporter of wool and fifth largest exporter of meat.

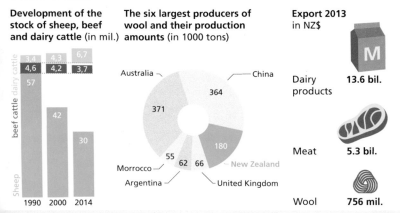

Development of the stock of sheep, beef and dairy cattle (in mil.)

dairy cattle: 3,4 | 4,3 | 6,7
beef cattle: 4,6 | 4,2 | 3,7
Sheep: 57 | 42 | 30
1990 | 2000 | 2014

The six largest producers of wool and their production amounts (in 1000 tons)

Australia 371
China 364
New Zealand 180
United Kingdom 66
Argentina 62
Morrocco 55

Export 2013 in NZ$

Dairy products **13.6 bil.**

Meat **5.3 bil.**

Wool **756 mil.**

alongside other types of trees. Growing very slowly, they can live for up to 1,000 years. The hard and resistant rimu wood is also much sought after as a **construction material**.

Christmas tree

Famed for its magnificent bright red blossom around Christmas time, the Pohutukawa is also known as »Christmas Tree« and can be found primarily on the beaches of North Island. The preferred habitat of the deep-red flowering **rata** is South Island. Another touch of colour in New Zealand forests is the yellow-flowering **kowhai**.

Gentian and orchids

High tussock, or tufted, grass cover is commonly found on the plains. The arid, **grassy landscapes** are found mainly in the lee of the New Zealand Alps. The so-called toetoe grass, a relative of South American pampas grass, is also very common. A particular feast for the eyes are the alpine meadows and pastures in their spectacular summer bloom. Alongside the daisy-like Celmisias look for bright blue gentian, various types of orchid and numerous other alpine flowers, amongst them the Mount Cook Lily, as well as another type of large white buttercup, the largest specimen of its kind. The **most common shrub** in New Zealand is the manuka, which can thrive nearly anywhere and is therefore appreciated as a valuable protection against erosion. It is also amongst the pioneer vegetation on cleared land. In former times, a kind of tea was prepared from its dried leaves, which is how it also came to be called »tea tree«.

Important flax

For the Maori, the New Zealand flax (*Phormium tenax*) was of major economic importance, having adapted very well to conditions on the wet plains. The fibres of these plants are made into baskets, textiles and the like. The Maori had already brought various crops from their **Polynesian homelands** to New Zealand, amongst them, for instance, the sweet potato called »kumara«.

More than 2,000 plants imported

When the white settlement of New Zealand began, hitherto **unknown plants** were imported in huge numbers. Well over 2,000 types of plant arrived here in this way, mostly without any forethought. Spread far and wide by now is the fast-growing Monterey pine (*Pinus radiata*), originally from California. The tree is planted in many places in New Zealand in monocultures, providing important raw materials to the timber industry. The Californian **mammoth tree** (Redwood: *Sequoia sempervirens*) has also been successfully introduced. Plants from different continents have been brought to New Zealand: trees (such as the oak), fruit plants (such as the Chinese gooseberry or kiwi), garden plants, decorative plants, clover and gorse. Several Australian eucalyptus and acacia species have found their way here too. These new arrivals have in many places already upset the fragile ecological balance.

The kea, a mountain parrot, is known for stealing so tourists shouldn't leave things laying around outside

FAUNA

The native fauna is represented primarily by the more than 250 types of bird, amongst them some rather odd customers, such as the **kiwi** (▶MARCOPOLO Insight p. 26), a nocturnal flightless bird. Before the arrival of humankind, the birds had no natural enemies, so that not just one but several species of flightless bird evolved.

Birds that can't fly

Other well-known flightless birds alongside the kiwi include the weka, the kakapo, the takahe and the moa, which is now extinct. The latter, an ostrich-like flightless bird, boasted over two dozen species. The largest moas would reach **over 4 m/13ft in height**. The early settlers of New Zealand – particularly the Maori – hunted these birds as a valuable addition to their diet, resulting in the moas being extinct by the time Europeans arrived.

Hunting for moas

Among the four species of New Zealand parrot, the **mountain parrot**, known as the »kea«, enjoys the worst reputation. It is said to attack and kill sheep. But nor are tents, sleeping bags and the suchlike safe from the attentions of the parrot, which is by now used to humans. Rubber parts of all kinds, such as **windscreen wipers and car tyres**, exert a particular fascination on this bird with its strong beak. Its adaptation to the rough conditions in the higher altitudes of the New Zealand Alps is surprising and atypical for its species.

Clever keas

Flightless night parrot Other New Zealand parrots include the bush parrot (kaka) and the parakeet. A bird that has become very rare now and is hence strictly protected is the **kakapo**, a flightless nocturnal parrot. Various types of honeyeaters are relatively common in natural forests, amongst them the bellbird and the so-called stitchbird. These birds feed primarily on nectar, but also on fruit and insects. Probably **New Zealand's most famous songbird** is the black-feathered tui, which also forms part of the honeyeater family.

The last of their kind **Rails** are also not uncommon in New Zealand, with the biggest example being the **takahe**. This flightless bird was already considered extinct when a large takahe colony was discovered in Fiordland after the Second World War. Another flightless bird is a type of **moor hen called weka**, which also forms part of the rail family. This duck-like and very curious bird can often be spotted at campsites and picnic areas where, in the manner of the magpie, it will look out for glittery objects.

Seagulls and more The world of seabirds bustling about New Zealand's coastline is particularly diverse. The most impressive amongst them is surely the royal albatross, boasting a wingspan of up to 3.5m/11.5ft. Further inhabitants of the coastal areas are various types of gulls, cormorants, storm petrels, terns and shearwaters. The shy **yellow-eyed penguin** only occurs in New Zealand, with its main habitat being South Island.

Insects New Zealand has countless types of insect, feeding numerous species of bird. One of the most interesting insects is the **fungus gnat**. The larvae of these microbes can be found mainly on the ceilings of dark caves. The way they go about procuring their food is fascinating. One place where this natural spectacle can be seen close-up is Waitomo Caves on North Island. The clouds of mosquitoes and sand flies appearing towards evening can become a veritable nuisance. Furthermore, New Zealand does have a few types of spider. In fact, the **most dangerous animal in New Zealand** for humans is a spider known as katipo, a close relation of the American »Black Widow« and the Australian »Redback«. The painful bite of an adult female may be fatal.

> **? How the fungus gnat feeds**
>
> MARCO ⊕ POLO INSIGHT
>
> The fungus gnat goes about feeding itself by producing spider web-like sticky threads; during digestion it emits a weak light, hence the label »glow worm«. Insects attracted by the light get caught in the sticky filaments of the »glow worms«.

Prehistoric reptiles In New Zealand, the reptile genus is represented by several types of gecko and smaller lizards. There are no snakes. The reptile called

»tuatara« belongs to the family of the bridge lizards. As the only living representative of a long-gone geological period, it is now only found in some earth caves on islands off the east of New Zealand. On every other continent this bridge lizard died out before the dinosaurs. Big-game anglers in particular appreciate the **abundance of fish in the waters** around New Zealand. Alongside numerous small fish, tiger sharks and hammerhead sharks, marlins, swordfish and tuna can be caught here.

The early isolation resulted in a **lack of mammals** – with the exception of two types of bat – on the islands making up New Zealand. Off the Kaikoura coast in the northeast of South Island entire schools of whales and dolphins may sometimes be seen, with sperm whales and even the so-called killer whales amongst them.

Whales and dolphins

The **European immigrants** in particular then brought many animals new to New Zealand, including farm animals and pets such as cattle, sheep, horses, goats, pigs, turkeys and peacocks, but also hunting game (including deer), as well as a number of freshwater fish. These animals were supposed to guarantee a food supply to the European immigrants.

Domestic animals from Europe

However, alongside them other animals came into the country, which were to pose a grave danger to the native fauna. This is particularly true in the case of the opossum (Australian oppossum), martens, cats, dogs, rats, as well as deer and roe deer, have had a devastating impact on **New Zealand's fragile ecosystem**. Thus the flightless kiwis are easy prey for hunting dogs and cats. The nesting places of many birds are sitting targets for martens. In the absence of any real natural enemies, deer have multiplied enormously, becoming a nuisance. The damage caused by their browsing has hindered the natural rejuvenation of the forests. Opossums have in recent times stripped bare entire patches of forest. The natural protection agencies employ costly operations (e. g. hunting by helicopter) to stem the explosive rate of individual species' propagation.

Easy prey without wings

Population · Politics · Economy

Why Auckland is the largest Polynesian settlement in the world, New Zealand's sheep wool is still in demand and ecology plays a central role in the life of the island nation.

The **New Zealand flag** shows the British Union Jack in the top left quarter and in the right-hand half the constellation of the Southern

National symbols

»Keewee Keewee«

Walking through New Zealand's forests, occasionally a shrill »keewee, keewee«, or a dull »quaak quaak« might be heard coming from the undergrowth. In fact, these sounds are often the only way to get to know New Zealand's most famous animal, which is mostly nocturnal and rather shy.

The kiwi is a **flightless bird** or »ratite« belonging to the Apterygidae family. Comparable in size to a regular domestic chicken, kiwis have a large curved sabre-like beak and grey-brown mottled feathers. The kiwi's wings are mere stumps, barely visible any more, leaving it unable to fly. However, it does boast an excellent **olfactory organ** located at the end of the beak, making it one of the world's few bird species with a good sense of smell. Kiwis also have bristly feelers beneath their beak, and an extremely keen sense of hearing – which is why the birds rarely miss a thing, including animals or other birds in their territory.

Shrill Calls

The New Zealand flightless bird, of which three types are known, prob-ably got its name from the call of the male bird, which from time to time emits a shrill »keewee, keewee«. The call of the female kiwi is more reminiscent of a frog's croaking. The females are larger than the males and lay sizeable eggs weighing about a fifth of their body weight. Known to be quite **solitary** and to reach ages of up to 25 years, the kiwi forages in darkness, roaming the New Zealand forests on carefully laid out and well-trodden paths. Using its curved and pointed beak, it un-

earths larvae and worms from the foliage or digs up tasty morsels with its powerful legs and claws. In the rainy season and when the forest berries ripen, kiwis are capable of covering fairly long distances at night.

Loner Seeks Companion

It is only during the mating season that the otherwise fervently solitary birds become sociable. A brace of kiwis spends its days in a **sleeping cave**, snoozing for up to 20 hours a day. At night, both go for-

Active at night: the kiwi

aging together. After the female kiwi has laid one to two eggs, which are very large in proportion to its body size, the male takes over the incubating. The baby kiwis hatch after about 80 days. Whilst the fledglings become independent relatively quickly, due to a certain lack of continued parental care, it might take five to six years for them to reach sexual maturity. New Zealand's native inhabitants, the Maori, have long prized the kiwi as a **noble game bird**, weaving its feathers into mats for their chiefs. Unfortunately, kiwi numbers have declined dramatically, particularly since the arrival of the Europeans, and they are now even threatened with extinction. As kiwis cannot fly or run fast they are

Give way to kiwis! And drive carefully wherever you see this road sign.

easy prey for humans and animals, in particular for the rats, martens, hedgehogs, cats and, most of all, the dogs brought in by the Europeans. Today, this national symbol of New Zealand enjoys strict protection.

Cross on a blue background. In a **referendum** on keeping this flag or a adopting a new »silver fern flag« held in March 2016 the current flag was chosen to remain.

In use since 1956, the **national coat of arms** includes a shield also displaying the Southern Cross as a symbol of the state, as well as a sheaf of corn, a sheep's fleece and mining tools as symbols of agriculture, husbandry and mining. The three sailing boats in the centre represent the importance of the maritime trade and the settlement of the islands from the sea. The left-hand part of the coat of arms shows a white woman with the flag of New Zealand in her hand, the symbol of the European immigrants, while to the right is a tattooed Maori in traditional dress bearing a lance, representing the native inhabitants. Both figures are shown standing on branches of the national plant, the silver fern. The British royal crown hovering above the shield symbolizes British sovereignty. The New Zealanders' **»national animal«** is the shy kiwi, which has given the New Zealanders their nickname, »kiwis«.

English tradition The English political tradition is particularly apparent in the fact that New Zealand has **no written constitution**; instead, case law from the British and New Zealand Supreme Courts forms the basis of constitutional law and constitutional tradition. However, the 1986 »Constitution Act« served to gather together and define more precisely constitutional law. Politically, New Zealand is entirely independent from Great Britain.

Legal system The country's legal system is modelled mainly on **British common law**, but complemented by distinctly homegrown laws. Until the 2004 establishment of the Supreme Court of New Zealand, the highest court of appeal in New Zealand law was the »Privy Council« in London. Since 1962, New Zealanders have been able to take their complaints about government agencies' misconduct to ombudsmen.

Trade unions During the turn of the 20th century, the New Zealand trade union movement was promoted in a major way **by the state**, allowing for a multitude of small trade unions. Until 1984 membership in a trade union was a legal requirement! In recent times their **influence has been increasingly curtailed**: with the industrial wage agreements expiring in 1991/1992, the collective agreements were abolished and replaced with individual or company wage agreements.

Nuclear-free zone New Zealand, a member of the Commonwealth and a founding member of the United Nations, maintains diplomatic and consular **relations with 41 states worldwide**. At international negotiations, the country, which in 1987 declared itself a **nuclear-free zone**, is working towards environmental protection and disarmament. Liber-

New Zealand's flag depicts the Union Jack and the Southern Cross

alization of commerce as well as the development of the Southern Pacific region form part of New Zealand's foreign policy.

Relations with the states of East and South-East Asia also play an important role for New Zealand, as evidenced by its involvement with the Asia Pacific Economic Cooperation (APEC), the World Trade Organisation (WTO), the International Monetary Fund (IMF) and the Organisation for Economic Co-Operation and Development (OECD). New Zealand also makes an important contribution to **security in the region** within the framework of a military alliance forged with Great Britain, Australia, Singapore and Malaysia, under the name of the »Five Power Defence Arrangement«.

Foreign policy

Some three quarters of all New Zealanders live on North Island, with only **a quarter based on South Island**. The fairly low average population density figures hide the fact that well over half the population live in highly urbanised areas with over 100,000 inhabitants. The urban areas also register high growth levels.

Population distribution

Regions and Districts

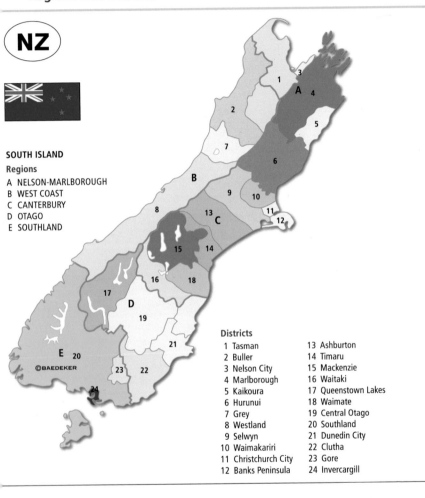

NZ

SOUTH ISLAND

Regions

A NELSON-MARLBOROUGH
B WEST COAST
C CANTERBURY
D OTAGO
E SOUTHLAND

©BAEDEKER

Districts

1 Tasman	13 Ashburton
2 Buller	14 Timaru
3 Nelson City	15 Mackenzie
4 Marlborough	16 Waitaki
5 Kaikoura	17 Queenstown Lakes
6 Hurunui	18 Waimate
7 Grey	19 Central Otago
8 Westland	20 Southland
9 Selwyn	21 Dunedin City
10 Waimakariri	22 Clutha
11 Christchurch City	23 Gore
12 Banks Peninsula	24 Invercargill

The process of **urbanisation** began some centuries ago, and is closely connected to economic development.

The enormous degree of rationalisation in agriculture has released
much of the workforce from the land, while the manufacturing industry and the service sector in the cities have offered new employ-
ment.

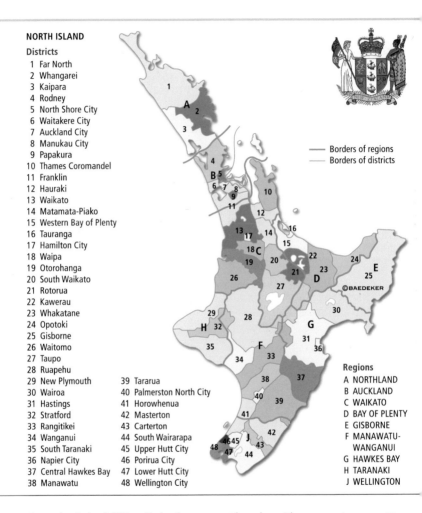

NORTH ISLAND

Districts

1 Far North
2 Whangarei
3 Kaipara
4 Rodney
5 North Shore City
6 Waitakere City
7 Auckland City
8 Manukau City
9 Papakura
10 Thames Coromandel
11 Franklin
12 Hauraki
13 Waikato
14 Matamata-Piako
15 Western Bay of Plenty
16 Tauranga
17 Hamilton City
18 Waipa
19 Otorohanga
20 South Waikato
21 Rotorua
22 Kawerau
23 Whakatane
24 Opotoki
25 Gisborne
26 Waitomo
27 Taupo
28 Ruapehu
29 New Plymouth
30 Wairoa
31 Hastings
32 Stratford
33 Rangitikei
34 Wanganui
35 South Taranaki
36 Napier City
37 Central Hawkes Bay
38 Manawatu

39 Tararua
40 Palmerston North City
41 Horowhenua
42 Masterton
43 Carterton
44 South Wairarapa
45 Upper Hutt City
46 Porirua City
47 Lower Hutt City
48 Wellington City

— Borders of regions
— Borders of districts

©BAEDEKER

Regions

A NORTHLAND
B AUCKLAND
C WAIKATO
D BAY OF PLENTY
E GISBORNE
F MANAWATU-
WANGANUI
G HAWKES BAY
H TARANAKI
J WELLINGTON

Around a sixth of all New Zealanders were not born here. The **many younger immigrants** of recent decades are evident, however, in the population's age pyramid. Just under a fifth of the population is made up of children and adolescents of up to 14 years of age, while about two thirds of the inhabitants of New Zealand are between 15 and 64, and roughly an eighth are 65 and over.

Age pyramid

Age structure In terms of the age structure, New Zealanders of European descent differ significantly from the Maori and the Pacific Islanders. Up to the 25-year-old age group, **Maori and Polynesians have a stronger representation**, in the 25 to 34-year-old group there is approximate parity, whereas the percentage of Europeans rises steeply within the older inhabitants of New Zealand.

Cultural melting pot Two thirds of the inhabitants of New Zealand are of European descent. Some 15 % of New Zealanders identify themselves as pure or mixed-race Maori, in other words belonging to the native population which immigrated from the Eastern Pacific centuries before the Europeans discovered New Zealand. Meanwhile, a good 7% of the population are »**Pacific Island Polynesians**«, who immigrated mainly from the tropical Cook Islands, as well as from the islands of Niue, Samoa, Tokelau and Tonga. They live primarily in Greater Auckland. The city itself is today considered the **world's largest Polynesian settlement**, with well over 190,000 inhabitants hailing from the Pacific islands. Many Chinese and Indians too have made New Zealand their home for generations.

Religion and faith In the last census, roughly a third of New Zealanders professed to have **no religion**. 14% of the population belonged to the Anglican church, 10% were Presbyterians, 13% Catholics, 3% Methodists and 2 % Baptists. The remaining 13 % of the population were shared between other religious groupings.

MAORI

Surpassed in number
(▶MARCO-POLO Insight p. 224) In terms of numbers, the Maori, New Zealand's native Polynesian population, are today far outweighed by the white immigrants. Only just under **15% of New Zealanders** call themselves Maori, whereby many do not have only Maori ancestors. Despite adapting to the lifestyle of the European immigrants, the Maori uphold many of their own **traditions**. At the time of the European settlement of New Zealand, some 100-120,000 Maori lived here, most of them on North Island, which they named »Aotearoa« (»Land of the Long White Cloud«). Only some 5% settled on South Island, with its less favourable climate. Around the mid-19th century, when inter-tribal conflicts, land wars against the British and diseases brought into the country by European settlers had severely decimated the Maori, leaving them uprooted and listless, they were expected to become **extinct**. Ferdinand von Hochstetter, in his extensive description of his research travels in New Zealand in 1863, declared himself very concerned by the decline in the Maori population (approx. 20% within 15 years). In the mid-19th century there were only 56,000 Maori left.

Black and white, red and green are the colours of the Maori –
a Maori couple poses for the camera

Hochstetter was convinced that the Maori faced complete extinction
by about the year 2000. For the same year, he projected the European
population of New Zealand, consisting of about 84,000 people in
1860, to reach half a million. In both
cases Hochstetter proved to be way
off the mark. Government measures
for the protection and **integration** of
the Maori and, in particular, a revival
of the culture through Maori role
models made the population grow
again and increased awareness of its
cultural identity.

The largest social unit, the tribe
(»iwi«), was subdivided into so-
called »hapu«, formed by some 500
people of various interrelated families. At the head of the iwi, a **chief**

? Maori - origins of the word

MARCO ⊕ POLO INSIGHT

The word »Maori« means something like »usual« or »common«?
The early white settlers in New
Zealand used it to distinguish the
natives from themselves. Later on,
the Maori adopted this designa-
tion. Before the arrival of the
white settlers the Maori had no
collective name for themselves,
with the tribe (iwi) constituting
the most extensive unit.

known as »ariki« would receive his authority for leadership through
his ancestors' »mana« (see below). However, he could also lose his
claim to leadership through misdemeanour. **Important decisions**
were not taken by the chief alone. He would call a meeting at the central place in front of the meeting house called **»marae«**. Every leader of a family was allowed to speak, the first and last word however
belonged to the chief.

Early settlements	The early inhabitants of New Zealand had initially lived in unfortified settlements called »kainga«. It was only from the 14th century onwards that fortified villages **fortified villages**, called »pa«, were laid out. They consisted of a number of houses grouped around a central meeting place called a »marae«. There was also a richly adorned meeting house, a storehouse, subterranean chambers or other suitable building where supplies were kept, cooking huts (eating was not allowed in the dwelling houses), as well as men's houses where tools would be made and repaired.
Animistic world view	The traditional Maori world view is shaped by **animism**, the belief that manifestations in nature are personified, and animated, by gods or ghosts. Tane, who separated his parents, heaven and earth, is the **most important Maori deity**. Creating the first woman from red earth, Tane is the God of the forest where the tall trees grow that are so important for building canoes and houses. Thus, he is also the God of craftspeople, and boat and house builders in particular. Anyone who wanted to fell a tree had to offer up a sacrifice to Tane, otherwise he would incur the **wrath of the god**.

Sacrificial offerings would mostly be food. The **human sacrifices** often occurring in Polynesian culture were only demanded by the war god, who also laid claim to the first killed enemy.

? MARCO ⊕ POLO INSIGHT

Ancestor cult

The wooden sculptures and carved figures on the meeting houses and war canoes do not represent gods, but purely the venerated ancestors. As founding fathers, they had to transfer their force, their »mana«, on to the »iwi« (tribe) or »hapu« (sub-tribe).

The **connection with the gods** was represented by a master, chosen one or priest called »tohunga«. Sometimes this could be a very experienced craftsman, such as a wood carver or tattoo artist. The **»tohunga«** would as a rule be of high descent, i.e. be a descendant of a long line of ancestors. Alongside the tohungas, the chiefs also fulfilled important religious functions. The so-called »karakia« chants of a magic formula, whose exact rendition was paramount, were performed as part of sacred rituals such as sacrificial celebrations, prayers and incantations.

Mana, tapu	Central concepts in Maori life are »mana« and »tapu «. »Mana«, which can roughly be translated as **»prestige« or »honour«**, was transferred as a force and a distinction by the Gods onto humankind and by them passed on through inheritance. Victories in battle were a way of augmenting it, whilst it could also be lost through mistakes during the celebration of ritual formula or violations of the »tapu«. When enemy chiefs were defeated and enslaved, they lost their mana. The Maori see »tapu« as **a positive force** which may not be dis-

turbed by anything. The holy objects of the priest were »tapu«, as well as the persons of the priest and chief themselves. The »tapu« commandment would also apply temporarily to manifestations of nature and the environment; there were **times of protection** for newly farmed sweet potato fields, for bird hunting and fishing, as well as for the harvest. However, things from daily life were »noa«, profane or ordinary – food for instance, or women for that matter! A broken »tapu« meant certain misfortune or, in the worst-case scenario, the death of the »tapu« breaker.

The first Maori, reaching the islands of New Zealand probably around the mid-8th century, brought various agricultural crops, most important among them the kumara, a kind of sweet potato, taro and yam roots. These **starch-rich crops** formed the basis of the Maori diet, supplemented by fish and birds. The meat of the rare Maori rat was also eaten, but all in all the protein supply was fairly sparse.

Vegetarian diet

There is still research to be completed on the subject of cannibalism. A lack of protein or of food in general, or **overpopulation** might have led the Maori to consume human flesh at certain times. Some contemporary reports mention the fact that in wartime the Maori would eat **enemies killed** in battle, in the hope of receiving the skills the adversary possessed.

Cannibalism

The personal property of a Maori included provisions, spears or fruit trees. The chiefs would be given **enemies taken in war**. Within the boundaries of the tribe, the »hapu« owned specific areas of land that they divided amongst individual families.

Property rights

Whilst the 19th century Maori were made to feel **strangers in their own country**, over the course of the 20th century, they increasingly gained self-confidence and demanded their rights. Since the 1970s there has been a real **renaissance of Maori culture**. Today, many Maori view their own traditions and culture with pride. Signs of this include the establishment of new »marae«, the transmission of Maori culture in kindergardens and primary schools, and the increased presence of the Maori language. Most Maori today might have English as their first language, but Maori, which has close links with other Polynesian languages, is now taught in various schools and educational institutions for adults. Some TV and radio programmes are also broadcast in Maori.

More self-confidence

The traditional values of Maori culture are embodied by **Tuheitia Paki**, who was crowned king of the Maoris in 2006 and who has his residence in Ngaruawahia. Tuheitia Paki is the oldest son of Te Arikinui Dame Te Atairangikaahu, who was crowned as the first

From adviser to king

Queen of the Maori in 1966 and died in 2006 at the age of 75. Before his **coronation** Tuheitia Paki worked as cultural adviser to the University of Wellington.

Maori King Movement

He is not the king of all the Maoris, only of the **Maori tribes on New Zealand's North Island** where he was elected by the tribal elders. The office of king is not hereditary but all kings have been direct descendants of Potatau, the first Maori king. In the 1858 »Maori King Movement« he tried to unite the many Maori tribes in order to confront the white majority.

The Maori in modern society

Whilst clearly in the minority compared to white New Zealanders, in today's society the Maori are no oppressed minority. Many white New Zealanders and especially tourists are very interested in the culture, artistic skills and craftsmanship of the Maori. Despite this, an enormous **cultural and economic divide** remains between the native inhabitants and the immigrants and their descendants. Many Maori are less well educated, have no work and often live off welfare.

The Maori youth has adopted a European lifestyle completely but is also often discriminated against in favour of descendants of the colonial powers

To this day, most Maori value ancestry and social values more than success and property, while **competitive thinking** is largely alien to them. Many Maori have been torn from their traditional large families and networks of relatives, instead living in small families that are widely scattered.

Community instead of possessions

ECONOMY

With the accession of the United Kingdom to the European Union in 1973 New Zealand lost what was traditionally its most important market, and the economy of the island state slid into a **deep crisis**, exacerbated by excessive state control, as well as an export-based dependency on world-market pricing.

Overview of the economy

From 1984 onwards, a **free market economy** began to be introduced. There was no more state control of interest and exchange rates, VAT was introduced, state subsidies slashed and **import restrictions** lifted. State-owned companies were privatised, including post and telecommunications, railways, banks and insurance, housing and electricity companies.

Businesses privatized

Privatisation, reduction in social spending and higher taxes managed to reduce inflation and new borrowing. In return however, the army of unemployed grew. After a period of recession, in **the 1990s a new economic growth** was again seen, but the high rate of unemployment initially remained. By 2005 then unemployment stood at a historical low of 3.7%; however, **especially Maori**, inhabitants of Polynesian descent and young people were disproportionately affected.

Many unemployed

The reforms were accompanied by a marked **structural change**. Industry gained an increasing share of gross domestic product, with agriculture's share decreasing sharply. Since the 1980s tourism developed into a very important economic sector. In 2013 foreign tourists numbered just about 2.7 mil. (of these more than 190,000 came from the U.K.); they spent about 7.5 bil. NZ dollars in the country.

Tourism grows

After bad experiences with the privatisation of the railway and utilities the government natioanlized them again in 2008. In other areas **privatisation is supposed to be stopped** or revoked.

The government takes over

New Zealand's **economy has suffered** until today from the effects of the recent worldwide financial and economic crisis. The number of visitors to the country sank temporarily and is currently recovering slowly. Prices of agricultural products plummeted. After the **gross domestic product sank** by several percentage points in the

World economic crisis

2008/2009 fiscal year it has risen again by 1.4%. The inflation rate, which had gone up to 4.3% in the 2008/2009 fiscal year, has in the meantime dropped below the 3% mark again. The job market is still problematical. **Unemployment** in September 2014 was at 5.4%.

Earthquake in Christchurch The catastrophic earthquake in Christchurch in September 2010 with 7.1 points on the Richter scale and in February 2011 with 6.3 points caused the country new economic problems. The **largest natural catastrophe** of the past 80 years, whose severity surprised even the experts, lead the country into a recession. The reconstruction has at least caused a boom in the building industry since 2011.

AGRICULTURE, FORESTRY, FISHING

Current situation In the 2013/2014 fiscal year, about 7% of the workforce were employed in **agriculture and forestry** as well as in **fishing**. This sector contributed just under 7,4% of New Zealand's GDP. Around 80,000 commercial operations, amongst them 7,000 large enterprises with over 400 ha/over 980 acres, were cultivating a total of 15 million ha/44 million acres of farmland. Some 14% of this land is employed as arable land and for permanent crops. Over the past few years, **low world market prices** for agricultural produce and import barriers have had a negative impact. Rigorous cuts in government subsidies and the heavy weight of debt led to farms going out of business.

A good New Zealand shearer can shear up to 300 sheep a day

Some 10 million cattle and dairy cows graze on New Zealand's pastures, bringing well over 500,000t of beef and 13,000t of veal onto the market. The dominant breed amongst the cattle is the strong **»Aberdeen Angus«**, originally from Scotland, which has been bred for over a century in this country and is highly valued for its robustness and the quality of its meat.

The current cliché that there are 20 sheep for every New Zealander no longer holds true. As a consequence of a catastrophic drought in 1988, but even more so through the fall in wool prices in the 1990s, the number of **sheep has been much reduced**. Between 1988 and the present, the sheep stock has fallen from 64.6 million to some 50 million animals. Despite this, New Zealand remains the world's **second largest wool exporter** after Australia.

Husbandry

Travelling across the islands visitors will see enclosures everywhere with large **herds of red deer** browsing. This game, introduced from Europe for hunting, soon became a disruptive factor in the ecology of New Zealand's forest areas, as they encounter **no natural predators**. In the nature reserves, the overgrown game stock was first hunted, then also captured and transferred to game parks. Meanwhile about half of the world's farmed game lives here. In 2008 about 7,500 tonnes of game was exported.

Meat a main export

The past few years have seen a substantial rise in the amount of **goatkeeping**, due to strong demand for their wool (mohair, cashmere), milk and meat. Goats are kept on pastures because of the way they feed, devouring **wild herbs and shrubbery** spurned by sheep and cattle.

New Zealand cashmere

Excellent pastures are eminently suitable for horse breeding, which a number of farms, primarily south of Auckland, have turned to. In New Zealand itself **racehorses** are highly prized, as nearly every urban settlement boasts a racecourse. Australia and the US are destinations for breeding horses, bringing in high dividends.

Prized thoroughbred horses

Alongside the endless pastures, the areas used for agriculture in New Zealand hardly make a dent in the statistics. However, the extremely **intensive special cultures** (fruit, especially kiwis and grapes, hops) in those relatively small parts of the islands with a favourable climate, are of great economic significance.

Agriculture, fruit and vegetable cultivation

Developed in New Zealand **from the Chinese gooseberry**, the kiwi fruit (►MARCOPOLO Insight p. 124) has become widespread over the past two decades, not only in the English-speaking world. Highly susceptible to wind damage, these climbing plants need trestles and hedges to shelter them. They thrive best on the **Bay of Plenty** in the east of North Island, where kiwi plantations dominate the landscape.

Kiwi – the fruit

Even today, a quarter of New Zealand is still covered in forest. The old kauri forests in Northland were thoroughly plundered by the early European lumberjacks, leaving only a few small, and now strictly protected, remnants of the **majestic kauri trees** (►MARCOPOLO Insight p. 212). The basis of modern forestry are the areas planted

Forest economy and management

with exotic types of wood not native to New Zealand. **Introduced conifers**, the Californian pine »Pinus radiata« in particular, thrive in New Zealand. These trees are ready for felling after 25 to 30 years, and their reforestation is easy. Of the islands' entire forested area (just under 8 million ha/20 acres), a good three quarters is used commercially. Two thirds of commercial woodlands are owned by the state, with a third in private hands.

Wood ahead of wool — Half of all logged timber is exported – as raw material for paper production, among other things – primarily to Australia and Japan. Wood is now third on the list of export goods, behind meat and dairy products – and ahead of wool!

Fisheries — As far back as 1978, New Zealand introduced an economic zone for fishing of 200 nautical miles around its islands. The coastal waters have been largely **overfished**. For the future, the fisheries sector and fish-processing industry are looking primarily to deep-sea fishing. **Oyster and mussel farms** have been doing well, while valuable catches include deep-sea perch, octopus, tuna and crawfish. Annual exports to the value of some 1 billion NZ$ are mainly destined for Japan, Australia and the US.

INDUSTRY, MINING AND ENERGY

Classifications — The secondary economic sector comprises the areas of energy and water supply, mining, the manufacturing industry and construction. This sector is responsible for just under 21% of New Zealand's gross domestic product, and **a quarter of the workforce**. The vast majority work in the manufacturing industry.

Industry losing jobs — The New Zealand industrial sector spans a broad range from heavy industry and mechanical engineering, structural and civil engineering, via wood processing, paper production, textile and leather goods production to food production. All in all, the manufacturing industry comprises around 20,000 companies, mainly smaller firms with up to five employees. Over the past two decades, the number of people employed in the sector has gone down by 40,000 to some 260,000, primarily because of ongoing **automation**.

Construction — The **detached house** with garden is a very common sight throughout New Zealand, including the suburbs of major urban centres. Most residential houses, of which well over 10,000 are built annually, are single storey and made of wood. In addition, offices and industrial buildings covering hundreds of thousands of square metres of floor space spring up each year.

Water is used to produce electricity in Wairakei on the North Island

In terms of energy policy, New Zealand is aiming to become **less dependent** on imported fuels – crude oil in particular. A considerable proportion of New Zealand's energy is obtained from domestic natural gas, with liquid gas or compressed gas fuel available everywhere. The **potential of hydraulic** and geothermal energy is harnessed by sophisticated technical facilities (reservoirs, geothermal power stations).

Energy, natural gas

However, the transformation of the previously **unspoiled landscape** in the course of damming and channelling has led to conflict with the nature and environment protection movement, which is very active in New Zealand. North Island, which uses **more electricity** than the sparsely-populated South Island, is dependent on combined heat and power plants, hydraulic power plants (along the Waikato River, amongst others) and on **geothermal power plants** (in the volcanic zone between Rotorua and Taupo). The geothermal power plants work with superheated steam obtained from bore holes in the volcanic region. The first geothermal power plants were established at

Conflict with conservation

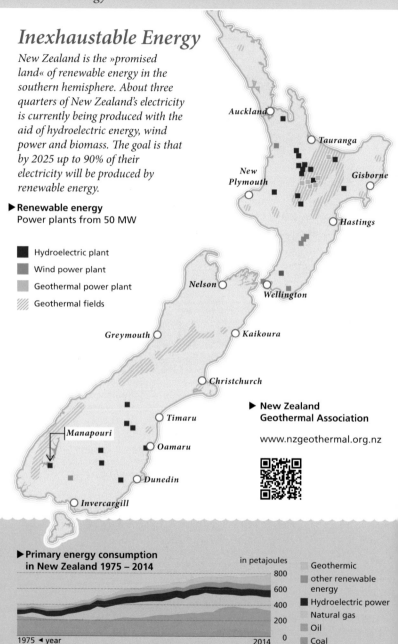

Inexhaustable Energy

New Zealand is the »promised land« of renewable energy in the southern hemisphere. About three quarters of New Zealand's electricity is currently being produced with the aid of hydroelectric energy, wind power and biomass. The goal is that by 2025 up to 90% of their electricity will be produced by renewable energy.

▶ **Renewable energy**
Power plants from 50 MW

- ■ Hydroelectric plant
- ■ Wind power plant
- ■ Geothermal power plant
- ▨ Geothermal fields

▶ **New Zealand Geothermal Association**

www.nzgeothermal.org.nz

Auckland
○ *Tauranga*
New Plymouth
Gisborne
○ *Hastings*
Nelson
○ *Wellington*
Greymouth
○ *Kaikoura*
○ *Christchurch*
Manapouri
○ *Timaru*
○ *Oamaru*
○ *Dunedin*
○ *Invercargill*

▶ **Primary energy consumption in New Zealand 1975 – 2014**

in petajoules

- Geothermic
- other renewable energy
- Hydroelectric power
- Natural gas
- Oil
- Coal

800
600
400
200
0

1975 ◀ year   2014

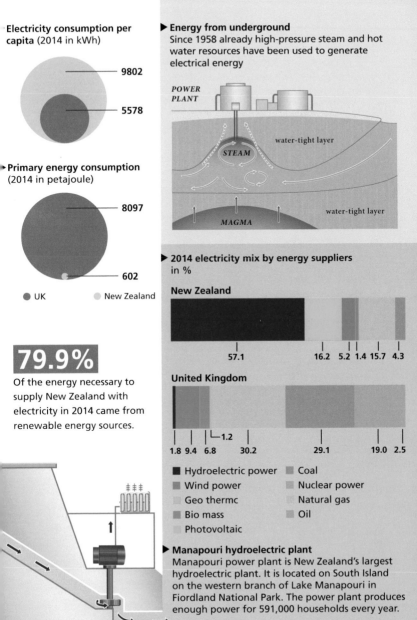

Electricity consumption per capita (2014 in kWh)

- 9802
- 5578

Primary energy consumption (2014 in petajoule)

- 8097
- 602

● UK ● New Zealand

79.9%

Of the energy necessary to supply New Zealand with electricity in 2014 came from renewable energy sources.

▶ Energy from underground

Since 1958 already high-pressure steam and hot water resources have been used to generate electrical energy

POWER PLANT

water-tight layer

STEAM

water-tight layer

MAGMA

▶ 2014 electricity mix by energy suppliers
in %

New Zealand

57.1 16.2 5.2 1.4 15.7 4.3

United Kingdom

1.8 9.4 6.8 └─1.2 30.2 29.1 19.0 2.5

- ■ Hydroelectric power
- ■ Wind power
- Geo thermc
- ■ Bio mass
- Photovoltaic
- ■ Coal
- Nuclear power
- Natural gas
- ■ Oil

▶ Manapouri hydroelectric plant

Manapouri power plant is New Zealand's largest hydroelectric plant. It is located on South Island on the western branch of Lake Manapouri in Fiordland National Park. The power plant produces enough power for 591,000 households every year.

Wairakei (1958) on the Waikato River, as well as at Ohaaki (1987). In the meantime numerous new power plants were built and about 15% of the primary energy used in New Zealand is produced by geothermics. More large projects are planned.

Energy from the south

Nuclear energy is not on the agenda in New Zealand. It is planned to intensify the use of domestic coal for energy generation and steel production. Due to the higher energy needs on North Island, a **cable has been laid down through Cook Strait**, bringing the excess electricity obtained from hydraulic power on South Island to the energy-hungry north.

Rich in raw materials

For a long time, New Zealand was considered a country with very few natural resources. Today however, substantial amounts of coal, oil, natural gas, iron, gold, sand and minerals are being extracted. The **coal reserves**, most of them on South Island, are estimated to run to several billion tons. Oil is obtained from the McKee Field off North Island and at Ngaere/Taranaki, natural gas from the Kupuni/Taranaki Field and the Maui Field (approx. 50km/30 miles off the Taranaki coast). They are used for generating electricity, and for producing synthetic fuels and petrochemicals. **Iron ore** is found extensively, in the form of black ironsand, on the western coasts of both islands. The existing deposits comprise a respectable several hundred million tons.

Shiny prospects

Gold was important for the development of New Zealand. In 1861, gold was found in Otago, and a short time later in Westland; the gold prospectors flocked into the country in their thousands. Today still, larger quantities of gold with a large value are mined every year, particularly on the **Coromandel Peninsula** (North Island), and in Otago and Westland (South Island).

Traditional jade jewllery

Called »**Pounamu**« in the Maori language, nephrite (New Zealand jade, greenstone) occurs in the west of South Island (►MARCOPOLO Insight p. 130). In the traditional Maori culture where metals were unknown, nephrite was an important trading commodity, providing the material for the production of weapons (axe blades, amongst others) and jewellery. Today, these stones are used in the manufacture of **pieces of jewellery** with **traditional Maori motifs**, primarily in Hokitika.

TRADE AND SERVICES

Service sector

The service sector is responsible for 70% of gross domestic product, and some **two thirds of the workforce** earn their living in this sec-

The production of beautiful jade jewellery is a tradition in New Zealand

tor. Amongst those working in the tertiary sector, 30% belong to the municipal, social and private services, 20% to commerce and the hospitality industry, 10% to banks, insurance companies and real estate and about 7% to transport and communications.

In the fiscal year 2010/2011, goods worth nearly 33 billion US$ were imported, primarily mechanical and electrical machinery, cars, oil and petrochemical products. The main countries supplying these goods were Australia, the USA, Japan, Great Britain, China and Germany.

Imported technology

In the same period, goods to the value of about 35 bil. US$ were exported, mainly **dairy products, meat, wood and paper**, crude oil, mechanical machinery, fruit, fish and seafood, and wine. The main export countries were Australia, the US, China, Japan, Great Britain and South Korea.

Exported worldwide

Tourism plays a major role in New Zealand. In 2014/2015 it brought in just about 10.6 bil. NZ$, almost 5 % of the GDP. The »white industry« currently supplies about **168,000 full-time jobs**.
The overall number of visitors rocketed from 2.45 million in 2009 to 2.95 million in 2015. About 7 % of these came from the UK.

Welcome visitors

Meanwhile, more and more New Zealanders are **concerned** about the invasion of holidaymakers from abroad. Fears that the hordes of visitors could damage the natural environment, which is still largely intact, are not merely figments of an over-worried imagination. Already there are demands to **severely restrict access** to particularly precious nature reserves or to introduce quotas for visitors.

Limited access

How **environmental protection** and tourism can be reconciled is the subject of much debate. By way of example, for some time there have been attempts to channel the streams of visitors at Milford Sound, one of the tourist highlights on South Island, in an environmentally sustainable way.

Sustainable planning

Excursion boat in Milford Sound – boating has also profited from the flourishing tourism

Welcome to Everyday Life

Experience New Zealand off the beaten tourist path – here you can meet completely »normal people«.

AT WORK

Picking fruit, milking cows, shearing sheep – your travel budget can be replenished in many different ways. People between 18 and 30 years can take advantage of the Working Holiday Visa. The New Zealand German Business Association posts jobs in its website:

www.newzealandnow.govt.nz/

LEISURE TIME

No matter where you're travelling in New Zealand there's usually an A&P show (agricultural & pastoral show) being held nearby. These agricultural trade shows are more like fairs, with rodeos, sheep-shearing contests or wood cutting contests and give opportunities to rub elbows with real New Zealanders.

SPORTS

Rich or poor, young or old, male or female, Maori or pakeha –New Zealanders or all sizes, colours or ages are rugby fans The members of the All Blacks national team are treated like heroes in the whole country. Anyone who wants to see a game has the choice of ITM cup or Super Rugby cup tournaments.

Information and tickets:
www.allblacks.com
("MARCOPOLO Insight p. 112)

HORSEWHISPERER

In the foothills of the New Zealand Southern Alps you can learn to ride under the eyes of local teachers, or go on rides in the countryside and get to know life at a New Zealand riding stable – a great place to meet New Zealanders.

Further info: Kowhai Equestrian Farm
Stay, 711 Island Rd. 7495 Oxford,
Tel. 64 3 3 124309

VOLUNTEERING IN CONSERVATION

The Department of Conservation is looking for volunteers who will help establish hiking and educational trails on Coromandel Peninsula; help maintain kauri forests, protect dunes or maintain the old Maori fort (pa) at Whitianga Rock.

Further info:
www.doc.govt.nz/getting-involved/
volunteer/

RESTORING AN HISTORIC WEEKEND COTTAGE

Rangitoto Island Historic Trust cares for the charmingly beautiful weekend cottages that were built in the 1920s and 1930s in the volcanic island landscape north-east of Auckland. As these are somewhat run down the trust welcomes working holiday guests.

Info: www.rangitoto.org,
also www.doc.govt.nz
or tel. 09 6 34 01 61 (Allan Godsall)

First came the Maori, and then the Europeans

From the native inhabitants to the arrival of the Europeans and British sovereignty, from the Treaty of Waitangi to the equal co-existence of immigrants and the Maori – in a similar way to the US, New Zealand is characterised by oppression and by the resistance of the native population.

around 0	Polynesian island dwellers arrive in New Zealand
around 1500	The classic Maori culture prevails everywhere
1642	Abel Tasman is the first European to sight New Zealand
8 Oct. 1769	The seafarer James Cook steps onto New Zealand soil
1769 / 1770	French seafarers land in New Zealand
6 Feb. 1840	Treaty of Waitangi
1841	New Zealand becomes a British crown colony

In contrast to the settlement of Australia by the Aborigines, who arrived about 40-50,000 years ago across land bridges existing at the time **from Southeast Asia**, the discovery and settlement of New Zealand is much more recent. It is thought that the Australian Aborigines and the New Zealand Maori, completely different groups in terms of descent and origins, were never in contact with each other.

Late settlement

The native population of New Zealand stems from the **Polynesian migrations** that started about 4,000 years ago in the western Pacific, leading via Samoa, Fiji, Tonga, the Society Islands and the Marquesas, on to the Cook Islands and – according to most recent research – reaching the remote islands of New Zealand **some 2,000 years ago**. The Polynesian islanders were excellent seafarers. Their long expeditions with outrigger boats and katamarans were not unintended extensions of fishing expeditions, but planned colonisation enterprises.

Arrival by boat

The former inhabitants of tropical islands found the climate of New Zealand unaccustomedly hard. They lived as **hunters and gatherers** off berries, fern roots, birds, fishing and hunting seals. On South Island they would hunt the local **moa**, a flightless ostrich measuring up to 3m/nearly 10ft, which soon died out due to changes in climate and vegetation, as well as from being the object of constant hunting. The inhabitants of Northland became familiar with the sweet potato

Unusual conditions

Maori culture is celebrated at the Maori Cultural Festival in Ruatahune

or **kumara** introduced from South America. It remains unclear where, when and how this transfer happened. Its cultivation and storage were prerequisites for the transition from the archaic non-sedentary culture of the moa hunters and gatherers to the classic Maori culture of groups living in unfortified or fortified villages.

From north to south
It is assumed that there was only one early immigration movement. It was from this archaic existence that the **classic Maori culture** would later develop, with its centre of gravity on the warmer North Island and more specifically in what is today Northland. From there, individual tribal groups would set out in canoe parties along the coast and on the rivers to more southerly regions. Around 1500, the classical Maori culture is said to have prevailed all over the main islands of New Zealand, with the earlier culture only persisting on Chatham Island, lying faraway to the east.

Maori legends
Maori tradition represents the **settlement of New Zealand** slightly differently. According to this, around the year 925 AD the seafarer Kupe, starting from the mythical island of Hawaiki near Tahiti was the first to reach New Zealand. He called this new country **Aotearoa (Land of the Long White Cloud)**. After having to fight against a huge octopus Kupe returned to Hawaiki.

The second to reach the New Zealand islands, 225 years later, and to have founded the **first Maori settlement** there, is said to have been Toi, a chief from Hawaiki. In Maori tradition, the extensive settlement of New Zealand is ascribed to a later large wave of immigration from Hawaiki. It is from there that around 1350 island dwellers are said to have started out in seven large **tribal canoes**, which the various Maori tribes still trace their heritage back to.

Seafarer Abel Tasman
In 1642, the Dutch seafarer Abel Janszoon Tasman (1603 – 1659), having been commissioned by Antonij van Diemen, the Dutch Governor General of Batavia (today's Jakarta, the capital of Indonesia), sailed around what is now Australia and discovered the island that today bears his name, **Tasmania**. On 13 December 1642 he became the **first European** to catch sight of New Zealand. The place where he landed was the north of South Island. However, after the Maori suddenly attacked his ship's boat and battered some seamen to death, avenged by the Europeans with cannon salvos, Tasman left what he called Murderers Bay, today's Golden Bay. He sailed along the west coast of North Island back to Batavia, assuming that the newly discovered country was the western coast of a large, hitherto unknown, **southern continent**. Dutch scholars introduced the name **»Nieuw Zeeland«** for the newly discovered South Pacific island world. In the further course of his South Sea journey Abel Tasman went on to discover the islands of Tonga and Fiji..

The great seafarer James Cook loved landing in Ship Cove in Queen Charlotte Sound

After the upheavals in Europe following the Thirty Year War, the conflict in the Netherlands and their sea war against England, the Dutch attempted **no further advances** into the southern Pacific. Instead, Great Britain and France now took the initiative. The decisive factor in unveiling the secrets surrounding the mythical southern continent were the **three voyages around the world** undertaken by James Cook (►Famous People) between 1768 and 1779, during which he made landfall in New Zealand.

James Cook's voyages of discovery

In early October 1769, during his search for the mythical southern continent, Cook reached the waters off New Zealand's North Island aboard his **ship Endeavour**. On 8 October Cook and his men stepped onto the island near today's Gisborne, hoisting the English flag shortly after at Mercury Bay on the Coromandel Peninsula, taking possession of the land **for King George III**. After that, Cook sailed for several months along the coastline of New Zealand, noting that it consisted in fact of **two main islands**. In the process, he also named many bays and promontories. In 1770 Cook anchored in Queen Charlotte Sound. During his second voyage around the world Cook returned to New Zealand, with the ships Resolution and Adventure, this time accompanied by the painter William Hogdes and the German natural scientist Johann Reinhold Forster with his son Georg . After spending time at Dusky Sound in South Island's Fiordland, he stopped over again at Ship Cove in Queen Charlotte Sound.

James Cook lands near Mercury Bay

Business with the Maori

Cook had contact with the traditional Maori culture and way of life on his first landing. New Zealand's native inhabitants loved the gifts and bartered goods of the Europeans, mainly iron nails, **iron axes and tobacco** (rather than alcohol, which they detested). When Cook came to New Zealand for the second time, the Maori were already well adjusted to **bartering**: they would keep the ship's crew in fish, sweet potatoes and fresh water in exchange for the coveted goods.

The French miss out

Hot on the heels of James Cook followed French seafarers. In 1769/1770, **Jean François de Surville** anchored, each time just after Cook to the north, in Doubtless Bay; in 1772 Marion du Fresne landed in the Bay of Islands, taking possession of the land for France as »France Australe«. An initially friendly encounter with the native inhabitants turned into **conflict**, with the Maori killing the captain and several of his crew. The Europeans that were left burned down three Maori villages, shooting dead many of the inhabitants.

Contact with Australia

The British government viewed Australia, also discovered by Cook, as an ideal **penal colony**. In 1788 the First Fleet arrived in Botany Bay, and the foundation of Sydney shortly afterwards marked the establishment of the first British colony. Ships soon left Australia for New Zealand, including the first **whaler** in 1791. And in 1792, seals were hunted in Dusky Sound for the first time. Others came to barter for flax with the natives and to cut down the rich woodlands.

New influence

For the Maori, **contact with the white people** brought changes and problems. Wheat and potatoes, pigs and horses were imported, but also hatchets, axes and, above all, the highly demanded firearms. The tribes living in Northland near the trading centre on the Bay of Islands would sell the traders almost anything to get hold of rifles.

Power-hungry chiefs

Having firearms meant that the Northland tribes held a powerful **superiority** over those that were not yet in direct contact with the white people. Hordes of rifle-wielding warriors under power-hungry chiefs such as **Te Rauparaha** (1819) subjected, killed or drove out defeated tribal groups, first on North Island, and later on South Island as well. Particular cruelty was displayed by Hongi Hika, who had visited England in 1820 and used the return trip via Australia for swapping the presents given by the English for rifles.

Breaking the rules

In the early 19th century, the number of the **pakeha**, i.e. the white people, was still relatively small; they came to agreements with and lived in close proximity to the Maori. However, over time the port settlement of Kororareka in the Bay of Islands deteriorated to become the **»Hellhole of the Pacific«**. White whalers and merchants exploited the naïve Maori, including breaking their customs and etiquette. The breaching of the Maori tapu laws led to violent conflicts and riots.

The founding of the first mission station in the Bay of Islands by Samuel Marsden (1765 – 1838) at Christmas 1814 marks the beginning of missionary work. As well as the **Anglicans**, **Methodists** also established a mission in 1823 in Whangaroa Harbour, and Catholic clergymen from France worked towards what they saw as the salvation of the Maori. However, the first successful conversions were few and far between, with the coexistence and competition of the Christian denominations scaring the Maori off. It was only with the increasing **impotence of the tribal priests** against the diseases introduced by the white people, and their perceived ability to breach the tapu rules without incurring divine retribution, that the number of successful **conversions** slowly rose, until by the mid-19th century most Maori professed some kind of Christianity.

Missionizing asnd colonizing

In 1823, once the number of white people in the Bay of Islands had grown, it was decreed from London that the British subjects in New Zealand would from now on be subject to the **jurisdiction of Sydney**. However, Sydney was over 2,000km/1,200 miles from New Zealand, and in Kororareka the law of the jungle, **arbitrariness and**

British sovereignty

The English artist Henry Williams depicted the Maori battle fleet with its long canoes in 1835

chaos continued to rule. In 1827, Hongi Hika and his warriors attacked and destroyed the mission of Whangaroa. In 1833, James Busby, as the official representative of British interests, arrived in the Bay of Islands, where already over 2,000 white settlers lived.

Pressure of the white settlers
The new settlers demanded land to cultivate and the Maori were prepared to give it to them. In exchange for rifles and tobacco however, the Maori would sometimes sell land that did not belong to them personally, but to the tribe collectively. **Bloody conflicts** ensued, as white settlers began to cultivate the land that they had acquired in good faith. Furthermore, they would often disregard the Maori's tapu commandments, unlawfully appropriating their land and inviting the revenge of the Maori.

Quarrels over land
In 1834, the conquest of Waimate Pa (Taranaki) saw the first clashes between British soldiers and Maori warriors. The fight for the land escalated following the foundation in 1838 of the **»New Zealand Colonisation Company«**. The company's driving force, Edward Gibbon Wakefield, was already well-known for his colonisation plans for southern Australia. The company would buy up land on a large scale, mostly from individual members of a tribe who did not have the approval of the tribe as a whole.

Arbitration efforts
The settlers, who were sold this land for a lot of money, then had to suffer the attacks of the tribe. In July 1839, in an attempt to bring order to this chaos, and also to forestall potential **French annexation plans**, Captain William Hobson (▶Famous People) was sent to New Zealand as representative of the governor of New South Wales. Hobson was supposed to protect both the Maori and the white settlers and proclaim the British crown's **sovereignty** in New Zealand, with the agreement of the Maori.

6 February 1840
On 6 February 1840, at Waitangi (Bay of Islands), Hobson and some 50 Maori chiefs from Northland signed the **Treaty of Waitangi**, which is considered the **»birth certificate«** of the state of New Zealand and its oldest constitutional document. In the treaty, the chiefs recognised the sovereignty of the British crown and in turn were guaranteed all existing private and collective property rights to their country, with the promise that only the English crown would be allowed to purchase Maori land, and given all the privileges of British subjects.

Afraid of losing power
Messengers took this **treaty** to all the tribes, so that eventually it bore over 500 signatures. Some tribal chiefs did however foresee the loss of political power and Maori autonomy and refused to sign. Today still, large sections of the Maori are hostile towards the treaty. Thus, the anniversary of the signing repeatedly provokes **protest demon-**

strations on the spot where it happened, in front of the historical Treaty House in Waitangi, in order to claim the rights granted by the treaty. A cruel pun turned the »Treaty of Waitangi« into the »Cheaty of Waitangi«. In 1975, the New Zealand government established a dedicated department looking at Maori complaints about breaches of the treaty, the **Waitangi Tribunal**.

Using the Treaty of Waitangi, the British annexed North Island in May 1840; they further inferred from the treaty the right to explore South Island and thus bring it into their possession. In May 1841 New Zealand became a crown colony, with Captain Hobson as its **first governor**. Hobson moved the capital from the Bay of Islands, which was still suffering some unrest, further south to the town of Auckland, founded in 1840.

New Zealand a crown colony

MAORI RESISTANCE

1839 – 1843	around 20,000 immigrants come into the country
1843 – 1881	Maori land wars against the colonial power
19th / 20th cent.	Renewal movements emerge within the Maori

Despite the refusal of some chiefs, the signing of the Treaty of Waitangi initially seemed to solve all problems between the pakeha and the Maori: the government had all disputed **land sales** checked by a commission, with the tribes partly getting their land back. In practice however, the government would sell on the land it had bought at substantial profit to the **thousands** of white settlers pouring into the country every year from 1840 onwards. This period saw the foundation of Wellington, Wanganui and New Plymouth on North Island, as well as Nelson and Akaroa on the Banks Peninsula near today's Christchurch by French immigrants.

Treaty of Waitangi

Whilst the **settlement plans**, led by the New Zealand Company, often proved to be empty promises, between 1839 and 1843 they did bring around 20,000 immigrants to New Zealand. In 1844 the company had to cease their activities due to lack of funds. The more land was transferred to the white settlers, the clearer it became to the Maori that they would soon be left empty-handed. The colony's **electoral law** also put them at a disadvantage, as at the time only personal owners of property were allowed to vote; with Maori land being the property of the tribe rather than of an individual, they remained excluded from elections. This inevitably led to conflicts.

20,000 immigrants

In 1843 the Wairau Valley near Nelson witnessed what came to be called the »**Wairau Affray**«. Despite previous warnings, a group of

The Maori rise up

white settlers from Nelson, led by Captain Arthur Wakefield, was travelling in the Wairau Valley to survey a heavily disputed land purchase. The local Maori saw this survey as a **provocation**, and the single bloodiest altercation about land rights on South Island ensued, with 21 settlers, Wakefield amongst them, being killed.

Settlers attacked

Unrest also started in the North; in 1844, chief Hone Heke felled the **British flagstaff** in Kororareka/Russell several times over and burned down the entire settlement in 1845. The following year, George Grey, governor since 1845, had Hone Heke's stronghold of Ruapekapeka taken by British soldiers. In 1846, the south of North Island, in the Hutt Valley near Wellington, also saw attacks by Maori tribes, and in 1847 there were **bloody clashes** near Wanganui in the southwest of North Island. After that things quietened down until 1860.

Constitution Act

Around this time, the beginnings of a government answerable to a **parliament** and of a regional self-administration began to take shape. The Constitution Act of 1852 cut back the power of the governor, as demanded by the settlers, and the provinces of Auckland, New Plymouth, Wellington, Nelson, Canterbury and Otago were founded, each with their own governments.

The Maori gather

As a reaction to the increased settlement by white people, the Maori tribes retreated into the remote interior. Towards the end of the 1850s, along the Waikato river in the centre of North Island, a **collective movement** came together, aiming for a unified front involving as many tribes as possible in order to counter the thirst for land of the white settlers. In 1857 this **king movement**, called »Maori Kingitanga« and mainly headed by the Waikato and Maniopoto tribes, elected chief Te Wherowhero as king. While he was not recognized by all the tribes, Potatau I, as he became known, and his Waikato tribes would for years fight tooth and nail against the government troops.

Battle for rights

Elsewhere too the indigenous people rebelled again. When a sub-chief sold land against the will of the tribe in 1860 on the northern slopes of the Taranaki (Mt Egmont) in New Plymouth, where the **lack of land** was particularly acute, the Maori attacked the white settlers. The government sent troops, and the fighting at Waitara marked the beginning of the land wars proper. After a **ceasefire** was negotiated in 1861, Taranaki still saw frequent Maori guerrilla attacks.

Driven south

From Taranaki, the theatre of war shifted to the Waikato River. Government troops drove the followers of the King's Movement south.

Mount Taranake rises up majestically; the land wars of 1860 began on its north slopes.

Cannon boats were used to attack positions in Meremere and Rangiriri from the Waikato River, and the **residence** of the Maori king was conquered. Eventually, British soldiers brutally drove out the rebellious Maori all the way down to the Punui River. South of the river was the start of **King Country**, as it is still called today, which the government ceded to the surviving followers of the retreated Maori king. The tribal land belonging to the rebels was confiscated.

Battles in the east

After the rebellions on the Waikato had been put down, the east coast was next to see revolt. In the battle for Gate Pa, the **Maori stronghold** near Tauranga in 1864, the government troops suffered **heavy losses**. Some weeks later however, the Maori were routed at Pa Te Ranga and their tribal lands confiscated by the state.

Hauhau movement

By the mid-1860s the character of the rebellion had changed. Now, religion was the main motivating force behind the rebelling Maori. The Hauhau movement, which took its name from its battle cry, was a Maori **revivalist movement**. They felt oppressed by the white settlers and wanted to chase them out of the country. Convinced that their strong faith would protect them from being hit by bullets, the Hauhau **ran into battle shouting**. Around 1865, the cult had spread over the whole of North Island. The Hauhau recruited new followers amongst the tribes loyal to the government on the eastern coast, and fought the government troops at Ruatoria and Gisborne, before eventually being defeated.

Moses of the Maori

Also native to the eastern coast, **Te Kooti** had a long line of ancestors; but he was no chief nor did he have a tattoo. He collaborated with the government in the fight against the Hauhau movement, but after being suspected of **collaborating** with the enemy, in 1866, along with 30 Hauhau followers, he was banished to the remote Chatham Isles without trial, where he founded a new **cult** called »Ringatu«. Te Kooti saw himself as the Moses of the Maori and wanted to be the one to get the Promised Land back for them. After fleeing from the island in 1868, Te Kooti and his followers battered to death 70 white settlers and Maori loyal to the government in Poverty Bay. The troops sent after him never caught him, and in 1872 he moved to King Country, where he lived under the protection of the Maori king Tawhiao, until being pardoned by the government in 1883.

Civil disobedience

The land wars came to an end with **peaceful acts of resistance** in Parihake at Taranaki (Mt Egmont): from 1866 onwards, the Maori prophets Te Whiti and Tohu called on their followers to pursue a campaign of civil disobedience against the white settlers and the government. Te Whiti would become one of the unifying figures of the Maori renewal movement.

The white settlers and the government had emerged clearly victorious from the land wars, with the coveted land now at their disposal. The Maori had not managed to present a united front. Whilst they were granted four seats in parliament as early as 1867, it was only in the 20th century that some of them received **compensation payments** for the injustices suffered in the land wars. In 1881, **peace was officially made** between the Maori king and the government, with the rebels receiving a pardon and allowed to leave King Country again.

The Maori are defeated

Whilst North Island was the theatre for the raging land wars, **sheep and cattle** herds were able to spread out across huge pastures. As early as 1847, the first shiploads of butter and cheese were transported from South Island to Sydney. However, it was gold mining rather than agriculture that brought wealth, and faster. After smaller finds at Milton in 1855 and in the Buller River in 1859, the major rush began in 1861, when Gabriel Read, a prospector from Tasmania who had gained previous experience in California and Australia, found the rich deposits of »Gabriel's Gully« at Lawrence, southwest of Dunedin.

Gold brings wealth

At that time most of the gold deposits in California and Victoria, Australia had already been exploited, so the **gold prospectors** flocked from there to Otago, in addition to many newcomers who

Up and coming Auckland

The gold prospector town of Clyde in Orago Region was much more lively during gold rush days

had quickly opened up the deposits of Clyde, Queenstown and Arrowtown. The gold finds turned Dunedin into a wealthy community of some importance; it was here that in 1869 New Zealand's **first university** was established. After the deposits were exhausted, the prospectors and adventurers moved on to the remote western coast. Hokitika grew, becoming an important supply port, but the passes across the high Southern Alps were also explored and connecting roads built. Thus, there was a **stagecoach connection** between Christchurch and Hokitika as early as 1866. With the end of the gold boom in the late 1860s the population migrated northwards, but not to the newly established capital of Wellington, but to Auckland, which now became the **economic capital**.

Wellington the capital

The gold wealth of South Island also awakened the desire for political independence from a North Island embroiled in the Maori wars. When Wellington was made capital in 1865, it was in order to confront these **separatist ambitions**. The general assembly decided against secession. In 1876, the centralists carried the day against the provincialists by abolishing the provincial governments. Now the **central government** once again held the initiative in terms of the development of the country.

1891 – 1912: Liberal era

The latter part of the 19th century was dominated by new developments in agriculture. By exporting **frozen meat**, the economy gained another mainstay; in 1882, a refrigerator ship left Port Chalmers to ship frozen meat to England for the first time. However, exports geared so heavily towards agricultural produce were subject to **price crashes** on the world markets. Also, New Zealand was heavily in debt through the borrowing which had financed the expansion of its infrastructure in the 1870s.

Exemplary social policy

With the economy in decline after the loss in value of the agricultural exports, unemployment rose steeply. The government, since 1891 in the hands of the Liberal Party, introduced a textbook social policy, which gave New Zealand a **pioneering role** in the wider world. New laws restricted the large-scale land holdings, which were particularly widespread on South Island, and allowed the rural workers to acquire land for themselves. The social and economic protection of the workers was strenghened by the introduction of the **8-hour working day** (1899), child labour safeguards, factory supervision, accident liability, health care and **state-guaranteed pensions**. However, only union members would benefit from this level of care. The electoral law had also been reformed in 1889, and in 1893 the goals of the **suffragettes** were achieved, with women receiving active voting rights.

Ngaruawahia is the official seat of the king of the Maori

While the overall population was steadily increasing – in 1901, New Zealand had 815,853 inhabitants – the **Maori population** fell alarmingly quickly to some 40,000 people. The Maori were like strangers in their own country, retreating or trying to make a living in competition with the white majority on the margins of society. Characteristic of the Maori's **self-abandonment** was the present that high chief Te Heuheu Tukino IV made the government: in the face of the Europeans' unstoppable progress in land use, he transferred the **volcanic peaks** of Tongariro, Ngauruhoe and Ruapehu, sacred to the Maori, to the government, with the caveat that a nature reserve be established there. This bequest formed the basis for New Zealand's **first national park**.

Strangers in their own country

Revivalist movements attempted to counter this development; some, such as the Hauhau, Ringatu, the movement led by Wiremu Ratana or the prophets of non-violent resistance, Te Whiti and Tohu, had religious foundations and messianic elements. The biggest impact was achieved by the charismatic Wiremu Ratana, whose **faith healings** attracted an enormous number of people and also gained political influence through the Ratana movement. **For decades**, the four seats in parliament due to the Maori were taken up by his followers.

Revivalist movements

A Maori unification movement with a long tradition is the Kingitanga **king movement** founded in 1858, but which remained re-

Social role: Kingitanga

stricted to the Waikato tribes. The king or queen does not fulfil any constitutional, administrative or political functions; what counts is solely the social and cultural role, the element of preservation and tradition so important to the »Maoritanga«. As was the case before the land wars, **today's king** at least officially resides again in Ngaruawahia at the confluence of the Waikato and Waipa rivers and is informally recognised by the government.

Political: Kotahitanga

A rival to Kingitanga in the 1890s was the Kotahitanga or **Maori Parliament** movement, started in Papawai near Masterton, which wanted an independent government for the Maori. Politically, these efforts found their expression in the Young Maori Party, which was set up primarily by pupils of the Te Aute College (near Hastings) in the early 1890s. Apirana Ngati, who was the first Maori to gain a university degree, used his position as secretary of the Young Maori Party to champion Maori rights in parliament. **James Carroll**, also known

Survival by assimilation

as Timi Kara, son of a chief's daughter and a white farmer from Wairoa, campaigned for »Maoritanga« as a member of parliament, minister and as prime minister. All advocates of »Maoritanga«, the preservation of Maori culture and traditions, saw the only chance for survival in **assimilation**. Thanks to government measures to promote Maori culture, the Maori were recovering. This resurgence was not to be dented by the terrible **flu epidemic** of 1918, which claimed a disproportionately high number of victims among the Maori, to the point that it was even interpreted as the revenge of their former deities.

NEW ZEALAND IN THE 20TH AND 21ST CENTURY

1907	The crown colony of New Zealand is given the status of a dominion
1911	The country's population exceeds one million
25 April 1915	Thousands of New Zealanders die at Gallipoli (Day of Remembrance)
World War II	New Zealand fights on the side of the Allies
1947	New Zealand attains full independence
1995	Compensation payments for the land expropriation of the Maori

New Zealand becomes a dominion

New Zealand did not join the British colonies on Australian soil that grouped together as the self-governing Commonwealth of Australia, instead remaining a crown colony until 1907, when it gained the status of a dominion. In 1911, the **population** passed the one million mark. When William F. Massey's Reform Party, supported by the farmers, took over government in 1912, the Liberal era was at an end.

Beautiful woodcarving is part of traditional Maori culture

In World War I, New Zealand supported the British mother country with troops. Together with Australia they fought as **»Australian & New Zealand Army Corps«** (ANZAC) in Egypt and in the Dardanelles against the Ottoman Empire, as well as in France and Belgium. On 25 April 1915, thousands of New Zealanders and Australians fell at Gallipoli, a day that has since become the **ANZAC Day of remembrance**. New Zealand's participation in the Conference of Versailles was an important appearance in the circle of sovereign nations, leading to membership of the League of Nations and the transferring of the mandate over the former German possession of Western Samoa in 1920. The inter-war period was dominated by **economic crises** and a fundamental political change, when in 1935 the **Labour Party** took over government for the first time.

All this faded into the background with the outbreak of World War II. Again, New Zealand sent troops, which from 1940 onwards were used in Greece and on Crete, in North Africa and later during the campaign in Italy. In contrast to the First World War, this time New Zealand was also subject to a **direct threat** from the Japanese. Only the intervention of US armed forces in the South Pacific averted this danger. The American assistance for New Zealand also signalled a fundamental shift in foreign policy towards the South Pacific region and the US, which found clear expression in the signing of the AN-

ZAC Pact between Australia and New Zealand 1944, and most of all in the 1951 **ANZUS Pact**, in which Australia, New Zealand and the US agreed a defence pact.

A sovereign New Zealand Four years previously, in 1947, New Zealand had achieved full independence, when parliament accepted the 1931 Statute of Westminster, making New Zealand a member of the Commonwealth of Nations. In the 20th century, England remained the true home for most of those who had moved from there and their descendants. Only in the recent past has the »Kiwis'« **view of the world** changed. The country began to align itself more with its South-East Asian, Australian and Pacific neighbours, first politically in treaties of protection and assistance such as SEATO, then also economically. Thus, New Zealand troops took part in the Korean and Vietnam Wars.

Relationship with USA changed In the 1980s however, New Zealand's stance towards the USA as its protector changed. The **anti-nuclear politics** of the Labour-led Lange government eventually led to the abrogation of the USA's ANZUS Pact responsibilities. The government also held a consistent line in denouncing French **nuclear weapons tests** on the Mururoa atoll, recalling its ambassador from Paris. Incidentally, on 10 July 1985, the **Greenpeace flagship** *Rainbow Warrior I* was sunk by French agents in the harbour of Auckland.

Maoritanga in the 20th century In the 20th century, the Maori renaissance movement was able to claim some successes. Established in 1975, the **Waitangi Tribunal** has been examining the claims of Maori tribes against the government, based on non-compliance with the rights and privileges granted in the Treaty of Waitangi. The tribunal is also a forum for matters regarding the contemporary scope for realising Maori tradition.

More self-respect A big step forward was made in 1987 with the introduction of the »Maori Language Act«, securing the **equal treatment** of English and Maori in New Zealand's public life. This also marked the turning point from an earlier assimilation phase to a **multicultural approach** more mindful of the respective cultures' distinct characters, thereby also responding to the difficult situation of the Pacific Islanders in New Zealand. Signs for the revival of Maori culture are the many new »marae« (meeting places) where Maori meet each other as well as white neighbours and guests. Old traditions are being revived in the arts of wood carving and handweaving, as well as the strong interest in Maori mythology and dances.

Public protests Since the end of the 1960s, **youth protest** has been a channel for the Maori movement to reach the public. There were protests against Eurocentric teaching at schools, plus land occupations and demonstration marches to Waitangi. Today's Maori do not want to be dependent on the welfare state any longer and are striving for **cultural and economic emancipation**. Given the difficult economic situation and the high levels of unemployment, which affect young Maori much more than white New Zealanders, achieving this is not an easy task. In May 1995, in the presence of the **Maori Queen Te Aiairangikaahu**, the New Zealand prime minister signed a document in which the government apologised for the 19th-century land expropriation by British troops. On top of that, the Tainui Maori association was granted 10 million US$ and 170 sq km/65 sq miles of land as reparation. This contract was confirmed in November 1995 by Queen Elizabeth II on the occasion of her visit to Rotorua.

In 1999, the electorate of New Zealand brought about a **shift in political direction**. After nine years of government by the conservative National Party, the Labour Party, led by the political scientist **Helen Clark** managed to swing the vote their way. Re-elected in 2005, the prime minister initiated wide-ranging adjustments to the free market economy, but was defeated in the 2008 general elections by the National Party under John Key, who now leads a coalition government.

Labour Party wins

Due to New Zealand's geological position in the collision area of two large continental plates, the country is no stranger to substantial **earthquakes** and **volcanic eruptions**. Thus, in February 1931 an earthquake in the town of Napier on North Island claimed the lives of 256 people. Active with irregular frequency is the volcano Ruapehu (in the Maori language = »exploding hell«) on North Island. On New Year's Eve 1953, an eruption claimed 151 lives.

Nature takes its toll

An earthquake shook South Island in July 2009 and the south-western coast moved 30cm/12in towards Australia. Three earthquakes in the region of Canterbury on south Island caused extensive damage in 2010/2011: on September 4, 2010 a quake that measured 7.1 points shook Christchurch. As the second most sever earthquake in New Zealand since 1931 it destroyed more than 500 buildings in the nation's second-largest city; there were no fatalities.

Severe earthquakes

There were countless aftershocks in the following months. The strongest – at 6.3 points – caused even more damage on February 22 than the main quake did since the epicentre was closer to the city. More than 180 people were killed and another 7,000 were injured. On June 13, 2011 about 50 houses collapsed in two more aftershocks; on September 4, 2011, a year after the first earthquake, Christchurch was again rocked. According to experts rebuilding the city will take about

Difficult reconstruction

20 years. Whole neighbourhoods have to be abandoned as the damage is too great and the ground is no longer suitable for building on it. Reconstructed buildings are to be limited to seven stories.

Successful sailors

In the spring of 2000 New Zealanders had reason to party when their yacht *Black Magic* NZL 60 successfully defended the **America's Cup** (►MARCO POLO Insight p. 146) it had won – to everybody's surprise – in 1995. However, in spring 2003 the New Zealand sailors failed to hold on to the trophy, having to concede victory to the Swiss *Alinghi* team.

New Maori king

On 15 August 2006 the Maori Queen Dame **Te Atairangikaahu** passed away only a few weeks after her 40th jubilee. Her son **Tuheitia Paki** became the new Maori king.

National Party rules

In fall 2008 there was a change in politics when **John Key (reelected in 2011 and 2014)** of the National Party became prime minister and replaced Helen Clark of the Labour Party. He immediately had to cope with the most **severe economic recession**, which New Zealand entered after the crisis on the financial markets that had been visible in 2007 already.

In 2011 the **container ship** *Rena* stranded on a reef in the Bay of Plenty and broke apart in early 2012. It caused New Zealand's worst **environmental catastrophe** to date.

Hot stuff: volcano eruptions are not unusual.
This one is on White Island off the coast of Whakatane.

Arts and Culture

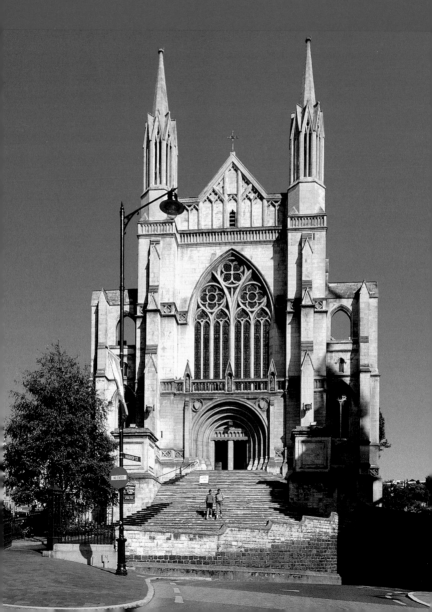

Maori Culture

Who is personified by the Maori meeting house? Where did New Zealand painting take its inspiration from? Who is the major influence on New Zealand theatre? Traditional Maori culture meets modern art by the descendants of the European immigrants.

The traditions and old art forms of the Maori become apparent to visitors in many New Zealand **museums**. The collections include meeting houses decorated with valuable carvings, old war canoes, sculptures carved from nephrite (greenstone) and much more. The skills, customs and traditions of the Maori may be experienced as part of special presentations as well, where **traditional songs** and dances are performed. Initiated by some Maori leaders, the Maoritanga movement aims to revive and nurture their people's **culture and history**.

Maoritanga (►MARCO-POLO Insight p. 224)

Today, a relatively high number of Maori still live on the **volcanic plateau** in the centre of North Island, including Rotorua and Taupo, in the Waikato area, in Northland, on the East Cape, on the Taranaki and in the Wanganui area. Here there is still plenty of visible evidence of their old culture, with the »marae« meeting places and their **richly decorated** communal and meeting houses.

Marae on North Island

The oldest meeting houses date back to the 19th century; however, in more recent times **new meeting sites** in the traditional style have been established all over the country. As in the past, these are places where greeting ceremonies and dances are held, where traditional speeches and chants are recited and weddings, christenings and birthdays are celebrated in style, and, above all, where very solemn tangihanga **mourning ceremonies** are held. Also as in the past, these meeting places are considered special sites which must be respected by visitors too.

Living tradition

Some of the **oldest evidence** of Maori culture are the rock drawings. These are found mainly on New Zealand's South Island, particularly in the south of the Canterbury region as well as in northern Otago. **Dating** them precisely has proven difficult, but they date back at least to the time before the arrival of the Europeans. So far, the meanings of many of these drawings have not been conclusively determined

Rock drawings

**An imposing monument to Neogothic architecture:
St Paul's Anglican Cathedral in Dunedin**

either. The drawings were mostly executed with **charcoal** or ochre and show various motifs, amongst them animals and humans.

Artistic carvings

Maori carvings are amongst the **highest achievements of South Sea art.** The preferred material was the durable yet easily worked wood of the native **totara tree.** Most of the richly decorated meeting and storage houses admired today are no older than 150 years and were crafted using modern iron tools.

Obsidian tools

Before making contact with the white people, the Maori only had access to carving tools made from stone. They relied on the glass-like volcanic obsidian to make razor-sharp scrapers and blades. Due to the importance of ancestor worship, **human figures** constitute some of the most important work of Maori woodcraft. Particularly conspicuous is the **over-emphasised head**, the part of the body that, according to Maori beliefs, was the most »tapu« and hence the most important. The feet presumably were considered less sacred and were

Southseas art: rich carvings by native inhabitants.

therefore represented in a shortened way. The hands of many figures mostly have only three fingers, similar to birds' claws. The slanting eyes are either hollow or decorated with inlaid **paua mother-of-pearl shells**. Often, figures are shown in a warrior pose with wide-open eyes and tongue sticking out, and wielding a stone club in their hand. The haka **war dance** also features this gesture, possibly intended to provoke or scare off evil spirits.

Most of the wood carvings – reliefs or free-standing figures – are painted in red or a reddish colour. All over Polynesia, the colour red had high symbolic value as the colour of the gods. To make the paint, red **ochre and fish oil** were mixed, with the colour allowing the grain of the wood and the **details** of the work to shine through. Unfortunately, in recent times many old carvings have been overlaid with thick oil paint, even in renowned museums.

Red – colour of the gods

The Maori would also decorate their canoes, paddles, musical instruments, weapons and objects of daily life **with rich ornaments**. The Maori meeting house, called »whare runanga«, personifies the highly revered ancestor. The gable of the house is crowned by the standing figure (»tekoteko«) of the ancestor, the mask (»koruru«) below showing his face. The roof boards form his outstretched arms (»maihi«) with fingers (»raparapa«). The interior of the meeting house represents his chest, the large beam running the length of the roof is seen as his **spine**, and the rafters his ribs. The rich **carvings inside** represent other personalities from the ancestor's circle, deities and mythical characters. In this way, the carvings served as a kind of **picture book**, a visual aid to representing the ancestors' deeds in song and stories.

Ancestors' house

A high degree of skill is also demonstrated by the jewellery and weapons crafted by Maori artists from the native »pounamu« (nephrite, greenstone, jade). This **semi-precious stone** (►MARCO POLO Insight p. 130) was only found along some rivers in the northwest of South Island. A very hard material, nephrite was polished for an interminably long time in order to create prestigious axes and clubs for chiefs or »hei-tiki«, **amulets** in human form. Today, nephrite jewellery is still manufactured following traditional patterns in Hokitika and Greymouth. The missionaries who sought to convert the Maori from 1814 did not appreciate the representations of **nudity** and particularly the sexual motifs.

Objects made from pounamu

At the end of the 19th century, along with the decline in the Maori population, their wood art almost fell into oblivion too. It was only through the Maoritanga movement and **new masters** such as Pine Taiapa that wood carving experienced a strong revival. Renowned

Maori carving as commercial goods

European collections, such as the British Museum in London (with 3,000 objects, almost certainly the finest in the world outside Aotearoa), include examples of classic Maori culture, as in the early 19th century these pieces were highly prized for trading and bartering.

Tattoos show status The Maori used the art of tattooing not to beautify the face but to mark a person's status. The men would have tattoos on the entire face, buttocks and thighs, women only on the **chin and lips**.

Music and speech The significance of Maori traditional music and speech developed due to the lack of a written tradition, and consists of the transmission of traditions, mythology and history. Music is comprised **almost exclusively of songs** (»waiata«), with a pitch that only alters slightly, but with very complex rhythms. The songs were accompanied by flutes, rhythms emerging from the singers stamping their feet and slapping their thighs or chest with their hands. Speech and song were intimately connected on **ceremonial occasions** at the meeting place (marae) and in the meeting house.

Songs were part of the formal rhetoric so to speak. Both found their subjects mainly in **mythology**. There were a variety of songs, but apart from the »karakia«, the sacred songs reserved for the priest during ritual ceremonies, it was mainly songs of mourning and love that were passed down. Modern Maori songs are often based on the Christian choral traditions of the European immigrants. Younger groups however are again reviving **traditional Maori music**.

Visual Arts

It took until the middle of the 20th century before painters and sculptors loosened their artistic orientation to Europe and let themselves be inspired by Maori themes.

Art of the immigrants The first white settlers came accompanied by cartographers and draughtsmen, meticulously recording what happened during the landing, and creating the first drawings of the natives, of the flora and fauna and also the landscapes. During his travels through New Zealand in 1844, George F Angas (1822 – 1886) committed many studies and images of the Maori to paper. Museum collections also keep the often **touchingly naïve** drawings from the times of the first settlers. The land surveyor **Charles Heaphy** (1820 – 1881) used his travels to create beautiful landscape portraits. Impressive too are the many lifelike portraits of the Maori and scenes from their lives by **Gottfried Lindauer** (1839 – 1926), a Czech from Pilzeň who lived in New Zea-

In good shape: traditional pottery in Nelson

land from 1873. **Charles Frederick Goldie** (1870 – 1947), born in Auckland, became one of the most famous painters in New Zealand, particularly because of his naturalistic depictions of the Maori.

20th century

Until the 20th century, New Zealand painting entirely followed **European examples**; New Zealand artists studied and worked mainly in London and would also exhibit there. The painter **Frances Hodgkins** (1869 – 1947) was from Dunedin, but became famous and successful only in England. Her still lifes and landscapes showed a European influence, Expressionism in particular. Other famous artists are the landscape painter Sir Mountford Tosswill Woollaston (1910 – 1998), Ralph Hotere (born in 1931), and the highly original Colin McCahon (1919 – 1987), whose large-format oil paintings with religious, mythological and social themes attract great interest.

Increase in Maori themes

Since the mid-20th century, the influence of Maori themes on New Zealand painting are unmistakable. Amongst the New Zealand sculptors, **Len Lye** (1901 – 1980) became famous for his **kinetic sculptures**. Two other artists who also became famous as sculptors and designers were Guy Ngan (born in 1926) and Molly McAlister (1920 – 1979).

Creative place

Many artists have settled in the sunny regions around Nelson on South Island and Northland (Bay of Islands in particular). One of them was the Austrian artist **Friedensreich Hundertwasser** (►Famous People), who from 1973 onwards lived partly on the Bay of Islands.

Arts and crafts

Because of the **carving and weaving skills** of the Maori, arts and crafts have had a long tradition in New Zealand. Over the years the whole country has seen the establishment of many arts and crafts potteries. Avant-garde arts and crafts shops and commercial galleries are doing well.

Architecture

From rushes to wood, stone to glass and steel: New zealand's architectural history is comparatively short. The immigrants preferred neogothic and neoclassicism for public buildings, but fans of modern buildings will also find something.

Maori architecture

At the time of the discovery of New Zealand by the white settlers, the Maori lived either in open villages (kainga) with simple huts or in fortified settlements (pa) surrounded by palisades. A **reconstructed Maori village**, Rewa's Village, can be found in Kerikeri and is well worth seeing. Maori houses are distinguished by the rich carvings, amongst them figures and masks with tongues sticking out.

Buildings of the white settlers

The first white whale and seal hunters erected tents and primitive huts made from reed (raupo) as living accommodation. Wealthy settlers brought prefabricated houses, and the widespread sawmills made wooden houses common. Stone houses were almost entirely restricted to public buildings. The **first European-style houses** were built in connection with the mission work on the Bay of Islands, such as the stations of Kerikeri and Waimate North. In the Auckland area, as well as around Christchurch, a number of 19th-century settler houses are preserved, some of them with wraparound balconies. Fancier residential buildings were realised in the **cottage style**. Attractive examples of this are Larnach Castle near Dunedin, Holly Lea in Christchurch and Alberton in Auckland.

Churches and secular buildings

For public building works in New Zealand, planners preferred the **neo-Gothic style**, whose forms borrowed from the English and Norman Gothic style. Most buildings were erected **from wood**. Under the guidance of the first Anglican bishop, Selwyn (1809 – 1878) and his architect **Frederick Thatcher** (1814 – 1890), a number of churches were built in this style, such as St Mary's Church in New Plymouth (1845/1846) and the All Saints Church in Howick (1847), but also secular buildings such as St John's College in Auckland (chapel 1847, College Hall 1849).

Neo-Gothic witnesses

Alongside Thatcher, **Benjamin W Mountfort** (1825 – 1898), who had immigrated to New Zealand in 1850, also made a name for himself as the architect of prestigious buildings in the neo-Gothic style. Amongst others, Mountfort designed Canterbury Museum and Canterbury College, both in Christchurch, as well as **St Mary's Pro-Cathedral** in Parnell/Auckland, built in 1888.

Neoclassicism was to become the second dominant style in 19th century New Zealand architecture. Auckland's **Government House** was
built following plans by William Mason and in 1876 William H Clayton designed the government building for the new capital, Wellington, also in the classicist style. William Armson (1834 – 1883), who
arrived in 1862 from Melbourne, contributed to the neoclassical aspect of towns like **Christchurch, Dunedin, Oamaru and Hokitika**.
One of the architects active in Dunedin and Oamaru was R A Lawson
(1833 – 1903), who left a number of neoclassical buildings.

Architecture in the English crown colony of New Zealand in the
early 20th century was still dominated by British and European
styles. In Europe as in New Zealand, the **neo-Baroque** style marks
the last vestiges of historicism. **John Campbell** chose neo-Baroque
as the appropriate style for the Public Trust in Wellington and the
main post office in Auckland. Of Campbell's 1911 design for the Parliament in Wellington that had burned down in 1907, only half was
executed; the left wing was only finally erected between 1964 and
1982 following designs by the London architect **Basil Spence**. Soon,
New Zealanders dubbed the building »Beehive«. Further prime examples for New Zealand's neo-Baroque style are the railway station
in Dunedin (1907) and Invercargill Town Hall (1906).

Architecture worth seeing: Willis Street in Wellington

Wellington's appearance is characterized by modern architecture: here the national museum Te Papa Tongarewa

Bauhaus influence

Functionalism gradually started to gain ground, as it had elsewhere, only after World War I. Under the influence of the German Bauhaus style, the 1920s saw the first steel-frame high-rises. The **massive 1931 earthquake** on Hawke's Bay on North Island destroyed most of Napier and Hastings; however, the two towns were rebuilt in a unified **Art Déco style**. The attractive Napier (pop. 60,000) in particular presents a unique cityscape to this day with pastel-coloured houses that one would ususally expect to find in Miami.

Critical architecture

In recent memory, two buildings have caused much controversy, the aforementioned government building in Wellington nicknamed »Beehive« and the Aotea Centre in Auckland, a concert hall built in 1989 in the style of the Finlandia Hall, which was completed as far back as 1971 in Helsinki from a design by architect **Alvar Aalto**.

Traditional dress

Today, the city centres of Auckland and Wellington are dominated by high-rises with **reflective glass façades**. The historic face of these cities can still be gleaned from the **old frontages** on the lower storeys of many modern buildings. Many old buildings were torn down because they were not earthquake-proof.

Literature

Three women are among the most important representatives of modern New Zealand literature: Katherine Mansfield invented the English short story, Keri Hulme was awarded the famous Booker Prize and Janet Frame became world famous when Jane Campion made a movie of her autobiography.

In a way, New Zealand's first literary product was published in 1854 by the governor at the time, **George Grey**. This was a collection of oral histories from New Zealand's native inhabitants. The first writer of some renown was **Frederick Maning** (1811 – 1883), an adventurer, saw mill owner and wood merchant, who at the time of the wood boom lived at Hokianga Harbour in the west of Northland and was married to a Maori. After 1860, using the **pseudonym of A Pakeha-Maori, Maning** wrote two books: *Old New Zealand, a Tale of Good Old Times* and *War in the North*, the story of the fight of Hone Heke against the British colonial power in the 1840s, told from the **perspective of a Maori**.

First literary work

At the age of 25, Samuel Butler (1835 – 1902) turned his back on his native England and settled on a farm on New Zealand's South Island, far from civilisation. After extended **voyages of exploration** he returned to England to dedicate himself fully to writing. Butler's narrative of his experiences, *A First Year in Canterbury Settlement* (1863), and his utopian novel *Erewhon* (1873) describe his travels into parts of South Island that at the time were still difficult to access.

Samuel Butler

20TH CENTURY LITERATURE

The **towering figure** of New Zealand literature at the beginning of the 20th century was the writer Katherine Mansfield (▶Famous People). Kathleen Mansfield Beauchamp, as she was christened, was born the daughter of a banker in Wellington. At 19 she moved to London. Moving to Germany for health reasons in 1909, she spent a few months in the small spa town of Bad Wörishofen. Artistically, this part of her life was to inform her first short stories, published in 1911 under the title In a German Pension. When her beloved younger brother Leslie died on the Western Front in World War I, she fell back on her **memories of her New Zealand childhood and adolescence** for the following short stories (*The Dolls House, Prelude* and *At the Bay*). It is for her stories that Mansfield is considered one of the

Katherine Mansfield

founders of the English short story. Her work The Garden Party now belongs to the canon of 20th-century literature classics.

Crime and Shakespeare Born and bred in Christchurch, **Ngaio Marsh** (1899 – 1982) started out in theatre before embarking on her **second career** in London as the author of detective novels. Amongst her most famous books are *A Man Lay Dead*, *The Nursing Home Murder* and *False Scent*. During World War II, Marsh went back to New Zealand, returning to the **theatre** and staging attention-grabbing Shakespeare productions. From 1950 onwards she lived in London again.

Maurice F R Shadbolt One of the older generation of contemporary writers is Maurice F R Shadbolt (1932 – 2004), who describes vividly the long-gone world of **gold prospectors**, lumberjacks and early settlers in his novel **Among the Cinders**. Shadbolt not only brings to life the world of the white settlers, but also the Maori and the rapprochement between the two extremely different groups.

James Baxter Considered New Zealand's **most famous poet**, James Baxter (1926 – 1972) was born in Dunedin. Through his father he was close to the pacifist movement, converted to Catholicism and in 1969 founded, in the remote village of Hiruharama (Jerusalem) on the Whanganui River, an **alternative community** for alcoholics, drug addicts and homeless people, which disbanded again after his early death.

Allen Thomas Curnow For years, the poet Allen Thomas Curnow (1911 – 2001) taught English literature in the metropolis of Auckland, writing **poems** from 1940. A selection of his work can be found in his very worthwhile *Selected Poems 1940-1989*.

Witi Ihimaera Maori author Witi Ihimaera (born 1944) attracted much attention with *Tangi* (1973) and *Bulibasha* (1994). His 1987 novel *The Whale Rider* was later made into a successful film (▶Film).

Patricia Grace Maori writer Patricia Grace (born 1937) received the **»New Zealand Fiction Award 1987«** for her book *Potiki*, which describes the Maoris' fight against the destruction of their living space. Grace also published other novels, amongst them *Mutuwhenua – The Moon Sleeps* (1978) and *Cousins* (1992).

Keri Hulme Born in 1947, the writer Keri Hulme is one of the few female New Zealand authors whose name is known in **other parts of the world** too. In her work, Hulme, who has some Maori blood, looks at problems rooted in New Zealand's **bicultural past**. Her novel *The Bone People* was awarded the prestigious British **Booker Prize** and depicts the isolation of the individual following the loss of traditional bonds.

Hulme also published a very successful collection of poems and prose *The Silence Between Moeraki Conversations* and the short stories *The Wind Eater*.

For Dunedin-born Janet Frame (1924 – 2004), writing was of **existential significance**. Frame spent years of her life in psychiatric institutions before her major literary talents were discovered, paving her **way to freedom**. Her first collection of short stories, *The Lagoon*, was published when she was 27. The successful film version of her autobiography ***An Angel at my Table*** (directed by Jane Campion), made the writer known to the rest of the world. She was nominated several times for the **Nobel prize for literature**, the last time in 2003. Frame died in 2004, shortly after receiving the New Zealand Prime Minister's Award for Literary Achievement.

Janet Frame

New Zealand's culture is influenced by old Maori dances and rites

Theatre

Theatre is one of the most important platforms on which the Maori have confidently returned to the roots of their culture.

Development New Zealand theatre was slower than other parts of the country's culture to leave behind the English and European models. It took a change in political direction in the Pacific region to trigger a gradual move away. The foundation in 1964 of the **Downstage Theatre in Wellington** created the first professional theatre in the country. Before, there had only been amateur stages and guest performances of foreign theatre troupes. In the 1970s, professional community theatres grew up in the larger cities like Auckland, Christchurch, Dunedin and Palmerston North.

Social drama New Zealand drama owes much to **Bruce Mason** (1921 – 1983). His first play, a sharp critique of white society, was published in 1953. Later, he would also grapple with the world of the Maori. Amongst his *Five Plays on Maori Themes*, the first piece, *The Pohutukawa Tree* (1957) is now considered a **classic**.

In a meeting house Maori perform age-old dances in traditional garb

On the whole, Mason had a **pessimistic** view of the future of Maori culture. In 1965, he wrote *Awatea* for the opera singer Inia Te Wiata, who had Maori heritage; this was the trigger for the foundation in 1966 of the **first professional Maori theatre troupe**. Since then, Maori theatre has been an integral part of the landscape of New Zealand drama.

In the late 1970s, a **new Maori theatre movement** emerged, differing from earlier movements in its political sense of mission. Performances with song, dance and speech, often in the Maori language, were staged at meeting places (marae), in universities, town halls and theatres. One **characteristic feature of Maori theatre** is that the distance between audience and performers is removed. Thus, theatre becomes a communal experience similar to the traditional Maori rhetoric and ceremonies during customary gatherings on the meeting place. In 1977, the **Maori poet and playwright Hone Tuwhare** wrote a play that was not staged until 1985 (*In the Wilderness without a Hat*). The plot's starting point is a funeral (tangi). A carved **ancestral figure (tapu) comes to life** to intervene in the discussions surrounding the way the funeral should be conducted. The fact that tapu was represented on stage was probably responsible for the worthwhile play only being staged some eight years after it was written.

Political consciousness

Film

Anything worth doing... the two New Zealand directors Jane Campion and Peter Jackson have received several Oscars – for films that were made in their home country.

The first films, made around the turn of the century, were documentaries, weekly news reels or silent movies where the Maori and the untouched nature of New Zealand served as an exotic backdrop for banal love stories. Rudall Hayward, **New Zealand's best-known director** of the 1920s and 1930s, invented his own camera and a sound system in order to make films with sound.

Exotic and mundane

After World War II, virtually nothing but Hollywood productions made it onto the country's screens. The New Zealand film industry only came to life in the 1970s. In 1977, **Roger Donaldson** made his movie *Sleeping Dogs*. The same year saw the creation of a Film Commission, in order to support the fledgling film industry with production, screenplay acquisition and marketing of New Zealand films through subsidies from taxpayers' money and revenue from the state lottery.

Film industry awakens

Middle Earth in New Zealand

The talented New Zealander Peter Jackson, director of the epic Lord of the Rings film trilogy, has good reason to be happy: not only did the films do great box office business worldwide, they won four Oscars as well. However, this success is also down to the film's fantastic New Zealand backdrop and the hard work put in by his countrymen and women.

With his hugely successful screen adaptation of the great imaginative world created by **J R R Tolkien**, director Peter Jackson not only filled the coffers of cinema owners but gave an immense boost to New Zealand tourism. Steady streams of globetrotting tourists visit the places where key scenes of the Tolkien adaptation were filmed, even though studio post-production clearly played a part in how the movies looked. The effect is similar to the hordes of visitors to Baker Street in London, on the trail of Sherlock Holmes.

Welcome to Hobbiton

Not far from Auckland, near Matamatae, the shy **Hobbits** have their home. The caves where the Hobbits live can be found here, together with a recent sign saying »Welcome to Hobbiton«.

The Land of Evil

And how could it be otherwise? In a place where the earth is particularly restless, where a sulphurous smell hovers, where mud pots bubble and hot waters hiss across rocks, here lies **Mordor**, the truly eerie land of evil. No wonder the volcanic landscape of the Tongariro National Park and the volcanoes of Ruapehu, Ngauruhoe and Tongariro seemed the perfect choice for dramatic cinematic scenes; Jackson fully understood the potential of his homeland.

Kingdom of Rohan

Of course it is not just New Zealand's geologically restless North Island that offers spectacular film locations, but also **South Island** with its landscapes ranging from the paradisiacal and climatically favourable Marlborough Sounds to the perpetual ice of the Southern Alps. Thus, Elrond's house may be found at the Marlborough Sounds, and the New Zealand Alps form part of the Kingdom of Rohan. And when dusk falls here, it seems entirely possible to make out a Black Knight or even Sauron in the distance.

Elf country, Lothlorien and Amon Hen

The area around Glenorchy and Lake Wakatipu has also been immortalised in the epic trilogy as elf country Lothlorien. The mountainous landscape around Queenstown, cleft by raging rivers, is set to become another hot spot for all Tolkien fans. This is where the mythical Misty Mountains rise, as well as Amon Hen, which nearly breaks up the Fellowship of the Ring.

Tolkien Trails

As you might expect from consummate tourism experts, the response in New Zealand to the success of the films has been swift. For a while there was even a Lord of the Rings Minister, and at Wellington airport a sign greets arrivals with the words »Welcome to Middle Earth«. In order to give visitors more background to the blockbuster, several Tolkien Trails have been set up where Lord of the Rings fans may follow in Gandalf's or Frodo's footsteps, or hunt rings and orcs. They can also get to know Hobbiton, Mordor and the river Anduin on a drive on **North Island** from Auckland to Wellington via Hamilton, Rotorua and Taupo.

South Island has three waymarked sections: the first trip, starting at the city of Nelson, leads into Chetwood Forest and the Dimrill Dale. Film locations at Takaka Hill, Mount Olympus and Mount Owen may be reached on foot. Christchurch is a good base for exploring Edoras and its **breathtaking views**. Several days are required to follow in Frodo's footsteps. Queenstown is the starting point for a trip taking in Glenorchy, Mount Cook, Te Anau, Twizel and Lake Wanaka.

These days, some tour operators also offer organized Lord of the Rings trips through New Zealand.

For more information:
www.newzealand.com
www.hobbitontours.com
Recommended reading: J.R.R. Tolkien, The Lord of the Rings, Harper Collins, UK, and Ian Brodie, The Lord of the Rings Location Guidebook, Harper Collins, Auckland 2003.

The key scenes of the epic films *The Lord of the Rings* were made in the beautiful mountain landscape of South Island

Protected films

Whilst between 1940 and 1970 there were a grand total of three films made in New Zealand, this figure had already risen to over 40 in the years between 1977 and 1985. Given the small domestic market, the Film Commission turned out to be an **important protector** of New Zealand film. Most productions subsidised by the Film Commission looked into the history of New Zealand, with the central event of the land wars and the problems of **bicultural society** in particular. Among the **better known directors** in New Zealand is Vincent Ward (*In Spring One Plants Alone*; *State of Siege*, from the novel by Janet Frame), Geoff Murphy (*Goodbye Pork Pie*), Michael Firth (*Off the Edge*) and Mereta Mita (*Patu*). Yvonne Mackay's award-winning film *The Silent One* in 1984 was the first New Zealand dramatic feature film to be directed solely by a woman and featured memorable soundtrack and underwater photography.

Jane Campion

One of the biggest successes in New Zealand cinema, and awarded 8 prizes at the 1990 **Venice Film Festival**, was ***An Angel at My Table***, the autobiography of the New Zealand writer Janet Frame (▶Literature), turned into a film by Jane Campion. Jane Campion went on to make ***The Piano***, a film that in 1994 was awarded several Oscars. That same year, back in New Zealand, the film *Once Were Warriors*, based on the book of Maori author Alan Duff achieved a new box of-

Dunedin's music scene includes Scots elements

fice record. Since *Jurassic Park* at least, New Zealand actor **Sam Neill** has become a well-known name.

Today, the **most successful New Zealand director** is Peter Jackson from Wellington, who made a name for himself with films like *Meet the Feebles* and *The Frighteners*. Recently, Jackson achieved worldwide fame with the incredibly successful film version of Tolkien's widely read ***Lord of the Rings*** trilogy, which was filmed at various locations in New Zealand (▶MARCOPOLO Insight p. 78). In 2011/2012 Peter Jackson also filmed ***The Hobbit***, the precursor tale.

World famous Peter Jackson

This young New Zealand filmmaker Niki Caro landed a surprise hit with her 2002 film ***Whalerider***, which was screened internationally. The movie is based on a story by the Maori author Witi Ihimaera.

Niki Caro

Music

No matter if classical or pop: musicians and singers don't have it easy in this little island nation. Many try their luck overseas – some with great success.

The problem of a relatively small island state with a fairly limited domestic market, is apparent not only in the visual arts but also in the music scene. Artists of international renown, such as the **opera diva Dame Kiri Te Kanawa** (▶Famous People) and the superb performer **Donald McIntyre** appear much more often on European and American stages than in New Zealand.

Classical music exported

Few pop music bands stay in New Zealand either, being unable to make a living there due to **low demand**. The New Zealand music scene, with its centres in Dunedin and Auckland, is subject to **constant change** and covers everything from Scottish bagpipes to hard rock. In 2011 Brooke Fraser charged to the top of the charts with *Something in the Water*. In 2013 Lorde from Auckland became the youngest solo artist to ever reach number one on the US singles chart with *Royals*. The song won two Grammy Awards in 2014.

Pop music

Famous People

JAMES COOK (1728 – 1779)

With his three sailing voyages around world, the English seafarer James Cook provided **ground breaking findings** on the Pacific and sub-Antarctic zones. Having been in the service of the Royal Navy since 1755, he participated in several sea voyages, was made lieutenant and appointed commander of the Endeavour in 1768. Cook's assignment on his first trip (1768 – 1771) was to observe the transit of Venus in front of the sun off Tahiti.

Afterwards, however, he sailed off on his own secret mission to look for the **southern continent, which was shrouded in myth**. He found the Society Islands and, on Abel Tasman's route, moved in the direction of New Zealand. On **8 October 1769**, Cook landed near today's town of Gisborne in a bay which he called Poverty Bay, as he found neither water nor sustenance there. The first encounter with the Maori ended lethally for some of them; although later Cook was able to make some progress towards the native inhabitants. It was Cook's circumnavigation of New Zealand which proved that the new country was indeed **made up of islands**. At the same time he discovered the strait between North and South Island, which was to bear his name.

During his **second expedition** (1772 – 1775), where he was accompanied by the German naturalist Johann Reinhold Forster, his son Georg and the English painter William Hodges, Captain James Cook sailed east around the globe. Three times he pushed south across the Antarctic Circle, exploring and naming New Hebrides, Norfolk Island and New Caledonia.

From New Zealand, where he took a break from exploring at Ship Cove in Queen Charlotte Sound, he sailed east to Patagonia, rounded Cape Horn and discovered South Georgia and the **Falkland Islands** in 1775. After returning to England, Captain Cook was made a member of the Royal Society.

During his **third trip** (1776 – 1780) he again headed for Queen Charlotte Sound in New Zealand, discovering Hawaii, amongst other places, landed on the coast of Alaska, passed the Bering Strait and reached the northern coast of Alaska. During his second stay on Hawaii he clashed with the inhabitants of the islands and was clubbed to death by them on 14 February 1779.

Cook is responsible for many **geographical designations** on New Zealand. His own name was given to, among other places, **Mount Cook**, the highest elevation of the Southern Alps, Mount Cook National Park and Cook River south of Fox Glacier in Westland.

James Cook never saw the mountain, but Mount Cook was named after him: New Zealand's highest peak

Her Majesty's seafarer

GEORGE EDWARD GREY (1812 – 1898)

Politician and friends of the Maoris

George Edward Grey, born in Lisbon, Portugal, was to become one of the most **influential personalities** in 19th-century New Zealand. Grey was Governor from 1845 to 1853 and again from 1861 to 1868, as well as **Prime Minister** between 1877 and 1879. His thinking shaped by an early deployment in Ireland, Grey turned towards political liberalism. After serving in Australia for three years, latterly as Governor of South Australia, in 1840 he succeeded Governor Fitz Roy of New Zealand, at a time when some of the Maori had taken up arms. Grey had more soldiers at his disposal than his predecessors, so he was able to put down the **uprising of Hone Heke and Kawiti** in the Bay of Islands with the help of allied Maori tribes. In 1853 he was sent as Governor of the Cape Colony to South Africa, returning to New Zealand and his old position in 1861, when the Taranaki land wars had flared up, and again he fought the insurgents successfully.

Hillary was the first to climb Mount Everest.

Grey's major achievement however, was his ability to understand and promote the culture of the Maori. He learned the Maori language, collected the mythology and tribal legends previously only transmitted orally and published them in London in 1854. Thanks to his **unique know-ledge** of »Maoritanga« and his empathetic understanding of New Zealand's native inhabitants, Grey enjoyed a high standing among the chiefs. George Edward Grey died on 19 September 1898 in London.

SIR EDMUND HILLARY (1919 – 2008)

Arguably the **most famous New Zealander** is Edmund Hillary, who came into the world on 20 July 1919 in Auckland. Hillary became world-famous through the **first ascent of Mount Everest**, the highest mountain on earth, alongside the Nepalese Sherpa Tenzing Norgay (1914 – 1986), managing to time his conquest to coincide with the coronation day of Queen Elizabeth II on 29 May 1953. This achievement earned him a knighthood. In 1957, Sir Hillary started out on a British expedition to Antartica, achieving the first overland journey with a vehicle to the **South Pole**. In the years 1960/1961 and 1963/1964 he returned to the Himalayas for research expeditions and lived there occassionally, devoting himself to social projects for the local people up to his death in 2008.

WILLIAM HOBSON (1792 – 1842)

Captain William Hobson was born in the Irish town of Waterford. When he came to New Zealand in July 1839, it was with a tricky mission: in his role as Lieutenant Governor, Hobson was supposed to negotiate with the Maori chiefs their recognition of England's sovereignty. These talks led to the signing of the **Treaty of Waitangi** on 6 February 1840, in which the Maori accepted British sovereignty and in exchange were guaranteed the property rights to their land. The treaty paved the way for the elevation of New Zealand to the rank of a crown colony, with Hobson as its first governor. His decision to buy land on Waitemata Harbour led in 1841 to the **capital being moved** from Russell to Auckland, which he named after the first Lord of the Admiralty.

First governor

During his time in office Hobson was caught in the middle. The new settlers of the New Zealand Company in Wellington besieged him with **demands for land**, which the Maori obviously did not want to give up as it had been guaranteed to them. Eventually some of the Maori took up arms. Hobson was ill-equipped to quell the uprising, as the young colony had no soldiers and no funds, and he had to resort to acting on his own authority to issue »**treasury bills**«, similar to treasury obligations.

Caught in the middle

Without **military backing** the sick man did not enjoy great standing with the Maori chiefs either, making him powerless to influence them. London was already planning to order Hobson back when he died on 10 September 1842 in Auckland.

No respect

HONE HEKE POKAI (C. 1810 – 1850)

Pakaraka near the Bay of Islands was the birthplace of Hone Heke Pokai, one of the signatories of the Treaty of Waitangi. Until the year 1841 his tribe, the **Ngapuhi**, had benefited from the charges that all ships entering the port of Kororareka (today Russell) had to pay. This boon came to an end when the government introduced duties in 1841. The **whaling ships** stopped coming. The loss in earnings, together with rising **suspicion** against the white government led to

Felled the flagpole

Maori chief Hone Heke with entourage

Hone Heke felling the flagstaff at the port, symbol of British supremacy, four times in succession. On the last occasion he combined cutting down the flagstaff with an attack on the white settlers there, who promptly fled the town. All the buildings apart from the churches and the mission stations were burned to the ground. This was the trigger for **war against the Maori** in the North, really Hone Heke's war, which only ended with his defeat by strong units of British troops at Ruapekapeka in 1846. Hone Heke Pokai died on 6 August 1850 in Kaikohe.

FRIEDENSREICH HUNDERTWASSER (1928 – 2000)

The Viennese Friedensreich Hundertwasser (real name Friedrich Stowasser) first came to fame as a painter and graphic artist. His art is characterised by ornamental-decorative and **curved lines** as well as bold use of colour. However, Hundertwasser began looking at architecture as early as the 1950s, and his Hundertwasser House (1983 – 1985), created in Vienna according to his ideas, is world famous.

Citizen of New Zealand

In 1973, the artist first visited his »dream destination« of New Zealand, and became a New Zealand citizen in 1986. Settling at Kawakawa on the **Bay of Islands**, Hundertwasser practised a way of living in tune with the environment, visible to this day most noticeably in his green guesthouse complete with **humus toilet**. Hundertwasser died in February 2000 during a cruise. His new **New Zealand flag** is known outside the country too, if not yet officially recognised: a green spiral on a white background. This design symbolises both an unfurling fern leaf, and an ornament much used by the Maori.

KIRI TE KANAWA (BORN 1944)

It was on 6 March 1944 that the world-famous soprano was born in Gisborne, on New Zealand's North Island. Early on, the daughter of an Irish mother and a **Maori father** was noticed for her singing. As a 20-year-old she had already won all the important prizes in the South Pacific area, amongst them the prestigious John Court Aria Prize. From 1965 onwards she studied at the London Opera Centre and soon after was offered a contract as Junior Principal at Covent Garden. Kiri Te Kanawa came to international attention as Xenia in *Boris Godunow* and as the Countess in *The Marriage of Figaro*. After her successes at London's Covent Garden, Kiri prepared for her debut at the **New York Metropolitan Opera**, where she shone as Desdemona in *Otello*.

Legendary soprano

Further triumphs included Violetta in *La Traviata*, Tosca in *Tosca*, as well as Pamina in Mozart's *Magic Flute* and, last but not least, Donna Elvira in Mozart's opera *Don Giovanni*. Few have forgotten Kiri Te Kanawa's 1981 performance in **London's St Paul's Cathedral**, where she sang *Let the Bright Seraphim* on the occasion of Prince Charles' and Lady Diana Spencer's wedding. The following year Queen Elizabeth II made her a Dame of the British Empire. For a long time, Kiri was considered one of the **best singers in the world**. She ended her opera career in 2009 and since then she has rarely performed in public.

Wedding song for Lady Di

TE KOOTI (1814 – 1893)

Te Kooti or Arikirangi Te Turuki was probably born on Poverty Bay. Without being a chief, Te Kooti was of **noble descent** and fought on the side of the government against the Hauhau movement until he was accused of **collaboration** with the enemy, imprisoned and deported to the Chatham Islands without trial or judgement together with 300 Hauhau followers.

Fought the Hauhau

It is presumed that his arrest was owed to envy and resentment. In exile he founded the **Ringatu cult** – which translates as »raised hand«, because he made his hand glow in the dark using phosphorus – which still today has a few thousand adherents. Te Kooti saw himself as the **Moses of the Maori** whom he wanted to guide into the Promised Land. After successfully fleeing the Chatham Islands, together with his followers he raided the Matawhero settlement near Gisborne in November 1868, killing 33 white settlers and 37 progovernment Maori. In 1872, having been pursued in vain for years by the government, he retreated back to King Country, where he lived

Into the Promised Land

under the protection of the Maori king until peace was officially declared. Subsequently Te Kooti was pardoned and in 1891 allocated land by the government at Ohiwa on the Bay of Plenty.

FELIX GRAF VON LUCKNER (1881 – 1966)

Sea devil with a heart

The **German marine officer**, who rose to fame as the »Sea Devil«, was born in Dresden. In the First World War (1916/1917), captaining the auxiliary cruiser Seeadler (Sea Eagle) he breached the British blockade, sinking or seizing several **enemy ships** in the Pacific, until having his ship wrecked by a tsunami. In a lifeboat, von Luckner sailed to the Cook Islands and on to the Fiji Islands. He was taken prisoner twice and interned; after the war he was released. When Count Luckner returned to New Zealand two decades later, it was to a surprisingly warm welcome. It had become known that during his sorties with the auxiliary cruiser Seeadler, he had always been concerned with the physical safety of enemy crews. Count Luckner died in 1966 in Malmö, Sweden.

KATHERINE MANSFIELD (1888 – 1923)

Vivacious writer

Born the daughter of a banker on 14 October 1888 in Wellington, Katherine Mansfield, real name Kathleen Mansfield Beauchamp, is the **most famous figure** in New Zealand literature. As a young girl she attended Queen's College in London, returning to New Zealand in 1906. After managing to persuade her father to let her move back to London, she arrived there again and from 1908 lived a very free-spirited life amongst a bohemian crowd.

From 1911 onwards she entered into a relationship with **literary critic** John Middleton Murray, whom she eventually married in 1918. Katherine Mansfield's wild lifestyle made no allowances for her health; finally she became ill with **respiratory disease** and had to undergo several treatments in France, Switzerland and Germany. She died on 9 January 1923, in a clinic in Fontainebleau, France.

Master of the short story

Katherine Mansfield's **literary fame** is due to her short stories, where she proved herself a master of the form, to the extent that Mansfield is credited with founding the English short story. Whilst her first publication in 1911, *In a German Pension* was still informed by the curative treatment in Bad Wörishofen, from 1915 memories of her

New Zealand childhood and adolescence became the themes of her work. The most famous amongst them are *Prelude, At the Bay* and *The Garden Party*.8

ERNEST RUTHERFORD (1871 – 1937)

Ernest Rutherford, born 30 August 1871 in Spring Grove near Nelson, is considered the **most important experimental physicist** of his time and the father of nuclear physics. His ground breaking scientific achievements were the discovery of **alpha and beta radiation** in 1898, and in 1900 of gamma radiation, as well as the identification of radioactivity as the spontaneous disintegration of atoms. Rutherford's findings led to the formulation of the **decay law** and the devising of the atomic model named after him. Rutherford had been awarded the **Nobel Prize** as early as 1908, at that time for chemistry. Elevated to the nobility, he held the honourable title Lord Rutherford of Nelson up to his death on 19 October 1937 in Cambridge, England.

Father of nuclear physics

WAKEFIELD BROTHERS (18TH/19TH CENTURIES)

Originally from England, the Wakefield Brothers have all, in their own way, left their mark on New Zealand's history. The most famous among them was **Edward Gibbon Wakefield** (1796 – 1862). As co-founder of the New Zealand Association, which later became the New Zealand Company, he was the main person responsible for the **influx of settlers** into the new colony. The uncontrolled immigration led to conflicts with the Maori, and a number of the settlers fell for Wakefield's not entirely reliable promises, as the Company mainly filled the pockets of its founders. Thus Edward Gibbon Wakefield himself stayed in London »to pull the strings«, and only came to Wellington in 1852, where he now lies buried in Bolton Street Memorial Park.

Legacy of four brothers

William Wakefield (1803 – 1848) brought the first colonists to Wellington in 1839/1840; he was considered to be the »Father of Wellington«. Arthur Wakefield (1799 – 1843) also worked on behalf of the New Zealand Company. He was killed during a land deal that lead to a fight. For many years Daniel Wakefield (1798 – 1858) worked as a judge in Wellington. Felix Wakefield (1807 – 1875), the youngest of the brothers, became an engineer and expert on horticulture on South Island.

Father of Wellington

ENJOY
NEW ZEALAND

What do New Zealanders eat? Where are the best Hiking Trails?
What kind of adventures can your kids have in New Zealand and
why should you always have a chocolate fish on hand in case
someone does you a favour?

Accommodation

Beyond Hustle and Bustle

Are you looking for a room in a hotel or would you prefer a motel? A backpacker hostel or a bed & breakfast? Boutique hotel or lodge? Or maybe camping? And if so – would you like a capmpground or a holiday park? Tent or hut? Standard, fully equipped, self-contained? The range of accommodation in New Zealand knows no end; it's attractive and sometimes a bit confusing.

The different standards for accommodation in New Zealand can mean just about anything. A hostel can be well-equipped and comfortable, but also shabby and cheap – it all depends on the owner. Boutique hotel can mean a special flair – or tasteless furnishings. The room price can include breakfast; or it might cost extra. And sometimes the price does not include the VAT either. Anyone looking for accommodation in New Zealand needs to read the fine print, or else there might be some unpleasant surprises.

Look closely when making reservations

The top of the highest price category are without a doubt the **luxury lodges**. They are in great locations and offer the best in comfort, which mere mortals can only dream of. But a night in a place like this can cost more than 1000 NZ$. If the accommodation is called a resort then it usually has a large spa. There's an overview at www.lodgesofnz. co.nz. **Boutique hotels** are excellent smaller and more individually run hotels with special themes. Most of the time, that is. Interesting addresses can be found at www.boutiquehotels.co.nz.

Luxurious and usually good

A **hotel** in New Zealand can mean anything from simple to luxurious. International hotel chains can be found in all of the locations frequented by tourists. **Motels, motor inns and motor lodges** can also be found in all categories, from inexpensive to top quality. Almost all of them can be booked ahead on the Internet. Be sure to **arrive at the agreed on time** or let the hotel know that you are arriving later because hotel rooms that are not claimed by 6pm can be passed on to other guests. Good to know: »Self-catering« means that no food is served.

For all budgets –

The selection of bed & breakfast accommodation has grown considerably in past years. They are mainly offered in **private homes**. Many very exclusive B&Bs have opened recently in carefully restored houses that are often listed monuments. They all have a **family atmos-**

Bed & breakfast

Accommodation can also be cheap like this backpacker hostel

Gold for the Environment – Ecologically Friendly Accommodation

Shimmering white mountains, fiery volcanoes, blue seas and green jungles – anyone who loves nature will find it in New Zealand, every thing from mighty glaciers to endlessly long, fine-grained sand beaches. Unfortunately this dreamland is about 23,000km (13,800 mi) away from Europe and anyone who wants to protect and conserve the environment can hardly justify an airplane flight to New Zealand anymore.

Can it even be called »green tourism« anymore when the flight to your destination alone already produces almost 14 t of CO2 per person? Can you call yourself a friend of nature when a trip like this produces as much carbon dioxide as driving 35km (21 mi) every day for seven years? This is a question that everyone has to answer for himself. But there are no real alternatives to flying either. Travelling to New Zealand from Europe takes four to six weeks, depending on the route.

Projects to Protect the Climate

But there are other ways to improve New Zealand's carbon footprint and to ease your conscience. Payments to Atmosfair or similar non-profit organizations financially support climate protection projects all over the world. A payment to balance a flight to New Zealand runs between 300 and 400 Euros. You can also reserve environmentally friendly accommodation in New Zealand, use means of transport with smaller carbon footprints or plan activities to support conservation of nature and preserve local traditions.

Green Quality Label

Protection of nature and climate change are common topics of conversation in New Zealand, especially in tourism. A country that advertises with the slogan »100% pure New Zealand« can't afford to lose its green image. The New Zealand Tourism Strategy 2015 makes it a goal to make New Zealand the world leader in environmental and nature protection. Quality labels like Earthcheck and Green Globe show that a certain hotel or B&B has committed itself to protecting the environment. The New Zealand quality label for tourism Qualmark also makes it much easier to find environmentally friendly accommodation. Use its website (www.qualmark.co.nz) to find details on the various categories of accommodation, regions, quality standards and level of quality label.

phere. There is a high demand for them and often the houses only have a few rooms for rent, so it is important to book early.

In New Zealand there are about 50 **youth hostels**, usually with well-equipped guest kitchens; infos at www.yha.co.nz. A night in a dormitory-style room starts at 25 NZ$. Anyone with an international youth hostel ID will get a discount; there is no age limit. Special hostels for **backpackers** are also inexpensive; there are around 300 of them in New Zealand. They vary quite a bit in quality and cater not only to backpackers. They also welcome families and people who would rather not spend their money on accommodation. Info at www.bbh.co.nz.

MARCO POLO TIP

Hotel passes **insider Tip**

Some hotel chains offer specific passes, which often allow an economical overnight stay in their members' hotels. The range of rooms offered by Flag Choice is particularly comprehensive. These passes usually have to be purchased before travel. For more information, consult a good travel agent.

New Zealand is the ideal place to travel with a **caravan** or a tent. Caravans can be rented from many travel or tourist agencies. There are hundreds of **camping and caravan grounds** available, both out in the middle of nature and near almost all of the sights and large cities. Anyone who does not have a rented caravan can often still find accommodation in one or in a **holiday cabin** on a camp ground. The around 250 campsites of the Department of Conservation usually have quite simple facilities but fabulous locations on both islands. Information at www.doc.govt.nz. The Holiday Accommodation Parks of New Zealand Association consists of about 300 campgrounds and offers accommodation from comfortable **tent places to holiday flats** at www.holidayparks.co.nz.

Camping

While it is possible to camp in the wild in New Zealand the **landowner's permission** is necessary. But »No Camping« signs are becoming more frequent.

wild camping

Children in New Zealand

Through Adventure Land in a Caravan

When the long flight is finally behind them New Zealand is a TOP destination for families with children. There's loads for them to experience! Great beaches where they can sunbathe with the seals, bubbling mud pools and geysers that shoot skywards, mysterious caves illuminated by thousands of glow-worms, theme parks with awesome rides as well as other at-tractions for large and small make New Zealand an adventure land that families with children can best explore in a caravan.

Travelling by caravan is ideal for families because it allows them to travel as it best suits their children. The camping grounds and holiday parks have the best facilities that are also **child-friendly**; they are lo-cated in attractive landscape and often near beaches. Most of these facilities offer family facilities with, for example, extra showers for families, horse riding for children etc. Most of these grounds also al-low children to play to their heart's content, collect treasures like sea-shells and stones, explore caves along the beach, watch interesting wild animals like **kiwis, penguins and dolphins**, drive through the jungle in a rail car and experience lots of other great things.

Families welcome

Great museums like the **Te Papa Tongarewa** (New Zealand's na-tional museum) in the capital city Wellington, Maori cultural sites like the Maori & Colonial Museum in Okains Bay (south of Christch-urch) and popular science facilities like Kelly Tarlton's Underwater & Antarctic Encounter in Auckland offer special programmes for chil-dren and youth of all ages.

Children's programmes

And then there are **outdoor adventures** like climbing or biking, rolling down a hill in a ball called a **Zorb**, skiing in the New Zealand Alps. But one thing should be remembered for outdoor activities in New Zealand: The intense sunshine in New Zealand makes sun pro-tection for children a must (including a hat with neck covering, sun-screen with a high sun protection factor).

The right sun protection

Attractions for kids

Black Cat Cruises
Akaroa Harbour Wharf

Akaroa 7520, NZ (South Island)
Tel. 03 3 04 76 41

Enjoy freedom with your kids and camper

http://blackcat.co.nz
daily 9am – 5pm
Tickets start at 74 NZ$
(children at 30 NZ$)
Boat trips and encounters with
dolphins

Blue Penguin Colony
Waterfront Rd.
Oamaru 9400
(South Island)
Tel. 03 4 33 11 95
www.penguins.co.nz
Tours all day
Admission: from 10 NZ$
(children from 5 NZ$)
About a one-hour drive north of
Dunedin there is a colony of the
world's smallest penguins.

Insider Tip

**Kelly Tarlton's Underwater &
Antarctic Encounter**
Orakei, Auckland 1071
(North Island)
Tel. 08 00 80 50 50
www.kellytarltons.co.nz
daily 9.30am – 4.30pm
Admission: 39 NZ $
(children 22 NZ$)
Here children can learn about ani-
mals that live at and in the waters
of the southern hemisphere.

Kowhai Park
Anzac Parade
Whanganui
(North Island)
Tel. 06 3 49 05 08
http://whanganuinz.com
At the moment one of the best
playgrounds in the world. The
park was severely damaged by
storms in 2015. While it has been
re-opened parts of it will probably
not be completely restored until
2017.

**Okains Bay Maori &
Colonial Museum**
Main Rd., Okains Bay 8161
(South Island)
Tel. 03 304 86 11
www.okainsbaymuseum.co.nz
daily 10am – 5pm
Admission: 10 NZ$
(children 2 NZ$)
Various children's programmes on
the world of the Maori

Orakei Korako Geyserland
494 Orakei Korako Rd.
Hidden Valley, Taupo,
NZ (North Island)
Tel. 07 378 31 31
www.orakeikorako.co.nz
Tours daily 8am – 4pm
Tickets: from 36 NZ$
(children from 15 NZ$)
Bubbling and stinking mud
springs and the chance to swim in
warm thermal springs.

Puzzling World Wanaka
88 Wanaka-Luggate Hwy.
Wanaka 9382 (South Island)
Tel. 03 443 74 89
www.puzzlingworld.co.nz
daily 8.30am – 5pm
Admission: 16 NZ$
(children 12 NZ$)
Optical illusions and exploring a
3D labyrinth.

**Rainbow Springs Kiwi
Wildlife Park**
192 Fairy Springs Rd.
Fairy Springs, Rotorua
(North Island)
Tel. 07 350 04 40
www.rainbowsprings.co.nz
daily 8am – 10pm
Admission: 40 NZ$
(Children 5 – 15 yrs. 20 NZ$)

Watch kiwis in their natural surroundings.

Te Papa Tongarewa Museum of New Zealand
55 Cable St.
Te Aro, Wellington 6011
(North Island)
Tel. 04 381 70 00
www.tepapa.govt.nz
daily 10am – 6pm, Thu until 9pm
Admission free
Various programmes for children and teens

Weta Film Studio / Weta Cave
1 Weka St., Miramar
Wellington 6022 (North Island)
Tel. 04 9 09 40 00
www.wetanz.com

daily 9am – 5.30pm
Admission: 24 NZ$
(children 12 NZ$)
Children will love the Orks and the Dark Lords from Lord of the Rings. The studio is named after a local and unusually large insect.

ZORB Rotorua
Western Rd./Hwy. 5
Ngongotaha, Rotorua 3010
(North Island)
Tel. 07 357 51 00
http://zorb.com
daily 10am – 5pm, in summer until 7pm
Admission from 78 NZ$
(for 3 rides)
Roll down a hill in a clear plastic ball.

Kids love to play on the high dunes of Ninety Mile Beach in the north of North Island

Festivals · Holidays · Events

Everything is a Reason to Celebrate

Holidays in New Zealand tend to be relaxed and uncompli-cated. If a holiday falls on the weekend then the following Monday and sometimes even the following Tuesday are also days off for employees and school children. And if those days coincide with other holidays then you just keep adding days to make a super-weekend out of it.

But when it comes to celebrating New Zealanders don't necessarily need a holiday. Any reason will do. Sports, music, art, culture, culinary delights – all of these can be a reason to celebrate. Every ethnic immigrant group in New Zealand also loves to celebrate its roots. And Kiwis of all origins celebrate the **birth of New Zealand** together, or the founding of their region or their city. the change of season can also be used as a reason to celebrate, just like any agricultural event.

Enough reasons

The N**ew Zealand International Arts Festival** ("Wellington) takes place in Wellington every two years and focuses on theatre, dance and music; it is a highlight of the New Zeland cultural calendar (www.festival.co.nz). In alternative years the International Jazz Festival is held in the capital city of New Zealand with world class international performers (www.jazzfestival.co.nz). In Wellington there is also the annual World of Wearable Arts Festival, a unique fashion show. The largest rock music festival is the spectacular **Big Day Out**, which gets crowds rocking every year in January or February in Auckland (www.bigdayout.com).

Arts and culture

Regional delicacies attract gourmets every February to the **Marlborough Wine and Food Festivals** in Blenheim. The Whitebait Festival in October in Greymouth small fish called whitebait are served ("Typical Dishes). Anyone who shudders already at the thought had better stay clear of the Wildfood Festival in Hokitika. Every March specialties like **candied beetles** and marinated maggots are served here (www.wildfoods.co.nz).

Culinary delights

Te Mataini is the name of a Maori dance contest, which takes place in odd-numbered years in various places. It is a chance to learn more about Maori dances and their background (www.tematatini.co.nz).

Maoris and Scots

New Zealanders love to celebrate and do it often

The **Maori Canoe Regatta** in March in Ngaruawahia is another highlight, in which colourful carved canoes shoot through the waves. The **Highland Games** on January 1 in Waipu present a completely different culture. For 140 years and in good old Scottish tradition tree trunks have been enthusiastically thrown through the air here to the sound of passionate bag pipe music.

Wood cutting contests, prizes for the fastest sheep shearer, dog shows, rodeos – the extremely popular agricultural & pastoral shows all look back on long traditions. The **agricultural fairs** were started already by the first settlers from Europe in the 19th cent. At that time already they were »the« event in the farmers' and sheep ranchers' calendar. Today you can still catch up on the latest in agricultural technology at the fairs. They usually resemble folk festivals, like the **Golden Shears Festival** in February/March in Masterton (www.goldenshears.co.nz). Gumboot Day is a unique spectacle that is held every year in March in Taihape – with the goal of breaking the world record in **throwing Wellington boots** (www.taihape.co.nz).

Rough rugby Rugby attracts thousands of spectators; it is a fast and sometimes rough team sport with a ball and relatively complicated rules. The atmosphere usually comes to a boil during test matches, most recently during the Rugby Union World Cup in fall 2015 when the New Zealand team, the **All Blacks**, won for the second time in a row and for the third time since 1987 (►MARCOPOLO Insight p. 112).

Traditional cricket Cricket, traditionally a British sport, is among the longest and most popular games in New Zealand and often captivates large crowds. Championship events in the host cities create an atmosphere similar to rugby games.

CALENDAR OF EVENTS

PUBLIC HOLIDAYS
National
New Year's Day (1 January), New Year Holiday (2 January), Waitangi Day (6 February: national holiday commemorating the founding of New Zealand), Good Friday (March/April), Easter Monday (March/April), Anzac Day (25 April, commemorating the battle of Gallipoli in 1915 where many lives were lost), Queen's Birthday (first Monday in June; birthday of the Queen of England), Labour Day (4th Monday in October), Christmas Day (25 December), Boxing Day (26 December)

Regional
Every province celebrates the day of its foundation: 22 January: Wellington; 29 January: Auckland, Northland; 1 February: Nelson; 23 March: Otago, Southland; 31

Sailing is very popular in New Zealand

March: Taranaki; 1 November: Hawke's Bay, Marlborough; 9 November: Canterbury; 1 December: Westland

JANUARY
Auckland (North Island)
Auckland Anniversary Day Regatta Sailing boat race honouring the day of the foundation of the city (29 January)

Glenorchy (South Island)
Horse Races & Rodeo
Rustic horse races and shepherd's games near Queenstown

FEBRUARY
Bay of Islands (North Island)
Waitangi Day: national holiday with a rather solemn aspect, commemorating the signing of the treaty between representatives of the British crown and some Maori chiefs on 6 February 1840.

Blenheim/Nelson (South Island)
Marlborough Wine & Food Festival. Wine festival with tasting of fine wines and food to match.

Kumara Beach/Sumner Beach (South Island)
Speights Coast to Coast Triathlon. Over 200km/125 miles of coast-to-coast running, cycling and kayaking (mid-February).

Napier (North Island)
Art Decó Weekend. Arts and cultural event with jazz festival.

Waikato (North Island)
Aotearoa Maori Festival. High-class Maori arts and cultural festival.

No. 1 National Sport

While New Zealand's soccer team has also taken part in World Cup tournaments rugby is still the number one national sport. Its national team, the All Blacks, is among the best in the world. They have something special to offer their opponents: before every game they dance the haka, the Maori war dance.

All Blacks Haka –
www.youtube.com

▶ **League teams**
The pro national championship is carried out in the ITM Cup. The Super Rugby Cup is played for by 15 teams from Australia, New Zealand and South Africa

122 m

22 m

8

7

6

5

4

HALF-WAY

3

2

22M LINE

10M LINE

1

2

3

GOAL LINE

68 – 70 m

DEAD BALL LINE

TOUCH LINE

Goal posts
The posts are 5.5m/ 18ft apart and 16m/53ft high. The cross bar is at 3m/10ft.

▶ **Rules**
The goal of the game is to carry or kick the ball past the opposing team and to gain points this way. Passing by hand is only allowed to the rear. Points can be made in the following ways:

TRY The ball has to be laid on the ground in the opponents' in-goal area.

CONVERSION After a successful try the ball is kicked from the point of the try between the goal posts and over the cross bar.

DROP KICK A kick during play between the goal posts and over the cross bar.

PENALTY KICK A kick towards the goal after a major infringement.

▶ **Rugby ball**
in compar

Ø≈78x60 cr

Ø≈65 cm

Ø≈70 cm

Men
Ø≈74,9 cm

Players' positions

1 Fullback
2 Left and Right Wing
3 Left and Right Centre
4 Stand-Off
5 Scrum-Half
6 Loose Forward
7 Second Row
8 Prop
9 Hooker

▶ All Blacks

The New Zealand Rugby Union national team is much better known by its nickname, the All Blacks, because the players' dress is black.

Coach: Steve Hanson
Captain: Richie McCaw

First test match: 15 August 1903
Australia 3:22 New Zealand

Highest win: 4 June 1995
New Zealand 145:17 Japan ●

Highest loss: 28 August 1999
Australia 28:7 New Zealand

World champion 1987, 2011, 2015

Dress

Home   Away

▶ **National and league teams**

www.allblacks.com

In-goal area
The area in which goals can be scored.

22m line
The defence team restarts play from here.

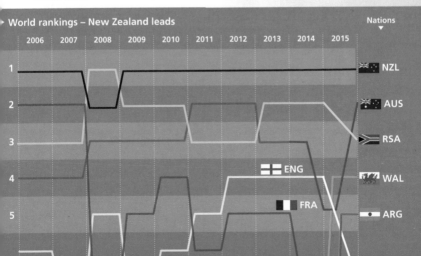

▶ World rankings – New Zealand leads

Nations ▼

	2006	2007	2008	2009	2010	2011	2012	2013	2014	2015	
1											NZL
2											AUS
3											RSA
4					ENG						WAL
5					FRA						ARG

Spectacular sight: Hot Air Balloon Festival, Hamilton

MARCH
Wellington (North Island)
Dragon Boat Festival.
A spectacular and colourful dragon boat regatta in Lambton Harbour celebrating Chinese New Year.

Auckland (North Island)
Round the Bay Run. One of the world's most popular traditional runs, with over 70,000 participants. The 8.4km/5mi-long route is flat and runs along Waitemata Harbour.

Hastings (North Island)
Highland Games. Sports contests in the Scottish tradition at Easter.

Hokitika (South Island)
Hokitika Festival. Traditional autumn (fall) festival with tasty food and drinks prepared as the first settlers would have known it.

Masterton (North Island)
Golden Shears. Most popular sheep shearing contest in New Zealand (early March).

Ngaruawahia (North Island)
Maori Canoe Regatta. Colourful regatta with carved warrior canoes at Ngaruawahia between Auckland and Hamilton

Taupo (North Island)
Ironman Triathlon. One of the oldest competitions of its kind in the world (first Saturday in March)

Wellington (North Island)
Wellington Festival. The largest cultural event in the country, with classical and modern music, theatre and poetry readings, takes place every other year (2018 etc.).

APRIL
Arrowtown (South Island)
Autumn (Fall) Festival in the former gold prospector settlement near Queenstown (mid-April)

Hamilton (North Island) *Insider Tip*
Hot Air Balloon Fiesta. Colourful balloon spectacle.

MAY
Te Puke (North Island)
Kiwi Festival. The tasty green fruit takes centre stage at this event in the »Kiwi Capital of the World« (mid-May)

JUNE
Wellington (North Island)
Film Festival. The country's most important film festival

JULY
Queenstown (South Island)
Winter Festival. A week-long winter party with night skiing and fireworks.

AUGUST
Bay of Islands (North Island)
Bay of Islands Jazz Festival. Most popular music festival in the country with famous performers.

SEPTEMBER
Alexandra (South Island)
Spring Festival. Spring is welcomed with a colourful programme of events.

Hastings (North Island)
Blossom Festival. Ten-day blossom festival with cultural events in New Zealand's largest fruit-growing area.

OCTOBER/NOVEMBER
New Plymouth (North Island)
Taranaki Rhododendron Festival. Colourful and sweet-smelling festival celebrating the rhododendron blossom (late October/early November)

Auckland (North Island)
Ellerslie Flower Show. One of the most beautiful flower shows in the southern hemisphere

DECEMBER
Auckland (North Island)
Air New Zealand/Shell Golf Open. Internationally known golfing tournament

Hangi – Maori Grill Party

There is no real translation for the Maori word »manaakitanga«. It could be hospitality, but not quite. Along with caring for the guests manaakitanga also includes the right attitude. This not only includes kindness and respect for others, but also something that is best described by the old-fashioned word »magnanimous«.

During a hangi, a traditional Maori feast, the hosts have a lot of time for manaakitanga. During this feast the food is cooked in a special oven in the ground and it can take up to seven hours before it is ready.

On Hot Stones

There are various rules for building hangi ovens, depending on the location and origin. But the principle is always the same: dig a hole in size according to the number of

Tasty part of a hangi feast: fresh fish

guests. Heat stones, preferably of volcanic origin, in a wood fire and lay them in the hole. Ashes and coal can also be added according to taste; they give the food a smoky aroma. Place baskets with the prepared food on the stones. In the past the baskets were woven with leaves and wood but now there are special metal baskets available. These baskets keep the food away from direct contact with the stones and thus keep it from burning. Finally the food is covered with wet cloths and sacks. When the hole is then filled with earth steam develops, which gently cooks the food.

Layering the food correctly in the baskets is important and depends on the cooking time of the individual components. Meat is in the lowest layer, followed by sweet potatoes, maize or pumpkin with fish and other vegetables on top. When the food is cooked it is tender and soft with a smoky and a bit earthy taste depending on the construction of the oven.

Hangi for All

Maori still prepare their food for large celebrations in a hangi. But strangers are rarely invited to these occasions. But anyone who still like to experience a hangi can make reservations in many of the Maori villages. For example in Tamaki Maori Village in Rotorua dance and singing is included in the three-hour event. In Mitai Maori Village you can experience the arrival of Maori warriors in a canoe in the jungle followed by dances and a tasty hangi dinner. In the evening you can walk to a beautifully lighted sacred spring after dinner. In Ko Tane Maori Village this special feast can be enjoyed after a kiwi-watching walk. Of course, these events have little to do with manaakitanga. But they are nonetheless interesting and a culinary event.

Addresses

Tamaki Maori Village
1220 Hinemaru Street, Rotorua
Tel. 07 349 2999
www.maoriculture.co.nz, 110 NZ$

Mitai Maori Village
196 Fairy Springs Rd, Rotorua
Tel. 07 3439132

www.mitai.co.nz
Hangi at night: 130 NZ$

Ko Tane Living Maori Village
60 Hussey Road, Harewood
Christchurch, Tel. 03 3596226
www.kotane.co.nz
Hangi plus kiwi tour, from 135 NZ$

Food and Drink

Multicultural Kiwi Cooking

Every New Zealand recipe raises the question: whose idea was it? The New Zealanders? The Maori? The Australians? Or even the Swiss? Many New Zealand specialities have their roots in other countries – and which ones is often grounds for debate.

Pavlova, for example the name of New Zealand's national dessert, is a meringue torte filled with cream and decorated with colourful fruit. The name of this sugary-sweet dietary nightmare sounds Russian but the recipe does not come from Moscow. It was named after the **Russian ballerina** Anna Pavlova who toured »down under« in the 1920s and had many fans there. But that is all we know for sure about the origins of this sweet delicacy. The rest is debated as the Australians also applauded the legendary Pavlova and made the creamy white dessert shaped like a tutu their national dessert.

National dessert - Pavlova

Or was it a German named **Herbert Sachse** who created the cultic torte in the 1920s? In Australia? After he read the New Zealand recipe in a newspaper and developed it further? Questions upon questions. But in New Zealand just like in Australia it's better not to look for answers! Just swallow your doubts with each sweet bite and without mentioning them. Pavlova is, after all, more than a dessert; it is a symbol. In Australia it is Australian, in New Zealand it is native New Zealand and that's all!

The true origins of many New Zealand dishes are no longer clear but that is not important either. No matter where the recipe comes from New Zealand usually gives it its **own special touch**. Kiwi cooking does not rely on complicated sauces, soufflés, soups and salad creations. The dishes are rather based on fresh ingredients and down-to-earth preparations. This does not make them boring either.

Creative and international

The number of **raw materials** that New Zealand's cooks can fall back on guarantees variety. There are roots, berries and sweet potatoes that don't grow anywhere else, fish, birds and seafood unknown on our side of the world. And even ingredients that are more common in other places have a unique aroma in New Zealand.

New Zealand lamb, for example, has an especially mild taste. In preparing it New Zealand's chefs confidently vary international trends. Influences come from the Pacific region, Asia, Britain and

Delicious: there's lots of fresh seafood in New Zealand

the Mediterranean, and of course there are many Maori recipes as well with **everything mixed together and combined into opulent meals**. Visitors wishing to try a broad selection of lamb dishes should look out for restaurants which have gained the »Lamb Award«. Popular lamb dishes are »lamb chops« (cutlets), »lamb kidney«, »lamb liver«, as well as sushi-style lamb meat rolls.

Meat pies are also very popular and New Zealanders' favourite fast food is **fish & chips**. This list shows that New Zealanders are real meat- and fish-eaters. But thanks to the rich fauna vegetarians don't suffer either. Here is a list of good restaurants with vegetarian menus: www.vegsoc.org.nz.

> **MARCO POLO TIP**
>
> **Tipping** *Insider Tip*
>
> Tipping is optional in New Zealand. Tips are in included in the bill in restaurants and hotels. But **for especially good service** the staff still hopes for something extra. Taxi drivers, baggage handlers etc. are also always happy to take tips.

Popular poultry — Kiwis have a special fondness for chicken and appreciate its many variations, especially for lunch.

Fish and seafood — Several dozen types of fish, many of them hardly known elsewhere, are lovingly prepared by New Zealand chefs. Hapuka, tarakihi and St Peter's fish are just a few of them. A particular speciality is a **small type of sardine** called whitebait. Crustaceans such as lobster and crayfish can be found on the menu alongside oysters and a multitude of mussels. Fish and seafood are usually served fresh, as nowhere in New Zealand is much over 150km/90 miles from the sea.

Exotic side dishes — New Zealand's good soils and favourable climate create ideal conditions for the cultivation of numerous types of **fruit and vegetables**. The kumara, a particularly soft and juicy sweet potato, is a popular side dish, while another tasty vegetable is the little-known tamarillo (tree tomato). Favourite fruits include apples, pears (amongst them the refreshing and very sweet nashi), strawberries, various citrus fruit, and of course kiwis, those Chinese gooseberries erst that moved out from New Zealand to conquer the world – very tasty and also very healthy.

EATING IN COMPANY

Cheaper to BYO — Restaurant prices in New Zealand are comparable to European prices. The bill becomes less when guests bring their own beer and wine. This is allowed in eateries with BYO (=bring your own) licence as they do not serve alcoholic drinks. Anyone who does bring his own pays a small corking fee. **Alcoholic beverages** may only be consumed from the age of 18, breaking this law is expensive.

There is a rich variety of **fruit and vegetable juices** as an alternative. The most populat ones include apple, pear, kiwi, cherry and citrus fruits.

The **national drink** is still **tea** as the British roots in New Zealand run deep.

The **coffee**-drinking culture has developed as well meanwhile. Especially in large cities there are a variety of bars and coffee shops that offer and prepare espresso and cappuccino like the Italians do.

Invitations to dinners or celebrations often ask guests to bring a plate. But the hosts would be amazed if the guests really showed up with their own empty plates. What is expected is a contribution to the buffet.

Bring a plate

Chef Evan Michelsen from Scarborough Fare Restaurant in Christchurch is a gourmet's delight

Sweet Potatoes and Blue Mussels

Exploring New Zealand's culinary landscape is fun, tastes good and offers no gastronomical landmines. Apart from a creamy paste that is served for breakfast and only looks like nougat cream.

Vegemite or Marmite: In New Zealand and Australia breakfast buffets usually include a dark creamy paste that at first glance could be confused with nougat cream. But be prepared: it is a salty yeast spread that takes some getting used to before you develop a taste for it. Many New Zealanders can't imagine starting the day without it but Europeans rarely start the day with it. But anyone who has not at least tasted it – is a coward! But it is not wise to spread it as thick as jam on your bread.

Kumara and tamarillo: While the kumara is not botanically related to the potato we still call it a sweet potato. It is used mainly in Maori dishes and tastes a little like chestnuts. Like the tomato the tamarillo is a member of the nightshade family. For this reason and also because of its red colour it is also called a tree tomato. The peel of this egg-shaped fruit is bitter and not eaten.

Whitebait: The bones of various varieties of tiny, young fish are so soft that the fish can be eaten whole; they are usually baked into potato pancakes or omelettes. They can only be caught during a very short season an under strict government regulations. They are considered to be a delicacy because of their slightly sweet taste, untypical for fish.

Paua, Pipi, Bluff oysters and green shell mussels: Gourmets rave about New Zealand's mussels. The noble oysters from the Bluff region with their unmistakable nut-like taste are available from April to August. Green shell mussels are available all year. In Europe they are mainly known as a dietary supplement for illnesses of the joints. They are a delicacy whether cooked, marinated or smoked. The pipi, which is popular among gourmets, is found mainly in Otago Harbour. The Paua is a delight to the eyes and the taste buds when it is prepared properly.

Popular Fruit

They taste sweet and are at the same time refreshingly tart. The kiwis, called Chinese gooseberries, are generally available in their green variety called Actinidia deliciosa and more recently also the golden yellow Actinidia chinensis

▶ Distribution

About sixty varieties of Chinese gooseberries thrive alone in south-western China, some also in Siberia, Japan and Malaysia. Today kiwis are mainly cultivated in New Zealand and the Mediterranean countries, the USA and Chile as well as in Russia and India.

China

1904

New Zealand

USA   1953

Europe   1975

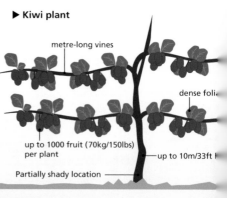

Kiwi Gree

▶ Cultivation areas

New Zealand is not the only producer of this sweet fruit. Many other countries are equally successful exporters. It is even cultivated in central Europe.

▶ Kiwi plant

metre-long vines

dense foli

NEW ZEALAND
ITALY
CHILE
FRANCE
JAPAN
GREECE

up to 1000 fruit (70kg/150lbs) per plant

up to 10m/33ft

Partially shady location

...ellow and green

...he most widely distributed variety worldwide is ...he green Hayward variety, which was bred in ...he 1920s in New Zealand. Since the 1970s it has ...old especially well in Europe. Since 2000 the new variety Kiwi Gold has conquered the produce sections of supermarkets. It is sweeter and less acidy.

smooth and not hairy, same size as green, hard protrusion at the blossom end

seed

fruit axis

Carpels (contain seeds)

fruit

Kiwi Gold

egg-shaped, hairy skin, up to 8cm/5in long and 5cm/2in wide

▶ Contents

A kiwi has about 50 calories per 100g/4oz

Vitamin C 0,07%
95% of RDA

Fat 0,6%
other minerals 6,3%
Carbohydrates 9%

Water 84%

▶ Also called Kiwi...

The nocturnal kiwi bird, New Zealand's national animal, is the smallest running bird in the world. It is not certain if its ancestors could not fly either.

Pelt-like feathers, underneath are 4-5cm (1.5-2in) long curved wings, no tail

Mustache-like whiskers

Muscular legs with large feet and sharp claws

About 20cm/8in long beak with nostrils (only bird to have them)

Largest bird egg relative to size of bird (15-30%), the female lays 1-2 eggs a year

▶ Endangered species

Before humans settled New Zealand the kiwi had no natural enemies. The Maori pushed them out of many areas and caused the extinction of dwarf kiwis. Hunting kiwis is forbidden since 1896 and the kiwi is a protected species since 1921.

Kiwi population

73,000 2008

63,000 2018 (expected)

Much-Praised »Late« Vintage

»New Zealand's climate and soil appear to be conducive to growing wine« noted the British missionary Samuel Marsden in 1819 already. He planted more than 100 vines near the mission station in Kerikeri on New Zealand's North Island, the first in the whole country. But even though these thrived it still took almost 100 years until New Zealand fruit of the vine could establish themselves worldwide as top quality wines.

Marsden was right: New Zealand's terroir is first class in many regions. But wine growing literally merely ailed along for many years as pests and diseases destroyed crops time and again and bizarre regulations made the marketing of their products difficult for wine growers. Until 1960 wine could only be sold in hotels in New Zealand; not even restaurants could serve wine. Wine has only been available in New Zealand supermarkets since 1990. But in the past 30 years New Zealand winegrowers have really caught up and even surpassed a few countries with old winegrowing traditions.

Vines from Europe

New Zealand winegrowers finally broke through in the late 1970s when they began to experiment with European varieties and growing methods. Sauvignon blanc wines from the Marlborough region, for example, have been export hits. Then in the 1980s the cultivation of Müller-Thurgau was tested. This is the most cultivated wine in cooler Germany. It was only in the 1990s that New Zealand winegrowers recognized the excellent conditions on South Island for growing French varieties like the demanding Chardonnay. They even successfully planted pinot noir grapes in Central Otago, the only area in New Zealand with a continental climate. Pinot noir from area gets wine connoisseurs worldwide raving.

Winegrowing Today

In the southern-most winegrowing nation in the world just about 700 winegrowers cultivate about 35,000 hectares (84,000 acres) and produce 235 mil. litres of wine a year. These figures doubled in the past 10 years. New Zealanders have also increased their consumption of wine: in 2011 every New Zealander drank about 21 litres of wine on average of which 15 litres were from New Zealand. In 2002 it was still 17 litres annually of which 8 litres were from New Zealand. By comparison German wine drinkers drink about 24 litres annually.

Regions and Varieties

The stony ground and large differences in day and night temperature make Marlborough the greatest winegrowing region in New Zealand; its best-selling variety is sauvignon blanc. Mainly Chardonnay and pinot noir are grown in Canterbury. Central Otago is considered to be the best region for pinot noir. Good red wines are also produced on the North Island, like the area around Hawke's Bay. An excellent cabernet sauvignon thrives near Auckland and a spicy Merlot in the Northland. For white wine fans Gisborne with its char-donnay is a good place to look. But in general, no matter where the wine is from they all come from a land with clean and clear air, where the sea is never far away. You can even taste it.

Adresses

Hawkes Bay
Mission Estate
198 Church Road, Napier
Tel. 06 845 93 50,
www.missionestate.co.nz
Mission Estate is the oldest still func-tioning vineyard in the country.

Craggy Range
253 Waimarama Road
Havelock North
Tel. 06 68 73 71 26
www.craggyrange.com

In the Terroir Restaurant here wines and dishes are matched perfectly.

Wellington
Johner Estate
East Taratahi RD7, Masterton
Tel. 06 3 70 82 17,
www.johner-estate.com
The German winegrower Karl Heinz has been growing wine here for ten years. Wine tasting.

New Zealand's winegrowers create fine wines: vineyard near Blenheim

Possum Fur and Hardwood

The nature and the people are what attract guests to holiday in the land of white clouds. Hardly anyone comes to New Zealand to go shopping. But it pays to take some time to shop while travelling around the country. You can find great souvenirs when you know where to look, including ones made of quality materials and ones you can#t find anywhere else in the world.

With around 30 mil. sheep New Zealand is one of the **world's largest producers of wool**. No wonder then that shops offer countless products connected somehow with sheep, from knit wear to sheepskins to lanolin-based toiletries. The »Swanny« a cross between a bush shirt and poncho in a typical plaid or check fabric is practically New Zealand's national dress. It is made of a specially woven wool fabric that lets rainwater just bead up. The original design is 100 years and comes from the Swanndri Company.

All sheep

Knitwear made from **possum-merino wool** are a unique rarity. Possum fur is spun together with fine merino wool. This makes a material that is especially soft, light-weight and still surprisingly warm.

Possum fur

Anyone opposed to fur clothing on principle should bear in mind: when it comes to possum even many animal activists support marketing these fur products. This nocturnal marsupial from Australia was able to multiply so much that it has become a threat to many ecosystems. Anyone who wants to support **natural animal husbandry** in New Zealand watch for the origins especially of wool and lambskin products like coats, jackets and boots. Products with the Zque label guarantee natural sheep husbandry and an environmentally friendly production process.

Sustainable shopping

There are not many good **deals** to be made when buying wool products in New Zealand since the prices are comparable to European ones. Outdoor clothing is cheaper in New Zealand.

European prices

But don't limit your shopping in New Zealand to wind- and weather-resistant clothing. Several New Zealand fashion designer have gained **international acclaim**. With the label Zambesi, for example, the two designers Elizabeth and Neville Findlay move confidently back and forth between everyday and not-your-everyday designs (www.zambesi.co.nz).

Outdoor and fine fashions

New Zealand fashion designers find international acclaim

The Green Philosopher's Stone

Seen from a purely scientific point of view jade, or pounamu, is not a mineral, but rather a mixture of jadeite or nephrite, which in turn consist of tremolite or actinolite. Got that? If not, it's not so bad. Hardly anyone looks at jade just from a scientific point of view. Ever since the stone age the mysterious green stone has inspired especially artists, healers and shamans.

Jade is created within the earth's crust as a product of volcanic processes. Even though it is only of medium hard consistency it breaks easily; drills and grinders are necessary to carve the green stone into jewellery and works of art. It is all the more astonishing that ancient, artistically designed works in jade have been found in every country of the world where jade occurs. This leads to the conclusion that jade has been seen as especially **valuable and magical** from early on. The green stone is still being used in natural medicine for illnesses of the kidney and bladder.

Jade from New Zealand

One of the Maori names for New Zealand's South Island is Te Wai Pounamu, which means as much as the »**land of jade water**«. And in fact there are rich occurrences of jade on the western coast of the island. This so-called greenstone is nephrite jade, not the more rare jadeite. Maoris group greenstone, which they call pounamu, according to colour and pattern. Inanga is a milky green, kahurangi is clear and translucent, kawakawa is dark green with dark specks like the leaves of a kawakawa tree and totoweka has reddish specks. There are also many special terms for different shades of colour according to the location where the stone was found. Along with precious axes the Maori made mainly amulets from pounamu stone. They did not make these for personal use, rather they gave them to guests as a valuable gift.

Mythical Fishhooks

Today many Maori carvers still make beautiful pendants out of nephrite jade. They often use traditional ancestral symbols as patterns. Many of the artistic amulets have, for example, the shape of a fishhook. These are called **hei matau**. They commemorate the demigod Maui who is supposed to have pulled North Island out of the sea with a fishing pole. They help wearers gain wealth and a strong will as well as safety on journeys across the water. Another common motif is the **koru**, a spiral-shaped symbol that symbolizes an opening fern leaf. It symbolizes new life and hope for the future. A **twist**, two strands that artistically cross and separate, symbolize eternal friendship and love. **Circles**, like eternal life, have no beginning or end and the three fingers of the bird-like **manaia** stand for birth, life and death. An especially powerful charm is the **tiki**, a figure with an enlarged head and huge eyes, which resembles an embryo. It gives wisdom and mana, that is spiritual power and energy.

Where to buy?

Nephrite pendants can be bought in every souvenir shop in New Zealand. But you can't always be sure that they are made of authentic nephrite stone and not cheap, imported jade. The jade city Hokitika on the west coast of South Island is a good and reliable address when it comes to handmade pieces by **authentic Maori artists**. There are many jade workshops here. Some even offer courses in which you can make your own piece of jade art under supervision. There are nice pieces to be found in Rotorua on North Island as well, where Maori carvers are trained. Expect to pay between 200 and 400 NZ$ for a piece handmade out of nephrite jade, depending on the size and work.

Jewellery made of green jade are popular souvenirs

From Tokyo
to New York Colour, patterns and flowing materials are emphasised by New Zealand designer Karen Walker. Her collections have made it to the **top catwalks** in London, New York, Tokyo and Sidney.

Anyone who wants to bring back »sweets for the sweet« as a souvenir should consider **honey**. This is just as much a gourmet speciality as wine, but it is much easier to transport. The amber-coloured manuka honey, for example, with its spicy taste was used by the Maori in the past as a natural antibiotic. Scientists have discovered meanwhile that **manuka honey** really does have antibacterial properties. The darker and very aromatic rewarewa honey comes from blossoms of the honeysuckle tree, which the Maori call rewarewa. This honey has an intensively **smoky and flowery aroma**.

MARCO POLO TIP

Delicious Honey   Insider Tip

The little beekeeping business »309 Honey« near Coromandel Town has become an insider's tip for its high quality but still reasonable manuka honey. Don't lett the drive on the gravel 309 Road put you off if you want to buy here.
309 Honey, Andrew & Sue Williams, 1644-309 Road, Coromandel Peninsula, tel. 07 8 66 48 00, www.309honey.co.nz.

Then there is another sweet speciality. Pohutukawa is a tree native to New Zealand that blossoms around Christmas every year with countless **bright red blossoms**. It turns New Zealand's beaches into a red sea of blossoms. Honey from these blossoms is light in colour and tastes a little like caramel, a rare and very fine delicacy.

Importing
not allowed Note: if you are planning on travelling back home via Australia bear in mind that honey may not be taken to Australia!
Maori woodcarvings make excellent gifts and are also easy to transport. In the shopping malls in larger cities beautiful and unique items of decoration and sculptures made of wood are available, but bear the shipping costs in mind when considering a purchase.

Worth shopping for: beautiful decorative accessories

Sports and Outdoors

From Trekking to Rafting

»No sports!« – Churchill's famous remark is probably not repeated very often by New Zealanders. For most of them recreation means either taking part in sports or watching others do it. Even though New Zealand is among the most sports-enthusiastic nations this still isn't enough for some people. A study was carried out recently to calculate the population's couch potato index so that measures could be undertaken to reduce it.

In hardly any country in the world is **sailing** as popular as it is in New Zealand. However, it is not only on the water that New Zealand sportsmen and women excel. New Zealand's **rugby** players have long been among the best in the world, while hockey, golf, tennis and cricket are other sports where New Zealanders perform to a high standard. The country is also home to many adrenaline-pumping outdoor activities such as **bungee jumping** and jetboat racing; friends of **rafting sports** will also get their money's worth here. If all this is too strenuous for you there are also gentler sports available in New Zealand like hiking and **trekking**. This is the only way to see the many rare but shy animals up close, which still live on the islands of New Zealand.

A sportsmad nation

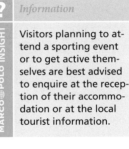

? **MARCO ☺ POLO INSIGHT** *Information*

Visitors planning to attend a sporting event or to get active themselves are best advised to enquire at the reception of their accommodation or at the local tourist information.

ACTIVITY SPORTS

Few areas on earth have as many horses per inhabitant as New Zealand. Little wonder then that horse riding is an extremely popular sport. Visitors can saddle up or sign up for a hack at many farms. Some farms and lodges offer »**horse trekking**« trail rides.

Horse riding

An increasing number of foreign tourists choose to explore New Zealand by touring bike or mountain bike. The best time for **cycling tours** is between October and April. Anyone planning a New Zealand cycling tour should really do some training beforehand. The

Mountain biking

Not a dry eye: rafting on the wild Shotover River

New Zealand is a paradise for cyclers in good condition

routes are predominantly hilly and **mountainous**, with near-constant winds and short, if sometimes fierce, rain showers to contend with.

Angler's paradise

One of New Zealand's favourite leisure activities is fishing. Some rivers and lakes – and even the waters off a few stretches of coast – teem with fish. While fishing in the sea is free, many inland bodies of water require a **fishing permit**, which may be bought at the local tourist information or in specialised shops selling fishing gear. Big-game fishing and **surfcasting** are very popular. The main season for big-game fishing is the months between January and May. One of the best areas for big-game anglers stretches off the northeastern coast of North Island.

TREKKING (HIKING, HILLWALKING)

Dream destination for trekkers

These days, a good third of New Zealand enjoys protected status. Little wonder that »trekking« (as the New Zealanders call it), **»bushwalking«** and »backpacking«, i.e. hiking and hillwalking – count amongst the most popular leisure activities.

There are opportunities everywhere, including the **green belts** of the larger cities, for shorter or longer hikes, »walks« or »tracks« taking just a few hours, or indeed several days. The New Zealand Department of Conservation maintains a great number of tracks, some of which are now **waymarked throughout**.

Walks, tracks

Everybody knows that **Sir Edmund Hillary** (▶Famous People), the first person to conquer Mount Everest, was a New Zealander. One of the places Hillary trained at before heading to the Himalayas was Mount Cook. Visitors who are into mountaineering will find peaks and rocky massifs in the New Zealand Alps that are challenging in the extreme.

Southern Alps for mountain climbers

Many tracks and walks can be tackled **all year round**. Only trails running through higher regions and those that receive a lot of snow are closed during the cold season. Many tracks require registration with the local DoC office. Also, for some trails it is recommended to take an experienced mountain guide.

Registration, guides

Along the tracks there are a good number of huts, usually between 4–6 hours apart. These huts might be fairly **spartan** but do offer tired hikers the basic facilities: **spaces for sleeping**, toilets, drinking water, sometimes cooking facilities too. As there can be **shortages** in high season, travellers are advised to always carry a small light tent for emergencies.

Huts

In New Zealand too, hikes led by knowledgeable guides are becoming increasingly popular. These excursions usually only require **light luggage** and weatherproof clothing, all other equipment, such as sleeping bags, is provided. Accommodation is usually in more comfortable huts, some of them equipped with **hot showers**. However, guides usually only take a very limited number of hikers.

Guided hikes

WILDLIFE WATCHING

In the past there were no land mammals in New Zealand. But there were many in the waters. Today all varieties of seals, like sea lions, fur seals, elephant seals but also whales and dolphins live here. The **hector dolphin** is a rarity. It is the smallest member of the whale family and can only be found around New Zealand's South Island.

Seals, whales and dolphins

Various varieties of sharks also live around New Zealand, including the feared great white shark, which is also on the list of protected species in New Zealand. Sharks are rarely seen near the beaches and they attack even more rarely. In the past 170 years, according to the Dept.

Protected: the great white shark

To Your Own Limits and Beyond

Adrenalin is actually a stress hormone. In dangerous situations it prepares the body for fighting or fleeing. The heart beats faster, blood pressure and breathing rate increase and within seconds energy reserves are released, which can make a person capable of the most strenuous feats. For some people this kick is practically an elixir of life that they can't do without.

Anyone who likes getting his blood pumping is in the right place in New Zealand. Faster, higher, farther – extreme sports are only limited by your own limits. There are thrills to be had here, on land, in the water and in the air.

The Wind in Your Hair

You are rarely as scared to death as when you are falling from a great height. The classic sports that play with this thrill are skydiving and bungee jumping. When skydiving you fall in free fall for a minute or longer, but only for a few seconds when bungee jumping. In the homeland of rubber rope jumping you can fall from buildings, towers, cranes, bridges or even a cable car. In a swoop, a close relative of the bungee, you are inside something like a sleeping bag when you fall into the deep and dangle at the end of the rope. And with rocket bungee you sit inside a ball that is anchored to the ground. The rope is then stretched and the anchorage is released so that you shoot into the air in the ball before falling back toward the ground. All of this is nothing for people whose health is not good. Anyone who wants to experience free fall without the risk should try bodyflying.

You float above the ground above a strong fan in a wind tunnel for several minutes. Or you can do this when paragliding or **parapenting** or when paraflying or parasailing. With the former you glide through the air with a parachute that you can steer; with the latter a boat pulls you through the air much like flying a kite.

A Sheer Drop

New Zealand is also the birthplace of **abseiling**. Anyone looking for the ultimate kick should go to the well-known karst regions on North Island (e.g. Waitomo Caves) and abseil into the unknown, mostly dark depths – the only light is from the lamp on your helmet. Depending on the cave you can continue your adventure by caving or by tubing down an underground stream. For people who like high ground but prefer to remain on it there is sand tobogganing: speeding down sand dunes on a sled. Then there is **zorbing**, rolling down a hillside in a large plastic ball. When the ball is filled with water the occupant stays more or less level. But in others you can roll with the motion of the ball.

Splashing Fun

White water adventures are part of a visit to New Zealand. Rafting is done in a rubber boat. The rivers used for this are not very long, but pretty wild. There are many organizers of rafting adventures, mostly from Queenstown, the rafting capital of New Zealand. **Kayaking** is more gentle. It is done throughout New Zealand in kayaks or canoes and makes it possible to admire the landscape while floating along. For people less interested in using muscles there's jet boating. These water vehicles suck in water through a pipe and blow it out again causing forward movement without a propeller. This makes it possible to ride through narrow canyons even in shallow water and close to the canyon wall.

Now there's no turning back

of Conservation, there were in all 17 serious **shark attacks** on humans. By comparison, every year 25 people worldwide have an unpleasant encounter with a shark. But even this does not make sharks into a dangerous species. Thousands of sharks die every year in **fishing nets** cast by humans.

Orcas hunting

In Raglan Harbour, on the west coast of New Zealand's North Island, you can sometimes watch a rare spectacle: **stingrays** retreat here now and then. The orca whales follow them and hunt them there.

Exotic birds

Many kinds of birds live on South Island, too: **royal albatrosses** live on Otago Peninsula near Dunedin, **penguins** live near Oamaru, mutton birds live off Stewart Island (south of the southern islands) and the smaller neighbouring islands; **gannets**, on the other hand, are at home on North Island near Auckland on Muriwai Beach, south-east of Hastings in Hawkes Bay on Cape Kidnappers.

Taking a break with a million-dollar view while hiking

WINTER SPORTS

Visitors are more or less guaranteed snow at higher reaches, above 1,000m/3,280ft–1,200m/3,937ft, in the period between July and September. The vast majority of New Zealand's ski areas lie **above the tree line** and are therefore extensive, with various lifts, ski huts, ski schools, etc. Many stations offer packages including lift passes and ski lessons, plus food and board. **Mount Ruapehu** in Tongariro National Park on North Island is a dedicated skiing region. The areas are Whakapapa and Turoa. Since the volcano is always rumbling **steaming mud springs** and holes in the slopes are not unusual.

Skiing from July

Ski clubs maintain their own »club fields« in sometimes fairly remote places. These ski areas do not usually have the same technical level as the aforementioned winter sports hot spots.

Club fields

Skiers who do not object to paying up to NZ$600 for three to five downhill runs per day, can charter a helicopter or ski plane to take them to more than 400 high-alpine slopes situated on South Island. New Zealand's **longest ski run**, of 24km/15 miles, can be found at Mount Tasman and the Tasman Glacier.

Heli skiing on South Island

Sporting Hot Spots

WALKS AND TRACKS

**Milford Track
(Fiordland National Park)**
Length: 50km/30mi long
Duration: 4 to 7 days
Simple huts as accommodation

**Routeburn Track
(Fiordland National Park)**
Length: 40km/24mi long
Duration: 4 to 6 days
Simple huts as accommodation

**Tuatapere Hump Ridge Track
(Fiordland National Park)**
Length: 53km/32mi long
Duration: 4 bis 7 days
Simple huts

**Coastal Track
(Abel Tasman National Park)**
Length: 30km/18mi
Duration: 3 days
Huts or tents

**Heaphy Track
(Abel Tasman National Park)**
Length: 80km/50mi long
Duration: 4 to 5 days,
Huts or tents

Volcanic mountains Ruapehu and Taranaki
Various tours possible

MOUNTAIN TOURS

North Island
Volcanic mountains Taranaki und Ruapehu

The Path is the Goal –
on Foot Through the Wilderness

Sir Edmund Hillary, who on May 29, 1953, was the first person to climb Mount Everest, was a New Zealander (▶ Famous People). Ever since he was a teenager he had trained in the mountains of New Zealand, among them Mount Cook, in order to get in shape for the hardship involved in this climb. But New Zealand is not just an optimal training ground for mountain climbers. It is also the right place for people who love hiking through wildly romantic jungles and national parks.

More than one third of New Zealand is under nature or landscape protection. Many of the hiking trails were originally **old Maori paths**. Later settlers, prospectors and hunters followed them and in this way preserved them. Today both native and foreign hikers are using them to get back to nature.

Short Tour, Long Tracks

Most of the trails run through nature preserves that are administered by the New Zealand Department of Conservation (DOC). It has divided the trails into various categories according to difficulty. Routes of about one hour on paved trails, which can be walked without any special equipment apart from walking shoes, are called **Short Walks**. **Walking Tracks** can take up to one day to cover. Hiking shoes or boots and slightly good physical condition are necessary for these as they can be muddy or rocky. Great Walks are tours that require real physical fitness; you might even have to cross streams or rivers without the help of a bridge. Tramping Tracks and Routes are a real challenge as they lead up and down mountains

through **untouched wilderness**. For these you need lots of experience, excellent physical condition and maybe even survival training. Most of the trails are on public land and accessible without an admission charge.

Great Walks

The **nine tours** that are called the Great Walks cover both North and South Island as well as the Stewart Islands and lead to great locations away from civilization. The most famous is Milfroed Track in Fiordland (▶p. 356). It runs through romantic valleys and to rugged waterfalls. Heaphy Track is the longest; it crosses breathtaking rope bridges through the wild jungles of the west coast. There are numerous huts along this track. But be aware: camping is not allowed along Milford Track even when the huts are full. Hikers must stay in the DOC huts. The number of hikers using certain tracks at one time is limited and reservations must be made.

The Best Time to Travel

The best time for trekking is late summer and early fall, the weeks after the main tourist season. The weather is still stable then, not so hot anymore and many of the tourists have left already. There is more room in the huts then as well. Detailed information on trekking and the condition of the tracks is available at the local and regional tourist offices as well as the NZ Department of Conservation (DOC; ▶national parks).

On security

There are no poisonous snakes or dangerous **wild animals** in New Zealand. But it is still important to find out about any possible dangers before each trek, like sudden changes in weather, rivers, infectious diseases, landslides or swarms of wasps. It is also easy to get lost in the extensive forests. Since there is often **no mobile reception**, in some regions it is possible to rent cheap emergency phones.

The growing number of hikers requires more careful use of **nature and the environment**. If everyone protects animals and plants, takes his own refuse with him, watches out for fire and is **considerate** of others New Zealand's national parks will remain incomparably beautiful for a long time.

The end of the trail: rope bridge in the jungle

South Island
Mount Cook, Mount Tasman
Mountains in Aspiring NP

SAILING
On an America's Cup yacht
Explore NZ, Auckland
www.explorenz.co.nz

Gourmet turns from Nelson
Gourmet Sailing
www.gourmetsailing.co.nz

In a catamaran in Abel Tasman National Park
Abel Tasman Sailing Adventures
Kaiteriteri Beach
www.sailingadventures.co.nz

On a dolphin tour
A-Class Sailing Akaroa
www.aclasssailing.co.nz

EXTREME SPORTS
Bungee jumping
A. J. Hackett Bungee
Queenstown
www.bungy.co.nz

Bodyflying and swooping
Agroventures, Rotorua
www.agroventures.co.nz

Abseiling/caving
Waitomo Caves Adventures
www.waitomo.co.nz

Sand tobogganing
Sand Safaris, Kaitaia
www.sandsafaris.co.nz

Jet boating
New Zealand Riverjet, Rotorua
www.riverjet.co.nz

SKI REGIONS
North Island: Mount Ruapehu
(Tongariro National Park)
South Island: Mount Hutt,
100km/60mi west of Christchurch

SEALS
South Island
along the quiet and deserted west coast

WHALES AND DOLPHINS
South Island
along Kaikoura Coast (east coast)

ROYAL ALBATROSSES
South Island
on Otago Peninsula

PENGUINS
South Island
near Oamaru

MUTTON BIRD
South Island
on Stewart Island

GANNET
North Island
near Auckland on Muriwai Beach,
in Hawkes Bay

New Zealand's higher elevations are relatively certain to have snow between July and September

After the Cup is Before the Cup – Sailing Nation New Zealand

When the Maori settled New Zealand they landed their sailboats on the beaches of Aotearoa, the land of the white cloud. The new Zealanders' passion for sailing has remained unbroken since then, hundreds of years ago. Auckland, for example, is called the city of sails; statistically there is one boat for every fourth resident of Auckland. And when a New Zealand team has one yet another international competition hundreds of thousands of people celebrate in the streets of Auckland.

For many New Zealanders May Day of 1995 is unforgettable; the New Zealand team led by Peter Blake with Russell Coutts at the helm of the **Black Magic**, won the America's Cup. Until then the world's most renowned sailing trophy had been firmly in American hands since 1851, with the exception of one single time. But now the kiwis showed that sailing is more than a very popular national sport in New Zealand. When it was time to defend the title in Auckland in the year 2000 the **America's Cup Village** was built in Auckland's harbour, with bars, restaurants and shops. A little later this party strip was opened festively when New Zealand's team again won the trophy.

Lost Title

Even though New Zealand made it to the finals two more times after this the cup was taken first by Switzerland and then again by the American team. The defeat in 2003 was especially painful for the New Zealanders because the skipper of the Swiss team was Russell Coutts; he had won both previous victories for New Zealand. He was then called a traitor. But the grief over the loss of the title did not diminish the New Zealanders passion for sailing. They are still confident that they will soon bring the coveted cup back home.

Close to the Wind

Anyone who would like to sail on a real America's Cup yacht can fulfil his dream at Viaduct Harbour in Auckland. Two boats that were used by the New Zealand team to train leave from here every day. The victorious boat of 1995, the Black Magic, can be seen in the exhibition Blue Water Black Magic in the New Zealand Maritime Museum. Along with Auckland New Zealand has many ideal sailing locations in the north and in the south. Explore picturesque natural harbours and with a little luck even see whales, dolphins, penguins or seals. A sailing license is not requires as many boats are rented with crews. The Bay of Islands and Marlborough Sounds are well-known sailing areas. **Gourmet tours** in Tasman Bay leaving from Nelson are an experience for all the senses. Boats take between eight and ten guests on board;

everything is possible from a three-hour harbour tour to a two-day gourmet weekend on the high seas.

Animals and Dream Beaches

In a harbour tour in Akaroa near Christchurch guests can also lend a hand in sailing the boat. The historic yacht SV Manutara is really a unique boat: it was built in 1953 from one giant kauri tree. Guests on the two-and-a-half hour sail learn not only the basics of sailing but also interesting facts about Akaroa. The rare hector dolphins, the smallest members of the whale family, can be seen on almost every trip. On a sailboat the playful animals are not bothered by the sound of motors. Anyone who would rather fly across the water on a modern catamaran and visit fabulous beaches can do this in Abel Tasman National Park. A visit to Adele Island, a bird sanctuary with a great variety of birds is a highlight of that park.

Winning the America's Cup has fuelled the New Zealand passion for sailing – Auckland is called the City of Sails

TOURS

Two islands with varied scenic appeal: mountain ranges and mighty glaciers on South Island, spectacular volcanic areas and gorgeous beaches on North Island. Here are a few ideas for individual tours through this unique country.

Tours Through New Zealand

Discover the most beautiful routes in the country, first on the map and then for real!

Tour 1 **Round Trip (North)**
This tour across North Island introduces travellers to all the most interesting sights, including dream beaches, volcanic areas and big cities.
▶page 155

Tour 2 **Round Trip (South)**
This route mainly follows the coast for a circuit of South Island. For those unable to decide between the two islands, tours 1 and 2 can also be combined.
▶page 157

Tour 3 **Taranaki Route**
This tour leads from Auckland to Wellington, past a picture-book volcano and a karst cave area with glow worm caves.
▶page 160

Tour 4 **East Cape Route**
This North Island route also focuses on a volcanic region, introducing visitors to one of the most fertile areas in New Zealand, an Art Déco town, and many dream beaches of course.
▶page 162

Tour 5 **Mackenzie – Arthur's Pass**
A drive through the breathtaking high mountain landscape of the interior, past small towns, lakes and a high plateau.
▶page 164

Travelling in New Zealand

Spoilt for choice

Travellers who make the long trip to the other side of the world rarely come to lay on the beach and stare at the sea for weeks. The country has much too much to offer for that: while the main attractions of New Zealand's North Island are the spectacular **volcanic areas**, beautiful dreamlike beaches and rich evidence of Maori culture, South Island's prime assets are the majestic snow-capped mountain tops and mighty glaciers of New Zealand's Southern Alps, **deep-cut fjords**. In New Zealand you can watch kiwis, discover prehistoric reptiles, watch penguins or swim with dolphins.

Plan well, see more

Anyone looking for a **surge of adrenalin** can jump from a bridge on a rubber rope in New Zealand, crawl into dark caves or chase across the water on a jetski. The land of the white cloud has an incomparable variety; anyone who wants to collect as many impressions as possible will have to plan his trip well.

Open-jaw flights

Generally speaking, New Zealand is relatively compact, allowing the main sights to be explored in about **3 weeks**. However, visitors should bear in mind that in terms of landscape the two islands are very different. Anyone wanting to gain a full appreciation of this

Along with spectacular snow-capped peaks and lush forests the southland offers plains with fertile pastures

country should be sure to visit **both islands**. It might be worth, for instance, flying in to Auckland on North Island and out again from Christchurch on South Island, in order to make the most of the time available.

Organizing a visit in this way means starting with Auckland, the country's **largest city**. The cosmopolitan »City of Sails« is dominated by the water which frames it. To the north and east of Auckland there are **magnificent beaches** and various opportunities for water sports, e. g. in the Bay of Islands or on the Coromandel Peninsula, but also ancient trees in the kauri forests near Dargaville. Further south, the **glow worm caves** near Te Kuiti captivate visitors. Bubbling geysers and hot thermal springs dominate the landscape around the »sulphur town« of Rotorua. A drive via the **Art Déco town of Napier** and through the famous national parks of Whanganui and Tongario leads eventually to the capital, Wellington.

Discover North Island

From Wellington, a ferry takes visitors across to South Island. The **fjord landscape** at Picton and Nelson is a paradise for boat trips and hikes. Abel Tasman National Park offers golden sandy beaches, only reachable on foot or by boat. From here, drive along the coast past the world-famous Pancake Rocks to Greymouth. Nearby Shanty-town, popular with visitors, recreates the gold rush fever of times past. Further south await the **mighty glaciers** of the New Zealand Alps. The Franz Josef and Fox Glaciers, alongside the breathtaking landscape of the Fiordland National Park and Milford Sound, count amongst the most **exciting natural monuments** of New Zealand. There are two options from here back to Christchurch: either a drive through the interior via Queenstown and Arrowtown, or down south via Invercargill and Dunedin.

Explore South Island

Recently, New Zealand has named and signposted a whole series of »Scenic Routes«, ideal for visitors who don't always feel like putting together their own routes. For instance, the northern tip of North Island is opened up by the **Twin Coast Discovery Highway**, run-ning through ancient kauri forests and past fantastic swimming beaches. The **Pacific Coast Highway** runs along the east of North Island and leads from Auckland via Napier to the Bay of Plenty and on to the Coromandel Peninsula. Also on North Island the Thermal Explorer Highway is a signposted drive from Napier into the **vol-canic area of Taupo** and on to Mount Ruapehu. On South Island, the Southern Scenic Route runs from Dunedin into Fiordland Na-tional Park. Over 100 Heritage Trails lead to the most interesting places for discovering New Zealand's cultural history. **Lots of mate-rial** on these routes can be picked up from local tourist information points.

Spectacular Scenic Routes

As New Zealand is a relatively **small country**, travellers face few problems reaching all parts of the islands without their own transport. Sometimes however, there can be a wait involved. In terms of public transport, the bus network is the most comprehensive, and nearly all tourist sights can be reached by bus. In most cases the tourist companies also offer special **tours** to individual attractions.
Visitors wanting to explore outside the tourist centres will need a **hire car**. The rail network has been thinned out over the years, really leaving only the larger cities as a viable option for train travel.

Relaxed travelling by bus

On the whole, New Zealand is an **all-year-round** destination, but it is only **in summer** that all the main tourist sights are guaranteed to be open. The New Zealanders' main travelling season is between Christmas and the end of January, leading to considerable traffic congestion. Unless absolutely unavoidable, it is perhaps best not to travel to New Zealand during that time.

When to go

Highlights North Island

Tour 1

Length of tour: approx. 1,800km/1,120mi
Duration of tour: approx. 2 weeks

This tour leads from Auckland to Wellington past most of North Island's main sights. Starting at the northern tip, it promises a journey past beautiful beaches, through ancient Kauri forests and volcanic areas to the country's charming capital.

The starting point of this trip is ❶****Auckland**, the »City of Sails« with its cosmopolitan flair. Highway 1 leads north along the Hauraki Gulf into the Northland region. Don't miss the picturesque little village of Puhoi, founded by Bohemian immigrants. A little further on, the lively town of ❷**Whangarei** appears, set in beautiful surroundings only marred by a large oil refinery.
This stage of the route ends at the ❸****Bay of Islands**, the cradle of modern New Zealand. Most interesting here are the old Maori settlements, as well as the whaling and mission stations, amongst them the towns of Paihia, Kerikeri and Russell. Waitangi was the place where in the 19th century the treaty between European immigrants and local Maori was signed; it is still in effect. From Paihia, Highway 1 leads on to finish at Kaitaia. From here, a detour along the fabulous 88km/54mi-long Ninety Mile Beach leads to **Cape Reinga**, supposed to be the northernmost tip of New Zealand.

Bohemian village

No other landscape in New Zealand is as charming as the Bay of Islands with its pleasant bays and sleepy villages

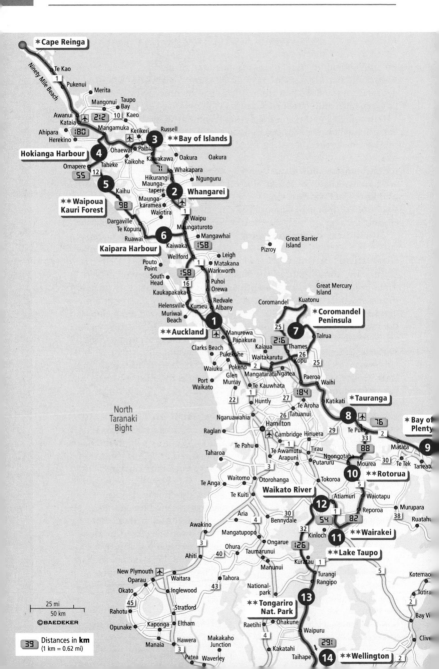

After returning from Cape Reinga, follow Highway 1 from Kaitaia a little bit further southeast and turn south at ❹**Hokianga Harbour** towards Taheke, where the road joins Highway 12. Follow it west to the mouth of Hokianga Harbour where the river joins the Tasman Sea and drive on south, more or less parallel to the coast. This involves crossing the magical ❺****Waipoua Kauri National Forest** (25km²/10sq mi), one of the last remaining ancient forests of New Zealand, with its imposing giant trees – and kiwis. Beautiful Bayly's Beach stretches further south and offers another opportunity for a swim. Not far from here, Dargaville is an up-and-coming tourist town keen to establish itself as »Gateway to the North«. Soon after, Highway 12 reaches the sunken valley system of ❻**Kaipara Harbour**, then joins Highway 1 leading south. At the town of Welisford, Highway 16 provides a useful alternative route back to Auckland.

On to the giant trees

Auckland is the starting point for a trip into the »hot heart« of North Island. Follow Highway 1 south to Pokeho, turning off east there and taking Highway 2 to the ❼***Coromandel Peninsula**. A good way to explore this peninsula is a circular drive on Highway 25, with the destination for this stage being the port town of ❽***Tauranga**, ❾* **on the Bay of Plenty**, its backcountry dominated by fruit-growing and forestry.
Past Te Puke, Highway 33 turns off south into the very active geothermal area of ❿****Rotorua**, where it joins Highway 5. A few days can easily be spent in and around Rotorua, experiencing volcanic and post-volcanic phenomena of all kinds – such as geysers, hot waterfalls, bubbling and steaming mud and sulphur springs – and soaking in the hot water pools. There are also some well-preserved traditional Maori villages giving a great insight into Maori culture. A relatively short drive further south on Highway 5 leads to the area of ⓫****Lake Taupo • Wairakei**, also extremely active in geothermal terms, with a large lake and an interesting geothermal power plant. Further north, the ⓬**Waikato** river squeezes through deep, especially picturesque gorges.

Feeling the earth's breath

Just a few miles south of Taupo, Highway 1 touches the ⓭** **Tongariro National Park**, a dual UNESCO Natural and Cultural World Heritage site. Rising up in this mountainous country shaped by active volcanism, the two volcanoes of Ruapehu and Ngauruhoe have long been held sacred by the Maori. However, these days they are increasingly becoming tourist centres for trekking and winter sports. From Tongariro, National Park Highway 1 leads south via Foxton (with pretty Foxton Beach nearby) and Levin to New Zealand's capital of ⓮****Wellington**, with its many fantastic restaurants and sights.

Holy fire mountains

Tour 2 Highlights South Island

Length of tour: approx. 2,700km/1,680mi
Duration of tour: approx. 3 weeks

Time permitting, this South Island tour can easily be added on to the North Island circuit. Otherwise, just start from Wellington and drive through South Island, hugging the coast nearly all the way, until reaching the capital again after almost a month.

Cross Cook Strait

From ❶ ****Wellington**, take the ferry across the storm-lashed Cook Strait and then drive through the beautifully scenic landscape of ❷ ****Marlborough Sounds** to the busy port of Picton, in the northeast of South Island. From Picton, the route leads west to Tasman Bay and the vibrant town of ❸ ***Nelson**. From here, a worthwhile detour on the Tasman–Heaphy Route leads into the magnificent ❹ ****Abel Tasman National Park**. Now follow Highway 6 through the Buller River Valley with its old gold prospector settlements to the river mouth at ❺ ***Westport**, and then continue south along the west coast sculpted by the wild swell of the Tasman Sea. An initial highlight on this stretch of coast is ❻ ****Paparoa National Park**, with its famous Pancake Rocks resembling stacks of pancakes turned into stone. The stage goal here is ❼ ***Greymouth**. Nearby, the restored gold mining settlement of Shantytown can be visited.

Cross the Alps

A drive via ❽ ***Hokitika** – where the Maori found the prized semi-precious nephrite (greenstone) with its green shimmer – and the town of Ross, around which gold has also been found, leads to ❾ ****Westland National Park** and the two natural wonders of Fox Glacier and Franz Josef Glacier. These two ice streams flow from the fern fields of the Southern Alps down into the evergreen rainforest on the west coast. Haast, further south, marks the end of the coastal stretch of Highway 6, which now turns inland to the southeast, following the Haast River upriver and crossing the New Zealand Alps at the ❿ ***Haast Pass**.
Between the two former glacial tongue basins today filled by the mountain lakes of ⓫ ***Lake Wanaka** and Lake Hawea, the highway winds its way into the lively tourist town of Wanaka.

Fun sports and natural wonders

From Wanaka, follow State Road 89 through beautiful landscape directly to ⓬ ***Arrowtown** and on to ⓭ ****Queenstown**, the two playgrounds for fans of adventure sports such as bungee jumping, rafting and jetboat trips. After visiting Queenstown and its charming surroundings – notably Lake Wakatipu, the Remarkables and Shotover Canyon – follow Highway 6 to Lumsden. From there, State

Road 94 leads as a cul-de-sac right into the highly scenic ⑭**Fiord-land National Park** with Lake Manapour and ⑮**Lake Te Anau**. The Milford Track begins on its north shore and can be walked in four days. It is one of the Great Walks.

From Te Anau, the State Road leads on to ⑯**Milford Sound** with Mitre Peak, which is often called the symbol of New Zealand. Don't

Way down south

miss a visit to the glow worm cave at Lake Te Anau, as well as the subterranean power plant at Lake Manapouri. Back in Te Anau, follow Highway 6 south to **⑰ Invercargill** in the extreme south of the island, the starting point for a worthwhile detour across to the southern **⑱ * Stewart Island**. With a bit of luck you can see a sea elephant lying on the beach. The mountainous island is a hiker's paradise.

Insider tip
Catlins

From the port of Invercargill, the scenic State Road 92 leads along the south- eastern (Pacific) coast of New Zealand's South Island through the enchanting landscape of the aboriginal **⑲ * Catlins** and past some particular points of interest, including Cathedral Cave and Nugget Point. At **⑳ Balclutha**, the road joins Highway 1, leading northeast on to **㉑ * *Dunedin**. Dunedin has a fair number of sights, while a day trip to the Otago Peninsula with its seals and bird colonies, and pretty Larnach's Castle, New Zealand's only castle and its famous gardens, is also well worth considering.

Dolphins and
whales

From Dunedin, Highway 1 leads north along the Pacific coast to **㉒ Oamaru**, passing the famous Moeraki Boulders. Via Waitaki, the road carries on to **㉓ * Timaru**, a good base for day trips into Peel Forest Park at Geraldine and the cave paintings at Cave. The route then crosses the Canterbury Plains, passing through the small town of Ashburton and eventually leading to **㉔ * *Christchurch**, the metropolis of South Island and well worth exploring even after the earthquake. From here, consider a day trip to the Banks Peninsula with the two natural harbours of Lyttelton and Akaroa. From Christchurch, Highway 1 leads north to Culverden, with a worthwhile detour inland to **㉕ * Hanmer Springs**. The journey carries on to **㉖ Kaikoura** at the feet of the eponymous mountain range. Kaikoura is the base for exciting boat trips, with a good chance of seeing whales and dolphins. The last stage on South Island leads north from Kaikoura into the famous wine-producing area of **㉗ Blenheim**, to eventually finish at the port of Picton.

Tour 3 **Taranaki Route**

Length of tour: 1,000km/620mi
Duration of tour: approx. 2 weeks

This alternative to the main route on North Island leads from the metropolis of Auckland to the as yet little known region on the Waikato River, past the town of Hamilton to the westerly point with the old volcano of Taranaki, and on to Wellington.

After several days of exploring and heading south from ❶**∗∗Auckland**, the route traverses a landscape shaped by the Waikato river. The first stage leads to the friendly town of ❷**∗Hamilton**, New Zealand's fourth largest city and site of a university and various research facilities. To the south of Hamilton, the large karst cave area of ❸**∗∗Te Kuiti** features the world-famous glow worm caves of Waitomo.

Further southwest, the port town of ❹**New Plymouth** on the Tasman Sea is dominated by the old and currently inactive volcano of ❺**∗Taranaki (Mount Egmont)**, which also forms the centrepiece of the eponymous national park. It is possible to drive all the way around this picture-book volcano. New Plymouth was once a hub for dairy products; today mainly raw materials for the petrochemical industry are shipped from here.

From Hawera on the southern foot of Taranaki, drive along the coast to ❻**Wanganui**, for an unmissable detour north into ❼**∗∗ Whanganui National Park**, not only for the magnificent ferns. The Whanganui River still follows its original riverbed here. The last stage of the route goes via Foxton and Levin to eventually reach New Zealand's capital, ❽**∗∗Wellington** with its many cultural and culinary highlights.

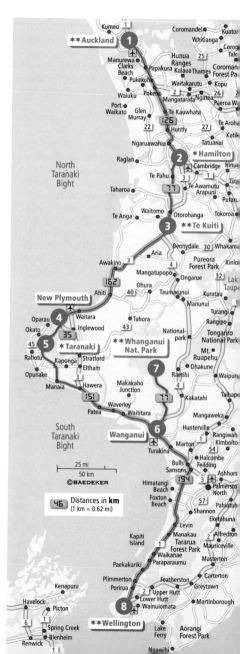

Tour 4 East Cape Route

Length of tour: 1,300km/810mi
Duration of tour: approx. 2 weeks

This alternative route from Auckland to Wellington heads east via the Bay of Plenty and the East Cape. It also gives an introduction to the fertile landscape of Hawkes Bay as well as the Art Déco town of Napier, finishing off with a drive through the »volcanic heart« of North Island to the south to Wellington.

Trip to a volcano   From ❶**Auckland**, drive southeast to the ❷*Bay of Plenty, which is steeped in history, with the two towns of Tauranga and

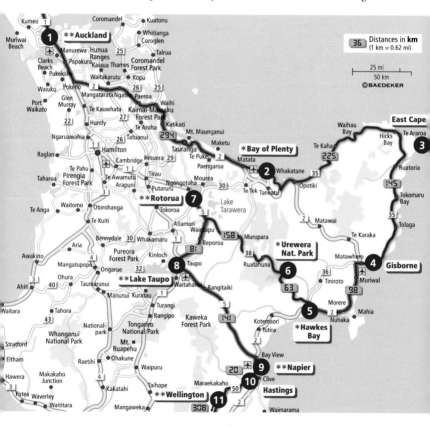

Distances in **km**
36 (1 km = 0.62 mi)

25 mi
50 km
©BAEDEKER

Floating along on a high bridge

Whakatane, alongside the old Maori settlement of Opotiki. Travellers with a bit of time on their hands might consider side trips to the beach at offshore Mayor Island or the still very young and active volcanic outcrop of White Island with its moon-like landscape.

The route leads on to ❸ **East Cape**, the eastern point of North Island and constantly ruffled by the swell of the Pacific. From there, turn south towards ❹ **Gisborne** on Poverty Bay and maybe consider a detour to the Mahia Peninsula south of Gisborne. On arrival at ❺ * **Hawkes Bay** drivers will encounter the town of Wairoa, from where the 180km/112-mile »Urewera Route« leads northwest and straight through ❻ ***Urewera National Park** into the volcanic area of ❼ **Rotorua**. At the southern fringe of Hawkes Bay, the Art Déco town of ❽ ***Napier**, is well worth a visit. From here, the 150km/93-mile »Napier–Taupo Route« leads northwest into the geothermal area of ❾ ***Taupo • Wairakei**, whilst the East Cape Route proper

Art Déco in Napier

runs inland from Napier through a charming landscape dominated by fruit trees and vineyards, via ⑩**Hastings** and Dannevirke to Masterton at the foot of the wild Tararua Range. The last stage leads via Greytown, Upper Hutt and Lower Hutt, eventually arriving at New Zealand's capital, ⑪****Wellington**.

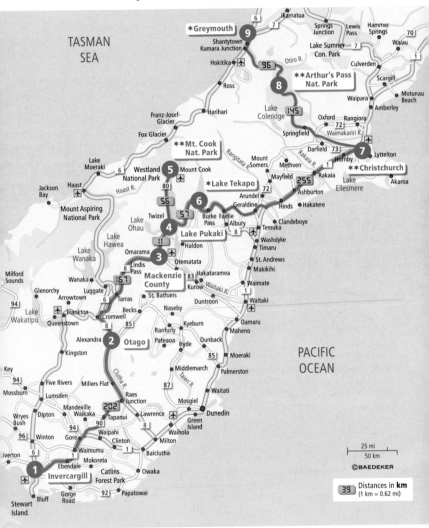

Mackenzie

Tour 5

Length of tour: 1,000km/620mi
Duration of tour: approx. 2 weeks

The southern half of New Zealand's South Island, from Invercargill to Christchurch, can also be traversed across the interior in order to take in Mackenzie Country and the magnificent alpine landscape of Mount Cook National Park, amongst other attractions. In addition, the charming route from Christchurch to Greymouth can be done on the well-kept road over Arthur's Pass.

From ❶**Invercargill**, head north via Gore into the mountain country of ❷**Otago**. One possible stop-off is Alexandra, the starting point for a round trip in the footsteps of the gold prospectors or a drive to the Clutha Hydro Electric Scheme. Carry on north via Cromwell and the Lindis Pass into ❸**Mackenzie Country**. Here, a detour from Twizel to ❹**Lake Pukaki** and ❺**Mount Cook National Park** is an absolute must. Heading northeast from the lively town of Twizel on Highway 8 leads past ❻**Lake Tekapo** and across Burke's Pass over to Fairlie and Geraldine. From here, follow State Road 72 into Peel Forest Park and on to Erewhon or Mesopotamia. The route's end point is ❼**Christ-church**, South Island's metropolis.

From Christchurch, follow State Road 73 northwest to Springfield and the eastern foothills of the New Zealand Alps. Now it's a steady climb through a rugged and romantic high mountain landscape to the crest of ❽**Arthur's Pass**, which is also the centrepiece of the eponymous national park. Beyond the pass summit, the drive carries on down into the wild Otira Canyon. Follow the Otira River all the way to its mouth at the re-stored gold prospectors settlement of Shantytown. From here it is not far to the final destination, ❾**Greymouth**.

SIGHTS FROM A TO Z

Natural spectacles of all kinds await travellers in New Zealand: alpine mountains covered in perpetual ice, miles of dreamy beach, volcanic areas with bubbling geysers and sleepy little islets ...

NORTH ISLAND

Surface: 113,729 sq km/43,911 sq mi
Population: approx. 3.1 million
Population density: 28 inh./sq km/ 20 inh./sq mile

** **Auckland**

✦ Se 127

Region: Auckland
Altitude: 0 – 260m/853ft
Population: 1.42 million

The only city with more than a million inhabitants has many faces. Some call New Zealand's largest city »Sydney for beginners«, referring to its skyline. But the city offers more than city life. The metropolis has in fact held on to its rural character to this day, while the suburbs spread out up to 70 kilometres/44 miles into the surrounding area. These offer beach resorts, tradional winegrowing, volcanos, rain forests and a enchanting island world.

Auckland lies on the isthmus occupied by numerous extinct volcanic cones between the bays of Manukau Harbour and Waitemata Harbour. With a height of 260m/ 853ft, **volcanic Rangitoto Island** divides Waitemata Harbour from the wide Hauraki Gulf with its string of islands. To the southwest rise the Waitakere Ranges. Since its foundation, the city has spread ever further south and north.

Between two bays

In 1891, Rudyard Kipling was still able to call Auckland **»last, loneliest, loveliest, exquisite, apart«**, whereas today the borders with the surrounding area are hardly visible anymore. Once-remote settlements have become autonomous outlying parts. Outside Auckland's inner city (CBD, Central Business District), the typical one-family house with small garden dominates.

> **! MARCO POLO TIP**
>
> *»City of Sails«*   Insider Tip
>
> On fine days, the Hauraki Golf is teeming with countless sailing boats. Statistics suggest that at least every fourth household in Auckland owns their own boat. Enthusiasm for sailing received a notable boost in 1995 when a New Zealand team won the coveted »America's Cup«.

The harbour of New Zealand's metropolis Auckland spreads out in front of an extremely impressive skyline.

Auckland

INFORMATION
Auckland i-Site Visitor Centre
Sky City, Atrium, Princes Wharf,
137 Quay St. and at the airport
Tel. 08 00 28 25 52
www.aucklandnz.com

SIGHTSEEING
The daily »**Explorer Bus**« leaves every
half hour between 9am–4pm in the summer (winters between 10am and 3pm)
from the Ferry Building. The bus stops at
14 stations and runs on a hop-on, hop-
off basis. Several times an hour, buses
operated by »The Link« offer a circular
trip taking in Symonds Street, New Market, Parnell, Railway Station, Mid Queen
Street, Casino, Victoria Park, Ponsonby
Road, K' Road, Myers Park, University.

EVENTS
Every year on the last weekend in January the city celebrates its foundation
with sailing regattas and open-air concerts. February sees the big »**Harbour
Festival**«, and at the end of March the
»**Round the Bays Run**« mobilizes tens
of thousands of people.

AUCKLAND SUPERPASS
This pass allows visitors to see 4 attractions (Sky Tower, Kelly Tarlton's Antarctic
Encounter & Underwater World, Rainbow's End Theme Park and a boat trip
with »Tuller Cruises« to Rangitoto Island)
relatively cheaply.
Available from the Auckland Visitor Information Centre for 125 NZ$.

WHERE TO EAT
❶ *Antoine's* £££ - ££££
333 Parnell Road

Tel. 09 379 8756
www.antoinesrestaurant.co.nz
Arguably the best (and most expensive)
restaurant in town, with excellent French
cuisine

❷ *Cin Cin on Quay*
£££ - ££££
in the Ferry Building
99 Quay Street
Tel. 09 307 6966
www.cincin.co.nz
Trendy quayside restaurant with fairly
varied cuisine

❸ *Esplanade*
£££ - ££££
1 Victoria Road, Devonport
Tel. 09 445 1291
www.esplanade_hotel.co.nz
High class restaurant with Mediterrane-
an-inspired cuisine

❹ *Hammerheads Seafood*
£££ - ££££
19 Tamaki Drive
Tel. 09 521 4400
www.hammerheads.co.nz
Popular with day trippers, this restaurant
on the scenic Tamaki Drive offers good
fish cuisine and a spectacular wine list

❺ *Harbourside* £££ - ££££
in the Ferry Building (1st floor)
99 Quay Street
Tel. 09 307 0486
www.harboursiderestaurant.co.nz
Good views and excellent seafood dishes
are on offer here

❻ *Curry Box* £ - ££
11 Beach Road

Tel. 09 3 73 55 56
www.currybox.co.nz
Fastfood restaurant with good Indian
cooking.

❼ Sal's Authentic New York Pizza
£ - ££
8 Commerce Street
Tel. 09 3 79 72 57
www.sals.co.nz
Legendary pizza and filled pizza rolls

❽ Sun World £ - ££
56 Wakefield Street
Tel. 09 373 5336
One of the best Chinese restaurants in
town, with mouth-watering Cantonese
dishes

WHERE TO STAY
❶ Auckland Hilton
££££
Princes Wharf, 147 Quay Street
Tel. 09 978 2000
www.hilton.com
Ultra-modern hotel with health club,
restaurant and bar

❷ Cotter House ££££
2 St Vincent Avenue
Remuera
Tel. 09 5 29 51 56
www.cotterhouse.com
Romantic trip into the past in a 1847
manor house.

❸ tHotel Pullman
££££
Corner Waterloo Quadrant & Princess
Street
Auckland Central
Tel. 09 35 31 00
www.pullmanauckland.co.nz
This luxury hotel with gym is situated in

a tranquil spot alongside the green spaces of the university campus and Albert
Park.

❹ Langham Hotel
££££
83 Symonds Street Auckland Central Tel.
09 379 5132 www.langhamhotels.com
Centrally located hotel with various bars,
restaurants, spa area and pool

❺ Copthorne Anzac Avenue
£££
150 Anzac Avenue
Tel. 09 379 8509
www.copthorneanzac.co.nz
Modern and functionally furnished
rooms, some of which give good views
of the Hauraki Gulf.

❻ Crowne Plaza Hotel £££
128 Albert Street
Tel. 08 00 15 41 81
www.crowneplazaauckland.co.nz
Centrally located hotel in the city centre
with large, comfortable rooms and a
small gym.

❼ Sky City Hotel £££
Cnr. Victoria and Federal Street
Auckland Central
Tel 09 363 6000
www.skycity.nz-hotels.com
This large modern hotel with its spacious
rooms forms part of the entertainment
complex at the Sky Tower.

❽ Kingsgate Hotel Parnell ££
92–102 Gladstone Road
Parnell, Auckland
Tel. 09 377 3619
www.millenniumhotels.co.nz
This modern hotel offers good-value
lodgings in the classy suburb of Parnell

»Capital of Polynesia« About a third of the New Zealand **population** lives on this narrow isthmus on North Island. Auckland, the main gateway to New Zealand, is also often called the »capital of Polynesia« due to the high percentage of Pacific islanders making up its population. The dense population of such a small space has given rise to enormous problems. It takes a Herculean effort, for instance, to guarantee the city's fresh water supply.

HISTORY

1840	The Waitangi Treaty securing British sovereignty of the region is signed, and Auckland becomes the capital
from 1842	Scottish immigrants land in Auckland
19th century	Gold is found on South Island, reducing Auckland's appeal
1865	The seat of government is transferred from Auckland to the up-and-coming city of Wellington
20th century	Renaissance of the city

Contested and popular The isthmus occupied by Auckland between the Tasman Sea and the South Pacific was hotly contested well into the 18th century.

Harbour Bridge arches across the harbour

Following many **tribal feuds** over the fertile volcanic soil, the Kiwi Tamaki tribe prevailed. In 1840, when British sovereignty had been secured by the Waitangi Treaty, governor Hobson decided to transfer the seat of government to the isthmus of Auckland, with Scottish immigrants following from 1842. The person credited with being Auckland's real »father« however is **John Logan Campbell** (1817–1912), one of the first European settlers in the Auckland region. As the co-founder of banks, insurance and shipping companies, and later on in his role as Mayor, he inspired the city's development. After the discovery of the rich **gold deposits on South Island**, Auckland lost its appeal, and in 1865 the capital was moved to **Wellington**. It took the gold finds on the Coromandel Peninsula and the lucrative agriculture south of Auckland to make the city grow strong again. Later on, the development of industry and the uniquely advantageous location in terms of commerce and transport ensured an economic boom lasting up to today.

> **MARCO POLO TIP** ⊕
>
> **!** *Sightseeing on foot* — Insider Tip
>
> Particularly charming is the 7km/4.3-mile »Waterfront Walk«, which starts at the Chief Post Office. Visitors who enjoy walking can follow the roughly 13km/8-mile signposted »Coast to Coast Walkway«, starting from the Ferry Building at the end of Queen Street.

Auckland's international airport lies 23km/just over 14 miles southwest of the city centre on Manukau Harbour. From Auckland, **express trains** go to ▶Hamilton (with connecting buses to ▶Rotorua) and ▶Wellington. The **road infrastructure** in and around Auckland is excellent, with motorways crossing the city in all directions. A fairly close-knit **public transport network** of city trains and buses allows visitors and residents to get around easily, with no need for a car.

Inexpensive connections

PORT OF AUCKLAND

The view of Waitemata Harbour with the volcanic **Rangitoto Island** is unforgettable. The buildings of the now very cosmopolitan-looking centre of the New Zealand metropolis with its **imposing skyline** formed by the Sky City skyscrapers and the Sky Tower, cluster around the port basin. All day long the port is thronged with passenger and freight boats, ferries, barges and smaller boats. In addition, the scene is enlivened by numerous white sailing yachts, especially in the **Hobson West Marina** and the **Viaduct Basin**, redesigned for the America's Cup races, the oldest and most prestigious regatta in the world.

***Waitemata Harbour*

Highlights Auckland

► **Waitemata Harbour**
Admire the throng of passenger and freight boats, ferries and barges.
►page 173

► **Sky City**
In the 328m/1,076-ft Sky Tower, visitors can get an overview of the city, dine with a view or climb to lofty heights.
►page 178

► **Auckland City Art Gallery**
Outside French Renaissance style, inside Old European Masters and contemporary New Zealand art
►page 181

► **Auckland Institute & Museum**
Houses the world's best collection of Maori art and art from the Pacific Islands
►page 182

► **One Tree Hill**
This volcanic cone offers one of the most stunning views across Auckland.
►page 183

► **Kelly Tarlton's Underwater World**
Eye to eye with the marine world: huge aquariums and a colony of penguins
►page 185

► **Devenport**
Thus upper class suburb can be reached by ferry and offers a holiday atmosphere with lively beaches.
►page 186

► **Hauraki Gulf**
Covered with many islets, this bay is a true paradise for sailors and anglers.
►page 188

Harbour Bridge The port is spanned by a **bridge** measuring a good 1km/3,280ft in length and approx. 43m/141ft in height. The particularly fearless can pay for the pleasure of a **bungee jump** into the void from the steel bridge arch, 243m/797ft long. Completed in 1959, the bridge was broadened a few years later, giving access to the parts of the city on the northern banks, as well as a few **pleasant bathing beaches and bays**.

Quay Street The port is bordered by lively Quay Street, where the very popular **Dockside Markets** and **China Oriental Markets** established themselves, taking in Princess Wharf. At weekends in particular things get very busy here.

*New Zealand National Maritime Museum A visit to this museum on the site of Hobson Wharf at the northwestern end of Quay Street gives a comprehensive insight into the **history of New Zealand seafaring**. It has Maori canoes and outrigger boats, as well as whaling paraphernalia, various traditional instruments and tools. Don't miss the sleek **Black Magic**: this is the boat that achieved a phenomenal victory in 1995 against the American team, winning the »America's Cup« with its New Zealand crew led by Sir Peter Blake and bringing the cup to New Zealand for the first time (▶MARCOPOLO Insight p. 146).

● Daily 9am to 5pm, guided tours: Mon Fri 10.30am and 1pm; admission NZ$ 17

The imposing old Ferry Building with its top-notch restaurant, situated at the point where Queen Street leads into Quay Street, is one of the harbour's most **handsome eye-catchers**. The building, a brick-and-sandstone construction on a base of Coromandel granite, was completed in 1912 following designs by architect Alexander Wiseman in the **English Baroque style**.

Ferry Building

Located next to the Ferry Building, the former main post office is an imposing edifice which was erected in 1911 following designs by John Campbell. The striking building leads into the Britomart Transport Centre; with the railway station and bus station it is the city's new traffic hub.

Chief Post Office

Located to the southwest of the Chief Post Office, the imposing Customs House was erected in 1889 in the **French Empire style** following designs by Thomas Mahoney. Initially the building was used to house officers, and later the customs authority itself. Today, **cultural institutions and shops** have made their home here.

Customs House

CITY CENTRE

Over the past decades, as a combination of busy main artery and **boulevard**, Queen Street has seen many new office towers housing banks, insurance companies, commercial and service companies reach up into the sky. Between Ferry Building and K' Road (see below), numerous **department stores, shops and restaurants** offer visitors a break from strolling. However, connoisseurs of art history will also find satisfaction here, with prestigious buildings from colonial times, Art Nouveau houses and Art Deco buildings, plus modern glass palaces all virtually side by side. Turning left from Queen Street is **Vulcan Lane**, Auckland's colourful food mile, busiest around lunch and dinner time.

Queen Street (Mall)

Insider Tip

MARCO ⊕ POLO TIP

! *Auckland Dockline Tram*

From late November to March an historic tram runs in the port area between 10am and 4pm, Fridays until 7pm. The ticket for an adult costs NZ$ 2. Infos: www.aucklandtram.co.nz.

** *Sky Tower*

Exactly 1,029 steps must be conquered in order to reach the largest viewing platform of Auckland's Sky Tower on foot. A faster and easier way is to catch one of the three glass lifts up to the new symbol of North Island's metropolis. Its revolving restaurant offers diners splendid views.

❶ Opening times:all year round daily 8.30am to late into the night..

❶ *Tower shop*
…so family and friends back home may also benefit from this visit to the Sky Tower!

❷ *Steps*
During a competition in 2009 the winner managed to run up the 1,000 plus steps in an incredible 4 minutes 53 seconds. How long will it take you?

❸ *Elevators*
very 15 minutes, three glass-fronted lifts (one of which has a glass bottom) whizz 225 people up to the viewing platform. The journey, travelling at 11 mph/ 18kmh, takes only 40 seconds.

❹ *Main observation level*
Here, visitors may use a computer or camera to learn more about the tower's technical specifications, or send a postcard from the highest letterbox in the southern hemisphere.

❺ *Orbit*
Enjoy New Zealand's cuisine at a height of 190m/over 220ft.

❻ *Sky lounge*
The highest café in the southern hemisphere serves coffee and snacks.

❼ *Sky Jump*
How does falling at speeds of up to 46 mph/75kmh for 16 seconds sound? The good news is there's a rope to break the fall. Extreme bungee jumping!

❽ *The Observatory*
A great variety of fish dishes are the speciality of this buffet with a pub atmosphere.

❾ *Vertigo Climb*
This climbing wall at lofty heights promises a very special thrill. The daring are rewarded by great views.

Take a stroll across the transparent glass floor, 186m/610ft above Auckland!

No other transmitter mast in the world broadcasts as many TV and radio stations

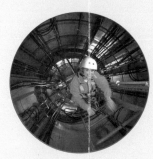

Those with enough stamina are rewarded by a magnificent panoramic view from the »Crows Nest«, at a height of 300m/nearly 1,000ft

On a clear day, the views from the Sky Deck, the highest viewing platform, reach far out to sea

A table with a view – and the risk that a good meal might become a sideshow

Take the leap!

©BAEDEKER

The so-called »Sky City«, with the Sky Tower in the middle, has become one of the main attractions of the metropolis

St Patrick's Cathedral   Standing to the west, off the lower part of Queen Street, at the corner of Hobson St/Wyndham St, the Catholic St Patrick's Cathedral was built in 1848, which makes it one of the **oldest churches** in New Zealand. It shelters a beautiful tabernacle given to the Catholic bishop Pompallier by the Maori; Pompallier had held the first Catholic religious service in New Zealand in 1838.

Sky Tower   Reaching up into the sky west of Queen Street, the 328m/1,076-ft concrete needle of the Sky Tower is the new **landmark of the **»City of Sails«**. The two viewing platforms, at a height of 192m/630ft and 220m/722ft respectively, or indeed the revolving restaurant of the tower, opened in 1997, provide stunning panoramic views. In addition, the Sky Tower also offers an **adrenaline rush**: this (fairly pricy) ultimate version of the regular bungee jump is here called »Sky Jump«. The **»Sky Walk«** activity, whilst not quite as expensive (NZ$ 145), still requires a degree of courage, as it walking around the outermost ring of the tower at a height of 192m/633ft. Security ropes guard against unplanned falls

> ● Sun – Thu 8.30am to 10.30pm, bungee jump NZ$ 225.

> [!] *South Sea feeling!*   *Insider Tip*
>
> **MARCO POLO TIP**
>
> Soak up some South Sea atmosphere! On the southern edge of the city centre, the corner of »K' Road« and Queen Street is particularly busy on Friday nights, when the shops stay open till 10pm and the many South Sea islanders create a special ambience.

Harrah's Sky City   The tower stands at the centre of a postmodern building complex conceived in Las Vegas style, with a luxury hotel, theatre, conference rooms, various restaurants and shops, as well as the largest casino in the southern hemisphere. Its deep-blue and green décor suggests the **underwater world** of the Polynesian demigod Maui. Introductory courses to the art of gambling are often held here in the mornings.

St Matthew's Church   Also west of Queen Street, on Wellesly Street, stands the Anglican St Matthew's Church, built in 1902 in the Old English style.

*Auckland Town Hall   **The Edge** is the name of the building complex around Aotea Square; it is the city's event centre. It includes the city hall on the southern side of Queen Street, which was built in 1911 following designs by the architect brothers Clark. The façade of the building, crowned by a tower, is composed of Oamaru marble, and the plinth of Melbourne bluestone. The city hall is not just the place where the city council meets; it also contains two concert halls that are known for their **outstanding acoustics**.

Auckland

America's Cup Facilities

National Maritime Museum

Lifting Bridge

Birkenhead
Stanley Bay, Devonport

Bledisloe Freight Terminal

Bledisloe West Wharf

Bledisloe East Wharf

Westhaven, Boat Harbour

Bus Depot

Freemans Bay

Viaduct Basin

Hobson Wharf

Princes Wharf

Queens Wharf

Captain Cook Wharf

Marsden Wharf

Kings Low Landing

Halsey Street

Pakenham Street

Sturdee Street

Quay Street West

Customs Street

Ferry Building

Queen Elizabeth Square

Bus Terminal

Galway Street

Tooley Street

Quay Street

Fanshawe Street

Maori Comm. Centre

Gandhi Hall

Hobson Street

St-Patricks Square

Cathedral

Wyndham Street

Fort Street

Shortland Street

Emily Place

Anzac Avenue

Society of Arts

Beach Road

Bus Terminal

Nile River's Underwater World

Victoria St. West

District Court

Sky Tower

Sky City Casino

Albert Street

Nelson Street

Victoria Street

AUCKLAND CITY

Queen Street

Freyberg Place

Bowen Avenue

Waterloo Quadrant

Old High Court

Old Auckland Station

Fraser Park

Parnell Rise

PARNELL

Parnell Road

Cook Street

Khartoum Place

Kitchener St.

High Street

Albert Park

Maclaurin Chapel

Old Government House

Wynyard Street

Allen Road

Carlaw Park

Mayoral Dr.

Aotea Centre

Aotea Square

Library

Art Gallery

Auckland University

Auckland Inst. of Technology

University

Symonds Street

Grafton Road

Stanley Street

Town Hall

Wellesley Street East

Rutland St.

Paul Street

Auckland Domain

Union Street

Vincent Street

Nelson Street

Hobson Street

Myers Park

Wakefield Street

Airedale Street

Domain Drive West

Pitt Street

Greys Avenue

YMCA

Queen Street

Liverpool Street

Symonds Street

Auckland Domain

Beresford St.

Karangahape Road

Cross St.

Motorway

Gov. Hobson's Grave

Grafton Bridge

Hospital

Auckland Hospital

Domain Drive North

Klox Road

The Crescent

War Memorial Museum

Football Rd.

Motorway

NEWTON

Kinnon Drive

Symonds Street

Grafton

YWCA

Winter-gardens

Auckland Domain

Newton Road

Waikato, Hamilton, Rotorua, Lake Taupo, Wellington

GRAFTON

Maori Mission

Eden Terrace

Carlton Gore Road

Outhwaite Park

Park Road

0,2 mi

300 m

©BAEDEKER

Victoria Park is not just a market place but also a lively stage for street musicians

Aotea Centre Extending to the right of the town hall, the flat **Aotea Centre** is the **largest concert hall in the country**. It was designed by star architect E Wainscott, who was probably inspired by Alvar Aalto's Finlandia Hall. The building work took a long time and was accompanied by fierce quarrels, so the cultural centre was only finally completed in 1990. On **Aotea Place**, a large sculpture honours **Lord Auckland**, who was chosen by governor Hobson at the time to give his name to the New Zealand capital.

The Civic To the north Aotea Square is bordered by The Civic, a large **rococo-style cinema** first that opened in 1929 and that re-opened in 2000. The auditorium seats 2378 on two levels; it is New Zealand's largest theatre and the venue of many concerts, musicals, plays and movies from the whole world.

ALBERT PARK · UNIVERSITY

Albert Park Extending to the east of the heart of the city centre is Albert Park with its old trees on a site formerly occupied by the town's first barracks. The eastern part of the shaded parkland is occupied by various institutes belonging to the renowned **Auckland University**. **St Andrew's Church**, which belongs to the university, was built in 1849.

An absolute must-see for any visitor to the city is the Auckland City Art Gallery in the southeast of Albert Park (Wellesly Street). This highly impressive building was built in 1887 following designs by the Melbourne architects office Grainger & D'Ebro with towers and high roofs in the style of the **French Renaissance**. It houses the famous »Grey Gallery«, a rich collection of Old European Masters and contemporary New Zealand art (by McCahon and Wollaston amongst others). The gallery also owns numerous oil paintings by artist Gottfried Lindauer (1839–1926), who arrived in New Zealand as an emigrant from Czechoslovakia, and went on to paint **wonderful Maori portraits** amongst other subjects. (Access to the gallery: corner of Kitchener Street/Wellesley East Street.)

✱✱Auckland City Art Gallery

❶ Daily 10am–5pm, guided tours daily 11.30am, 12.30pm and 1.30pm, free admission

The former government building was constructed of wood in the neoclassical style in 1856 after designs by William Mason. Following the transfer of the seat of government to ▶Wellington in 1865 it served as a summer residence and guesthouse for high-ranking visitors. Today it belongs to the University of Auckland.

✱Old Government House

Opposite the Old Government House, the former synagogue, built in 1884 following designs by Edward Bartley, today serves as a space for **cultural events** (music, theatre).

Old Synagogue

The architectural inspiration for this richly decorated 1868 brick building was **Warwick Castle**, hence the number of turrets, gargoyles and grotesques. The portraits were carried out by a travelling German engraver called Anton Teutenberg. A new modern extension of the Court of Appeal for the district courts somewhat lessens the visual effect of the old building on the Waterloo Quadrant.

High Court

VICTORIA PARK · PONSONBY

To the west of the city centre lies **Victoria Park** (1905). The site of a former waste incinerator today serves as a market place selling all kinds of bric-a-brac, but also fresh fruit and vegetables. Friendly restaurants and a wide range of entertainments attract visitors.

Favourite market

To the west of the City, the part of town called Ponsonby has preserved, particularly in Renall Street, a row of small 19th-century houses which were once inhabited by workers from the nearby port and are now much sought-after townhouses. The **Ponsonby Post Office** (1912), a highly original building in the English Baroque style, was designed by John Campbell.

Ponsonby

AUCKLAND DOMAIN

Park

The extensive recreation area of Auckland Domain southeast of the city centre offers varied leisure activities.

**Auckland
Institute &
Museum
(War Memorial Museum)

At the highest point of the park stands the monumental War Memorial Museum. Its outside staircase offers **splendid views** over the city and the busy Waitemata Harbour. The neoclassical building was erected in 1929 as both a memorial site for the New Zealand soldiers killed in World War I and an exhibition area for the collections of the Auckland Museum, originally established as early as 1852. In the 1960s, comprehensive extension works were carried out. Today, the **»War Memorial Hall«** serves as a memorial to the fallen of all wars that New Zealand soldiers took part in. The museum itself contains **collections on the natural and cultural history** of the southern Pacific region as well as the history of the city of Auckland. The so-called **Maori Court**, a meeting house decorated with rich carvings dating back to 1878, comes from the Thames area. The wonderful Maori doorway was brought here from the Rotorua area. Also worthy of note is a **storeroom** decorated with carvings. Particularly interesting is the canoe, measuring 25m/82ft in length and dating back to around 1836, which was once used by Maori warriors to cross Manukau Harbour. A **planetarium** forms part of the museum too. The wings of the so-called **Winter Gardens** (glasshouses with temperate and tropical plants) were built for the 1913 Auckland Exhibition and today form part of the city's Botanical Gardens.

MARCO ⊕ POLO TIP

Don't miss *Insider Tip*

- The Maori doors in the ground floor
- Storeroom with carvings
- Canoe from around 1836, in which Maori warriors first crossed Manukau Harbour

❶ Museum and planetarium: daily 10am – 5pm, Maori dance performances: Nov. - Mar. daily 12.45pm and 2.30pm, following guided tours through the Maori collection, admission NZ\$ 25

PARNELL

Historic suburb

East of the city centre, the old suburb of Parnell stretches to Hobson Bay and has preserved numerous buildings from Victorian times, **lovingly restored** in recent years. Crowds of tourists browse in the many nostalgic shops (selling arts and crafts in particular) and restaurants line up like a string of pearls along **Parnell Road**.

In 1856/1857, a house for the priest **John Kinder** was erected at the beginning of Ayr Street (no. 2; east below the Auckland Domain). Kinder, who also excelled as a painter and photographer, had arrived in Auckland in 1855. The building was designed by **Frederick Thatcher**, Bishop Selwyn's much sought-after architect. Inside Kinder House fine views of Auckland, captured by the owner of the house over the years, can be seen.

*Kinder House

❶ Wed – Sun 12pm–3pm, free admission

It was in the **little wooden church**, built in 1856/1857 near Point Resolution following designs by Frederick Thatcher that the constitution of the Anglican church was agreed upon. The small ecclesiastical building commands views over Judges Bay. Many citizens and soldiers from Auckland's early days are buried in the old cemetery.

*St Stephen's Chapel

The wooden **neo-Gothic building** (1888), one of the largest of its kind, used to stand on the other side of the street and was only moved to its current location next to the new Holy Trinity Cathedral in 1982.

*St Mary's Pro-Cathedral

WHAT TO SEE IN AUCKLAND'S OUTLYING AREAS

Taking its title from Lord Auckland's family name and 196m/643ft high, this volcano in the southern part of the city offers attractive **views** and was the southernmost point of an area purchased in 1840 by the Maori for the establishment of the town. Razed to the ground and barely visible anymore, the fortification is said to have been around as early as the 16th century. The extensive **Eden Garden** nearby contains some beautiful trees and an extensive collection of camellias.

? *Tamaki Makau Rau*

MARCO ⊕ POLO INSIGHT

is the name of the city that the Maori founded around 1350 on the site of present-day Auckland. Anyone who would like to explore Auckland from a Maori perspective can book city tours with a Maori culture emphasis with various tour organizers, like Tamaki Hikoi, tel. 02 11 46 95 93, www.tamakihikoi.co.nz, or T.I.M.E. Tours, tel. 09 8 46 34 69 www.newzealandtours.travel

Further south, one of the **most charming viewpoints of Auckland** is the One Tree Hill volcanic peak, rising up 183m/600ft. Still visible from up here are the old fortification trenches and walls of the large Maori »pa« from the 17th/18th centuries, said to have sheltered up to 4,000 people. A **sacred totara tree** standing on top of the mountain before the arrival of the European immigrants was unthinkingly

**One Tree Hill, Cornwall Park

felled by the first white settlers. This park contains Auckland's oldest known building, **»Acacia Cottage«**, built in 1841 by John Logan Campbell. When he died at a ripe old age in 1912, his body was buried on the summit of One Tree Hill. The obelisk standing next to his grave symbolizes his esteem for the Maori and their unusual achievements. One Tree Hill is also the home of the **Stardome Observatory**, which is well worth visiting.

ⓘ Mon 9.30am – 3pm, Tue – Fri 9.30am – 4.30pm, 6.30pm – 9.30pm, Sat 12.30pm – 5pm, 6.30pm – 11pm, Sun 11.30am – 9.30pm, admission: NZ$ 10, www.stardome.org.nz

Ellerslie Racecourse
The most famous **horse races** in New Zealand are held below One Tree Hill to the west in a park. A small museum tells the story of horse racing.

Alberton House
Situated in the southwest of the city on the slopes of Mount Albert, this gabled manor house was erected in 1862. In 1870, the owner, Allan Kerr Taylor, having made his fortune during the **gold rush**, had the property extended with further rooms as well as a ballroom (100 Mt Albert Rd.).

ⓘ Wed – Sun 10.30am – 4.30pm, admission: NZ$ 10, www.heritage.org.nz

A glass tunnel leads through the rich underwater world of Kelly Tarlton

This museum in the Western Springs part of the city (Great North Road) presents the story of technology and transport in New Zealand. Visitors are usually most interested in the flying contraptions belonging to the **pioneer of flight Richard Pearse** (1877–1953), who was making his first attempts to fly at around the same time as the Wright Brothers. A vintage tram connects the museum with the nearby zoo.

**Museum of Transport & Technology (MOTAT)

❶ Daily 10am – 5pm, admission NZ$ 16, www.motat.org.nz

? **MARCO ⊕ POLO INSIGHT**	**Special Conditions!** In the **Antarctic Encounter**, a reconstructed research station with a small colony of penguins, visitors to Kelly Tarlton's Underwater World can enter a »Snow Cat« to get a feel for the difficult conditions scientists work under in the Antarctic.

Auckland's extensive **zoo** is also to be found in the Western Springs part of the city. A much-visited attraction here is the **Kiwi House**, one of the few places in the country where New Zealand's emblematic animal may be seen. Landscapes from the coast to the barren highlands have been reproduced here in a convincing manor.

❶ Daily 9.30am – 5.30pm, winter only until 5pm, admission: NZ$ 28, www.aucklandzoo.co.nz

Located in the Orakei part of the city, east of Hobson Bay, Kelly Tarlton's Underwater World is well worth a visit. Opened in 1985, this marine aquarium on Tamaki Drive/Orakei Wharf is a great tourist attraction. Visitors move through huge aquariums in long acrylic tunnels, admiring fish great and small, amongst them sharks and rays. An interactive room tells the story of the **explorations of diver Kelly Tarlton** (1935 – 1985), who researched the fauna of the Southern Pacific ocean as well as the shipwrecks off New Zealand's coastline.

**Kelly Tarlton's Underwater World

❶ Daily 9.30am – 5pm, admission: NZ$ 39, www.kellytarltons.co.nz

Situated in a very picturesque spot on the Hauraki Gulf some 23km/14 miles southeast of Auckland, Howick (pop 15,000) is a suburb of the New Zealand metropolis. **Howick Colonial Village** was founded in 1847 as a military settlement, belonging to the chain of fortified »fencible settlements« planned by Governor Grey. Its many well-preserved historic buildings have earned Howick listed status and it is now an **outdoor museum**. Particularly noteworthy is **All Saints Anglican Church** (1847), which – as nearly all churches built under Bishop Selwyn – was designed by the architect Frederick Thatcher. The church nave was extended in 1862. The old cemetery with headstones from the time of the early settlers is well preserved. Also of interest are the courthouse (1848) and the Bell House, built in 1852 and now housing a restaurant.

*Howick

Howick Colonial Village: daily 10am – 4pm, admission: NZ$ 15, www.fencible.org.nz

Auckland • Surroundings

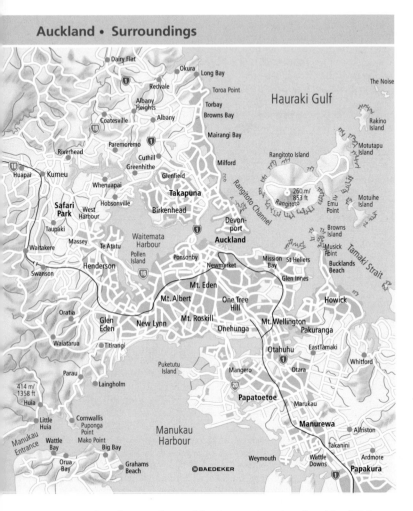

*Devonport Stretching northeast of the city centre, on the other side of Waitemata Harbour, the **well-to do residential suburb** of Devonport boasts elegant villas and well-kept gardens. Founded back in 1840 and one of Auckland's oldest suburbs, it is still accessible from the city centre by ferry. With its beach life, yachting marina and expensive boutiques, Devonport has a **real holiday atmosphere** and commands the most beautiful view of the City of Auckland's skyline. The **Naval Museum** located on the northern side of Waitemata Harbour in

Devonport tells the story of the Royal New Zealand Navy with exhibits including uniforms, medals, ship's bells and ships in a bottle (Spring Street). The pavilions set up today along Montgomery Road near the airport, and much admired at the Brisbane Expo in 1988, showcase the mythology, history, nature and environment of New Zealand.

❶ **Naval Museum:** daily 10am – 5pm, free admission

AROUND AUCKLAND

Thanks to its position on two wide-branching harbours, Auckland boasts many beautiful beaches. The beaches on the northern bank of Waitemata Harbour from Cheltenham to Long Bay are favourites. The best beaches can be found at **Takapuna and Milford**. Unfortunately, the very beautiful beaches on the western coast are quite dangerous, with their steep rocks, the strong swell of the tempestuous Tasman Sea and some treacherous rip currents.

Beaches

Strong swimmers can try the following: the **beach at Piha** (approx. 40km/25 miles to the west), **Karekare Beach**, **Whites Beach**, **Bethells Beach** as well as the **beach at Whatipu** at the mouth of Manukau Harbour. There are several good bathing beaches on the Hauraki Gulf, and some **popular ones on the Whangaparaoa Peninsula** (approx. 40km/25 miles, accessible via Highway 1), as well as at **Orewa** and **Waiwera**.

Recommended beaches

This **tourist route** starts at the Ferry Building in Auckland and leads on past Waitemata Harbour to Judges Bay below Parnell Park. Crossing Hobson Bay, drivers reach Ohaku Bay, where many yachts are moored. In Orakei, a »marae« (built by Maori and white settlers working together) and a Maori meeting house are well worth a visit.

*Tamaki Drive

The headland at Bastion Point shelters the tomb of **Michael Joseph Savage** (1872–1940), the Labour Prime Minister much loved by the people at the time. The memorial column stands in stark contrast to the volcanic silhouette of Rangitoto Island opposite. Eventually Mission Bay is reached, with its pretty bathing beach. The mission, founded by Bishop Selwyn, has now been turned into a culinary enterprise and the bay recently acquired a chic residential area. At the eastern end of Heliers Bay, Tamaki Drive ends at **Achilles Point**.

Mission Bay

The green trees of the Waitakere Ranges southwest of Auckland are very popular as a recreational space near the city. This holds true in

Waitakere Ranges

particular for the 6,400ha/15,800-acre Auckland **Centennial Park** in the south. The information office situated some 5km/3.1 miles west of Titirangi teaches visitors about the flora, above all the last of the local **kauri trees**.

Western coast
The rugged west coast, with its rocks battered by the Tasman Sea, boasts some very scenic spots, amongst them the **beaches of Piha** (approx. 40km/25 miles west of Auckland). Piha and Karekare are also good bases for hikes in the Waitakere Ranges, here beguilingly green and ferny. A worthwhile destination further north is **Muriwai Beach**, where colonies of gannets have recently spread from the offshore islands to the mainland.

**Hauraki Gulf
Right on Auckland's doorstep the Hauraki Gulf opens out, framed by Northland on one side and the promontory of the Coromandel Peninsula reaching up north on the other. Littered with numerous islets, the bay is a **true paradise** for amateur sailors and anglers. A large part of the gulf is protected, with the Hauraki Gulf Maritime Park still offering the opportunity to see rare birds, insects and sea creatures. Several of the Gulf islands may only be visited in daytime, and even then often require special authorization.

Rangitoto
Accessible by ferry from Auckland, the **volcanic island** Rangitoto is likely to have been active during the time of the Polynesian settlement of New Zealand some 700 years ago, as there are no signs of the remains of Maori fortifications. Situated right in front of Waitemata Harbour, the island with its charming contours was bought by the government as early as 1857 and has been a popular day trip destination ever since. The top of the 260m/853-ft island volcano commands fabulous views across the Hauraki Gulf. Located in the Hauraki Gulf, **Waiheke** Island presents itself predominantly as a holiday island, but has over 5,000 inhabitants, giving it a fairly dense population. The magnificent bathing beaches in the north of the island have evocative names such as Oneroa Beach, Palm Beach and Onetangi Beach. East of Waiheke, **Pakatoa** Island is a **delightful spot**, excellent for unwinding from busy Auckland.

> **?**
>
> MARCO ◉ POLO INSIGHT
>
> *Shipwreck*
>
> The name »Achilles Point« was chosen in memory of the cruiser HMS Achilles, which in December 1939, together with two other British war ships, blocked the mouth of the Plate river, leading to the scuttling of the German battleship Admiral Graf Spee by its crew.

Motuihe Island
This tiny island forms part of the Maritime Park and is a popular day trip destination for city dwellers. During World War I there was a prisoner-of-war camp here. The island became famous through **Felix Graf**

von Luckner (►Famous People), interned here after being captured on the Cook Islands. It was from here that the »Sea Devil« undertook his daredevil escape, as he hijacked the commander's yacht during an event, seized the Moa and, sailing under the German flag, managed to proceed to the Kermadec Islands. Further north, **Kawau Island** is accessible by boat from Sandsplit and Snell's Beach. Governor Grey had bought the island – on which copper had previously

MARCO ⊕ POLO INSIGHT

?   *A drop of the good stuff ...*

The »**Auckland Wine Trail**« passes some of New Zealand's most famous wineries: Henderson (approx. 20km/12.5 miles west) and Kumeu (approx. 25km/15.5 miles northwest), where visitors can take part in guided tours and tastings. The vineyards here are cultivated mainly by immigrants from Dalmatia in Croatia.

been mined – in 1862 and extended the house of the mine administrator to a castle-like stately home. He also had a kind of »Garden of Eden« laid out here, with **many exotic plants and animals**. The restored mansion, furnished in period style, may be visited.

❶ **Mansion Kawau Island:** Mon – Fri 12pm – 2pm, Sat, Sun 12pm – 3.30pm, admission: NZ$ 4, www.doc.govt.nz

Inhabited by some 600 people, the roughly 28,000ha/69,000-acre **Great Barrier Island**, was named thus by James Cook because it appeared to him like a mighty barrier blocking the bay. Once inhabited by kauri lumberjacks, gold prospectors and copper miners, today this is home to a multitude of dairy cows and sheep.

Great Barrier Island

Little Barrier Island is a true **refuge for rare plant and bird species**, which is today lovingly protected as a natural gem and can only be visited with special authorization by the Department of Conservation.

Little Barrier Island

Measuring only 207ha/511 acres, with its lighthouse visible from afar, this island lies off Whangaparaoa. Previously the land here was pasture, whereas today the island has the status of a **nature reserve**, and is gradually regaining its natural forest cover. Apart from one good sandy beach, the coast is very steep. The island can only be visited in the daytime.

Tiritiri Matangi Island

Situated just under 50km/31 miles north of Auckland and easily accessible via Highway 1, the spa town of Waiwera was known back in the 19th century for its curative thermal springs and relaxing beaches. At that time already the spa hotels and bath houses were doing brisk business. A visit to the state-of-the-art **thermal baths** of Waiwera (opening times: daily 9am – 9pm) comes highly recommended.

*Waiwera

❶ Sun – Thu 9am – 8pm, Fri, Sat 9am – 9pm, admission: NZ$ 26, www. waiwera.co.nz

*Puhoi   Situated just under an hour's drive north of Auckland, the small town of Puhoi was founded in the 1860s by immigrants from the (formerly German, today Czech) Egerland region. The **Bohemian immigrants** received parcels of land for clearance northwest of the Hauraki Gulf, built a village in their traditional style with a church (the altarpiece, created in 1885, is a reminder of the old country) and set up a field cross at the entrance to the village.

»German   Today's **Puhoi Hotel** used to be called »German Hotel«. The local
Hotel«   pub received a licence to serve alcohol as early as 1879, and photos on the walls bring the old times to life again.

** Bay of Islands

—————————————————— ✦ Se 126

Region: Northland
Altitude: 0 – 300m/984ft
Population: approx. 15,000

This verdant paradise for holidaymakers in the northeast of North Island consists of more than 150 islets. There are green jungles, blue lagoons and white beaches, so it's no wonder that the rich and beautiful have their own holiday homes here. The bay is also very popular among sailors and deep-sea anglers. But not only the paradise-like nature and the sub-tropical climate make the Bay attractive. The contract that established the colony of New Zealand was signed here in 1847.

Bay of Islands   Stretching across a very scenic landscape to the northeast of North
Maritime &   Island, the island was named Bay of Islands by James Cook in 1759.
Historic Park   The first European settlers settled here. In terms of the **history of its origins**, the bay represents an entire system of river valleys drowned by the sea. This flooding was caused by rising sea levels following the last Ice Age. The area between Whangaruru in the south and Whangaroa in the north both on the coast and in the interior holds more than three dozen fascinating **natural monuments as well as historically and culturally important sites** grouped together in the Bay of Islands Maritime & Historic Park.

WHAT TO SEE IN THE BAY OF ISLANDS

Paihia   Counting some 2000 inhabitants, the small town of Paihia in the southwest of the Bay of Islands emerged from a mission founded in

1823. Look out for St Paul's Church, built in 1926, and the decommissioned Bark Tui ship, today housing a restaurant. Pahia is a good base for **boat trips full of interest**, amongst them the »Cream Trip« through the island-studded Bay of Islands, or the »Cape Brett Trip« to Piercy Island and the Cape Brett promontory on the southern entrance to the bay. Absolutely spectacular is a **boat trip through the »Hole in the Rock«** of the 140m/459-ft Motukokako. Otehei Bay (outer part of the Bay of Islands) offers the chance to try a »Subsea Adventure«: experiencing the colourful underwater world aboard a diving boat.

Some 3km/1.8 miles west of Paihia, the impressive Haruru Falls roar at their most spectacular after longer periods of rain. **Haruru Falls**

Situated north of Paihia, this is the place where the eponymous **historic treaty** was signed on 6 February 1840, after negotiations between British emissaries and some Maori chiefs from the nearby **Waitangi**

The coastal landscape of Bay of Islands near the town of Russel

Bay of Islands

INFORMATION
The Wharf
Marsden Road, Paihia
Tel. 09 402 7345
www.visitnorthland.co.nz

DAY TRIPS
Paihia is the starting point for bus trips to Cape Reinga, New Zealand's northern tip, with a detour to Ninety Mile Beach. A nostalgic steam train runs between the two settlements further south, Opua and Kawakawa.

WHERE TO EAT
❶ *The Gables* **£££**
The Strand, Russell
Tel 09 403 7670
www.thegablesrestaurant.co.nz
One of the best restaurants on the Bay of Islands serves up typical New Zealand specialities, such as lamb and game dishes, but also excellent fish and seafood.

❷ *The Black Olive*
££
308 Kerikeri Road, Kerikeri
Tel. 09 407 9693
As the name suggests, the cuisine has a Mediterranean flavour, but exotic dishes such as »Cajun Chicken« are also on offer.

❸ *Waitangi Restaurant*
£££
Tau Henare Drive, Paihia
in the Copthorne Hotel
Tel. 09 402 74 11
Fine food in a relaxed atmosphere and a wonderful view to enjoy.

❹ *Waterfront Restaurant & Bar* **££**
Marsden Road, Paihia
Tel. 09 402 6701
Very good cooking at relatively reasonable prices

WHERE TO STAY

❶ *Duke of Marlborough*
££ - £££
35 The Strand
Russell, Bay of Islands
Tel. 09 403 7829
www.theduke.co.nz
Comfortable and traditional Victorian house on Russell's promenade. Especially nice: the rooms with a seaview

❷ *Kingsgate Hotel Autolodge Paihia* **££ – £££**
104 Marsden Road
Paihia, Bay of Islands
Tel 08 00 65 29 29
www.kingsgateautolodge.co.nz
Well equipped mid-range hotel right on the beach

area. (This was the time of the foundation of the British colony of New Zealand, ▶History p.54). Other chiefs however refused to sign the treaty. The Maori had issues with the British sovereignty, as their system of organization did not recognise any sovereign rights above tribal level. Every year, the signing of the treaty is solemnly commemorated in Waitangi on **Waitangi Day** (6 February). In the more recent past, representatives of the Maori have repeatedly expressed their protest against this treaty. Incidentally, the originals of the Treaty of Waitangi are kept in the national archive in Wellington. The house where the treaty was negotiated – **Treaty House** – was built in 1833 following designs by Sydney architect John Verge. This was the residence of **James Busby**, the representative of the British government. The lateral wings were only added later. In 1932, the governor general at the time purchased the property and gifted it to the people of New Zealand.

> **MARCO ⊕ POLO TIP**
>
> !
>
> *Cream Trip*   Insider Tip
>
> The best way to experience the enchanting world of the Bay of Islands is on a »Cream Trip«. This round trip by boat – with the opportunity to observe dolphins – goes back to the days when milk gathered on the individual islands was picked up by boat, and the post delivered at the same time. The modern pleasure boats leave daily at 9.30am in Paihia (9.40am in Russell) between September and May. A tasty lunch is served during the trip. For more information: www.fullers-bay-of- islands. co.nz

In 1940, centenary year of the signing of the Treaty of Waitangi, a large ***Maori meeting house** was inaugurated, completed with the collaboration of the gifted wood carver **Pine Taiapa**. Displaying all the regional styles, it bears witness to the new-found confidence of the Maori. Don't miss the **huge carved canoe** put together from three large kauri trunks. The local Waitangi visitor centre has extensive information on this historic place.

❶ **Maori meeting house:** Jan./Feb. daily 9am – 7pm, otherwise daily 9am – 7pm, admission: NZ$ 25, www.waitangi.org.nz

Situated in an extremely scenic position at the tip of a side bay of the **Kerikeri** Bay of Islands, the small town of Kerikeri, with 4,300 inhabitants, is today primarily known as a **refuge for artists and wealthy retirees**. In 1819 the second mission on New Zealand soil was established here, led by John Butler, who was to carry on his work some two decades later in the new settlement of ▶Wellington. Also known as »Kerikeri Mission Building«, **Kemp House** was completed in 1822. John Butler, for whom the house was originally built, was only to live here for one year before being called away. In 1832, James Kemp moved in with his family, and the house was inhabited by his de-

Maori Meeting House

Fortified Maori villages, so-called »pas«, started to emerge in 14th-century New Zealand. They consisted of a number of houses clustering around a meeting place called »marae«. At the centre of this, the »whare runanga« meeting house personified the highly revered ancestors.

North Island in particular boasts many richly decorated communal houses, which now serve once again for the celebration of major feasts, greeting ceremonies and dances, or the recital of traditional speeches and songs. The oldest preserved meeting places date back to the 19th century.

❶ »Tekoteko«

The standing figure of the highly revered ancestor crowns the roof ridge of the meeting house.

❷ Roof ridge

Below the roof ridge, the face of the ancestor is represented as a mask, with the ancestor's arms (»maihi«) outstretched to the left and right of the mask to form sloping bargeboards.

❸ The Interior

The interior and the roof ridge beams and rafters represent the chest and the spine of the ancestor.

❹ Side posts

The side posts of the meeting house symbolise the ancestor's ribs.

❺ Myths and stories

The elaborate carvings on the interior walls of the meeting houses tell Maori myths. For instance, often they might represent the fight between Kupe the seafarer and a giant squid during the discovery of New Zealand.

The most famous Maori meeting house stands in the Bay of Islands near Waitangi. Erected between 1934 and 1940, it commemorates the 1840 Treaty of Waitangi

Human figures count amongst the most important artistic traditions of Maori carving. Rather than gods, they represent the ancestors. The head, the most important part of the body in Maori culture, is usually shown as being disproportionately large.

Near the Waitangi meeting house, the world's largest warrior canoe can be admired. Building this 35m/115-ft boat took two years. Once a year, on Waitangi Day, the impressive vessel is set afloat and rowed by eight warriors.

©BAEDEKER

Today, the Maori also use the meeting houses and places to perform drama and dances. Often, the distance between the audience and the performers is removed, turning the piece into a communal experience.

The numerous carvings in the meeting houses are lovingly crafted by hand, as seen here in Rotorua's Arts and Crafts Institute.

scendants until 1974. Today it is a **museum**, giving an idea not only of the aesthetics of the time around 1840, but also of the Victorian period. Right next door stands the **Stone Store**, which is claimed to be the **oldest stone house in New Zealand**, which also used to belong to the Kemp family. It was built from 1832 onwards on the site of a previous building that had burnt down, and housed for a while the library of Bishop Selwyn. During the conflict with the Maori, led by Hone Heke, ammunition was kept here. Today, the building houses a small museum with interesting exhibits from the early day of the mission. On the opposite side of the bay a so-called »kainga«, i. e. a »normal«, non-fortified Maori village, has been reconstructed. The lovingly designed complex gives a good insight into the conditions of Maori life before the Europeans arrived. There is a conspicuous lack of carvings though. The carved and highly revered artworks of the meeting houses were kept more securely in the fortified »pa« village. The name **»Rewa«** refers to the second-most powerful man of the tribe, whose chief was **Hongi Hika**. Situated on the terraced hill above the bay, the fortified Maori village of **Kororipo Pa** is accessible via a footpath starting at the Stone Store. It was from up here that the Maori leader Hongi Hika would set off for his raids, which led him all the way to ▶Wellington and the ▶East Cape. In Sydney in 1814 he met the missionary Samuel Marsden, whom he helped in the setting up of missions in Rangihoua 1814 and later also in Kerikeri. Situated approx. 3km/1.8 miles outside Kerikeri, the spectacular **Rainbow Falls** attract many visitors.

❶ **Kemp House and Stone Store:** tours daily 10am – 5pm, winter until 4pm, NZ\$ 10, www.heritage.org.nz

Rewa's Village: daily 9 am – 5pm, winter until 4pm, admission: NZ\$ 5, http://rewasvillage.co.nz

Russell Opposite Paihia, the village of Russell (pop 1,200) sits on a promontory in the Bay of Islands. The best way to get there is by ferry from Pahia (15 mins). Travelling to Russell by car involves a major detour via Whakapara. For a short time Russell was the capital of New Zealand, until the seat of government was transferred to ▶Auckland in 1841. When the Bay of Islands lost its importance, many inhabitants moved away. In Russell time stood still – which explains why the 19th-century atmosphere has been preserved so well to this day. **Christ Church** was built in 1836, making it the **oldest preserved Christian church in New Zealand**. However, unlike other ecclesiastical buildings on the bay, it did not start life as a missionary church but

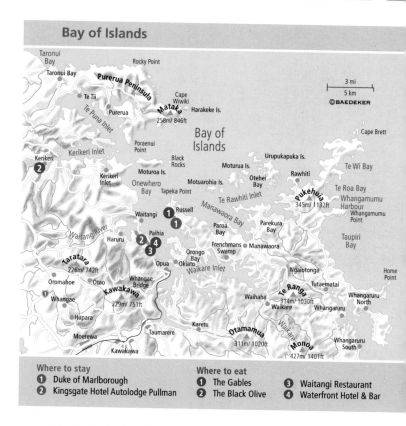

Bay of Islands

Where to stay
1 Duke of Marlborough
2 Kingsgate Hotel Autolodge Pullman

Where to eat
1 The Gables
2 The Black Olive
3 Waitangi Restaurant
4 Waterfront Hotel & Bar

as a parish church for the white settlers. Look out for the old head-stones around the church, marking the graves of whalers, seafarers, Maori and early settlers buried here. Erected in 1841/1842, **Pompal-lier House** was not – as the name might suggest – the residence of the Catholic bishop Pompallier, who in 1838 established the first Catholic mission in New Zealand, but the site of the **mission's print-ing press**. Originally the house would have been less elegant than it is now. It was only when the Catholic mission moved away to Auck-land that the new owners had it remodelled and a veranda and fire-place added. The listed building is furnished in 19th-century style and still contains the old printing press. The **Russell Museum** on York Street recalls the time of the **great seafarer** Captain Cook. Look out for the model of his ship Endeavour (opening times: 10am–4pm). The charming old **harbour front** has many a reminder of the early days of the settlement, including the police station in the former

The public toilet designed by the Viennese artist Friedensreich Hundertwasser is Kawakawa's main attraction

Customs house, the Duke of Marlborough pub (said to **have the oldest alcohol licence in New Zealand**) and an old cannon. Yachts and catamarans of all sizes moor on the pier. During holiday season and in the evenings when the deep-sea anglers return with their catch, the scene gets more animated.

Pompallier House: daily 10am – 5pm, winter until 4pm, admission: NZ$ 10, www.heritage.org.nz

Russell Museum: daily 10am – 4pm, in January until 5pm admission NZ$ 10, www.russellnz.co.nz

Kawakawa
Situated on Highway 1, Kawakawa is today the administrative headquarters of the Bay of Islands district. In this town of 2,000 inhabitants, **flax processing** initially played a major role, to be replaced later on by coal.

Hundertwasser was here
Today Kawakawa is predominantly known as the adopted hometown of the Austrian artist **Friedensreich Hundertwasser** (▶Famous People). The Austrian-born artist not only lived on a former farm nearby where he planted thousands of trees, he also gifted the town a public toilet built in his style, without corners or edges. Now Kawakawa's biggest tourist attraction stands on the main road (driving north).

Vintage Railway
A further attraction is the Bay of Islands Vintage Railway, which runs down the high street, **competing with car traffic**. The heritage rail-

way reopened in 2006 and its route is gradually being lengthened to complete the historic rail link to the former coal port of Opua.

A few miles south of Kawakawa lie the Waiomio Caves, also called Kawiti Caves, a large and intricate cave system famous for its karst features and varied stalactites and stalagmites. The main attraction is the spectacular **glow worm grotto**, which draws many visitors into this intricate cave system each year. The caves belong to the descendants of Chief Kawiti, who fought with Hone Heke at Ruapekapeka. The grotto can be seen in a tour that lasts about half an hour. A wooden walkway leads through the limestone caves. Thanks to the glow worms the visitors feel like they are under a starry sky.

*Waiomio Caves

The **old Maori fortification** of Ruapekapeka is well worth seeing, if not easily accessible. It can be reached 16km/10 miles south of Kawakawa off Highway 1. In 1846, this pa was the site of the last conflict between Hone Heke and government troops. The fortification was unable to withstand the sustained fire of the government soldiers. After the storming of the pa, Governor Grey called for peace, allowing the Ngapuhi to return to their tribal lands. Remains of the fortification walls, the underground emplacements and tunnels can easily be made out, as can the positions of the British cannons. The battleground also offers **fine views over the mountains** of Northland.

*Ruapekapeka

? **MARCO POLO INSIGHT**

Trenches and Maoris

The old Maori fortress Ruapekapeka is one of the largest and most complex pas (fortified Maori village) in New Zealand. Their ingenious system of tunnels and trenches served as a model for the trenches built in world War I.

Some 20km/12.5 miles west of Paihia (see p. 191), in 1830 Samuel Marsden established the first Anglican settlement in the island's interior. Marsden ordered the building of a farm following the English model so the indigenous people would not only be converted but also instructed in a useful way. The farm developed enormously and in 1835 impressed the naturalist **Charles Darwin** who, after travelling through the jungle for a long time, thought he had emerged into an English village. Under Bishop Selwyn the farm was temporarily the seat of a bishopric and the site of a theological college. The only building still standing from the time of the mission's foundation is **Mission House**, built in 1832, which today makes it **New Zealand's second-oldest building**. A good example of the early colonial architectural style, it can be visited daily in the summer. Next to the Mission House, **St John's Church**, the third church built on this site in 1871 still stands, and its cemetery preserves several 19th-century tombstones.

Waimate North

* Bay of Plenty

✦ Sg–Sh 128

Region: Bay of Plenty
Altitude: 0 – 232 m/761ft
Population: 277,000
❶ Tauranga Visitor Centre , 97 Willow Street, Tauranga
Tel. 07 5 78 81 03, Fax 07 5 78 70 20
www.tauranga.govt.nz

The softly sweeping bay, today also known as »Kiwi Coast«, stretches between the Coromandel Peninsula in the west and the East Cape. The Thanks to the mild climate and the fertile ground New Zealand's largest kiwi plantations can be found here. The most important towns here are Tauranga, Whakatane and Opotiki.

Dramatic history

The »Bay of Plenty« owes its name to James Cook (►Famous People), who was able to stock up on provisions here after nearly running out in the appropriately named **Poverty Bay** at ►Gisborne. In the 19th century, bloody conflict was raging between individual Maori tribes, severely decimating the Bay of Plenty population. Nor did the settlement by white immigrants and the mission work proceed as planned. More **fear and suffering** was brought about by the Hauhau movement and Te Kooti's subsequent guerrilla war. After the land wars, soldiers were settled on confiscated Maori land in the Bay of Plenty. The white settlers lived initially off pasture farming, until fruit-growing took over in the 20 th century. The best yields were achieved from citrus fruits. As early as the 1960s, cultivation of the newly **fashionable kiwi fruit** started, with the kiwi soon becoming a major export success. In the interior of the Bay of Plenty and on the volcanic plateau, pine tree monocultures were established with the Californian pinus radiata shrub. Thus, ►Tauranga was able to develop into a **major port for exporting wood**.

Shipwreck Rena

On October 5, 2011 the ship Rena, which was loaded with more than 1300 containers ran aground on a reef in the Bay of Plenty and lay at a sharp angle. Many of the containers fell overboard and some of them were washed ashore; large amounts of oil also ran out of the ship. In early January 2012 the ship broke apart and sank. This caused the worst environmental disaster that New Zealand has ever experienced. The beaches on the Bay of Plenty, but also as far away as **Waihau Bay** and the **East Cape** became polluted. Thousands of volunteers cleaned the beaches and countless oil-soiled birds. By April 2012 only half of the containers could be salvaged. The consequences of the use of Corexit to bind the spilt oil cannot be determined yet.

DESTINATIONS IN THE BAY OF PLENTY AND FURTHER INLAND

The town of Te Puke (pop 6,000) has earned a name for itself as the **kiwi capital of the world**. In April and May huge quantities of the vitamin-rich fruit are harvested in the surrounding area. Some plantations offer guided tours.

Te Puke

With a population of 15,000, the town lies at the point where the river of the same name flows into the bay, and acts as the **logistical centre** for a region dominated by agriculture. Large kiwi cultures have been established in the back country of Whakatane, where pasture farming (dairy cattle, sheep and red deer farms) also plays a major role. Large plains in the surrounding area have been reforested with fast-growing conifers to supply, among other things, the raw materials for the wood-processing industry on the edge of town. In summer the attractive bathing beach is deservedly popular. The sa-

Whakatane

They are keeping an eye on beach life at the Bay of Plenty

cred **Pohaturoa Rock** right in the middle of the town centre features a **tapu cave** in front of which the Maori used to celebrate important festivities. Next to the rock, look for a model of the Mataatua Maori ancestor canoe. Since 1927 this has also been a place of commemoration for the New Zealand soldiers who died in the First World War. The almost sheer-faced summit above the sacred rock offers fantastic views across the town. In good weather, even the vapour trails of steam coming from White Island can be seen. The small **Whakatane Museum** on Boon Street displays very pretty Maori crafts.

❶ **Whakatane Museum:** Mon – Fri 10am – 5pm, Sat, Sun 10am – 2pm, admission: donation requested, www.whakatanemuseum.org.nz

Ohope Beach   This beach, popular with surfers, extends some 6km/nearly 4 miles east of Whakatane, and is separated from a protected area inside the natural harbour by the narrow Ohiwa peninsula. On the road to ▶Rotorua, some 12km/7.5 miles southwest, lies the small thermal spa of **Awakeri Hot Springs**.

Kawerau   Situated at the foot of Mount Edgecumbe, around halfway between Rotorua and the Bay of Plenty, Kawerau (population 8,000) was founded in 1953, with the pine monocultures of **Kaingaroa State Forest** spreading out nearby. Kawerau is the site of a factory which produces newspaper and wood pulp for export. The **Tasman Pulp & Paper Mill** processes 2 million cubic metres/some 21.5 million cubic feet of material annually from the surrounding pine forests. A nearby geothermal field was one important reason for the construction of this industrial complex. Natural steam is used here as a source of energy. At a height of 805m/2,641ft, the extinct **volcano Mount Edgcumbe** is easy to climb under normal conditions; however, due to the extensive cutting of timber there are currently only rudimentary paths. The summit offers stunning panoramic views. Anyone who wants to climb to the peak needs a permit. It is available at the Maori Investments House in Waterhouse Street (weekdays)

? A mountain as a cemetery

MARCO POLO INSIGHT

Mount Edgecumbe is considered sacred by the Ngatiawa Maori tribe as a burial site. There have been long-running attempts to have the mountain given back to the Maori and to stop its exploitation by the wood industry.

* Tawawera Falls   Some 22km/13.5 miles southwest of Kawerau, the massed power of the Tarawera River bursts over a **60m/196-ft set of rock ledges** – after the river has run a longer stretch underground in a system of karst caves. A **lovely hiking trail** leads through the forest to the waterfalls.

The eastern town of Opotiki (pop 4,000) used to be one of the largest Maori settlements on the bay. The small church on the edge of town, built in 1864 on behalf of the **German missionary Carl Volkner**, is worth a look. Volkner had been in Opotiki since 1859, but on his return from a visit to Auckland in 1865 he was murdered in this very church by Hauhau followers. The Maori suspected the priest of being a traitor and a spy for the government. Due to the proximity of the town to the impenetrable Urewera hills, Opotiki continued to be exposed to **attacks** by Hauhau groups or the guerrilla fighters of Maori chief Te Kooti.

Opotiki

About 8km/5mi south of the town is Hukutaia Domain, a c. 4.5ha/11.1ac **park with ancient trees**. There are estimated to be 7000 of them from 1500 varieties. The oldest is a puriri tree with a circumference of 21m/69ft, which the Maori used to use as a burial site. It is more than 2000 years old.

Hukutaia Domain

✴ WHITE ISLAND

Some 50km/31 miles off the coast of Whakatane, this volcanic island rises up to 300m/985ft out of the sea (accessible by boat or plane from Whakatane and Tauranga). An eruption in 1914 literally blasted off the eastern flank of the volcano.
Since then White Island no longer has a crater lake, although there are still **considerable levels of thermal activity**: plumes of steam constantly drifting by, hissing fumaroles, boiling and bubbling pools, alongside sulphur holes with a rather dubious smell. The island was given its name by James Cook for its long **white vapour clouds.**

Thermal activity

✴ Coromandel Peninsula
✴ **Sf 127/128**

Region: Waikato
Altitude: 0 – 892m/2,926ft

The Coromandel Peninsula sticks out northwards like a tongue, dividing the Hauraki Gulf (and the Firth of Thames) in the west from the ▸Bay of Plenty in the east. The volcanic landscape is full of extraordinary contrasts, as craggy rocks alternate with fine sandy bays along the coast. Whilst the west coast is very well sheltered, on the Firth of Thames in particular, the strong swell shapes the heavily indented eastern coast.

The uneven coastline of Coromandel Peninsula is beaten by waves, wind and weather

Unspoiled nature

On both sides of the peninsula sailors, deep-sea anglers and divers can truly get their money's worth. Visitors penetrating further into the interior of the peninsula will find a largely untouched natural landscape with difficult-to-access mountains, rugged valleys and dense forests. The ridge of the peninsula is formed by the **Coromandel Range** stretching to the northern tip of the promontory at Port Jackson. Its up to 800m/2640ft-high mountains forms a **weather divide** between the east and west side of the peninsula – bright sunshine along the coast while the mountains disappear into the clouds is not unusual.

Kauri wood, kauri resin and gold

Before the Europeans arrived, the Coromandel Peninsula was covered in mighty **kauri forests**, but they fell under the immigrants' axes back in the early 19th century. Incidentally, the peninsula owes its name to the British supply ship Coromandel, which was used around 1820 to transport kauri wood. After the lumberjacks had finished, the kauri resin prospectors dug up the area, finding plenty of the sought-after raw material. Eventually the news spread like wild-fire that there was gold to be found on the Coromandel Peninsula. Fortune hunters from all corners of the earth made sure that the easily accessible deposits of the precious metal did not last long. Today, visitors can still come across numerous **abandoned pits, in most cases not secured**.

DESTINATIONS ON THE COROMANDEL PENINSULA

Situated on the western side of the Coromandel Peninsula, on the mouth of the Waihau River, is its most important settlement, the small town of Thames (population 7,000). The town developed from the old port of Shortland and the former **gold prospectors settlement** of Grahamtown. Housed in the former »School of Mines«, the **Thames Mineralogical Museum** displays a fairly extensive collection of rocks and minerals alongside models of mines and so-called Stamper Batteries, which were used for smashing rocks. During the gold mining period, the **»Queen of Beauty Pump«**, set up behind the local power station, used to pump water from the mines, at depths of up to 300m/984ft.

Thames

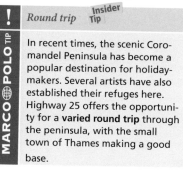

MARCO POLO TIP

Round trip Insider Tip

In recent times, the scenic Coromandel Peninsula has become a popular destination for holiday-makers. Several artists have also established their refuges here. Highway 25 offers the opportunity for a **varied round trip** through the peninsula, with the small town of Thames making a good base.

❶ **Thames Mineralogical Museum:** summer 10am – 3pm, spring and fall until 1pm, winter by appointment, admission: NZ$ 10, www.nzmuseums. co.nz

The nature reserve north and southeast of Thames comprises 63,400 ha/156,660 acres, of which over 8,000 ha/19,768 acres are sustainable kauri plantations. Large areas of the craggy highlands are covered with **natural rainforest**. Information on the forest and hiking options can be picked up from the park administration (13km/8 miles east of Thames on the road to Kauaeranga).

*Coromandel Forest Park

In the 1860s there was also gold mining in the area surrounding the port of Coromandel (pop 1,500) on the northwest coast of the peninsula. These times are recalled in the former **School of Mines**; also look out for the former **Court House** (1860) and an old battery for smashing the auriferous ore.

Coromandel (port)

Day trips from Coromandel

Starting at Coromandel, the winding but highly scenic **Highway 25** leads via the largely abandoned old goldmining settlement of Kuaotunu to Whitianga (48km/30 miles; see below). The road rises gradually to 347m/1,138ft, yielding magnificent views of the natural ports of Coromandel and Whangapoua, as well as Mercury Bay. The shortcut from Coromandel to Whitianga (33km/20.5 miles) is very narrow and full of bends, passing the **Waiau Waterfalls** and ancient kauri trees. A rewarding option on the way is to climb **Castle Rock** (525m/1,722ft), which offers excellent views. The road from Tapu to Coroglen further south (29km/18 miles) winds through the valleys of Tapu and Waiwawa with the double summit of the 819m/158-ft Camels Back rising in the background. A nearly **square kauri tree** can be spotted 8km/5 miles from Tapu on the road to Coroglen. North of Coromandel the coastal road deteriorates and becomes narrower, making it extremely hard work to get to **Cape Colville** on the northern tip.

Mount Moehau

Up in the north, rising 892m/2.926ft above sea level, Mount Moehau is considered a **sacred mountain** by the Maori. Its summit is said to

The English seafarer James Cook anchored here in the picturesque Mercury Bay

hold the grave of the leader of the Arawa tribe. The climb is heavy going and only worth attempting for the views in good weather. .

Some 70km/44 miles north of Thames, the popular holiday town of Whitianga occupies a scenic position on beautiful **Mercury Bay**. Legendary Polynesian seafarer Kupe is said to have fished here once. James Cook (►Famous People) made anchor in this bay in 1769, taking possession of New Zealand for Great Britain by hoisting the British flag. Later, Whitianga was a base for shipping large quantities of kauri wood and kauri resin all over the world. During Cook's time, the promontory of Whitianga Rock held an important Maori fortification (»pa«). Although it was easy to defend, little of it is still visible today. At **Shakespeare Cliffs**, a monument commemorates James Cook, who set down anchor here with his **Endeavour**. In the luxurious wellness spa The Lost Spring relax in hot thermal water under palm trees (121A Cook Drive). Extending near Whitianga, **Buffalo Beach** gets its name from a ship which ran aground here in 1840. A few miles east of Whitianga, the day trip destination of **Hahei** has a pretty beach. From the centre of Hahei, a little road leads to a car park, from which it is about an hour's walk to Cathedral Cove. This **imposing rock cave** was hollowed out by the ocean swell. One of the scenic highlights of the Coromandel coast, it is only accessible by foot at low tide. Located south of Hahei, **Hot Water Beach** is a natural phenomenon to impress the most jaded traveller. Either side of low tide, underground hot springs erupt right onto the beach. These springs are eloquent proof of the **volcanic origin** of the Coromandel Peninsula.

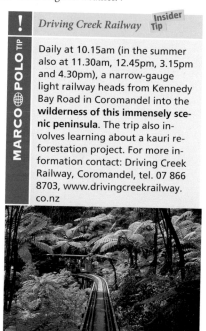

MARCO POLO TIP

! *Driving Creek Railway* **Insider Tip**

Daily at 10.15am (in the summer also at 11.30am, 12.45pm, 3.15pm and 4.30pm), a narrow-gauge light railway heads from Kennedy Bay Road in Coromandel into the **wilderness of this immensely scenic peninsula**. The trip also involves learning about a kauri reforestation project. For more information contact: Driving Creek Railway, Coromandel, tel. 07 866 8703, www.drivingcreekrailway.co.nz

❶ The Lost Spring: daily from 10.30am, latest admission at 6pm, admission: per hour NZ$ 36, per day NZ$ 60.

Pauanui, Tairua

The two holiday destinations of Pauanui and Tairua occupy a very scenic position close to each other on the eastern coast between Whitianga and Whangamata, divided only by Tairua Harbour. In season, their **beaches** are fairly popular.

Coromandel Penisula

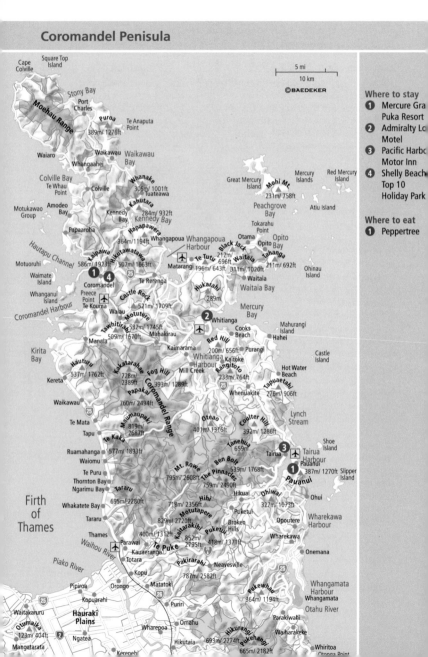

5 mi
10 km

©BAEDEKER

Where to stay
1. Mercure Gra
   Puka Resort
2. Admiralty Lo
   Motel
3. Pacific Harbo
   Motor Inn
4. Shelly Beach
   Top 10
   Holiday Park

Where to eat
1. Peppertree

Only 3,500 people live permanently in this popular holiday town on the southeastern coast of the Coromandel Peninsula. The town started life as a lumberjack and gold prospector settlement; today, during high season, it appears to burst at the seams. The harbour bay has a good bathing beach, whilst more pretty beaches can be found further north at Onemana and Opoutere, as well as to the south at Whirirtoa. A **variety of hikes** lead through Taitua State Forest, situated further north, as well as the two valleys crossing the interior of the peninsula, Wentworth Valley and Parakowhai Valley.

Whangamata

Formerly a thriving gold prospectors settlement, these days has only 5,000 inhabitants. The town lies in the southern foothills of the Coromandel Range, not far from the ▶Bay of Plenty. It was here that the coveted precious metal was first found in 1878. In use until 1952, the mine at Martha Hill used to be the **most productive gold mine in New Zealand**. Its deepest pit reaches down 550m/1,804ft beneath the surface of the earth. Below ground no less than 160km/100 miles of tunnels were dug out. The year 1912 saw bitter conflicts between the mine workers and mine owners, one of the consequences being the foundation of the **New Zealand Labour Party**. When the Martha Hill Mine ceased operating in 1952 due to low productivity, there were fears for the survival of the settlement. However, Waihi was able to develop into the central hub for an extensive area. Some industrial units established themselves, and in 1988 gold mining was even taken up again. The local **Arts Centre & Museum** recalls the time of the gold boom. The model of a gold mine, old and new mining equipment alongside numerous photographs document all aspects of gold mining.

Waihi

Waihi Arts Centre & Museum: summer Tue – Fri 10am – 3pm, Sat – Mon 12pm until 3pm, winter Thu – Mon 10am – 3pm, admission: NZ$ 5, www.waihimuseum.co.nz.

Many buildings in the town date back to the time when the first gold mine was flourishing. On Martha Hill, the ruins of the pump house stand as a reminder of the old days. The new Waihi Gold Mining Co. mines the gold in large-scale open cast mining. There are plans to convert a **200m/656ft-deep hole** into a NZ$20 million Waihi Gold Discovery Centre. Guided tours of the site can be arranged by appointment.

*Martha Hill Gold Mine

Old trains run back and forth between the old railway station of Waihi on Wrigley Street and Waikino.

Goldfields Railway

❶ Round trip ticket NZ$ 18, www.waihirail.co.nz

This gorge between Waihi and Paeroa functions as a kind of open-air museum of bygone mining times. The **Karangahake Gorge His-**

*Karangaha-ke Gorge

Coromandel Peninsula

INFORMATION
Coromandel Information Centre
355 Kapanga Road Coromandel
Tel. 07 866 8598
www.the coromandel.com

WHERE TO EAT
❶ Peppertree ££-£££
31 Kapanga Rd, Coromandel
Tel. 07 866 8211
www.peppertreerestaurant.co.nz
Fish fresh from the boat to the pot –
perfection!

WHERE TO STAY
❶ Mercure Grand Puka Resort £££
Mount Aneue, Pauanui Beach
Coromandel Peninsula
Tel. 07 864 8088
www.pukapark.co.nz
This holiday complex in the rainforest
offers excellent views over the charming
beach of Pauanui.

❷ Admiralty Lodge Motel ££-£££
69–71 Buffalo Beach Road
Tel. 07 866 0181

www.admiraltylodge.co.nz
Lying on the Coromandel Peninsula and
roughly 15 minutes' drive from Whitianga, this motel on Buffalo Beach is well-
run and functionally furnished.

❸ Pacific Harbour *Insider Tip*
Motor Inn ££-£££
233 Main Road, Tairua Beach 2853
Coromandel Peninsula
Tel. 07 864 8581
www.pacificharbour.co.nz
Very well-kept holiday accommodation
in picturesque Tairua on the eastern
coast of the Coromandel Peninsula.
Good starting point for exploring; many
attractions immediately nearby.

**❹ Shelly Beach Top 10 Holiday
Park £-££**
243 Colville Rd., Coromandel
Tel. 08 00 42 46 55
This holiday park sits right on the beach,
which is both safe and pretty, just a few
minutes' drive from the small town of
Coromandel.

toric **Walkway** (approx. 2 hrs) runs along the old railway line, passing the monster machines once used to smash up the rock. During
the main tourist season a **heritage railway** travels the 13km/8-mile
stretch through the gorge from Waihi to Paeroa.

*Waihi Beach   Approx. 11km/7 miles east of the main town lies the beautiful, sandy
10km/6 mile-long Waihi Beach The village was founded in 1920,
when the mining company had the first cottages built at the northern
end of the beach. They were meant for workers who had respiratory
illnesses caused by the hard work in the mines.
Today Waihi Beach is an Eldorado for nature lovers and water sports
fans. Surfers especially appreciate the perfect conditions here as the
beach is considered to be one of the **safest surf spots in New Zealand**.

** Dargaville · Kauri Coast

—————————————— ✦ **Sd 126**

Region: Northland
Altitude: 0 – 774m/2539ft
Population: 4,500

From the outset the heart of the Kauri Coast was an important hub for buying and selling kauri wood and kauri resin, the sought-after raw materials which were so abundant in the surrounding area. Today, the town serves as a base for trips into the kauri forests further north, which are designated nature reserves (▶MARCOPOLO Insight p. 212).

Laid out on a hill above Wairoa River, **Harding Park**'s main attraction is a well-stocked museum bringing together items from the time of the Maori and the early days of European settlement. Worthy of note is a warrior canoe that was buried some 70km/44 miles south of Dargaville in 1809 following tribal wars, and only **rediscovered a few decades ago**. Exhibits from more recent times include the remains of the Greenpeace vessel **Rainbow Warrior**, sunk by French agents in 1985 in the harbour of Auckland. Also look out for the interesting exhibition on the processing of kauri resin.

❶ daily 10am–4pm, admission: NZ$ 15, www.dargavillemuseum.co.nz

*Dargaville Museum

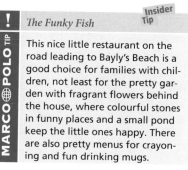

MARCO◉POLO TIP

The Funky Fish   Insider Tip

This nice little restaurant on the road leading to Bayly's Beach is a good choice for families with children, not least for the pretty garden with fragrant flowers behind the house, where colourful stones in funny places and a small pond keep the little ones happy. There are also pretty menus for crayoning and fun drinking mugs.

Some 13km/8 miles west of Dargaville, the beautiful and popular **Bayly's Beach** forms part of Ripiro Ocean Beach, which still appears quite untouched, with its tall, **shifting dunes** stretching some 100km/62 miles along the Tasman Sea.

*Bayly's Beach, Ripiro Ocean Beach

From Dargaville, State Road 12 leads into **New Zealand's most beautiful, yet preserved kauri forests**. An approx. 40km/25-mile drive leads to Trounson Kauri Park, which covers just under 600ha/1,490 acres, with a very dense crop of kauri trees. The nature reserve was established in 1919 and features **hiking trails, picnic and camp sites**. Stretching out further northwest, Waipoua Kauri Forest preserves the largest area of kauri trees in New Zea-land. Waymarked trails lead from the road to the impressive giant trees of M **Tane Mahuta** (= God of the Forest) and M **Te Matua Ngahere** (= Father of the Forest).

Trounson Kauri Park

An Evergreen Tree

The New Zealand kauri tree is among the most massive trees in the world. It can grow to be more than 50m/165ft tall and the circumference of its trunk can reach 16m/53ft. Kauri trees can live more than 2000 years. From time immemorial especially large trees, like the Tāne Mahuta, have been venerated by the Maori as woodland gods.

▶ »Agathis australis«
New Zealand's largest variety of tree, the evergreen kauri tree or kauri fir, is in the family of the Araucariaceae, which have been verified for the Jura period 200 – 150 mil. years ago.

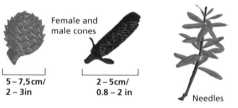

Female and male cones

5 – 7,5cm/
2 – 3in

2 – 5cm/
0.8 – 2 in

Needles

▶ Age
Kauris can reach an age of more than 2000 years.

1 – 4m/
3 – 13ft
diameter

2016
today

1824
Tree variety
first described

1612
A. Tasman discovers
New Zealand

c. AD 12
Tree began
to grow

For comparison
Mammoth tree

Kauri

▶ Kauri in the past

The Maori already knew the advantages of kauri wood. Since it is quite solid but still easy to work they used it to build boats and houses and also to carve works of art. The aromatic the sap (copal) was used to light fires, to make the colours for their tattoos as well as to heal wounds.

Carving

Schiffbau

Hausbau

▶ Kauri today

Today the kauri tree is protected and may only be cut by Maoris in exceptional cases for ritual or religious use. The wood of swamp kauris may be used; these sank into the mud in the past 50,000 years and were thus conserved. This wood is used to make high quality and exclusive furniture, music instruments etc.

Instruments

Furniture

10 – 20m/
33 – 66ft
to crown

30 – 50m/
100 – 165ft
total height

▶ »Tāne Mahuta«

The largest known kauri tree in New Zealand stands in Waipoua Forest.

	m/ft
Total height	**51.5/170**
Circumference of trunk	**13.8/45.5**
Diameter of trunk	**4.4/14.5**

	years
Age	**1,500**

by comparison
oak

▶ Where do kauri grow?

Kauri forests once covered more than 1.2 mil ha (almost 3 mil. ac) of land. Today there are only 9000 ha (more than 22,000 ac) in the northern part of North Island. The best known area is in Waipoua Forest in Northland.

Tāne Mahuta
Waipoua Forest

Auckland ○

Kauri border

■ growth areas

Dargaville and the Kauri Coast

INFORMATION
Normanby Street, Dargaville
Tel. 09 4 39 49 75
www.kauriinfocentre.co.nz

WHERE TO STAY
Parkview Motel
36 Carrington Street

Dargaville
Tel. 09 4 39 83 38
www.parkviewmotel.co.nz
This very quiet motel is known to be especially family-oriented; it has 16 rooms with modern furnishing – a pleasant accommodation in Dargaville.

Matakohe   In the town of Matakohe, 72km/45 miles southeast of Dargaville on Hwy 12, the well-endowed **Kauri & Pioneer Museum** has extensive information on the history and significance of the kauri felling industry, and on the uses of kauri resin.

East Cape

✦ Sj 128

Regions: Bay of Plenty, Gisborne
Altitude: 0 – 1,754m/5,754ft
❶ Gisborne Visitor Information Centre, 209 Grey Street, Gisborne, Tel. 06 8 68 61 39,
www.gisbornenz.com

Until some years ago, the landscape of the East Cape, where James Cook and his companions were the first Europeans to set foot on New Zealand soil on 9 October 1769, was little-known. Today, it is an insider's tip on the tourist circuit. As the eastern-most point of New zealand it is a wonderful place to watch the sun rise. The East Cape is at its most beautiful at Christmas time, when the pohutukawa trees display the glowing red colours of the southern summer.

Masterpieces of Maori woodcraft   Some truly magnificent examples of **Maori woodcraft** come from the East Cape, amongst them the meeting and store houses, as well as the warrior canoes which can be seen today in the famous ethnographic museums of ▶Wellington and ▶Auckland. Some **wonderfully carved meeting houses** are preserved here, for instance in Hicks Bay, Te Kaha, Tikitiki and ▶Gisborne.

Omaio Beach   Omaio Beach, 56km/35 miles northeast of Opotiki, boasts a **splendid beach** and these days a good infrastructure too.

Situated just under 70km/43 miles northeast of Opotiki, the town of **Te Kaha**
Te Kaha lies on a particularly **charming bay**. A Maori »pa« once
stood on the site where various Maori tribes over the course of history fought numerous feuds. Between the 1830s and the 1930s many
whalers moved here from the
▶Bay of Islands to hunt the huge
sea mammals as they passed. The
newer, richly decorated Tukaki
meeting house (1950) is particularly worth a look. Older cultural
artefacts from Te Kaha are today
displayed in the very worthwhile
War Memorial Museum in
▶Auckland.

Extending nearly 100km/62 miles
northeast of Opotiki is the tiny
settlement of **Waihau Bay**, its
guesthouse, established as far back
as 1914, offering a great view of
the coast to **Cape Runaway**. This

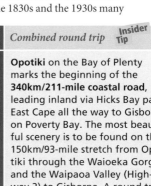

! MARCO ◉ POLO TIP *Combined round trip*   Insider Tip

Opotiki on the Bay of Plenty
marks the beginning of the
340km/211-mile coastal road,
leading inland via Hicks Bay past
East Cape all the way to Gisborne
on Poverty Bay. The most beautiful scenery is to be found on the
150km/93-mile stretch from Opotiki through the Waioeka Gorge
and the Waipaoa Valley (Highway 2) to Gisborne. A round trip
combining both routes is recommended.

cape is effectively the eastern border of the ▶Bay of Plenty. Cape
Runaway owes its name to James Cook, who christened it as such
when he was travelling between Poverty Bay and the Bay of Plenty.
He fired a mighty cannon shot into the air to dispel the Maori's warrior canoes.

Situated some 120km/75 miles northeast of Opotiki, the name of the   **Whangapa-**
town of Whangaparaoa means something along the lines of »**Bay of**   **raoa**
the Whales«. It was from here that whalers would hunt their prey in
former times.

Approx. 150km/93 miles northeast of Opotiki (190km/118 miles   **Hicks Bay**
north of ▶Gisborne), Hicks Bay was named by James Cook in honour
of one of his officers. The local beach is popular, particularly the
stretch on Horseshoe Bay. Worth seeing especially are the meeting
house of Tuwhakairiora (1872) and the **glow worm cave** near the
local motel.

The easternmost point of New Zealand is only accessible using a   **East Cape**
dead-end road via Te Araroa. A lighthouse 140m/nearly 460ft
above the sea yields spectacular panoramic views. **Numerous**
shipwrecks dot the sea around the cape, waiting to be discovered.
It is called the place where the sun's rays first touch New Zealand,
even though this is not exactly true as there are some islands further east.

Te Araroa In Te Araroa stands one of New Zealand's oldest and largest **pohutu-kawa trees**. In 1820, ferocious attacks took place here by the Ngapuhi from Northland, who were already armed with rifles. Several thousand local Maori were killed or enslaved.

*Tikitiki Lying a few miles south of Te Araroa beyond the Raukumara Mountain Range, the town of Tikitiki boasts **one of the most beautiful Maori churches in New Zealand**. Dedicated to Our Lady, the church was built in 1924 in honour of the Maori soldiers killed in the First World War.

Waipiro Bay, Te Puia Springs Lower down the coast, Waipiro Bay was still one of the largest settlements on the eastern shores at the beginning of the 20th century. However, the town's position a long way from any transport links led to its decline. A few miles further south, the town of Te Puia is famed for its **curative thermal springs**. Nearby **Mount Molly** offers an especially expansive and beautiful view of the whole region.

This small church is still standing on Waipiro Bay

On the north end of the picturesque bay, Anaura Bay Walkway, just under 4km/2.5 miles long, also offers some very fine views. Tolaga Bay with its fabulous beach is popular with swimmers as well as anglers. A hiking trail leads to Cook's Cove, which is privately owned and closed in August and September.

*Anaura Bay, Tolaga Bay

Just under 30km/18.5 miles north of Gisborne, the small Maori settlement of **Whangara** lies right on the sea. The carved figure on the gable of the meeting house represents a whale with a human sitting on its back. Tribal legends tell how the ancient ancestor of the local Maori was carried here riding a whale. Only a few miles further north the **beautiful Waihau Beach** unfolds.

*Waihau Beach

The very hilly and densely forested nature reserve between East Cape and the ▶Bay of Plenty extends across more than 115,000ha/284,100 acres and is **hardly touched by tourism**. The highest elevations here are the Hikurangi (1,754m/5,754ft) and the Raukumara (1,413m/ 4,635ft). The **nature reserve** is traversed by the Motu River. The best access is from the old road to Motu, about 35km/22 miles east of Opotiki. For information, contact the Forest Service offices in ▶Gisborne, Opotiki (▶Bay of Plenty) or Ruatoria.

Raukumara Forest Park

Gisborne · Poverty Bay
✦ Sh–Sj 129

Regions: Gisborne
Population: 47,000

Due to its location on Poverty Bay, far from the most important transport routes and markets, the town of Gisborne was long derided as the »end of the world«.

This all changes each year on New Year's Eve and New Year's Day, when Gisborne becomes a cauldron of activity as the city in eastern New Zealand is the first to enter the new year. Gisborne is, incidentally, the birthplace of the world famous soprano Dame Kiri Te Kanawa (" Famous People). The mountain, at the feet of which James Cook came ashore, commands magnificent views across the town and its surroundings. Looking southwards, the view takes in Poverty Bay to the promontory of Young Nicks Head. An **observatory** has been set up on the mountain.

Kaiti Hill (Titirangi)

Standing at the foot of Kaiti Hill, the Poko-O-Rawiri meeting house was erected in 1925. Whilst one of the largest and most modern of its kind, it was not constructed following the traditional method. The

Poko-O-Rawiri

Gisborne · Poverty Bay

INFORMATION
Gisborne Visitor Information Centre
209 Grey Street, Gisborne
Tel. 06 868 6139,
Fax 06 868 6138
www.gisbornenz.com

WHERE TO EAT
The Marina £££
1 Vogel Street
Tel. 06 868 5919
The clue is in the name: excellent fish dishes and lobsters!

WHERE TO STAY
Cedar House ££
4 Clifford Street
Tel. 06 868 1902, fax 06 867 1932
www.cedarhouse.co.nz
Built in 1909 in the Edwardian Style, this handsomely furnished villa serves guests as a base for the still little-known area around Gisborne.

White Heron Motor Lodge ££
474 Gladstone Road
Tel. 06 867 1108, fax 06 867 1019
www.whml.co.nz
Modern and well-run accommodation with friendly service on the western edge of town.

handsome carvings are all in the Rotorua style. The **Maori church** near the meeting house is also worth seeing.

Museums The **Tairawhiti Museum** on Stout Street looks at the cultural development on the eastern coast, showcasing works by contemporary New Zealand artists. On the river, the **Maritime Museum** is worth visiting; the remains of the Star of Canada, stranded on Kaiti Beach, can be seen here.

Both museums: daily 9am – 5pm, admission: NZ$ 15,
www.tairawhitimuseum.org.nz, www.maritimemuseum.co.nz

Church of Matawhero The church of Matawhero, situated approx. 7km/just under 4.5 miles west of Gisborne, is the **oldest church in the area**. Built in 1862, this ecclesiastical building, constructed entirely from kauri wood, initially served Captain Read as a base for one of the first settlers. Subsequently it was converted into an Anglican church, which the Presbyterians purchased in 1872. This is the only building that was spared Maori leader Te Kooti's attention.

*Manutuke Some 14km/8.5 miles southwest of Gisborne, the town of Manutuke boasts two very beautifully carved Maori meeting houses. The bargeboards of the **Te Mana-ki-Turanga** meeting house (1883) show how the god Tane divided heaven and earth and how Maui pulled his great fish out of the sea. The second house, **Te Poho Rukupo**, was built in 1887 in honour of the Maori chief and famous woodcarver Ruku-po. A third meeting house, built nearby in 1842, **Te Hau-ki-Turanga**, can today be viewed in the new and very worthwhile Museum of New Zealand, Te Papa Tongarewa, in ▶Wellington.

In 1888, a meeting house was erected with the utmost urgency in **Rongopai**, northwest of Gisborne, when the Maori leader **Te Kooti**, by then pardoned, announced his visit. However, he never turned up. The paintings inside show a radical break with tradition in favour of strong European influences.

North of Gisborne, the coastal road to ▶East Cape boasts a few **very pretty beaches, arranged like a string of pearls**: Wainui Beach (5km/3 miles from Gisborne), Makorori (14km/8.5 miles), Whangara (28km/17 miles), Waihau (45km/28 miles) and Tolaga Bay (55km/34 miles). More fine beaches and quiet holiday resorts can be found on the **Mahia Peninsula**, 80km/nearly 50 miles south of Gisborne, which divides Hawkes Bay from Poverty Bay.

Bathing beaches

> **MARCO POLO TIP**
>
> **!** *Perfect Chardonnay* — Insider Tip
>
> Poverty Bay is New Zealand's most famous Chardonnay-growing wine region. The wines produced at the »Millton Vineyards« near Manutuke count among the best in the country. Information: The **Millton Vineyards** Ltd, 119 Papatu Road, Manutuke, Gisborne, tel. 06 862 8680, www.millton.co.nz

✴ Hamilton

✦ Sf 128

Regions: Waikato
Altitude: 75m/246ft
Population: 170,000

The fourth-largest city in New Zealand – and the only inland city – lies in the eminently fertile plain of the Waikato River. Since 1950, the city has developed particularly dynamically, boasting a university as well as renowned research institutes (amongst them the Meat Industry Research Institute of New Zealand).

The main attraction in town is the well-endowed Waikato Museum of Art & History, which primarily tells the story of the Tainui Maori tribe. The highlight of the exhibition is a **carved Maori warrior canoe** dating back to 1845. Also worth seeing are modern wood carvings and weavings from Ngaruawahia.

*Waikato Museum of Art & History (▶MARCO POLO Insight p. 224)

 Victoria & Gantham St., daily 10am–4.30pm, admission: donation requested, http://waikatomuseum.co.nz

Historic buildings	In 1878, the Bank of New Zealand was established on the corner of Hood Street/Victoria Street. Today the building serves as a **cultural centre**. Erected in 1893, Hockin House on Selwyn Street houses the Waikato Historical Society. A good example of **Victorian architecture** in New Zealand is Lake House, built in 1873 on Lake Crescent.
Hamilton Gardens	Lying on the shore of Waikato River, the relaxing Hamilton Gardens are well-maintained in all their splendour. The best time to see them is when the roses are in bloom.

AROUND HAMILTON

Nikau Cave	About 70km/40mi north-east of Hamilton lies Nikau Cave; exploring this dripstone cave is a real adventure. It means climbing ladders and squeezing through narrow passages. But it's worth it as the depths of the cave hold glow worms and fantastic dripstone formations. ❶ Mon – Sat 9.30am – 4.30pm, Sun 10am – 4.30pm, admission: NZ$ 40, http://nikaucave.co.nz
Temple View	Around 7km/4.5 miles southwest of Hamilton, it is difficult to miss the mighty temple and headquarters of the New Zealand **Mormons**.
Raglan	Situated just under 50km/31 miles west of Hamilton on the Tasman Sea, the town was named after an English lord and commander in the Crimean War. It was here that in the 1830s the first white missionary settlement in the Waikato area was founded. Today, Raglan is a **popular holiday destination** where holidaymakers enjoy themselves on a pretty beach of dark sand. In the harbour **orcas** sometimes can be seen hunting stingrays. A worthwhile detour heading south from Raglan leads to the charming **Bridal Veil Falls**, which do indeed sway in the wind like a white bridal veil. When the sun hits them they also shine in all the colours of the rainbow.
*Ngaruawahia	Located just under 20km/12.5 miles northwest of Hamilton, Ngaruawahia is the former **capital of a Maori kingdom** of the Waikato tribes. It was here that in 1858 Chief Te Wherowhero was elected King Potatau I. The current king (since 2006) Tuheitia Paki is the seventh head of the Waikato tribes. Over the course of the land wars it became evident that the residence was more endangered than protected by its position on the two rivers. In 1863, after the British cannon boats on the Waikato River had conquered the Maori fortifica-

Fabulously beautiful: Bridal Veil Falls by Raglan

Hamilton

INFORMATION
Hamilton i-Site
5 Garden Place
Tel. 08 00 24 26 45
www.visithamilton.co.nz

WHERE TO EAT
Angus Road Eatery **££– £££**
Mystery Creek Rd./Angus Road
Tel. 07 8 23 64 11
http://www.angusrd.co.nz
In the newly renovated restaurant a fire
roars in the fireplace and dominates the
room; the pizza oven is also fired with
wood. For anyone not interested in pizza
there is also a dinner menu. The view of
the Waikato River is on the house.

WHERE TO STAY
Atrium on Ulster **££**
281 / 283 Ulster Street
Tel. 07 8 39 08 39
http://atriumonulster.co.nz
Elegant, new motel, centrally located,
good value for money.

SHOPPING
Main Street/Victoria Street
The two busy major streets of the city
are Main Street and Victoria Street,
which runs parallel to the Waikato River; both boast not only pretty shops,
but also several art galleries and show-
rooms.

tions of Meremere and Rangiriri, Ngaruawahia was given up without
a fight. Following the battle at Orakau the king looked for refuge with
the tribes in King Country. The Maori lands were surveyed by the
colonial government and sold. Even after the white settlers had made
official peace with the Maori in 1881, it was still to be decades until a
new Maori residence was established here. Since 1920, plots of land
on the river have been bought back by white settlers, and the
Turangawaewae Pa fortification built. First to be erected was the
Arehurewa reliquary shrine, with the **Kiwikiwi Meeting House**
three years later.

Mahinarangi Meeting House   The first post for the **Mahinarangi Meeting House**, with its ornate
carvings, was driven into the ground by the famous Maori politician
Apirana Ngati. Finally, in 1933 the royal residence called **Turongo**
was built, following ideas by Princess Te Pua. Its tower-like extension has some fine carvings, while the »Kimiora Cultural Complex«,
built in 1974, boasts a **large-scale mural**. A monument here honours
Maori King Potatau I. The gun turret of a cannon boat set up here
dates back to the 1863 land wars.

Taupiri Mountain   Some 7km/just under 4.5 miles north of Ngaruawahia, the 288m/945-
ft Taupiri Mountain rises above the Waikato River. The Maori con-
sider it a **sacred mountain**, but only saw its restitution by the government in 1975. One part of the mountain slope, which has been

fortified since ancient times, holds a »tapu« burial site for Maori kings.

A town of 7,000 inhabitants on the lower reaches of the Waikato River, Huntly lies 33km/20.5 miles north of Hamilton. Here, the river cuts through rich coal deposits which have been exploited since the 1840s. In 1859, the geologist **Ferdinand von Hochstetter** carried out a systematic exploration of the deposits. The Huntly coal-fired power station was completed in 1981. With their height of **150m/492ft, its chimneys** have become landmarks visible from afar.

Coal mining and coal-fired power station at Huntly

Lying some 17km/10.5 miles north of Huntly is Rangiriri. In 1863, during the time of the land wars, this was the site of a battle between British troops and the Maori with great loss of life. It took the British two fruitless assaults before they were able to take the Maori fortification, a little of which remains west of Highway 1.

Rangiriri

Situated 53km/33 miles northeast of Hamilton (Hwy 26), the little spa town of Te Aroha (pop 3,500) lies at the foot of the mountain of the same name on the edge of the Kaimai mountains. The **bath houses** and spa facilities, built in the Victorian style and dating back to the turn of the century, are worth seeing here. Today, the facilities are complemented by modern baths. The curative spring waters are administered in the shape of drinking and bathing treatments. The summit of the 952m/3,123-ft Te Aroha commands **spectacular views**. Several scenic hiking trails lead up to the mountain top, but there is also the option of a shuttle bus for people who prefer not to walk.

***Te Aroha**

> **MARCO ☉ POLO TIP**
>
> *Ngaruawahia Regatta*   Insider Tip
>
> Every year since 1896, a colourful canoe regatta has been held at the confluence of the Waikato and Waipa rivers, with the absolute highlight the passage of the traditional large warrior canoes of the Maori. The event takes place on the Saturday which falls closest to 17 March.

Worthwhile destinations for day trips into the surrounding area are the **Kaimai Mountains**, accessible by several hiking tracks, as well as the impressive 150m/492-ft **Wairere Waterfalls**.

Situated some 30km/18.5 miles south of Hamilton (Hwy 3), the old Maori settlement of **Te Awamutu** on the Waipa River today has just under 9,000 inhabitants. A mission was established here in 1839, and in the late summer of 1864 this is where the last battles of the land wars in the Waikato area were fought. After the end of the Waikato wars, soldiers were settled on the confiscated tribal area. The **Puniu River** to the south formed the border with King Country, which no white settler dared set foot in before a peace accord with King Tawhi-

***Te Awamutu**

A Special Culture

Far more than 600,000 Maori stills live in New Zealand today. Despite all adversities during colonial times they were able to preserve their Maoritanga, i.e. their values and special cultural characteristics until today

▶ **»Ta Moko« (tattoo)**
The traditional body decorations are worn mainly in the face, on the thighs and on the buttocks. They are an important step towards adulthood. The right half of the face shows information about the father, the left half about the mother.

1 **Ngakaipikirau:** rank

2 **Ngunga:** position in life

3 **Uirere:** tribal information
Nose: person's tribe
Cheek: parents' tribe

4 **Ulma:** descent (whether from first or second marriage)

5 **Raurau:** person's signature and position

6 **Taiohou:** person's work

7 **Wairua:** person's power

8 **Taitoto:** birth status

▶ **»Waka« (canoe)**
The range runs from smaller fishing boats up to 40m/130ft-long war canoes that were paddled by 80 people.

▶ **»Marae« (meeting house)**
Most Maori tribes had the own marae, where greetings, speeches and other ceremonial activitie took place.

How is a moko made?
A moko is not injected but worked into the skin with a scratching and scraping tool. Thick scars are formed.

Deep cuts are made in the skin. Then with the aid of a comb the pigment is added.

▶ **»Hongi« (greeting)**
Maoris press their noses against each other gently to greet each other. They do this to feel the other person's (life)breath.

Maori Haka – www.youtube.com

▶ **»Haka« (dance)**
Haka actually just means dance, but it also stands for a special war dance. It has become a regular part of a welcome or entertainment ceremony.

Passion
Hands, feet, arms, legs, voice, eyes and tongue are used to express feelings when dancing.

»Whetero«
Sticking out the tongue and opening the eyes wide is supposed to scare the opponent off.

▶ **Weapons**
There were many wars between individual Maori tribes. Deadly weapons were developed for this.

»Mere«
Club made of wood, bone or jade

»Taiaha«
1.5m/5ft-long hardwood stick for hitting or throwing

ao was signed in 1881- although by 1880, the construction of the railway had reached as far as Te Awamutu. **St John's Anglican Church**, built in 1854, is worth seeing with its beautiful old stained-glass windows and interesting tombstones. Standing in marked contrast next to the old church is a modern example of ecclesiastical architecture from 1965.

Museum   The Civic Centre on Roche Street houses the **Te Awamutu Museum**, speciali-sing in the Maori and the land wars.
i Mon–Fri 10am–4pm, Sat 10am to 1pm, Sun 1 to 4pm, free admission, http://tamuseum.org.nz

Pirongia Forest Park   Pirongia Forest Park, extending approx. 15km/9 miles west of Te Awamutu around **three extinct volcanos** Mount Pirongia (959m/3165ft), Mount Kariori (756m/2495ft) and The Cone (945m/3118ft), has been developed for hikers with trails and lodges, and boasts beautiful views.

Kawhia Harbour   Some 100km/62 miles southwest of Hamilton , the natural feature of Kawhia Harbour opens out on the west coast. The area once had great significance for the Maori as a **resting place for the Tainui ancestors' canoe**. Nowadays a small settlement, Kawhia (pop 650) used to be an important 19th-century trading centre for wood, flax and grain. Exports would go to Sydney and even as far as California. After the land wars and the peace treaty of 1881, the town fell into obscurity. On **Te Puia Hot Water Beach** the stretch of beach located some 4km/2.5 miles west of Kawhia, low tide sees hot springs rising from the sand. So anybody can dig their own **personal thermal pool**!

Waikato River   Hamilton forms the centre of the Waikato Region , crossed by **New Zealand's longest river**. The river's Maori name, »Waikato-taniwha-rau« means something along the lines of »Flowing Water of the 100 Water Monsters«. Up to the point when it was tamed by reservoirs, power stations and flood dams in the 20th century, the river lived up to its name, with waterfalls, whirlpools and rapids, swamps and floods. Today, the Waikato's enormous hydroelectric potential is put to good use, with a whole cascade of barrages and hydroelectric power stations being built. One example south of Lake Taupo, the Tongariro Hydro-Electric Power Scheme, is followed by a succession of eight hydroelectric power stations past the point where the Waikato flows out of Lake Taupo. Further projects are the geothermal power station of Wairakei, as well as the two coal-fired power stations of Huntly and Mercer, which need the water of the Waikato for cooling rather than energy production.

Hastings

————————————————— ✧ Sg 130

Region: Hawkes Bay
Altitude: 25m/82ft
Population: 76,000

Situated some 20km/12.5 miles south ►Napier, the town of Hastings lies amidst the fertile Heretaunga Plain with its many orchards and vineyards. The economy is dominated by the food industry (canning plants, fruit processing, brewery, storage freezers for meat). Hastings profits from a mild, sunny climate and is considered to be one of the warmest cities in New Zealand.

In 1864, a group of 12 settlers nicknamed the »12 Apostles« purchased land in the Heretaunga Plain. One of them, Francis Hicks, in 1873 founded the settlement that was supposed to take the name

History

Vegetables, fruit and grapes flourish in the fertile Heretaunga Plain near Hastings

Hastings

INFORMATION
Hastings Visitor Centre
Russell Street,
Hastings
Tel. 06 873 5526
www.visithastings.co.nz

WHERE TO STAY
Hawthorne House £££
1420 Railway Road South
Tel. 06 878 00 35
www.hawthorne.co.nz
Well-run accommodation in an elegant
and very well-kept older country house a
few miles south of town.

Hicksville. Instead the name that stuck was the one referring to Warren Hastings, the first British Governor General of the East India
Company. As with the neighbouring town of ▶Napier, Hastings also
became a victim of the devastating earthquake of 1931. Several dozen
people died and many houses were totally destroyed. The rebuilding
was mainly carried out in the **Art Déco** style.

WHAT TO SEE IN AND AROUND HASTINGS

Exhibition
Centre
A remarkably extensive collection of **Maori works of art** can be admired at the Hastings Exhibition Centre. The centre also houses the
art collection put together by a former mayor (Civic Centre, Eastbourne St.
❶ Mon – Fri 10am – 4.30pm, Sat, Sun 11am – 4pm, admission prices vary
according to exhibition, www.creativehastings.org.nz

Havelock
North
Spreading southeast of Hastings, the **well-to-do residential suburb**
of Havelock North (pop 10,000) is named after a British Major Gen-
eral who distinguished himself in the Indian uprising of 1857/1858.
The town is home to prestigious private schools.

Lourdes
Chapel
On the road to Te Mata, the modern chapel dedicated to the Virgin
Mary was completed in 1960. The **influence of Le Corbusier** on its
architect John Scott is unmistakable. The wooden interior is very
reminiscent of the churches commissioned by Bishop Selwyn, such
as All Saints in Howick or Old St Paul's in Wellington.

*Te Mata
The summit of Te Mata, just under 400m/1,312ft high, offers beautiful views of **Hawkes Bay**. The mountain can be accessed via a narrow road or a charming hiking trail. Lying on the slopes of the mountain and blessed with good views, the Te Mata Estate is one of the
oldest vineyards in New Zealand, producing exceedingly fine

wines since 1896. A lot of care has gone into the restoration of the old buildings making up this fine property. These are complemented by some remarkable new buildings that have gone up on the site since 1987, designed by renowned Wellington architect **Ian Athfield**.

In acknowledgement of the fact that wine and poetry are inextricably linked, every other year the Te Mata Estate honours a writer who has made a valuable contribution to **New Zealand literature**.

Te Mata poet laureate

A particular attraction of the area around Hastings and ▶Napier, with its favourable climate, are its numerous **wine cellars**. A number of them may be explored during a hike on the Hawkes Bay Wine Trail. The tourist information offices in Hastings and Napier have brochures and information.

*Hawkes Bay Wine Trail

Amongst the wine cellars with an excellent reputation are **Vidal's Vineyard** (Hastings), **Te Mata Estate** (Havelock North), **Corbans Winery** (Napier), **Esk Valley Estate** (north of Napier), **Brookfields Vineyards** (Meeanee, between Napier and Hastings).

In this water park children of all ages can play on slides and in the fantasyland.

Splash Planet

❶ daily 10am – 5.30pm, admission: NZ$ 28, www.splashplanet.co.nz

Lying a good 30km/18.5 miles southeast of Hastings, **Waimarama** (accessible via Havelock North) boasts a splendid sandy beach with views of the high cliffs of Bare Island. Havelock North is also on the way to **Ocean Beach**.

*Beaches

The Maori village of Pakipaki, lying about 6km/3.7 miles south of Hastings on Highway 2, is worth a visit for the **Houngara** meeting house, built in 1916 and decorated with rich carvings.

Pakipaki

Situated just under 30km/18.5 miles south of Hastings, Te Aute College was established in 1854 for Maori students. The school became famous through the achievements of Maui Pomare, Apirana Ngata and Peter Buck, who all went on to become Maori leaders and were educated here. This is also why it is considered the **breeding ground of the influential Young Maori Party**. Look out for the school's impressive assembly hall, decorated in the 1930s with wonderful carvings by Pine Taiapa.

Te Aute College

Situated some 43km/just under 27 miles (50km/31 miles) southwest of Hastings, the two towns of Waipawa (pop 1,700) and Waipukurau (pop 3,700), were founded in the 1860s by the owners of **huge sheep farms**. Pasture farming still plays an important role here today.

Waipawa, Waipukurau

✳ Hawke's Bay

✦ Sg–Sh 130

Region: Hawke's Bay
Altitude: 0 – 403m/1,322ft
Population: 160,000

The sunny bay on the east side of North Island is a popular destination for gourmets and wine lovers. Its location in the lee of mountain ranges make it the warmest region of New Zealand and create optimal conditions for growing fruit and wine. But water lovers will also appreciate the area here.

Vast estates

The interior of the Hawke's Bay area is very hilly, even mountainous in places. The only lowland is **Heretaunga Plain** at ▶Hastings, which, having been drained, was divided up into parcels of land and sold off. The typical model for the European settlement of Hawke's Bay and its interior was not penniless emigrants arriving here but rather **well-funded entrepreneurs** who were able to buy huge estates off the Maori and establish farms on them. Instead of working the estates themselves, they employed administrators to do so for them. In February 1931 a **severe earthquake** shook the area around Hawke's Bay, affecting the two towns of ▶Napier and ▶Hastings particularly badly. Over 200 people died in the rubble. One consequence of the quake was a lifting of the ocean floor, creating over 3,000ha/7,400 acres of new land.

Cape Kidnappers

Today's name for the cape, **Cape Kidnappers**, comes from James Cook (▶Famous People), who, after his first disappointing landing at Poverty Bay, turned around and sailed south in order to put down anchor at the cape. The next morning, while Cook was negotiating barter deals with the indigenous inhabitants who had come to join him in canoes, some Maori attempted to kidnap a Tahiti-born **ship's boy, Taiata**. The boy, however, was able to jump out of the canoe and dive back to the ship.

The name chosen by Captain Cook for the steep promontory, **Cape Kidnappers**, stuck. It was not until half a century after Cook that the first Europeans arrived at Hawke's Bay.

In the 1840s, the missionary **William Colenso** established a station near Clive, where he introduced the native inhabitants to the cultivation of **grains** and **fruit**.

? On the hook

MARCO ◉ POLO INSIGHT

In Maori mythology the Cape was the magical fishing hook of Maui, which he used to pull the entire North Island out of the sea like a huge fish. Tofay bird lovers from all over the world visit the large colony of gannets here.

Located 21km/69 miles east of ▶Hastings, near Clifton at the end of Hawke's Bay, the Cape is particularly well known as a **breeding site for gannets**. The Australian gannet can grow to a respectable size, 84 to 91 cm (32 to 36 in). The gannets arrive at the reserve towards the end of July, lay their eggs between October and November, and six weeks later the chicks are hatched. From February onwards the birds leave the breeding area, and by April the gannets are nearly all gone.

* Gannet colony

Access to the gannet colony is only possible **at low tide** from Clifton, on an 8km/26 mile-long path across the beach to a large observa-tion platform. Guided tours from Te Awanga lead visitors close to the breeding colony, from where the birds can easily be watched.

Lying between ▶Napier and ▶Gisborne on Hawke's Bay, the settle-ment of Wairoa (pop 5,000) is a good base for exploring **Te Urewera National Park** with **Lake Waikaremoana**.

Wairoa

The pride and joy of Wairoa's **Marine Parade** is an old lighthouse made from kauri wood, which stood on Portland Island (off the southern tip of the Mahia Peninsula) between 1877 and 1958.

Kauri wood lighthouse

The small Wairoa Museum houses exponents of natural and cultural history for a thousand years of settlement history, from its begin-nings until today. There is also an attractive **collection of Maori art**. From the bridge the carved meeting house of Takitimu may be seen upriver.

Wairoa Museum

❶ Mon – Fri 10am – 4pm, Sat 10am – 12pm, admission: donation requested, http://wairoamuseum.org.nz

▶Gisborne, ▶Hastings, ▶Napier

Other destinations

Hokianga Harbour

✳ Sd 126

Region: Northland
Altitude: 0 – 222m/728ft
Population: approx. 20,000
❶ P.O. Box 6, Omapere, South Hokianga, Tel. 09 4 05 88 69,
http://hokiangatourism.org.nz

The bay on the Tasman Sea to the far north is effectively di-vided in two: tall sand dunes tower on the barren northern side of the bay, while pretty beaches span the green southern side, with its two holiday towns of Omapere and Opononi.

Kauri wood and kauri resin

It is likely that around the same time they arrived in the ►Bay of Islands, ships bearing European whalers and lumber merchants sailed into **Hokianga Harbour**. Until the early 20th century lumberjacks and collectors of kauri resin ruled. As time went on, they were gradually replaced by farmers who turned the cleared areas into pasture for cattle and sheep. Remains of the original **kauri forest** are only preserved south and north of Hokianga Harbour, for instance in **Waipoua Forest** and **Trounson Forest** (►Dargaville · Kauri Coast)

PLACES IN AND AROUND HOKIANGA HARBOUR

Omapere, Opononi

The main town on the southern side of the **natural harbour** of Hokianga is Omapere. The Information Centre building houses a small museum of local history, showing, amongst other things, a film about »Opo« the tame dolphin who created a stir in the 1950s. Opononi is also a good base for an **exciting cruise** through the extensive **Hokianga Harbour** aboard a renovated old steamboat.

> **?** MARCO POLO INSIGHT
>
> *Plays with a dolphin*
>
> In the summers of 1955 and 1956 a tame dolphin named »Opo« turned up at Opononi and proceeded to play with holidaymakers in the shallow waters? Opo's antics kept the whole nation entertained at the time, and until his death the small holiday town used to burst at the seams.

The former loggers settlement of **Rawene** occupies a very picturesque position on a promontory a few miles further east. Some of the houses still stand on stilts in the water. In the more recent past, the town of has seen a revival, as **artists and people seeking an alternative way of life** have moved here. Buildings worth looking out for are the Old Hotel, the former hospital next to the jetty, and above all **Clendon House**, which was built in the 1860s for the English merchant James R Clendon. Today lovingly restored with period furnishings, Clendon House on the esplanade in Rawene functions as a museum.

❶ Clendon House: summer Sat – Mon 10am – 4pm, admission: NZ$ 10, www.heritage.org.nz

Horeke

Even further east, this small town with its **houses on stilts** presents a decidedly picturesque image. Around 1827/1828 there was a shipyard here, but by 1830 the Australian enterprise had hit the rocks financially. Followers of John Wesley, the founder of Methodism, established the **Mangungu Mission House** west of Horeke in around 1838. The former mission church has disappeared now, but the cemetery with its old tombstones has survived. The Mission House is now a museum open to the public.

❶ summer holidays Sat and Sun, winters only Sun midday–4pm, at other times by appointment, admission: NZ$ 10, www.heritage.org.nz

Stretching some 3km/1.5 miles south of Horeke the wild, romantic Wairere Boulders Nature Park boasts spectacular **basalt boulders** up to 20m/65ft in diameter. These are the remnants of volcanic activity that took place some 2.5 million years ago. The park has a nature trail with shorter and longer routes leads over 23 bridges through shady rain forest (walking time: 1 – 2 hrs).

*Wairere Boulders

In the former logging settlement of **Kohukohu** on the northern side of the natural harbour, the **first Catholic Mass** on New Zealand soil was held in 1838, as evidenced by a memorial stone at Totara Point. Today, Kohukohu is well known as an artists' colony and refuge for

Kohukohu

Ngawha Hot Springs: anyone who swims here should remove jewellery, watches and metal objects first as the sulphur darkens them

those weary of city life. Kohukohu is **connected by ferry** with the neighbouring town of **Rawene** to the south.

Kaikohe

In the 19th century, the area around the small town of Kaikohe (pop 4,000) still had some well-fortified Maori settlements. It was here during the **Northland Land War** (1844 – 1846) that bloody conflicts took place between the warriors led by Maori chief Hone Heke and British troops, with much loss of life. Hone Heke was living in Kaikohe when he died in 1850.

Pioneer Village

Here in Pioneer Village the old courthouse of Waimate North (1862), a tiny prison, a blacksmith's workshop and a **completely stocked shop** can be visited, along with other 19th-century buildings and a completely restored narrow-gauge railway (1907) for transporting wood.

❶ Mon – Sat 10am – 4pm, Sun 12pm – 4pm, admission: NZ$ 12, www.pioneervillage.co.nz

The sand beach of Ninety Mile Beach at Kaitaia seems endless – in fact it is »only« 64 miles long

Some 7km/4.5 miles east of Kaikohe (fork off Hwy 12), **mineral-rich thermal water** emerges from the ground, and is used very successfully for the treatment of skin diseases and rheumatism. The water temperature in the different pools varies from luke warm to pretty hot.

Ngawha Hot Springs

✳ Kaitaia · Far North

✧ **Sd 126**

Region: Northland
Altitude: 40m/131ft
Population: 6,000
❶ Kaitaia Visitor Information Centre, Te Ahu, Corner Matthews Avenue and South Road Tel. 09 4 08 94 50, www.kaitaia.net.nz

The gateway to the north of New Zealand's North Island is the tourist base of Kaitaia. The town is normally the starting point for a trip to the northernmost point »Far North«, with its famous Ninety Mile Beach and Cape Reinga.

The exhibition on Kaitaia's South Road preserves some unusual items, amongst them an anchor lost by French seafarer de Surville in 1769 in Doubtless Bay during a storm. Look out also for the huge **skeleton of a moa**. A collection of photographs shows the way of life in Far North around 1900.
❶ Mon–Fri 10am–4pm, admission: NZ$ 5, www.teahuheritage.co.nz

Far North Regional Museum

A typical Maori »marae«, **beautiful wood carvings and weavings** and much more can be admired (and some of it purchased) in the arts centre dedicated to New Zealand's native inhabitants. Visitors have the opportunity to watch craftspeople at work or even take part themselves. Every year in March, a well-respected **Arts & Crafts Festival** is held here.

∗Te Wero Nui Maori Cultural Centre

Just under 15km/some 9 miles southwest of Kaitaia, on the southernmost tip of Ninety Mile Beach, lies the **Maori settlement** of Ahipara, where visitors can not only learn about the daily life of New Zealand's native inhabitants, but also pursue various sports and activities, such as surfing, horse-riding and fishing.

Ahipara

Just under 40km/25 miles southeast of Kaitaia, Omahuta Forest Sanctuary protects a larger stand of **ancient kauri trees**. Numerous **types of bird** may be observed here too. Access by car is from Hwy 1 south of Mangamuka Bridge. A beautiful hiking trail leads into the forest.

∗Omahuta Forest Sanctuary

*Ninety Mile Beach Appearing unendingly long, the **sandy beach** on the western side of the northern »finger« has a breadth of up to 200m/656ft and lends itself to all kinds of activities, including hair-raising car races. In January 1932, the Australian Norman Smith set a world speed record of 164m/h/264km/h on the stretch of beach at Hukatere. Every year in January, the **Surfcasting Fishing Contest** attracts thousands of enthusiastic surfcasters to the area. In March, the long-distance running competitions of the **Ninety Mile Beach Te Houtawea Challenge** are held here.

> **?** MARCO ⊕ POLO INSIGHT
>
> *The trick with the miles*
>
> The legendary »Ninety Mile Beach« does not in fact measure 90 miles but just 64. It is not clear where the name of the beach came from. Presumably »Sixty Mile Beach« did not sound spectacular enough.

Shifting dunes The sand dunes north of Kaitaia tend to shift inland. Successful efforts have been made to stabilise them by sowing **grass seeds and lupins**, as well as through planting conifers.

Aupouri Forest A narrow side road leads from Kaitaia to the tip of the **Aupouri Peninsula**, whose western side is **largely forested**. In the past, it was kauri trees growing to maturity here, whereas today it is mainly pines. The historic search for kauri resin resulted in larger areas being literally dug up. At the northern edge of the forested area the road meets **volcanic rock**, here called »The Bluff«. There are some Maori still living here too.

Wagener Museum At Houhora, approx. 40km/25 miles north of Kaitaia, the Wagener Holiday Park right on the water offers camping and activities including kayaking and cycling. The Memorial Park is ideal for a long walk and picnic.

Subritzky House Practically right next to the museum, look out for the house erected around 1860 from kauri wood by a Polish immigrant and lovingly restored by his descendants.

*Cape Reinga A narrow tourist road leads from Kaitaia to the northwestern point of North Island, Cape Reinga (165m/541ft). The lighthouse atop the cape, pounded by the wind and the elements, offers **magnificent views**: westwards along the coast to Cape Maria van Diemen, named thus by seafarer Abel Tasman, and eastwards to North Cape. On a clear day, **Three Kings Islands** can be made out in the distance, so named by Tasman because he sailed past here on Epiphany (6 January) 1643. The lighthouse was erected in 1941. Below the lighthouse and hanging over the steep cliffs which drop down towards the sea, is an ancient **Pohutukawa tree** that the Maori hold sacred. This is the place where the souls of the dead are said to dive into the underworld (Reinga) at sunset in preparation for returning home to Hawaiki.

Well worth exploring, this long-distance trail (134km/83 miles) leads east from Cape Reinga towards Spirits Bay and south past Cape Maria van Diemen taking in the entire length of Ninety Mile Beach, before turning inland again to Te Paki. However, bear in mind that there is **no accommodation** in the Cape Reinga area.

*Cape Reinga Walkway

Doubtless Bay stretches around 35km/22 miles northeast from Kaitaia and is accessible to visitors via Hwy 10. Beautiful beaches, such as Coopers Beach, plus excellent **fishing and diving spots** have turned the bay into a tourist hot spot. In Maori mythology **Kupe, the legendary seafarer** from Hawaiki is said to have stepped ashore here for the first time. But the name »Doubtless Bay« was coined by James Cook, who, sailing past here in 1769, decided that this was without a doubt – »doubtless« – a bay, and not an island.

*Doubtless Bay

With its little old kauri wood huts, the small fishing port of Mangonui (= huge shark) presents a rather picturesque image. A **Heritage Trail**

Mangonui

The little lighthouse at the point of New Zealand's North Island can be seen from far off

leads to the most beautiful places. In pretty **Mill Bay**, where today colourful boats bob up and down, the first immigrants from Europe arrived and stocked up on fresh water. Once there used to be a saw-mill here as well as a loading point for kauri wood. To the west, above Mill Bay, the remains of the old **Rangikapiti Pa Maori fortification** are still preserved. From up here there is also a **fantastic view** of Doubtless Bay.

*Whangaroa Harbour

East of Mangonui, the road reaches Whangaroa Harbour (Hwy 10, then a cul-de-sac). This wonderful bay, framed by high cliffs, forms part of a **system of sunken valleys** on the Pacific coast, home today predominantly to holidaymakers looking for peace and quiet and dedicated deep-sea anglers.

Massacre on the Boyd

In 1809, the Boyd, coming from Sydney, sailed into **Whangaroa Harbour** in order to load kauri wood. Several of the ship's crew were Maori, among them a young chief who was said to have been beaten

The fastest shearer wins the golden sheep

by white seamen during the voyage across the Tasman Sea. In order to avenge this, all **whites that went ashore were slaughtered**, and the following night the ship was plundered by the Maori. After an explosion of gunpowder the whole ship burnt out, with only four of the crew surviving. The news spread like wildfire, and from then on the white settlers avoided the harbours and bays of Northland. Even the missionaries stayed back. To this day, the **wreck of the Boyd** lies at the bottom of the sea off Red Island, forming a destination for summer boat trips.

The small picturesque bays of Matauri Bay, Tauranga Bay and Wainui Bay harbour **wonderful beaches**, accessible via a coastal road which affords many pretty views.

Bathing beaches

It was off Matauri Bay that the **Rainbow Warrior** was sunk. As is well known, the Greenpeace boat was destroyed in 1985 in the port of ▶Auckland by French agents. Today, the wreck lies as an artificial reef at a depth of 27m/89ft at the most and is home to countless maritime inhabitants. No diver will pass up this chance for a dive to a shipwreck.

Rainbow Warrior

Masterton

 ✦ **Sf 131**

Region: Wellington
Altitude: 112m/367ft
Population: 23,000

The town of Masterton lies east of the Tararua Range in the agricultural Wairarapa region. In recent years the city was able to develop from a regional market town to a garden town. Visitors who happen to be here in March will get to see the annual Golden Shears sheep shearing competition, the Olympics of the sheep shearing business.

Queen Elisabeth Park, which was established in 1874, is the heart of the town. The Wairarapa Arts Centre in Masterton is also well worth a visit. Incorporating the 1878 Methodist church on Bruce Street, this interesting gallery showcases local and regional art. Nearby in Dixon Street, in the **Shear Discovery Centre**, everything revolves around wool and sheepherding in the history of New Zealand.

The heart of the town

Wairarapa Arts Centre: daily 10.30am – 4.30pm, free admission, www.aratoi.org.nz
Shear Discovery Centre: daily 10am – 4pm, admission: NZ$ 10, www.nzmuseums.co.nz

Masterton

INFORMATION
Masterton Visitor Centre
Cnr Bruce & Dixon Sts. Masterton, NZ
Tel. 06 370 0900
www.cityofmasterton.co.nz

WHERE TO STAY
Fernside ££££   *Insider Tip*
Road 1, Wairarapa
Tel. 06 308 8265, www.fernside.co.nz
An hour's drive north of Wellington, this
hotel feels like an English stately home
set amidst a 14ha/34.5-acre park. The
gatehouse can be rented as a holiday
house. Everything has an opulent flair.
The lake in the park was used as a film
setting for Lord of the Rings.

**Copthorne Resort Solway Park
££–£££**
High Street South
Tel. 06 370 0500
www.millenniumhotels.co.nz/copthorne
wairarapa
Generous holiday complex featuring all
the necessary comforts.

Bird breeding station
About 30km/18.5 miles north on Highway 2, **Pukaka Mount Bruce Wildlife Centre** is run by the Department of Conservation and is well known for its breeding station for birds, particularly focusing on the threatened **takahe**. Among the many bird houses there is also a nocturnal house for kiwis.

❶ daily 9am – 4.30pm, admission: NZ$ 20, www.pukaha.org.nz

Tararua Range
Looming up west of Masterton, the **wild and rugged mountains** of the densely forested Tararua Range separate the Wairarapa area from the west coast. Visitors here will find a number of **impressive peaks** towering above them, including the Mitre, at 1,571m/5,154ft. Just under 100,000ha/247,100 acres of the mountain range are designated as **Tararua Forest Park**, where several hiking trails have been established. Simple lodges give shelter for the night.

Mount Hildsworth
Rising up 1,474m/4,836ft on the eastern edge of Tararua Forest Park, about 22km/13.5 miles west of Masterton, Mount Holdsworth is recognised as an area deserving special protection.

*Honeycomb Rock Walkway
Some 50km/31 miles south of Masterton, at Fault Point, an 8km/5-mile **hiking trail along the Pacific coast** gives access to strange rock formations resembling beehives.

Castlepoint, Riversdale
The two beach resorts of Castlepoint (just under 70km/44 miles northeast) and Riversdale (approx. 60km/37 miles east) are the only ones to be found on this long, steep, inaccessible coastline. A detour to the **lighthouse** on Klippe Castle Point as well as climbing **Castle Rock** is worthwhile.

A trip to the **wild coast** of Palliser Bay or Cape Palliser, reached by driving east past Lake Wairarapa and then south, is definitely worthwhile. The place achieved sad notoriety in 1942, when an uprising of Japanese prisoners of war was brutally quelled.

Palliser Bay, Cape Palliser

Some 20km/12.5 miles southwest of Masterton, a lot of fruit and vegetables are cultivated in the former centre of the **fertile Wairarapa area**. Founded in 1854 by small farmers, the settlement was named after **governor George Grey**. Grey had supported the »Small Farms Association«, which aimed to help the rural workers acquire their own businesses.

Greytown

The once dense virgin forest was long since cut down, but due to the unpredictable Waiohine River the railway was routed past Greytown, stopping further development of the town. Greytown is supposed to be the first planned town in the New Zealand interior.

Waiohine River

Some 20km/12.5 miles northwest of Greytown, the wild Waiohine Gorge at the edge of Tararua Forest Park marks the starting point for **adventurous hiking trails** up to the 1,182m/3,878-ft **Mount Omega**, as well as to the 1,474m/4,836-ft **Mount Holdsworth**.

*Waiohine Gorge

** Napier

✳ Sg 130

Region: Hawkes Bay
Altitude: 0 – 141m/462ft
Population: 58,000

After a devastating earthquake in 1931, it was decided to rebuild Napier in a quakeproof way. Instead of the architecture that had dominated previously, simpler and more geometric forms came to the fore, inspired by the American Art Deco and Spanish Mission Revival styles. The architectonic coherence of the buildings have made them unique in this part of the world. The pastel colours were chosen out of necessity at one time – water was added to the paint because there wasn't enough to go around.

Running right along the seafront, Marine Parade is an attractive **boulevard** ideal for a stroll. The **waterfront promenade**, lined with Norfolk pines, looks particularly resplendent in the morning sunlight. These days, the obligatory tourist attractions have gone up all along the road.

*Marine Parade

Napier

INFORMATION
Napier Visitor Information Centre
100 Marine Parade Napier, NZ
Tel. 06 834 1911
www.visitus.co.nz

WHERE TO EAT
❶ *Fox on the Quay* £££
14 West Quay
Tel. 06 8 33 65 20
The special charm of this otherwise modest restaurant is not revealed to the eyes but to the taste: regional cooking with that certain something is served here.

❷ *Bluewater* £££
10 West Quay Ahuriri Napier
Tel. 06 8 35 86 68
The menu has a broad selection and the various local wines are excellent.

WHERE TO STAY
❶ *Mon Logis* ££–£££
415 Marine Parade
Tel. 06 835 2125
www.monlogis.co.nz
Right on the Pacific and only five minutes from the city centre, this boutique hotel run by a genial Frenchman is a good choice. The boutique hotel dates back to the 1860s and has kept its original charm.

❷ *BK's Fountain Court Motor Inn* £
411 Hastings Street
Tel. 06 8 35 73 87
www.fountaincourt.co.nz
This family-friendly motel has large, comfortable rooms and a pool, the prices are inexpensive. There are lots of attractions here for children.

Colonnade, Sunken Gardens
The lively heart of Marine Parade is situated immediately in front of the city centre. **Well-kept gardens**, amongst them the imposing »Sunken Gardens«, as well as mini-golf and a skating rink, offer fun for old and young. The colonnade with its bandshell built in the Mediterranean style exhibits the **ship's bell** from HMS Veronica. It was this ship that provided the first emergency aid after the devastating 1931 earthquake.

Mardi Gras Area
Further south look out for the site of the **Mardi Gras Area**, the **Can Am Cars**, as well as a small boating lake. A few steps further along is the **National Aquarium of New Zealand & Kiwi House**, with an oceanarium spreading over three storeys and housing numerous marine animals from the Pacific, alongside various types of lizard. Things get particularly busy for the interesting **shark feedings**! The Kiwi House offers the chance to observe the flightless kiwi bird (►MARCOPOLO Insight p. 26), and other representatives of New Zealand's nocturnal fauna.

National Aquarium: daily 9am – 5pm, summer evenings as well, feedings daily 10am and 2pm, admission: NZ$ 20,
www.nationalaquarium.co.nz

An extensive exhibition in the **Hawkes Bay Art Gallery & Museum** looks at the development of culture and art in the east of New Zealand's North Island. The **colonial history** of Hawke's Bay is told on the ground floor, with a lot of space also given to contemporary art. However, the audiovisual exhibition on the terrible 1931 **earthquake** and the city's rebuilding, explored through old photographs and eyewitness accounts, is particularly impressive.

❶ www.hbmag.co.nz

The sculpture of the **mermaid Pania** in the green space opposite the art gallery commemorates a famous character from the world of Maori legend. Pania was living on land with a man she loved whilst her relatives living on the reef asked her to return. When she swam out to visit the relatives, they pulled her into the depths with them and Pania was never more allowed back to dry land. Catching the eye right next to the statue is the **Tom Parker Fountain**, illuminated at night to great effect. The fountain makes an ideal starting point for a 1 to 2-hour walk round the city's Art Deco quarter (see below, Art Deco Walk). Relax and enjoy the warm water in the **Ocean Spa** on Marine Parade.

Ocean Spa: Mon – Sat 6am – 10pm, Sun 8am – 10pm, admission: NZ$ 10.70, www.oceanspa.co.nz

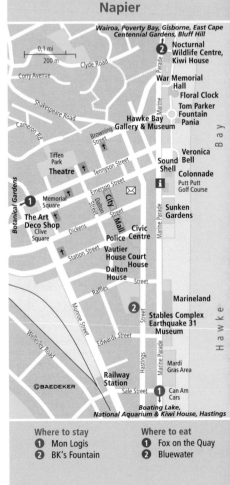

Napier

Wairoa, Poverty Bay, Gisborne, East Cape
Centennial Gardens, Bluff Hill

0.1 mi
200 m

Clyde Road

Corry Avenue

❷ Nocturnal Wildlife Centre, Kiwi House

War Memorial Hall

Floral Clock

Tom Parker Fountain

Pania

Shakespeare Road

Cameron Rd.

Hawke Bay Gallery & Museum

Browning Street

Marine Parade

Veronica Bell

Tiffen Park

Tennyson Street

Sound Shell

Colonnade

Theatre

Emerson Street

Putt Putt Golf Course

Botanical Gardens

Memorial Square

Dalton Street

City Mall

Sunken Gardens

The Art Deco Shop

Clive Square

Dickens

Civic Centre

Police Centre

Station Street

Vautier House Court House

Dalton House

Raffles

Street

Marineland

Munroe Street

❷

Stables Complex Earthquake 31 Museum

Wellesley Road

Edwards Street

Hastings

Marine Parade

Mardi Gras Area

Railway Station

© BAEDEKER

Sale Street

Can Am Cars

Boating Lake,
National Aquarium & Kiwi House, Hastings

Hawke   Bay

Where to stay
❶ Mon Logis
❷ BK's Fountain

Where to eat
❶ Fox on the Quay
❷ Bluewater

The adjoining **War Memorial Hall** commemorates the New Zealand soldiers killed in both world wars. Incidentally, the **beautiful floral clock** in front of the memorial site is a **popular photo subject**.

War Memorial Hall, Floral Clock

From Hawke's Bay Museum, broad Tennyson Street leads the way into the city centre. This is where to find the **Cathedral of St John**

St John the Evangelist

the Evangelist. Its roof collapsed during a service on the day of the devastating earthquake. Part of the church is a small chapel dedicated to clergyman Bennett, the first bishop of Maori descent, as well as Maori politician Apirana Ngata.

**Art Deco Walk
After the devastating earthquake of February 1931, Napier's city centre was quickly rebuilt using two architectural styles in vogue at the time in the US – **Art Deco** and the so-called **Mission Revival Style** – as reference points. The architectural ensemble thereby created is unique, at least in the southern hemisphere, and may be compared to the Art Deco quarter of Florida's tourist magnet Miami Beach. Today, the entire neighbourhood enjoys **listed status**. Napier-born architect **Louis Hay**, who played a major role in the reconstruction of his hometown, looked to the buildings of US-American architects Henry H Richardson, Frank Lloyd Wright and Louis Sullivan for inspiration.

> **MARCO POLO TIP**
>
> *Art Deco Weekend* **Insider Tip**
>
> The highlight in Napier's calendar of events is the Art Deco Weekend, held annually on the third weekend of February. There is a colourful programme of events ranging from a fashion show to an egg and spoon race. Accommodation for this weekend should be reserved early!

Among the first post-quake buildings erected in Napier were the 1932 Masonic Hotel, designed by Wellington architect W J Prouse, and the Criterion Hotel, designed by E A Williams. Further **architectural highlights** are the Daily Telegraph Building (1932) with its sun symbols and ornaments, the Country Wide Bank erected the same year, the 1936 A & B Building, its domed structure forming one of the landmarks of Napier's Marine Parade, and last but not least, the 1938 theatre with its Egyptian-style pillars and arches and a foyer adorned with pretty nymphs. It is also worth a look inside the ASB Bank building to admire the wonderful carvings created by Maori artists.

*Deco Centre
Originally built for the fire service, the Deco Centre today houses both the **Art Deco Trust**, which champions the protection of historic monuments, and the **Art Deco Shop**, which offers a selection of richly informative material on the Art Deco style. There are also guided Art Deco tours (163 Tennyson St & Clive Square East).
❶ daily 9am to 5pm; guided Art Deco tours: June – Oct Wed, Sat and Sun 2pm; Oct – June daily 10am and 2pm, free admission, www.artdeconapier.com

*Bluff Hill
Rising north of the city is Bluff Hill, with the worthwhile Centennial Gardens and the Domain. Bluff Hill Lookout (access via Lighthouse Road) offers a quite **spectacular view**. Weather permitting, the **Mahia Peninsula** can be made out to the northeast and **Cape Kidnappers** to the southeast.

Just under 20km/12.5 miles northwest of Napier, on the road to ▶Taupo (Hwy 5), Eskdale Park is a popular **destination for excursions**, with its romantic river valley, ancient trees and well-kept vineyards. The year of 1866 saw fierce conflict here between white settlers and Hauhau rebels.

Eskdale Park

Lying some 40km/25 miles north of Napier on Highway 2, the old sheep station of Tutira lies on a lake immortalised by the works of **farmer and writer Herbert Guthrie-Smith** (1861–1940). The charming **Tutira Walkway** leads visitors on a 9km/5.5-mile circular walk which is very steep in parts. The lake itself and its banks are a designated bird reserve.

Tutira

▶Hastings, ▶ Hawke's Bay

Further destinations

New Plymouth

✶ Se 130

Region: Taranaki
Altitude: 0 – 177m/580ft
Population: 75,000

Situated at the foot of the Taranaki volcano, the now heavily industrialized port town of New Plymouth is also the centre of fertile farming country. Its port was once a busy commercial hub for dairy products; today, the main shipping goods are raw materials for the petrochemical industry from the rich oil and natural gas deposits off the coast. But the city is interesting for tourists as well. There are excellent conditions for surfing and Mount Taraniki is not far away. Egmont National Park located there is great for skiing and snowboarding.

Named after the **English version**, the port town was founded in 1841. At the time, the first white settlers supposedly encountered few native inhabitants, although several fortified Maori villages and larger kumara fields suggest a slightly different reality. It is likely that in the first half of the 19th century the badly-equipped Taranaki tribes were put under such pressure by the Waikato tribes – who were already using firearms – that they were driven further south, where they aimed to join forces with chief **Te Rauparaha** in order to get their own hands on rifles and resettle in their tribal areas. **Conflicts** soon erupted between the returning Maori tribes and the »pakeha« (whites) who were by now living here. In 1860 these conflicts were to escalate into nationwide fighting.

History

New Plymouth

INFORMATION
New Plymouth i Site
65 St Aubyn Street, New Plymouth
Tel. 06 759 08 97
www.newplymouthnz.com

Insider
Tip

WHERE TO STAY
One Burgess Hill ££ – £££
One Burgess Hill Road
Tel. 06 7 57 20 56
www.oneburgesshill.co.nz
About ten minutes away from the centre of town, in small bungalows in a quiet location on the river are these 15 bright rooms with varying furnishings for self-caterers: The »classic« variation is with WC and shower, »elite« is with a bath-tub in front of a glass wall and the pent-house apartment even has a whirlpool on the terrace.

WHAT TO SEE IN AND AROUND NEW PLYMOUTH

Pretty parks
Designed in the Victorian style, **Pukekura Park** on Liardet Street has a fountain, illuminated at night, and a waterfall. Next to Pukekura Park, **Brookland Park** offers pleasant green spaces for leisure and relaxation.

The Gables
An interesting-looking gabled wooden house nearby, built in 1848 as a hospital, is today a venue for various **cultural events**, such as art exhibitions.

Taranaki Museum
This museum houses an extensive collection of **Maori objects** from the region, amongst them a stone axe from the ancestors' canoe, a chief's robe, several old stone sculptures and wood carvings. There is also documentation on the European settlement.
❶ Mon, Tue, Thu, Fri 9am – 6pm, Wed until 9pm, Sat, Sun 9am – 5pm, tours NZ$ 10, www.pukeariki.com

Richmond Cottage
Standing next to the museum, Richmond Cottage was erected in 1853 as a **school house**. Furnished in the style of the time it shows the kind of environment a wealthy 19th-century family was able to create for itself.
❶ Sat, Sun, hol. 11am – 3.30pm, free admission, www.pukeariki.com

St Mary's Church
Standing on Marsland Hill, right in the city centre, is one of the **oldest stone churches in New Zealand**, with a remarkable interior. Its

When the rhododendron blooms Pukeiti Park becomes colourful

construction was ordered by Bishop Selwyn in 1842. In the confusion of the land wars the church was also used as a military post and **ammunition depot**. The cemetery preserves some of the tombs of early white settlers.

Marsland Hill

Marsland Hill, with its good all-round view, used to have a fortified »pa« Maori village. At the time of the land wars **soldiers were stationed** up here. The hill is best climbed from Robe Street or from St Mary's Church.

Govett-Brewster Art Gallery

This gallery on Queen Street exhibits contemporary New Zealand art, with particularly interesting objects – sculptures, paintings and graphic works – created by **Len Lye**.
❶ daily 10am – 5pm, admission: donation requested, www.govettbrewster.com

Tupare Garden

South of New Plymouth on Mangorei Road lies Tupare, a garden on a hill on the banks of the Waiwhakaiho River that was created by the entrepreneur Sir Russell Matthews and his wife in 1932. Tupare is considered to be **one of the most beautiful gardens** in New

Zealand, with picturesque glades, pretty hothouses, old fruit trees and splashing waterfalls. On a clear day the snow-capped peak of Mount Taranaki can be seen from many parts of the gerden.

❶ daily 9am – 8pm, free admission, www.trc.govt.nz/tupare-home/

Pukeiti Rhododend-ron Park

In the nearby rainforest between the Patuha (683m/2,240ft) and Pouakai (1,400m/4,593ft) mountains is a major designated nature reserve: Pukeiti Rhododendron Park, which is worth visiting. In the springtime its **spectacular blossoms** attract visitors from near and far.

Pungarehu, Cape Egmont

In Pungarehu, some 40km/25 miles southwest of New Plymouth, taking the turning to Cape Egmont is worth the detour. The cape is the western-most point of Taranaki on North Island's west coast. The huge lighthouse was erected in 1881, and the cape boasts numerous **conical lava formations**.

Waitara

About 17km/10.5 miles northeast of Plymouth, Waitara (pop 6,000) was the place where the **land wars** started in 1860. A few petrochemical and food industry companies (such as frozen meat) have since settled in the town.

Urenui

Approx. 15km/9 miles further east, the road reaches Urenui, birthplace of famous Maori scholar and politician **Peter Buck**. His remains lie buried beneath the prow of a stone canoe at the former Okoki Pa Maori defensive settlement.

King Country

Heading northeast from New Plymouth the road initially crosses the softly undulating grassland of Taranaki before reaching the jagged mountain landscape of King Country. From here the colonial troops drove the Maoris of the King Movement further south in the 1860s.

Hawera

On the southern foot of the ▶Taranaki volcano, some 70km/44 miles south of New Plymouth, lies the small town of Hawera (pop 11,000). Of the **Turuturu-mokai Pa** fortification, both in and north of Hawera, only protective walls, deep trenches and a storage pit remain.

The best overview of the town and surrounding area can be had from the **water tower** on the corner of High Street & Albion Street. It was built in order to increase the water pressure since there were many fires here between 1884 and 1912.

Established in a former dairy, the **Tawhiti Museum** tells the chequered history of Te Hawera as a place of settlement. The dioramas, some very tiny and others life-sized, are amazing for their attention to detail.

Tawhiti Museum: Fri – Sun 10am – 4pm, winter only Sun, admission: NZ$ 15, www.tawhitimuseum.co.nz

Palmerston North

—————————— ✦ Sf 131

Region: Manawatu-Wanganui
Altitude: 10m/33ft – 760m/2,493ft
Population: 85,000

Situated about 150km/93 miles northeast of ►Wellington on the Manawatu River, the town was named after the former British Prime Minister Lord Palmerston. Today, the old logging settlement is a regional hub, in terms of infrastructure and commerce, for an area dominated by pasture farming, large dairies and frozen-meat factories. Palmerston North is one of New Zealand's largest cities; because of its comprehensive selection of educational opportunities it is also a major university city with several institutions of higher education.

However, Palmerston North is best known as the home of the **»Massey University of Manawatu«**, which in 1928 grew out of an agricultural school named after the local farmer **William Ferguson Massey** (1856–1925). The leader of the Reform Party, Massey served as New Zealand 's prime minister between 1912 and 1925. The university 's major emphasis is agricultural sciences and it houses several **agricultural research institutes** for veterinary medicine, nutrition-

Agricultural research

Palmerston North

INFORMATION
Palmerston North
Visitor Centre
52 The Square
Tel. 06 350 1922
www.manawatunz.co.nz

WHERE TO STAY
Hacienda Motor Lodge
£££
27 Victoria Avenue
Tel. 06 357 3109
www.hacienda.co.nz
This motel personally run by Debbie and Stuart Suisted with comfortable guest rooms lies only a few minutes' walk from the town centre.

Arena Lodge **£££**
74 Pascal Street
Tel. 06 357 5577
www.arenalodge.co.nz
Opened only a few years ago, this establishment boasts suites whose furnishings border on the luxurious, and is popular with business travellers as much as with tourists.

Colonial Court Motel **£££**
305 – 307 Fitzherbert Avenue
Tel. 06 359 3888
www.colonialcourtmotel.co.nz
Friendly accommodation with functional rooms in the southern part of the town.

al science and biotechnology. Additional research is carried out into pasture and dairy farming, the quality standards of seeds produced in New Zealand, plus the rearing of bulls.

WHAT TO SEE IN PALMERSTON NORTH

The Square The busy heart of the town is »The Square«, an open area once measuring nearly 7ha/7.2 acres and previously cut in two by the railway, but now a park with fountain. This is also where the modern **Civic Centre** can be found. The **Square Edge** building, which used to house the municipal administration and city council, is today home to a **crafts centre**, artists studios, shops and galleries.

Museums In Main Street, the **Te Manawa Museum**, specialising in regional history, is worth visiting. Amongst many other things, the museum

In the Rotorua thermal region there are many places that steam and bubble, like in the Waimangu Valley where a small lake »boils«

displays impressive Maori cultural artefacts, as well as reminders of the early years of white settlement. The **Manawatu Art Gallery** concentrates on collecting and showing work by contemporary New Zealand artists. New Zealand's hard-hitting national sport is the subject of the **Rugby Museum** on Cuba Street.

> ● All museums: Main Street 326, daily 10am – 5pm, admission: NZ$ 12.50 (Rugby-Museum), the other museums are free of charge, www.rugbymuseum.co.nz

From Monro Hill, named after a British immigrant who settled here in 1870 and founded **New Zealand's first Rugby Club**, the view ranges across the Massey University campus (see above).

Monro Hill

This viewpoint on the southern outskirts (at the end of Cliff Road) gives a **nice view** of the town; on a clear day it is even possible to catch sight of the **volcanoes** Taranaki and Ruapehu.

ANZAC Park Viewpoint

AROUND PALMERSTON NORTH

About 20km/12.5 miles northwest of Palmerston North, the town of Feilding was founded in the 1870s as a **»Special Settlement«**. At the time, the »Emigrants & Colonists Aid Corporation«, led by Colonel William Feilding, purchased land for penniless immigrants and settled them here as labourers on small parcels of land. In 1874 the first 250 settlers arrived, razed the forest and established farms. Alongside sheep and cattle rearing, fruit and vegetables are also successfully grown here. Despite the relatively short distance from Palmerston North, Feilding has managed to preserve a character all of its own, including several buildings dating back to the late 19th century, including the **1904 Building**, which was built – not surprisingly – in 1904 and is on the monuments list. Feilding has been voted **New Zealand's most beautiful town** several times.

Feilding

? MARCO ●POLO INSIGHT   *Magic flute*

There is another Arawa legend surrounding Lake Rotorua and Mokoia Island in its centre. Hinemoa, a girl standing on the banks of the lake, was so enchanted by the island chief's flute playing that she managed to reach the island by swimming across the lake using empty pumpkins as swimming aids. Her parents had betrothed her to another and hidden all the canoes.

Stretching northeast of Palmerston North, the 936 sq km/361-sq mile Ruahine Forest Park is a **nature reserve famous for its unspoilt wildness**. Here, those in the know can still find numerous examples of the native New Zealand flora and fauna which has become rare

*Ruahine Forest Park

elsewhere. The few access roads lead to huts and picnic areas, which form the starting points for **hiking trails leading into the wilderness**. Driving from Palmerston North, the way to the reserve leads via Ashhurst through the Pohangina Valley.

*Manawatu Gorge

About 16km/10 miles northeast of Palmerston North (travelling in the direction of Woodville), Highway 3 leads to the **wild, romantic gorge** dug out by the Manawatu River. Dividing the Ruahine Range to the north from the Tararua Range to the south, this rugged gorge is a **mecca for jetboat enthusiasts and wildwater rafters**. The river is classified as being level II, that is middle difficulty. A bit further to the north the turbines of **Te Wapiti Wind Farm** can be seen; it is one of the largest windpower complexes in the country.

Norsewood

Situated around 20km/12.5 miles north of Dannevirke, the village of Norsewood (pop 300) grew out of a **lumberjack settlement** founded by Scandinavian immigrants which burnt down in 1888. Later, the »Norsewear« textile business was established here. Worth a visit is the **Pioneer Museum** in Upper Norsewood. West of Norsewood, look out for the Cistercian **Seven Star Abbey**.

Pioneer Museum: daily 8.30am – 4.30pm, admission: NZ$ 5

Waihi Falls

The picturesque **Waihi Falls** lie right in the middle of the jungle, some 40km/25 miles southeast of Dannevirke on the Horoeka road via Waipatiki.

** Rotorua

✦ Sg 129

Region: Bay of Plenty
Altitude: 297m/974ft – 757m/2,483ft
Population: **72**,000

Hot steam rises from cracks in the earth, geysers erupt in fountains, mud holes bubble away, and iridescent deposits shimmer in all colours on the hot soil. And hanging over it all is a strong smell of sulphur. Located south of the ►Bay of Plenty and dominated by volcanic features, the landscape around Lake Rotorua and Lake Tarawera is the most popular tourist destination in New Zealand.

Geysers, sinter terraces and thermal springs

As far back as the 19th century, European settlers would visit this downright **unearthly area** filled with curiosity, admiration and a frisson of fear. The Maori living here had adapted to their »hot« environment long ago, bathing in the thermal water, using it for heating

Rotorua

INFORMATION
Tourism Rotorua
1167 Fenton Street, Rotorua
Tel. 08 00 76 86 78
www.rotoruanz.com

WHERE TO EAT
Pig & Whistle Historic Pub £
Haupapa Street/Tutanekai Street
Tel. 07 3 47 30 25
www.pigandwhistle.co.nz
In the former police station you get Ki-
wi-style burgers, pizza, steaks and pasta.

Sabroso ££
1184 Haupapa Street
Tel. 07 3 49 05 91
www.sabroso.co.nz
Sabroso is Spanish for »tasty«, and that's
what the Latin American cooking in this
tiny restaurant is. The menu offers Mexi-
can and South American dishes and tapas

Rendezvous ££
1282 Hinemoa Street
Tel. 07 348 9273
This colonial-era building in the centre of
town provides a great setting for delicious fish dishes and grill specialities.

WHERE TO STAY   **Insider Tip**
Koura Lodge ££££
207–209 Kawaha Point Road

P.O. Box 1600
Rotorua
Tel. 07 3 48 58 68
www.kouralodge.co.nz
This comfortable lodge is a wonderful
place to relax, with its well-tended gardens on the western shore of Lake Rotorua, restaurant, beach, tennis and golf
nearby.

Princes Gate Hotel £££ – ££££
1057 Arawa Street
Tel. 07 348 1179
www.princesgate.co.nz
This traditional and time-honoured hotel
was built at the end of the 19th century
right at the entrance to the world-
famous Government Gardens. Each of
the rooms has its own individual style
and is furnished to high standards of
taste. Amenities include a restaurant,
bar, conference rooms, thermal pool and
sauna.

*Springwaters Lodge Bed and
Breakfast* ££ – £££
9 Te Waerenga Road
Hamurana
www.springwaterslodge.co.nz
Modern bed and breakfast with family
atmosphere near Lake Rotorua. The
owners are proud of the fact that the
place does not smell of sulphur!

and even for cooking. Later, they would prove indispensable as
guides for the white tourists. Highlights of **19th-century volcano
tourism** were the sinter terraces on **Lake Rotomahana** with their
pink-and-white glow, considered a **wonder of the world** at the
time.

The **legends of the Arawa** tribes provide their own explanation of
how the volcanic and thermal activities originated. Immediately after

Creation
myth

the landing of the ancestors' canoe, a Tohunga priest and his companion climbed the snow-covered summit of Tongariro, where they were in danger of freezing. So Tohunga asked the gods in their ancient homeland of Hawaiki to send him **warming fire**. The fire arrived – beneath the sea – and hit the surface of the earth for the first time at White Island, then at various points at Rotorua and Taupo, until it poured out of the summit of Tongariro, finally reaching the freezing Tohunga. Tohunga was saved, but his companion had already frozen to death.

ROTORUA (CITY)

A spa is born   During the **land wars**, local Arawa tribes were loyal allies of the government. They even stopped Maori groups from the ▶Bay of Plenty from marching through their area, when the latter tried to come to the aid of the Waikato tribes. In thanks, the **Duke of Edinburgh** visited in 1870 to offer a bust of his mother, Queen Victoria, which today still stands on the »marae« meeting place in **Ohinemutu**, the old Maori settlement on the southern banks of Lake Rotorua. At the time, the duke was welcomed by the Maori with a party and dances

A masterpiece of carving art: the attractive meeting house in Ohinemutu

and also enjoyed the **healing sulphurous waters** rising here, which were to become an enormous boost for **tourism**. Rotorua went on to become an extremely popular **spa**, in the manner of the elegant European spa towns of the time.

The Tarawera volcano erupted with little warning on 10 June 1886. However, an old Tohunga priest from the local Maori community had been warning of a **major disaster** for some time, while tourists accompanied by Maori had reported strange occurrences on Lake Tarawera, where they claimed to have seen a **ghost canoe**. When it happened, the northern summit of Mount Tarawera opened up, and a rift in the ground was created across a stretch of 20km/12.5 miles. The Maori village of Te Wairoa and other Maori settlements were buried under layers of lava and ash. Over 150 lives were lost, and the sinter terraces, the former **wonder of the world**, were no longer. The eruption did create new attractions however, particularly in **Waimangu Valley**.

The Tarawera erupts

WHAT TO SEE IN ROTORUA CITY

The charming gardens – **recreation park and sports facilities** in one – lie right next to the lake. The park is very well looked after, with flowering plants of many colours, and offers the chance not just to stroll, but also to play golf and cricket. The visual highlight of Government Gardens, as well as Rotorua's **world-famous landmark**, is the **MM Tudor Towers (bath house)**. Rotorua's timber-framed former bathing house was built in the 19th century and opened in 1908. Since the inauguration of new thermal baths, it has been used to house the extensive collections of the local **Rotorua Museum**, which has comprehensive information on the natural and cultural history of the area. The park also houses the municipal **art gallery**, which preserves wonderful Maori works of art, amongst other things.

*Government Gardens

❶ Daily 9am – 6pm, winter only until 5pm, admission: NZ$ 20, www.rotoruamuseum.co.nz

Erected in 1927, the **memorial** honouring the dead of World War I includes many Maori names and shows the manifold connections between the Maori and the white communities, like the Arawa ancestor canoe, the signing of the Waitangi Treaty, the English kings and the preaching missionary.

Te Arawa Soldiers' Memorial

Behind the Tudor Towers a modern **spa centre** has been set up, with the »Polynesian Baths« fed by three different healing springs as a special attraction. The perfume of orchids fills the air.

*Polynesian Pools

❶ Daily 8am – 11pm, admission: NZ$ 52, www.polynesianspa.co.nz

Rotarua

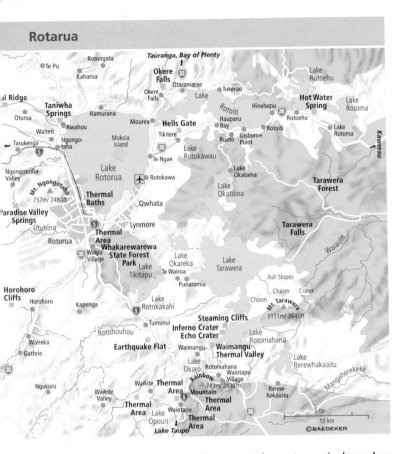

Te Pu
Rotongata
Tauranga, Bay of Plenty
Okere Falls
Lake Rotoehu
Kaharoa
Okere Falls
Otaramarae
Tokerau
ui Ridge
Taniwha Springs
Hamurana
Lake Rotoiti
Hinehopu
Hot Water Spring
Lake Rotoma
Oturoa
Awahou
Mourea
Hells Gate
Hauparu Bay
Rotoehu
Lake Rotoma
Waiteti
Ngongo-taha
Tikitere
Gisborne Point
Rotoiti
Tarukenga
Mokoia Island
Ruato
Ngongotaha Valley
Te Ngae
Lake Rotokawau
Lake Okataina
Kawerau
Mt. Ngongotaha
757m/2484ft
Lake Rotorua
Rotokawa
Lake Okataina
Tarawera Forest
Thermal Baths
Qwhata
aradise Valley Springs
Utuhina
Lynmore
Tarawera Falls
Waiaute
Thermal Rotorua
Thermal Area
Whakarewarewa State Forest Park
Waipa Village
Lake Tikitapu
Lake Okareka
Te Wairoa
Lake Tarawera
Horohoro Cliffs
Horohoro
Kapenga
Lake Rotokakahi
Punaromia
Ash Slopes
Chasm
Crater
Tumunui
Rotohouhou
Steaming Cliffs
Inferno Crater
Echo Crater
Mt. Tarawera
1111m/3645ft
Waireka
Guthrie
Earthquake Flat
Waimangu
Lake Rotomahana
Waimangu Thermal Valley
Lake Rerewhakaaitu
Ngakuru
Lake Okaro
Rotomahana
Waiotapu Village
Mangaherekeke
Waikite
Thermal Area
Rainbow Mountain
743m/2438ft
Rere-hakaaitu
Waikite Valley
Thermal Area
Thermal Area
Waiotapu
Lake Opouri
Thermal Area
Lake Taupo
5 mi
10 km
©BAEDEKER

Lake Rotorua Rotorua is a good base for romantic boat trips to the **legendary Mokoia Island** rising out of the centre of the lake.

*Ohinemutu Adjoining Rotorua's extensive Government Gardens to the north, look out for the **Maori village** of Ohinemutu. Between the houses and in the tiny gardens, steam can be seen rising everywhere here from the geothermically active ground. Ohinemutu was once the most important Maori settlement in the Rotorua area. On the **marae** (meeting place) a very skilfully carved canopy protects the bust of Queen Victoria brought over by her son, the Duke of Edinburgh, in 1870. A masterpiece of the art of carving is the Maori **meeting house** (see image p. 261), richly decorated both outside and in. Inside the Anglican **St Faith's Church**, erected in 1910 in the same neighbourhood, look out for beautiful carvings and weavings produced by the Maori. A stained-glass window shows Jesus as a Maori chief walking across Rotorua Lake. Next to the church, the last resting place of the dead are massive, whitewashed stone and concrete coffins protecting them from the hot earth. Amongst those buried here are the missionary **S. M. Spencer** (1810 – 1898) and **Captain Gilbert Mair** (1843 – 1923), who was a close friend of the Te Arawa and the only white person to be made **chief**, having defended Ohine-mutu against Hauhau raids and attacks by Te Kooti.

Rising northwest of the city, 757m/2,483-ft Mount Ngongotaha offers splendid views of the city and the lake. The **Skyline Gondola**, with its valley station located on Fairy Spring Road, is a popular way to ease the strain of getting up there. The mountain station has a **panoramic restaurant** as well as a small **amusement park** with a go kart track, flight simulator and further attractions.

Mount Ngongotaha

❶ Skyline Gondola: 9am until late evening, admission: NZ$ 27, www.skyline.co.nz/rotorua/

Stretching across the eastern slopes of the mountain, this nature park boasts idyllic walking trails under high tree ferns. The ponds and brooks support swarms of **rainbow trout**. There is also an exemplary animal enclosure laid out to provide the ideal conditions for different species. Local birds like the kea and tui can be seen here. One highlight is the **Kiwi Encounter** kiwi brooding station, where visitors can watch some of these flightless nocturnal birds foraging for food.

Rainbow Springs Nature Park

❶ Tours: daily 10am – 4pm, NZ$ 40, www.rainbowsprings.co.nz

At the northern foot of the mountain, in the village of Ngongotaha, **New Zealand sheep** of all breeds are daily shown to visitors of the Agrodome. New Zealand's masters of sheep shearing show their skills here, accompanied by some self-styled German shepherd trainers.

Agrodome

❶ Shows: daily 9.30am, 11am and 2.30pm, NZ$ 32.50, www.agrodome.co.nz

TE PUIA · WHAKAREWAREWA

The northern part of the hissing and bubbling geothermal field is accessible via the Maori village of **Whakarewarewa**. In Thermal Village see how the Maori live today. The southern part of the geothermal field is accessible via **Te Puia Maori Arts & Crafts Institute**. Here young Maoris are trained in the traditional crafts of carving and

* Thermal Village

weaving. As in Whakarewarewa dance and singing performances are held here as well. **Pohutu Geyser** is also accessible from here.

Thermal Village: daily 8.30am – 5pm, admission: NZ$ 35, www.whakarewarewa.com

Arts Institute: daily 8am – 6pm, admission: NZ$ 49.90

Whakare-warewa Forest Park	Covering about 3,800ha/9,390 acres, the forest lies southeast, adjacent to the geothermal field of Whakarewarewa. Hiking trails lead to the **Blue Lake** and **Green Lake**.

WAIMANGU VALLEY · LAKE TARAWERA

Volcanic landscape The Waimangu Valley, southeast of Whakarewarewa Forest, was completely altered by the eruption of the **Tarawera volcano in 1886. Old photos show the sinter terraces, described by Ferdinand von Hochstetter, that were no longer there after the eruption. The Maori settlements of **Te Waiora**, **Te Arihi** and **Moura** disappeared beneath a mass of lava and ash, with roads and bridges destroyed. Today, the volcanic phenomena in the Waimangu Valley can be visited as part of an organized trip (NZ$ 35). The tour also comprises a walk along the banks of **Lake Rotomahana**, past the **Waimangu Geyser**, which is currently inactive but whose fountain allegedly used to reach up to 400m/1,312ft. Other points of interest for visitors are the **Waimangu Cauldron**, a »boiling lake« some 4ha/nearly 10 acres in size, the **Cathedral Rocks** and **Warbrick Terrace**.

> ! **MARCO POLO TIP**
>
> *Waikite* **Insider Tip**
>
> Hidden a few miles south of Rotorua, west of Highway 5, the charming Waikite Thermal Valley is crossed by a »boiling« brook. The fantastic and very well equipped local campsite boasts a thermal pool and a restaurant.

At Lake Tarawera, protected by the 1,111m/3,608-ft **Mount Tarawera**, visitors can admire – at **Tarawera Landing** in particular – some highly impressive Maori **rock paintings**. A boat takes visitors across Lake Tarawera to the Maori village of **Te Wairoa**, which was buried under the debris, but has now been at least partially uncovered again. This buried Maori village at the southwestern edge of Lake Tarawera may also be visited independently. Fourteen kilometres/just under nine miles southeast of Rotorua there is a small **exhibition**, using revealing photographs and objects found beneath the lava to give an idea of what it once would have looked like here. One of the excavated Maori houses used to belong to the ancient **Tohunga priest** who had warned of a great misfortune. Also visible are the remains of a mill and a tourist hotel. Look out for the very old stone-built Maori **storage house** decorated with archaic figures.

WAIOTAPU

Roughly a 20-min drive south of Rotorua on Highway 5 leads to the geothermal field of **Waiotapu** with its numerous volcanic and post-volcanic sights. One of the main attractions is the Lady Knox Geyser (east of SH 5), which starts foaming and ejecting a **jet of water** at around 10.15am every day. However, knowing that these days this natural spectacle is induced by artificial aids possibly tarnishes the experience slightly. Detergent is channelled into the soil, and the sodium carbonate contained in the soap alters the surface tension of the highly pressured underground water; thus activated, the thermal water sprays through an opening high into the air.

*Lady Knox Geyser

> **? Did you know**
>
> MARCO ⊕ POLO INSIGHT
>
> ... that it was prisoners washing their clothes with soap in the stagnant thermal waters of the Lady Knox Geyser a few decades ago who unwittingly caused the geyser to erupt? Soap reduces the surface tension of water.

Shimmering in all the colours of the rainbow, the nearby **silica** terraces of the Artist's Palette pool are a reminder of the sinter terraces lost to the eruption of the Tarawera.

Artist's Palette

A short distance behind Artist's Palette and via a narrow walkway hot and heavily mineralised thermal water forms bubbles in the **Champagne Pool**, imitating the celebratory drink. At the same time this pond and neighbouring ones glow in many colours – yellow, green and blue – while the banks are coloured in bright orange. The bubbling hot spring was formed about 900 years ago. It has a diameter of about 60m/200ft, is also 60m/200ft deep and has a constant water temperature of 74°C/165°F. Water froths over from the circular, steam-shrouded cauldron onto **The Terraces**.

*Champagne Pool

The most recent attraction is the Wai-O-Tapu Geothermal Wonderland opened up south of the geothermal area (approx. 27km/just under 17 miles south of Rotorua), with its informative **Visitor Centre**. From the centre, hiking trails and boardwalks lead to some particularly **impressive natural wonders**, such as Rainbow Crater, Devil's Ink Pot, Opal Pool, Jean Batten Geyser, Frying Pan Flat, Oyster Pool and Sulphur Cave.

*Wai-O-Tapu Geothermal Wonderland

❶ Daily 8.30am–5pm, admission: NZ$ 35, www.waiotapu.co.nz

TIKITERE · HELL'S GATE THERMAL RESERVE

Situated in the northern Rotorua area, only a five-minute drive from the airport, **Tikitere** owes its nickname, **»Hell's Gate«**, to its strong-

»Hell's Gate«

Textbook volcano peak: Taranaki or Mount Egmont

ly sulphurous and therefore highly **malodorous springs** and boiling mud holes. There is a small geothermal field with bubbling mud springs, one hot water fall (**Kakahi Falls**) and various pools and ponds. At most times, **evil-smelling steam clouds** waft above the primeval forest-like vegetation. A small exhibition informs visitors about the vagaries of the local nature. In the new spa **Hell's Gate Wai Ora Spa**, visitors can lower themselves into New Zealand's largest whirlpool or take a restorative mud or sulphur bath.

❶ Daily 9am – 8.30pm, admission: NZ$ 20, www.hellsgate.co.nz

FURTHER PLACES TO VISIT AROUND ROTORUA

Lake Rotoiti   Situated northwest of Lake Rotorua, some 20km/12.5 miles from the city of Rotorua, Lake Rotoiti is a popular **destination** for day trips. There are several interesting carved Maori meeting houses around the lake. Another popular place to visit are the **Okere Falls** on the northwestern arm of Lake Rotoiti.

Hongi's Track   East of Lake Rotoiti, a large **forested area** stretches all the way to Lake Rotoehu, with »Hongi's Track« winding its way through it. During their **campaigns of conquest** in 1823, the warriors of Ngapuhi chief Hongi Hika hauled their warrior canoes overland from one lake to the other on this dirt track. Today, it has been turned into a beautiful 3km/1.8-mile hiking trail (walking time: just under 2 hrs there and back) through the bush. Along the way look out for a **sacred tree**, said by the Maori to have been planted some 400 years ago by a chief's wife named Hinehopu.

✳ Taranaki · Mount Egmont

✳ Sd–Se 130

Region: Taranaki
Altitude: 2,518m/8,261ft
❶ Stratford Information Centre, Prospero Place, Boradway, Stratford,
Tel. 08 00 76 56 70, www.stratford.govt.nz

The western region of North Island takes its name from the soaring, isolated volcanic cone of Taranaki (Mount Egmont). Shrouded in legend, the high mountain attracts the rain clouds of the Tasman Sea like a magnet, causing numerous watercourses to run down its slopes.

As early as the 19th century the summit area was declared a **nature reserve**, meaning that forest clearance and agricultural use were prohibited above a certain altitude. However, large swathes of virginal forest were cut down on the lower slopes. Today, lush green pastures for dairy cattle unfold here. The Taranaki region ranks among the **most densely populated areas of New Zealand**. The capital and administrative seat of the district is ▶Stratford.

Densely populated

The economic centre and largest city of the Taranaki region is ▶New Plymouth, situated on the coast north of the old volcano. In the 19th century, land seizures by white settlers led to severe conflicts with the local Maori, which escalated from 1860 onwards into the Taranaki land wars. Whilst **oil** was found near New Plymouth as far back as the 19th century, more economically relevant were the **natural gas fields** off the Taranaki coast at Maui and at Kapuni, south of the volcanic mountain.

Petroleum and natural gas

The centre of the 33,534ha/82,864-acre nature reserve is formed by the almost symmetrical **Taranaki** volcano, whose highest summit rises up to 2,518m/8,261ft. Thanks to its perfect conical shape, this volcano is often compared to Japan's Fujiyama. Today, the Maori name of »Taranaki« for the impressive volcano has prevailed over »Mount Egmont«, the name chosen by Cook to honour the former Lord of the Admiralty. Only the national park itself still bears the name of the admiral. The fully protected zone of the mountain, comprising the main summit and the northern secondary summits of

＊＊Egmont National Park

MARCO ⊕ POLO INSIGHT

?

Holy peak

The Maori thought that Taranaki was a mountain god, which is why they never climbed above the snow line. When the peak is hidden in clouds, Maori mythology says, Taranaki is crying for his lost love the volcano woman Pihanga.

Pouakai (1,400m/4,593ft) and Patuha (684m/2,244ft), still preserves the **primeval forest and bush vegetation**. Whilst in summer, whole flocks of hikers conquer the summit (starting from the mountain stations, it is possible to go up and down in a day), **skiers** throng the slopes of the Taranaki in winter. At an altitude of about 900m/2,952ft, **mountain houses** have been set up for visitors to drive to and spend the night. Including both ascent and descent, a summit tour takes approx. 10 hours.

Curtis Falls, Dawson Falls Signposted hiking trails lead to the **impressive cascades** of the Curtis Falls and Dawson Falls. The latter has a well-run **lodge**, with hiking paths to Lake Dive and Stratford Mountain House.

North Egmont Some 25km/15.5 miles south of ▶New Plymouth, North Egmont lies at an altitude of 936m/3,070ft. The local visitor centre has comprehensive information on the national park. **Charming hiking trails** lead to **Holly Hut** and the **Bells Falls**.

Kori Pa Lying a little way inland, south of the village of Oakura, the old Maori settlement Kori Pa had a **fortification high above the river** that was hard to conquer. The settlement was only abandoned after 1820, when the local Taranaki tribes were fleeing from the Waikato tribes and their firearms.

Puniho Some 30km/18.5 miles southwest of ▶New Plymouth, in the village of Puniho, visitors can find the **rock** said in Maori mythology to have led the Taranaki volcano during its flight from the central plateau. **Sacred** to the Maori, for certain festivities the rock was dressed in a chief's attire. **Touching the rock could have fatal consequences**, so 70 enemy warriors who had taken it away with them are said to have died the very same day. The rock is said to have then returned to its old position by itself. The appearance of the white man on the scene has dramatically diminished the rock's magic powers, so that these days it can be touched with impunity.

!

MARCO ⊕ POLO TIP

Anglers' Paradise **Insider Tip**

The best fishing spots on the lake shore can be found at the mouth of the Waitahanui River (approx. 15km/9 miles south of Taupo on Highway 1) and in Hatepe (approx. 10km/6 miles further south, also on Highway 1). Here, anglers can sometimes be seen standing next to each other in long rows hoping to catch trout and other fish. The fishing season lasts all year round.

Some 3km/1.8 miles uphill (from Pungarehu) the two Maori leaders **Parihaka** Te Whiti and Tohu established a village. From 1866, the inhabitants of the village practised **passive resistance and civil disobedience** against white rule. In 1881 the two leaders were arrested and kept prisoner for nearly two years without trial, while their village was razed. The conflict between the Maori and the white settlers were only resolved in 1926, when the New Zealand government agreed to reparation payments. Today, the village is a **centre of the Maori Renaissance**, also boasting the **tomb** of their leader Te Whiti.

Short walks lead to Dawson Falls in Egmont National Park

Oaonui Around 50km/31 miles southwest of ▶New Plymouth, Oaonui provides the logistical base for the two offshore platforms belonging to the »Maui« gas field. The visitor centre has information on **gas extraction in the shelf zone**. A high-pressure pipeline transports gas all the way to Auckland.

Manaia Forming the centre of an area dominated by agriculture, the village of Manaia (pop 1,000) lies 90km/56 miles south of ▶New Plymouth. The two **blockhouses** on the golf course were erected in 1880 to serve as protection against the assaults of Te Whiti.
In 1868, 12km/7.5 miles northeast of Manaia a bloody skirmish took place between Maori warriors and British soldiers. The latter were led into an ambush by Maori leader Titokowaru and annihilated.

Kapuni North of Manaia, visitors may see the Kapuni **natural gas fields** being exploited, as evidenced by flames from excess gas being burnt off, pipelines and a fertiliser plant.

Stratford Situated on the southeastern slope of Taranaki, the **market town** of **Stratford** (pop 6,000) was founded in 1877 on an old Maori trail. Initially, the processing of wood from forest clearances played an important role. Originally the small town was called Stratford-on-Patea reminiscent of **William Shakespeare's** birthplace Stratford-upon-Avon. Many of the streets are named after figures from the great playwright's dramas. Stratford's **glockenspiel** – New Zealand's first – shows three Romeos and three Julias at 10am, 1pm and 3pm.

Today, Stratford is a **base for mountain tours** around the Taranaki, which every summer regularly becomes New Zealand's most frequently climbed mountain (access for drivers is via Pembroke to the Stratford Mountain House). Completed in 1976, Stratford's power plant works with natural gas from the nearby Kapuni field. The town is also the starting point of the »Forgotten World Highway« SH 43, New Zealand's first so-called Heritage Highway. It runs for more than 155km/90mi through remote areas, over four mountains and along a river to Taumarunui.

Manukorihi Pa The fortified **Maori village** of Manukorihi Pa is worth seeing, with its beautiful **meeting house** erected in 1936 in honour of influential Maori politician Maui Wiremu Pomare.

The model village Taranaki Pioneer Village with around 50 completely furnished buildings south of Stratford shows how hard life was in the good old times of New Zealand's first settlers.

Taranaki Pioneer Village

❶ daily 10am – 4pm, admission: NZ$ 12, www.pioneervillage.co.nz

** Taupo · Wairakei

✦ Sg 129

Region: Waikato
Altitude: 370m/1,214ft – 1,088m/3,569ft
Population: (region) 380,000

Situated at the heart of North Island and spanning over 600 sq km/230 sq miles, Lake Taupo forms New Zealand's largest inland body of water. Its depths hide not one but several volcanic craters. The seclusion and peace around it give few clues as to the raging inferno that would have reigned in the area at the time of its creation.

Imposing Maori witnesses: rock carvings at Lake Taupo

Formation Following some 300,000 years of relative calm, in the second century AD this area saw a whole series of the most violent volcanic eruptions, releasing enormous quantities of volcanic ash and pumice over a huge surface area. After the **collapse of the empty crater** a massive caldera formed, but the accumulations of debris stopped the water collecting here from draining: Lake Taupo was formed. The last major **volcanic eruption** in the area of today's Lake Taupo happened at a time when New Zealand was probably only sparsely populated, if at all. However, the **atmospheric fallout** from this major eruption was observed in faraway parts of the world, as evidenced by records from ancient China and the Roman Empire. And the **mighty layers of pumice and ash** that can be seen today are an **impressive testimony to this natural disaster**. Rivers flow into Lake Taupo from nearly all points of the compass, the largest among them being the **Tongariro**, which runs into the lake through a delta at Turangi in the south. The water-rich **Waikato River** also emerges from the lake near the town of Turangi.

Settlement Due to the plentiful fish and birdlife, the Maori settled fairly early on the shores of Lake Taupo. However, they feared the water because of the **monsters** said to be living in it. In 1839 the first white missionaries arrived in the area, but immigrants from Europe initially had little interest in the seemingly barren landscape around the lake. In 1869, well-armed police forces were stationed here to counter Te Kooti's guerrilla warriors. Around this time the healing powers of the local **thermal waters** were also discovered and the first **bathhouses** erected. One man who was swept away by the charms of Lake Taupo and its surroundings was the natural scientist **Ernst Dieffenbach**, who in 1841 was commissioned by London's New Zealand Company to explore this area. However, it was to be a few more years before roads started to be built here.

Boat trips Crossing Lake Taupo, an armada of steam boats, motorboats and sailing boats start out from all the larger tourist places. Many boat trips lead to the **spectacular Karangahape Cliffs** or to the masks engraved into the layered rock some time ago by young Maori artists. Trips for all tastes are on offer – ranging from basic options to stylish motor yachts.

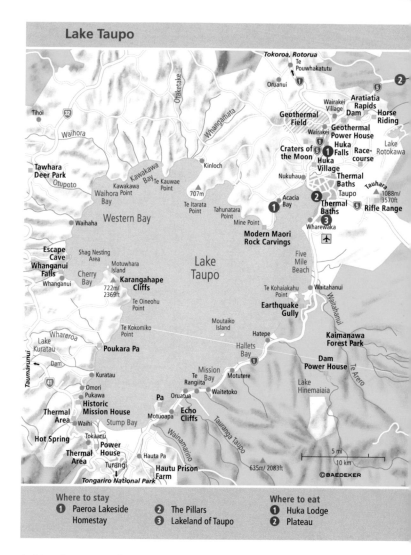

Lake Taupo

Tokoroa, Rotorua
Te Pouwhakatutu
Oruanui
Wairakei Village
Geothermal Field
Aratiatia Rapids
Wairakei Dam
Horse Riding
Geothermal Power House
Wairakei
Craters of the Moon
Huka Falls
Race-course
Lake Rotokawa
Huka Village
Thermal Baths
Tihoi
Waihora
Tawhara Deer Park
Otupoto
Kawakawa Point
Waihora Bay
Te Kauwae Point
Kinloch
Nukuhau
Taupo
Tauhara 1088m/3570ft
Thermal Baths
Rifle Range
Te Itarata Point
707m
Tahunatara Point
Acacia Bay
Thermal Baths
Western Bay
Waihaha
Mine Point
Wharewaka
Modern Maori Rock Carvings
Escape Cave
Shag Nesting Area
Motuwhara Island
Five Mile Beach
Whanganui Falls
Cherry Bay
Karangahape Cliffs
722m/2369ft
Lake Taupo
Whanganui
Te Oineohu Point
Te Kohaiakahu Point
Waitahanui
Moutaiko Island
Earthquake Gully
Te Kokomiko Point
Hatepe
Whareroa
Lake Kuratau
Poukara Pa
Hallets Bay
Kaimanawa Forest Park
Dam
Dam Power House
Waiahanui
Kuratau
Mission Bay
Motutere
Te Areto
Omori
Te Rangiita
Lake Hinemaiaia
Pukawa
Historic Mission House
Pa
Oruatua
Waitetoko
Thermal Area
Waihi
Motuoapa
Echo Cliffs
Stump Bay
Tokaanu
Hot Spring
Power House
Thermal Area
Hauta Pa
Turangi
Hautu Prison Farm
Tongariro National Park
635m/2083ft
5 mi
10 km
©BAEDEKER

Where to stay
1 Paeroa Lakeside Homestay
2 The Pillars
3 Lakeland of Taupo

Where to eat
1 Huka Lodge
2 Plateau

A drive of approx. 150km/93 miles leads around Lake Taupo. To the east and south the road nearly always hugs the lake, giving many **fine views** along the way. A number of holiday homes also lie along the road, most of them right on the lakeshore. Past Waihi, drivers have to navigate around the mountains which reach down to the lake.

Around the lake by car

Taupo · Wairakei

INFORMATION
Taupo Visitor Centre
Tongariro Street, Taupo
Tel. 07 376 0027
www.laketaupo.com

WHERE TO EAT
❶ *Huka Lodge* **££££**
Huka Falls Road
Tel. 07 378 5791
Wonderful multi-course menus with creations by an ambitious team dedicated to Pacific cuisine

❷ *Plateau* **££** Insider Tip
64 Tuwharetoa St, Taupo
Tel. 073 77 24 25
Here you can taste New Zealand: typical local specialities are served here along with seven different New Zealand beers on tap. The music is by New Zealand artists and the restaurant furniture is made form local materials.

WHERE TO STAY
❶ *Paeroa Lakeside Homestay* **££££**
21 Te Kopua Street, Acacia Bay
Tel. 07 378 8449

www.taupohomestay.com
Situated in a beautiful location on the western lake shore with fantastic views, this relaxed accommodation offers everything for a proper New Zealand dream holiday: bathing, sailing, fishing, and a dramatic volcanic landscape to explore.

❷ *The Pillars* **££££**
7 Deborah Rise Bonshaw Park
Tel. 07 378 1512
www.pillarshomestay.co.nz
Some ten minutes north of Lake Taupo near Highway 5 (in the direction of Napier), a modern, Mediterranean-style guesthouse promises a relaxing stay. The rooms are very spacious and have all modern conveniences, complemented by a pool and tennis court.

❸ *Lakeland of Taupo*
Lake Taupo
Tel. 07 378 3893
www.lakeland.co.nz
Holiday hotel offering good views, modern furnished rooms, restaurant and bar, conference rooms, swimming pool and tennis

TAUPO

Vibrant holiday resort

Lying on the northeastern shores of the lake, Taupo has around 25,000 inhabitants. Tourism has been an important factor from the beginning, alongside forestry and the use of geothermal energy. Today, Taupo is a **popular holiday resort** with numerous accommodation options (hotels, motels, motor camps, etc.), some of them with their **own thermal swimming pools**. Spreading out right along the lake, which is very popular among sailors and anglers, is the modern if slightly soulless town centre, which does at least afford **magnificent views**. The finely carved **Maori gateway** is worth seeing, while at night the contours of a huge artificial trout are enhanced by countless lightbulbs. A protective wall and the old **courthouse (1881)** are a reminder of the time of the settlement's foundation by the security forces.

Taupo's main draw are its thermal baths. This is true in particular for **De Brett's Spa Resort**, with its comfortably equipped spa and pampering facilities. The **A. C. Baths** on Spa Road started life as the bath houses once used by the members of the »A(rmed) C(onstabulary)« to recuperate from their demanding missions

*Thermal baths

A.C. Baths: daily 6am – 9pm, admission: NZ$ 10, www.greatlaketaupo.com

Starting at Taupo, this hiking trail leads along the Waikato River to the **Huka Falls** (4km/2.5 miles), where the river plunges into the deep for 10m/33ft after several cascades, and further on to the **Aratiatia Rapids** (11km/just under 7 miles). Beautiful vistas open up along the way. From the mouth of the Huka Falls, Loop Road leads to the **Taupo Lookout**, situated at the local radio station. From here, there is an excellent view of the town and lake stretching all the way to the mountains beyond. **Waikato River Lookout**, often also called »Hell's Gate«, is best accessed from Spa Road. The view down to the river is across **steaming rock cliffs**.

*Taupo Walkway

WAIRAKEI

A particular attraction is Wairakei's geothermal field, lying just under 10km/6.2 miles north of the town of Taupo and easily accessible to tourists with their own transport as **»Wairakei Park«**. The circular drive might only be around 40km/25 miles long, but due to the **wealth of sights**, drivers should allow a whole day for it. Heading north on Highway 1, directly past Taupo the Huka Falls Loop Road turns off east. At **Huka Falls**, the swollen Waikato River thunders across an 11m/36-ft rock ledge. More than 220,000 litres (58,000 gal.) of water are carried over every second. A little further on, drivers reach the **Volcanic Activity Centre**, where they can learn interactively about the Taupo Volcano Zone and find out what an earthquake feels like in an earthquake simulator.

*Geothermal Field

The Volcanic Activity Centre has taken over the function of observation station of the New Zealand Institute of Geological & Nuclear Sciences. It shares comprehensive information on New Zealand's **volcanic past and present**, explaining both the various manifestations of volcanic and geothermal activity and the state of geo-scientific research. There is also information on how **volcanic activity is monitored**.

❶ Mon – Fri 10am – 5pm, Sat, Sun 10am – 4pm, admission: NZ$ 12, www.volcanoes.co.nz/Volcanic-Activity-Centre

Wairaki region is a natural heating plant. Steam rising from the ground here is channelled to power plant turbines.

*Geothermal-Power Project

The **geothermal power station**'s visitor centre explains how the steam coming out of the earth is converted into energy. The educational video gives basic explanations on the construction and operation of Wairakei's geothermal power station.

❶ daily 9am – 12pm and 1pm – 4pm, www.nzgeothermal.org.nz

Thermal Valley Lookout

Armed with the necessary background knowledge, visitors can then drive through the »**ordered chaos**« of hissing steam pipes and tubes to the viewing platform. The Wairakei Thermal Valley offers a few **post-volcanic phenomena**, including a small geyser, hot waterfall, bubbling mud pools and multicoloured deposits.

Aratiatia Dam

A good 5km/3.1 miles north of Wairakei lies the Aratiatia Dam and the first of a whole **string of hydraulic power stations** lining the Waikato River. Because of the amount of water being taken out by the power station, the Aratiatia Rapids run dry most of the time, but twice daily water is allowed to rush through the former river bed.

❶ Demonstration: daily 10am, 12pm, 2pm, summer also 4pm, www.greatlaketaupo.com

The **»Craters of the Moon«** can be found south of Wairakei. They were formed in the 1950s when a geothermal power plant lowered the ground water level. Here too there is a lot of steaming, hissing and bubbling, accompanied by a frequent strong smell of rotten eggs. A word of warning: for safety reasons visitors must not leave the marked trails that lead to the various observation points.

Craters of the Moon

The **»Hidden Valley«** is secreted away some 30km/18.5 miles from Taupo and only accessible via a side road from Highway 1 (or 5). Here too there is a **geothermal field**, accessible **only by boat** via the Waikato River. Whilst a part of the area is flooded by the dammed Waikato, a **circular hike** allows geysers, sinter terraces, mud pots and hot springs to be explored. Particularly impressive are the sinter terraces that have been given the evocative epithet of **»The Great Golden Fleece«**.

*Orakei Korako (Hidden Valley)

❶ Boat departures: daily 8am – 4.30pm, from NZ$ 40, www.orakeikorako.co.nz

TURANGI

Lying at the southern end of Lake Taupo, **Turangi** (pop 3,000) has seen rapid development since 1964, when work began on the »Tongariro Hydro-Electric Power Scheme«, but has since begun to shrink again. Loggers, construction workers and engineers have settled here, and tourism has brought affluence to the place. Turangi not only serves as the **starting point for explorations** of the area around Lake Taupo, but also for tours into ▶Tongariro National Park.

From workers' settlement to tourist town

Driving from Turangi on to Tokaanu, the cables for the Tongariro Hydro-Electric Power Scheme are visible on the hillside. This project serves to connect the watercourses of the Whanganui, the Tongariro and other rivers by **canals and tunnels**. Before the water flows into **Lake Taupo**, it is used to drive the turbines of a hydraulic power station.

Tongariro Hydro-Electric Power Scheme

Turangi is dominated by 1,325m/4,347-ft Pihanga. The Pihanga Saddle Road Viewpoint commands a **wonderful view** of **Lake Taupo**, which is valued by angles for its rich supply of trout. Hiding not far from here is **idyllic Lake Rotopounamu**.

Pihanga

Situated 5km/just over 3 miles west of Turangi, the township of Tokaanu owes its fame to the local curative thermal springs, the **Tokaanu Thermal Pools**. The beautiful complex consists of open-air public thermal baths with steaming pools and the even hotter, partly enclosed and chlorine-free private pools.

Tokaanu

In the Anglican **St Paul's Church**, look out for the furnishings made by Maori craftspeople.

Waihi   In a very idyllic if dangerous location, the **Maori settlement** of **Waihi**, northwest of Turangi, has already been the victim of several rubble and mud avalanches. In 1846 many inhabitants lost their lives when the village was buried under tonnes of debris. Unfortunately tourists are not welcome here, as they may read on a sign at the entrance to the village.

Dating from 1889 and furnished in the best Maori traditions, the **church** and the **meeting house** decorated with impressive Maori carvings are only accessible to visitors who have obtained special authorization. Outside the village, the **Waihi Falls** roar over a steep 90m/295-ft precipice.

> **?** MARCO⊛POLO INSIGHT
>
> *Female volcano*
>
> Pihanga is the only »female« volcano in Maori mythology. Understandably »she« had all the more fervent admirers in the shape of her »male« counterparts Tongariro, Ruapehu, Taranaki, etc.

✶ Tauranga

✦ Sg 128

Region: Bay of Plenty
Altitude: 0 – 252m/826ft
Population: 121,000

Thanks to its sheltered position behind Mount Maunganui and the offshore Matakana Island, in addition to its rich supply of wood from the interior, Tauranga has become one of the most important ports of North Island. In recent times, the port town has also become a popular holiday and retirement resort, primarily due to the quiet beaches nearby and the rich fishing grounds of the Bay of Plenty. In early Ocotober 2011 the container ship Rena ran aground on a reef 20km/12mi before Tauranga port in the Bay of Plenty. This led to the worst environmental disaster in the history of New Zealand so far ▶Bay of Plenty.

*»The Elms«   »The Elms« mission **with its chapel and a small library in the garden** has been preserved almost unchanged since its foundation in 1838. The old trees – two Norfolk pines and an English oak – have grown enormous by now.

❶ Tours: daily 2pm and 4pm, NZ$ 8, www.theelms.org.nz

In the southern part of the city (17th Ave West) about 90 **buildings from pioneer times** were reconstructed. In the 50 shops and businesses that opened here you can buy souvenirs or watch craftsmen at work.

Historical Village on 17th

❶ Daily about 10am – 4pm, free admission, www.villageon17.co.nz

This **1864 fortification** with earthworks and cannons, named after the Monmouth Light Infantry that were stationed here, may be reached from the northern end of the beach. The handsome **Maori war canoe**, carved in 1970, is a real eyecatcher here. The fort was also the beginning of the later town of Tauranga.

Monmouth Redoubt

Just a few miles from Tauranga and nowadays **easily accessible via the new harbour bridge**, the independent port town of Mount Maunganui (pop 12,000) lies on the other side of the natural harbour, which here boasts state-of-the-art transport facilities. In summertime, the town at the foot of Mount Maunganui, rising up steeply 252m/826ft from the sea, is a **popular day trip destination.** Surfers love the artificial reef that was constructed there in order to guarantee regular waves. Accessible via hiking trails, **Mount Maunganui** once supported a Maori fortification.

Mount Maunganui

Several bathing beaches can be found at the foot of Mount Maunganui, such as **Ocean Beach** and **Papamoa Beach**. Furthermore, there are a number of **springs** in the surrounding area that release thermal water.

Bathing beaches, thermal springs

Contrasts: deep sea port in front of Mount Maunganui

Tauranga

INFORMATION
Tauranga Visitor Centre
95 Willow Street, Tauranga
Tel. 07 578 8103
www.tauranga.govt.nz

WHERE TO EAT
Somerset Cottage £££
30 Bethlehem Road,
Tauranga
Tel. 07 5 76 68 89
www.somersetcottage.co.nz
Somerset Cottage is one of the city's
best restaurants, if not the island's. The
excellent food is served in an elegant
ambience. Outstanding wines from New
Zealand are served with it.

WHERE TO STAY
Belle Mer £££ – ££££
53 Marine Parade Mount Maunganui
Tel. 07 575 0011
www.bellemer.co.nz
Luxurious holiday complex right on the
beach with splendid sea views plus a
beautiful swimming pool and a wonderful spa facility

Bay Palm Motel ££ – £££
84 Girven Rd., Mt. Manganui
Tel. 07 574 5972 Fax 07 574 5972
www.baypalmmotel.co.nz
New, exceedingly comfortable and
barrier-free beach accommodation.
With swimming pool, spa and golf

Mayor Island A **pleasure boat trip** takes visitors to this island of volcanic origin,
which rises to a height of 387m/1,269ft some 35km/22 miles north of
Tauranga from the northwestern ▶Bay of Plenty. The **two volcanic
crater lakes** are well preserved, and here too the Maori once had a
fort, a few remains of which can still be seen.

The waters around Mayor Island are renowned as **rich fishing**
grounds. Every year in late summer and autumn, major **deep-sea
angling** competitions are held here.

** Te Kuiti · Waitomo Caves
Sf 129

Region: Waikato
Altitude: 140m/459ft
Population: 4000
❶ Waitomo Visitor Information Centre, 21 Caves Road,
Waitomo Caves, Tel. 07 8 78 76 40, www.waitomocaves.com,
www.waitomo-museum.co.nz

Te Kuiti is the sheep shearing capital of the world – the annual
national championships take place here every year – and the
centre of King Country, dominated by the agricultural and forestry sectors.

In the aftermath of the **Battle of Orakau**, the followers of the Maori king fled to Waitomo. For 17 years the king was to live here undisturbed, as white settlers did not dare set foot into King Country. In 1872, the Maori leader Te Kooti also looked for shelter here, after his actions in the east had been unsuccessful. In 1887, when the railway line from Wellington to Auckland was built, a construction workers camp grew up here.

Shelter

WHAT TO SEE IN AND AROUND TE KUITI

The pride and joy of the village is a beautiful **Maori meeting house**, erected in 1878 for the Maori leader Te Kooti. After being pardoned in 1883, out of **gratitude** he presented the house as a gift to the tribe that had taken him in.

Maori meeting house

Some 20km/12.5 miles northwest of Te Kuiti, don't miss the extensive **karst cave system** of the Waitomo Caves. Famous for their bizarre stalagmite, stalactite and sinter formations, the **subterranean cavities** attract scores of tourists, particularly in the high summer season. The visitor centre has information on the origins and unique features of the caves. Traversed by a stream and fully explored for the first time in 1887, the main cave offers a particular attraction: so-called glow worms. In truth, these »**glow worms**« are actually **insect larvae**, which can only survive in high levels of humidity and use their long, sticky, glowing filaments to lure their prey. From a boat in the darkness of the cave, visitors can make out the myriad tiny beads of light hanging down from the cave ceiling – just like an **overhanging firmament of night stars**. Lying 2km/1.2 miles from the main Waitomo cave, **M Aranui Cave** was discovered by a Maori in 1911. This dry subterranean passage may not have any glow worms, but it does have pretty stalactites and stalagmites as well as sinter formations. Next to Aranui Cave is the so-called »Cave of the Dogs«, **MRuakuri Cave**, the largest of the Waitomo caves. This one also has a stream running through it and boasts a colony of glow worms.

**Waitomo Caves

MARCO POLO TIP

! *Abseiling* Insider Tip

A special thrill for adrenaline junkies: abseiling and blackwater rafting through the wild Ruakuri Cave. Visitors booking such a tour can expect to abseil down to the cave floor, be swept along the cave stream on a dinghy and to clamber across various obstacles, with whole galaxies of glow worms along the way. Information: Black Water Rafting, Waitomo Caves, tel. (07) 878 - 62 19

Waitomo main cave: tours daily 9am – 5pm, summer until 5.30pm, NZ$ 49, www.waitomo.com

Aranui Cave: tours daily 9am – 4pm, NZ$ 49, www.waitomo.com

Waitomo Walkway Starting at the car park in front of the main cave, this **fascinating trail** leads through forest and limestone formations past the steep gorge of the Waitomo stream to the ancient cave fragment preserved as **Ruakiri Natural Bridge** (walking time: approx. 4 hrs).

*Ohaki Village Weaving Centre The route from Te Kuiti to the caves leads past a **reconstructed Maori village**, looking much as it would have before the arrival of the Europeans. Here, visitors can watch the skilled New Zealand indigenous inhabitants in action (weaving, in particular) and purchase a souvenir or two.

Just under 20km/12.5 miles north of Te Kuiti, in the village of **Otorohanga** (pop 2,500) the main attractions are a **bird park with kiwi night house** and a few aviaries with native birds.

❶ Daily 9am – 4.30pm, winter until 4pm, tours from NZ$ 40

Aranui Cave fascinates visitors with its dripstone and sinter formations

Extending approx. 60km/37 miles southeast of Te Kuiti, **Pureora Forest Park** is famous for its unusually **diverse bird life** and is reasonably accessible through hiking trails. The pumice soils here formed after the last eruption of the Taupo volcano some 1,900 years ago.

Pureora Forest Park

Te Urewera National Park
─────────────────── ✳ G–Sh 129

▶Urewera National Park

✶✶ Tongariro National Park
─────────────────── ✳ Sf 130

Region: Manawatu-Wanganui
Surface area: 79,598 ha/196,690 acres
Altitude: 500m/1,640ft – 2,797m/9,276ft

A listed UNESCO World Heritage site, the most impressive feature of this national park are its scenic contrasts. The summit plateau resembles a bizarre lunar landscape. Bare lava fields, rocky precipices and areas covered in brown tussock grass alternate with mountains and rainforests.

Tongariro National Park extends across the heart of North Island. By car, coming from the north take Hwy 47 from Lake Taupo via Turangi to National Park and carry on using Highways 4 and 49 to Ohakune and Waiouru. Highway 1, the infamous **»Desert Road«**, takes drivers back to Turangi. This round trip is approx. 180km/112 miles long (not counting detours and side trips). Scheduled buses run from Turangi to National Park, Ohakune and Waiouru. The nearest railway stations are Waiouru, Ohakune and National Park.

How to get there

The national park is an excellent year-round destination. The **skiing season** on Ruapehu normally lasts from June to October. As the weather in the national park is very changeable and can switch rapidly, make sure to take **rain protection and warm clothes** on longer excursions. Solid footwear is important, particularly above the snow line, and good maps are absolutely essential, as there are long stretches that are not adequately marked. **Provisions** (especially enough liquids) should be taken too, and remember to boil water taken from wild sources in order to kill off any parasites.

When to go, special tips

The centre of the national park is formed by three volcanoes: **Tongariro** (1,968m/6,456ft), **Ngauruhoe** (2,291m/7,516ft) and **Ruape-**

✶✶Volcanic landscape

Tongariro National Park

INFORMATION
Department of Conservation, Whakapapa Visitor Centre
Whakapapa Village
State Highway 48, Mt Ruapehu
Tel. 07 8 92 37 29
www.doc.govt.nz

WHERE TO EAT
❶ *The Grand Chateau* £££ – ££££
Highway 48
Private Bag, Mount Ruapehu
Tel. 07 892 3809
www.chateau.co.nz
In the famous hotel's »Ruapehu Room«, delicious game and lamb specialities are served up in style.

WHERE TO STAY
9 km/5.5 miles from where Bruce Road forks off Highway 47 (Turangi – Tongariro National Park), at the halfway point, the »Château Tongariro« luxury hotel was built in 1929. Apart from this hotel there are further guesthouses and simpler accommodation in Whakapapa,

Turangi, Ohakune, Waiouru, as well as at the National Park railway station. The entire national park has only a few huts with sleeping bag accommodation. The skiing huts at Iwikau and Tukino are unfortunately reserved for ski club members only.

❶ *The Grand Chateau* ££££
Highway 48
Private Bag, Mount Ruapehu
Tel. 07 892 3809
www.chateau.co.nz
This comfortable mountain hotel has been around since 1929; today, apart from mountaineers, it largely attracts passionate skiers.

❷ *Powderhorn Chateau* £££
Bottom of Mountain Road
PO Box 222, Ohakune
Tel. 06 385 8888
www.powderhorn.co.nz
Built of wood, this rustic mountain hotel offers truly snug rooms.

hu (2,797m/9,176ft). These belong to a whole chain of volcanoes that can be traced northwards beyond the volcanic White Island (▶Bay of Plenty) to the **Kermadec Islands and Tonga**. Fairly recent in geological terms, New Zealand's volcanoes have erupted time and again over the centuries, as shown by Maori legends and traditions, plus observations made since the European settlement. However, catastrophic damage has been rare. The worst consequences followed the **overflowing of a crater lake** on the Ruapehu summit over the Christmas period of 1953, when the descending mud and water plunged into the railway bridge at Tangiwai. The bridge collapsed, derailing the Wellington – Auckland express train and killing 151 people. Covered in snow all year round, the summit of Ruapehu last showed strong **volcanic activity** in 1995 and 1996, when it spat out large amounts of rock and lava, and mud streams poured down its slopes. **Tongariro**, jutting up in the north of the national park, is the lowest of the three volcanoes. Its summit is already split into several craters. On the slopes at Ketetahi visitors come across an **active geothermal field** with hot springs, steaming fumaroles and boiling mud pots. One volcano which is almost constantly active is the composite volcano **Ngauruhoe** (2291m/7560ft high), which can often be seen blowing smoke and steam skywards. A whole series of smaller eruptions since 1954 has changed the appearance of the mountain, particularly towards the west.

The Maori both feared and revered the smoking mountain summits, which to them were invested with a sacred force, »tapu«. The volcanoes entered many **legends and traditions**. Thus, the subterranean fire was said to have been created after the children of the gods had forcibly separated their parents, Papa (Mother Earth) and Rangi (Father Sky). They decided to turn Mother Earth in such a way as to stop the floods of tears and laments. However, the youngest of her children, Ruaumoko, was still nursing at her mother's breast and so was also turned, lying under her. In order to get warm he received the subterranean fire, becoming the god of volcanoes and earthquakes. In the traditions of the Taupo and Rotorua tribes, their ancestor **Ngatoro**, leader of the Arawea tribal canoe, marched inland after landing on the coast of the Bay of Plenty, in order to take possession of the land. Deciding to climb the Tongariro mountain with a female slave, he asked his followers to fast until he returned. His people broke the commandment, so the gods became angry, sending a **snowstorm** which nearly killed

Mythology

MARCO POLO TIP

Serpentine bends **Insider Tip**

Railway buffs will not want to miss the two-hour trip through the park aboard the little Raurimu Spiral railway. This amazing feat of engineering involves bridges and tunnels running across and over each other like hairpins. Information and tickets can be found at the Visitor Centre in Taumarunui station.

Ngatoro and his companion. In his distress, Ngatoro called on his own gods in faraway Hawaiki to send him fire. The fire arrived, creating along the way the geothermal fields of Rotorua and Taupo, and then erupted from the volcanic summits in order to warm the ancestor. He threw the body of his dead slave Auruhoe into the Ngauruhoe crater, which since then has borne her name.

The health resort of Whakapapa contains the visitor centre of the national park administration. The highlights here are the carefully composed presentations laying out the fascinating **natural history and development** of this active geothermal area, as well as its plant and animal life. Worth mentioning among the latter are the numerous varieties of native birds. **Audiovisual educational programmes** are shown daily. The conservation centre shop also has brochures and

Whakapapa, Tongariro National Park Headquarters

maps, alongside detailed descriptions of the individual tracks leading through the reserve. Note that the national park administration runs **two more information points**, one in Turangi (►Lake Taupo) and one on Mountain Road in Ohakune in the south. These two information points are only open Mon–Fri 8am–4pm.

❶ Visitor centre: daily 8am – 5pm, summer until 6pm
Educational programmes: daily 11am, 2pm and 4pm; NZ$ 3

Turoa The Turoa **skiing area** on the southwestern slopes of Ruapehu has only recently been opened up and is accessible from Ohakune via the Ohakune Mountain Road. People coming in cars should have snow chains along. There are several pistes here for beginners and advanced skiers.

Te Porere Pa The **Maori fortification** on the western edge of the national park is signposted from Highway 47 (Turangi). This is the site of Te Kooti's defeat in 1869 during the last great battle of the land wars. The fortifications have partly worn away over time.

Red-brown gravel and lava are typical of the crater landscape at Mount Ruapehu

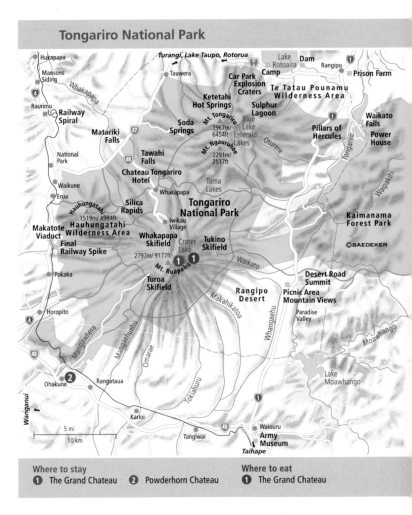

Tongariro National Park

Where to stay
1 The Grand Chateau **2** Powderhorn Chateau

Where to eat
1 The Grand Chateau

It was from this earthwork west of Rangipo on Lake Rotoaira that **government troops attacked** the Te Porere Pa position held by Te Kooti.

Poutu Redoubt

HIKES IN THE TONGARIRO NATIONAL PARK

The **most popular hiking trails** starting from the Visitor Centre in Whakapapa Village are: Alpine Garden Track (2km/1.2 miles),

Around Whakapapa

Taranaki Falls Track (circular route: 7km/4.3 miles), Whakapapanui Track (3km/1.8 miles), Silica Rapids Track (7km/4.3 miles) and Waihohonu Track (a day's walk from the Desert Road/Highway 1 to Château Tongariro, a luxury hotel, or vice versa). Tongariro Peak is crossed at Tongariro Alpine Crossing; the route can be hiked in six to eight hours. In the winter this is New Zealand's largest skiing region, at around 1050 ha./2600ac.

Tongariro Crossing

The area around the Tongariro volcano allows for the crossing of a part of the national park which is fascinating in terms of the landscapes' history. Some **9 hours** are required for this 19.4km/11.6mi trail, discounting breaks. The reward is spectacular views en route, including the Emerald Lakes and Blue Lake.

Round the Mountain Track

Some **four to five days** are needed for the »Round the Mountain Track«, which leads from the end of the Ohakune Mountain Road in the south via Whakapapa, making an arc around Ngauruhoe and Tongariro to the Desert Road.

The Emerald Lakes and Blue Lake glitter like gemstones between the two volcanos Ngauruhoe and Tongariro

Situated on the southwestern rim of Tongariro National Park (Hwy 49) is the village of Ohakune (pop 1,500). After the forests were cleared, the good volcanic soils of this area allowed for the **highly productive cultivation of vegetables**. The coming of the **railway** had a major impact on the development of the settlement. Today, Ohakune is a tourist resort popular all year round as a good base for **exciting tours** into the national park and to Mount Ruapehu.

Ohakune

Blessed with extremely attractive scenery, the Ohakune Mountain Road winds its way upwards through the forest of the national park to the **Mangawhero Falls**, and then on to the **Turoa ski area** on the western slopes of the 2,797m/9,176-ft **Mount Ruapehu**. The road ascends from 600m/1,968ft to 1,600m/5,249ft. Up here, there is snow between June and October.

*Ohakune Mountain Road

Beginning at the start of the **Ohakune Mountain Road** (Park Ranger Station), an approx. 3km/1.8-mile circular hiking trail gives access to part of the **Mangawhero Forest**. About 2 hours are required for a hike to the imposing **Waitonga Falls**, which, at a height of 63m/206ft, are amongst the highest in the Tongariro national park.

Some 20km/12.5 miles north of Ohakune, a rather imposing railway bridge spans a cleft valley crossed by Highway 4. This **monument to technology**, 79m/259ft high, was constructed in 1907.

Railway bridge

Approximately 11km/6.8 miles west of Ohakune, the village of Raetihi, with its 1,300 inhabitants, lies on Highway 4. In former times, the village used to mark the boundary between the Whanganui area and King Country. Its heyday was around 1900 when about 4,500 people lived here. In 1918, a **terrible forest fire** claimed nine sawmills and 150 houses. The timber economy in the area took a long time to recover from this severe blow. Today, the **twin towers of a church** of the Ratana cult lend visual interest to the village.

Raetihi

Starting from Raetihi, an endlessly interesting drive leads through the **wild, romantic valley** of the Whanganui River. This involves first heading west to Pipiriki, and then following the river along its **winding course**.

Whanganui River Road

A few miles south, outside Tongariro National Park, the settlement of Waiouru (pop 3,000) on Highway 1 forms the southern end of the volcanic central plateau. Sprawling here in the inhospitable, tussock-covered highlands (approx. 800m/2,624ft above sea level) is **New Zealand's largest military camp**, with a large training area. The

Waiouru

town itself boasts the **highest railway station** on North Island. On a clear day it offers an excellent view of the volcanic mountains in the Tongariro area. The **Army Memorial Museum** shows uniforms and armaments of the New Zealand army as well as various kinds of military equipment. Dioramas of world-famous theatres of war complement the exhibits.

❶ Army Memorial Museum: daily 9am – 4.30pm, admission: NZ$ 15, www.armymuseum.co.nz

Rangipo Desert Extending north of Waiouru, the Rangipo Desert is not a real desert, but rather an area barren due to dry winds and bad soils.

✳ Urewera National Park

———————— ✤ Sg–Sh 129

Regions: Bay of Plenty, Hawke Bay, Gisborne
Surface area: 212,672ha/535,408 acres
❶ Department of Conservation Aniwaniwa Visitor Centre, State Highway 38 Aniwaniwa, Tel. 06 8 37 38 03, www.doc.govt.nz

New Zealand's fourth-largest national park, comprising the North Island's last major area of virginal forest, is today a sheer paradise for outdoor enthusiasts, attracting keen wilderness walkers, kayakers, anglers and hunters. So far, over 650 different types of plant have been identified in the densely-forested area between the Bay of Plenty and Hawke's Bay. Some kiwi birds still live in the wild here, as well as a number of parrots called »kaka«.

Getting there The main access road is the **winding Highway** 38, crossing the mountainous national park from northwest (Rotorua) to southeast (Wairoa, Hawkes Bay). Access from the north can be found starting from ►Whakatane along the Whakatane River. Occasionally, there are day trips into the reserve by bus from ►Rotorua.

Natural space The foundations of this mountainous landscape are formed by young sediments deposited 10–15 million years ago on the ocean floor and lifted up about 2 million years ago. Since that time, erosion has resulted in **distinctive mountain ridges** and deep valleys, some studded with lakes. What is unusual for New Zealand is that the area is almost completely covered in vegetation – even the highest summits hardly manage to break through the **dense forest cover**.

Isolated area The **Tuhoe** Maori, native to the Te Urewera area, were already living in isolation in pre-European times, having little contact with other

tribes. Until the 20th century, the local Maori lived mainly on roots, berries, birds and fish. Given the lack of
any significant bartering or trading
goods of any kind, European immigrants had little interest in this area.
Even the missionaries soon gave up.

Maori leader **Te Kooti**, who had
supported the government in their
fight against the Hauhau rebels until
his arrest and exile in 1866, found
sanctuary and new followers in the
Urewera mountains. The **Ringatu cult** founded by Te Kooti also met
with an enthusiastic reception here.

? MARCO POLO INSIGHT

Children of the mist

According to an ancient tradition,
members of the Tuhoe Maori
tribe living in the Te Urewera area
are known as »Children of the
Mist«. According to legend they
are the descendants of the human
son of Tuhoepotiki, who was born
to the heavenly mist woman
Hinepukohurangi and the mountain Te Maunga.

The second leading figure of the area was Rua Kenana (1869–1937),
who founded a **religious community** similar to the Mormons and
saw himself as a kind of younger brother of Jesus, or a prophet. Rua
Kenana viewed his »Te Wairau Tapu« cult as a **revival of Maori confidence** and way of living. His brethren, who from 1905 onwards
gathered around him in a large round temple on Maungapohatu,
venerating him as the heir of Te Kooti, reached a modest degree of
prosperity through shared ownership of all worldly goods and modern ways of working. However, Rua Kenana looked for confrontation
with the New Zealand government, protesting against conscription.
When police came to arrest him in 1916, they were drawn into a gun
battle with his followers which entered the history books as effectively the **»last battle«** between Maori and pakeha (= whites).

Rua Kenana

WHAT TO SEE IN UREWERA NATIONAL PARK

In the village of Aniwaniwa on Highway 38, the national park administration runs a **Visitor Centre with museum**. This is the place to
pick up lots of important information about hikes in this still largely
primal forest. The **imposing mural** by Colin McCahon in the Visitor
Centre reflects the reverence still afforded today in the Urewera area
to the two Maori leaders Te Kooti and Rua Kenana.

Aniwaniwa

Starting at the visitor centre, the 12km/7mi-long Hinerau's Track is
a beautiful **hiking trail** along the Aniwaniwa River, giving access to
the imposing landscape of the national park and wonderful views of
Aniwaniwa Falls. Numerous rare birds can be spotted along the way.
Other very worthwhile hikes lead to the **Bridal Veil Falls** and **Aniwaniwa Falls**, as well as the small **Lake Waikareiti** higher up.

**Hinerau's
Track*

*Lake Waikare-moana

Lying in the centre of the national park, 614m/2,014ft above sea level, charming Lake Waikaremoana reaches depths of **up to 248m/813ft**. The lake was formed some 2,200 years ago, when a massive rockfall blocked a narrow gorge of the Waikaretaheke River, creating a natural reservoir. The **Visitor Centre** and the **Waikaremoana Motor Camp** are equipped to help hikers. The **isolated natural reservoir** is popular with holidaymakers who value seclusion and quietness.

A hike around the lake on the long **Waikaremoana Track** along the lakeshore requires 3 to 4 days. This well-maintained and signposted hiking trail measures 46km/28 miles and must rank **among the most beautiful** on New Zealand's North Island. Several basic huts offer shelter to wilderness hikers and kayakers.

Urewera National Park has a unique atmosphere in the fall when the leaves change colours

Accessible via Highway 38, the scattered Maori settlement of Ruatahuna lies on the western slopes of the Huiarau Range in the upper reaches of the Whakatane River. From here, a worthwhile 4km/2.5-mile detour leads to **Mataatua**, to admire a beautiful **Maori meeting house** with impressive carvings. Mataatua was the name of one of the large tribal canoes that once carried the Polynesians to New Zealand. Its crew settled east of the Bay of Plenty.

! **MARCO POLO TIP**

Insider Tip

Trout for everybody ...

Among anglers Lake Waikaremoanga is a well-kept secret, as there can be few places in the whole of New Zealand better suited to trout fishing. Rainbow trout in particular thrive in the lake. It is just a question of finding a spot on the lakeshore or chartering a boat to cast the line. Visitors who fancy themselves as anglers do require a fishing permit, available from any Campground Store or boat hire place.

Wanganui

✦ Se–Sf 130

Region: Wanganui
Altitude: 0 – 135m/443ft
Population: 45,000

This well-kept little town is one of the oldest in New Zealand, owing its foundation to a favourable position on the Whanganui River. Today, the port has lost its significance whilst the town has undergone a revival of its colonial past. The late-Victorian frontages for instance have been renovated, old lanterns put up and flower beds laid out everywhere.

The town of Wanganui lies on the southwestern coast of North Island, in the area of the **mouth of the Whanganui River**. Even before the arrival of the Europeans, this river was an important transit route for Maori canoes. It saw many conflicts between individual Maori tribes. Particularly brutal were the fights between the local Maori and the warriors led by Te Rauparaha. In 1840, the **New Zealand Company**, led by William Wakefield, »bought« a few thousand hectares of land off the Maori. The indigenous inhabitants take a different view of this however. In any case, the Company started settling immigrants here the same year. The **fertile plains** around the mouth of the Whanganui were easily cleared and cultivated. The broad river made it unnecessary to build roads to transport goods and people. However, **confrontations** with the local Maori did occur. In 1847 a sizeable number of British troops came to the assistance of the white settlers.

Contested region

A year later, the Maori received a contract and 1,000 pounds sterling for 32,000ha/79,073 acres of land. This meant that the conflicts between Maori and »pakeha« (= whites) were solved for the time being. Thus, the local Maori tribes did not take part in the land wars that had flared up in the meantime, **allowing Wanganui to develop undisturbed**.

WHAT TO SEE IN AND AROUND WANGANUI

Queen's Park A fortification established by the early settlers was turned into this centrally located park, which has now become the **cultural heart** of the town, boasting the Wanganui Museum, the Sarjeant Gallery and the War Memorial Hall. **Wanganui Museum** houses an **excellent collection of Maori decorative art objects**, amongst them jewellery made from greenstone, while the 23m/75-ft long war canoe exhibited here was still manned by 70 men as recently as 1810. A series of **chief portraits** by the painter Gottfried Lindauer can also be seen here, and last but not least, the time of the first white settlers is recalled too.

ⓘ Daily 10am – 4.30pm, admission: NZ$ 8.50

Sarjeant Gallery Named after a wealthy city family, the Sarjeant Gallery art collection is housed in an imposing building with large skylights. It originally focussed on works by English and New Zealand artists of the 19th and early 20th centuries; now the gallery covers everything from the 16th cent. to contemporary art. It shows more than 5500 works of the most different kinds.

❶ Daily 10.30am – 4.30pm, free admission

Cook's Gardens The best **view of Queen's Park** can be had from neighbouring Cook's Gardens. Part of a military fortification at the time of the land wars, today they feature green spaces and sports facilities, with a wooden 19th-century **fire lookout tower** and an **observatory** pointing skywards. It was here in Cook's Gardens in 1962 that New Zealand running sensation **Peter Snell** set his first world record in middle distance running.

Moutoa Gardens Whanganui River has a small **historic park** marking the site where the land purchases were carried out. Originally the idea was to have the town's market place here. Monuments commemorate historic events, such as the **Battle of Moutoa** (1864), where local Maori beat off Hauhau fighters bent on destroying Wanganui. The Maori who died in World War I have been honoured by a monument, as has Putiki chief **Te Rangihiwinui Kepa**, known as »Major Kemp«, who fought on the side of the government army in the land wars.

Wanganui

INFORMATION
Wanganui Information Centre
31 Taupo Quay
Tel. 06 349 0508
www.wanganui.com

WHERE TO EAT
Redeye £ – ££
96 Guyton Street
Tel. 06 345 5646

Town-centre restaurant particularly popular with younger people

WHERE TO STAY
B-K's Magnolia Motor Lodge ££
240 St Hill Street
Tel. 06 348 0020
www.nzmotels.co.nz
Motel in the heart of town equipped with modern comforts

Durie Hill, with viewing tower and war memorial, offers **pretty views** of the town, the coast and the volcanoes of Ruapehu und Taranaki rising in the distance.

Durie Hill

The Maori fortification established on the river withstood enemy attacks up into the 19th century – until 1829 when Te Rauparaha and his warriors overpowered its defenses and instigated a **terrible bloodbath**. In 1891, a flood washed away the meeting house and numerous Maori canoes. After that the Maori set up a new meeting house as well as a storage house. The interior of the Maori church, erected in 1937, boasts **wonderful carvings** by the great master Pine Taiapa.

Putiki Pa

DAY TRIPS FURTHER AFIELD

Just under 50km/31 miles northwest of Wanganui, the village of Waverley counts 1,500 inhabitants and was made famous by **ancient rock drawings** discovered nearby.

Waverley

Approx. 23km/14 miles southeast of Wanganui, the Maori settlement of Ratana became famous through a **religious movement** which had a major influence on the new direction of Maori thinking. Look out for the double-towered church of 1927. The museum commemorates **Wiremu Ratana** (1870–1939), the founder of the Ratana religion, who helped many a sick fellow citizen. His birthday is celebrated every year on the 25th of January as a popular fair. The large meeting house displays models of the seven Maori ancestor canoes and two ships, Abel Tasman's **Heemskerck** and James Cook's **Endeavour**.

Ratana

★★ Wellington

Se 132 Se 132

Region: Wellington
Altitude: 0 – 495m/1,624ft
Population: 191,000 (Greater Wellington: 380,000)

The capital of New Zealand, Wellington, has many faces. At first sight already it captivates visitors with the unique beauty of its surroundings and its location right on the water. There are glittering bays, steep cliffs and the picturesque natural harbour of Port Nicholson. But the city itself has its own charm, both nostalgic and sleepy as well as cosmopolitan and modern.

A shortage of level ground

The city's unique topography comes with an inherent problem: Wellington is short of level ground. So its buildings are spread across widely spaced areas between bays and hills, connected by a serpentine network of roads. Land gains through the **tectonic lifts** that followed the devastating earthquake of 1855 – at the time the area bordering the port rose 1.5m/nearly 5ft – and artificial landfills created more space for the city, as well as a site for the airport. However, in the city centre planners were forced to build upwards.

As a consequence, Wellington has an **ultramodern skyline**, but has paid the price in having to sacrifice much of its Victorian fabric. Instead of traditional commercial buildings, glass and steel structures sprouted up, turning many commercial streets of the city centre into pure **wind tunnels** – a characteristic trait of the city. The often strong westerly wind almost constantly blowing in from the Cook Strait gave Wellington the nickname **»Windy City«**.

The residential areas have now shifted to faraway dormitory towns, such as those in Hutt Valley to the northeast and on the Kapiti Coast to the north. City highways and railway lines give access to the centre. The tunnels that had to be dug through the mountains to accommodate them again claimed many old buildings in the process.

Seat of government and port

Thanks to its position on the northern side of Cook Strait, in addition to being the seat of parliament and government Wellington fulfils an important role as a **port connecting the North and South Islands**. However, in terms of being an urban metropolis, New Zealand's capital has been overtaken by ►Auckland – quite a reversal of fortune: Wellington had to fight for years to take Auckland's capital city status.

The most beautiful view of Wellington is from Mount Victoria

1776	James Cook discovers Bay of Wellington
around 1840	European settlement begins
1865	Wellington becomes capital of New Zealand
1897	Foundation of Victoria University
20th/21st cent.	As capital, Wellington experiences an enormous boom

Maori mythology has it that **Kupe, the legendary discoverer of New Zealand**, entered the bay and camped on the Miramar Peninsula. The **first sedentary settler** however is said to have been Tara, a son of Whatonga who had come from Hawaiki. Tara had started out from Hawke's Bay in order to look for new areas to settle. He gave the protected harbour its Maori name, **Te Whanganui-a-Tara**, and his descendents formed the tribe of the Ngai-Tara, who fortified all the hills around the port. During his first voyage around the world in 1770, **James Cook** overlooked the entrance to the harbour basin. It was only during the second trip that he noticed the arm of the sea leading deep inland, which he took to be a natural harbour. However, wind and tides made the Resolution drift back out to sea again. **Georg Forster** described bare, blackish mountains rising high, and curious Maori approaching the Resolution with their canoes.

Mythology

Wellington

INFORMATION
Wellington Visitor Centre
Civic Square
(corner Wakefield Street/Victoria Street)
Tel. 04 802 4860
www.wellingtonnz.com

EVENTS
Wellington is home to the New Zealand Symphony Orchestra and the New Zealand Ballet Company. The **New Zealand International Arts Festival** takes place in February and March every other year (2016, 2018, etc.), with numerous events and exhibitions. However, the lifeguards pull in an even bigger audience each January with their rowing competition from South Island via the Cook Strait. Further highlights in Wellington's calendar are the ceremonial state opening of Parliament and **Tulip Sunday** in early October, when the Botanic Gardens show off their splendour.

SIGHTSEEING
Bus trips taking in the harbour, going along the coast or heading into the mountains of the interior are usually offered in conjunction with a cable car trip or a trip around the harbour. The Public Relations Office has information on these trips. An individual and inexpensive way to explore the sights is a Day-tripper Ticket for the inner city Stagecoach buses (NZ$ 9). Following the huge success of the **Lord of the Rings** film trilogy, which was shot in New Zealand, visitors can now explore the locations in and around Wellington through a »Lord of the Rings Locations Itinerary« or by taking a »Lord of the Rings Self Drive Tour«. Extensive information material can be picked up from Wellington's Visi-

tor Centre (see above) and online (www.wellingtonnz.com).

SHOPPING
Wakefields Market (at weekends) on the corner of Jervois Quay and Taranaki Street offers a colourful mix of clothes and crafts. Shopping centres, large department stores and elegant boutiques can be found along Lambton Quay. Shopping with historic flair is also possible in the »Old Bank Arcade«, an historic bank building where designer fashions and cosmetics are now sold.

WHERE TO EAT
❶ *Martin Bosley's*
££££
103 Oriental Parade, Oriental Bay
in the Royal Port Nicholson Yacht Club
Tel. 04 9 20 83 02
www.martin-bosley.com
One of New Zealand's finest addresses: enjoy oysters, duck liver mousse and seafood in a noble setting on the water, with a panoramic view of Wellington.

❷ *Logan Brown*
££££
192 Cuba Street/Vivian Street
Tel. 04 8 01 51 14
www.loganbrown.co.nz
A former 1920s bank building was converted into a top restaurant. What has remained are the nostalgic charm of the high ceilings and the fact that klarge anounts of money change hands. The relaxed atmosphere and the creative cooking are new.

❸ *The Whitebait*
££££
Clyde Quay Wharf

Tel. 04 3 85 85 55
www.white-bait.nz
Its known for its excellent organic cooking. The decor is all in white.

❹ Ortega Fish Shack   Insider Tip
£££
18 Majoribanks Street
Tel. 04 3 82 95 59
http://ortega.co.nz/
In this small but fine restaurant the best in fish cuisine is served. But there are also meat dishes.

❺ CQ Restaurant
££
213 Cuba Street
Tel. 04 3 85 21 56
Thiss restaurant in Wellington's entertainment quarter is recommended for good-value food.

❻ Mekong
££
138 Vivian St, Cuba
Tel. 04 801 8099
Excellently prepared Vietnamese and Cambodian specialities are served here

❼ Scopa Caffé Cucina
££
Ghuznee Street/Cuba Street
Tel. 04 3 84 60 20
www.scopa.co.nz
Probably the city's most popular Italian restaurant.

❽ Shed 5
££
Queens Wharf (Maritime Museum)
Tel. 04 499 9069
www.shed5.co.nz
Original culinary creations served in a former warehouse

❾ Satay Kingdom
£
Cuba St, Shop 212, Cuba Mall
Tel. 04 38 13 7 30
Malay cooking, good and really cheap.

WHERE TO STAY
❶ Bolton Hotel
£££– ££££
Bolton Street/Mowbay Street
Tel. 04 4 72 99 66
www.boltonhotel.co.nz
Luxury rooms with friendly service. The city with all its sights, shops, bars and restaurants is only a few minutes' walk away.

❷ Lambton Heights
£££
20 Talavera Terrace, Kelburn
Tel. 04 4 72 47 10
www.lambtonheights.co.nz
Located a little outside of the centre, this boutique hotel in Kelburn has a spa, beautiful garden and a view of the harbour and the city.

❸ Copthorne Hotel Wellington
££
100 Oriental Parade
Tel. 04 3 85 02 79
www.milleniumhotels.co.nz
Modern-styled city hotel with friendly service near the port.

❹ Ibis £
153 Featherston Street
Lambton Quarter
P O Box 3556
Tel. 04 496 1880
www.ibishotels.com
This central guesthouse near the port offers pleasantly furnished rooms.

Settlers arrive and city is founded Half a century after Cook, **Te Rauparaha** and his warriors attacked the unsuspecting tribes in the south from Kapiti Island. The survivors fled into the forests while the Te Ati Awa from Taranaki moved south to occupy the newly available space, having themselves been driven out of their tribal lands. Thus, at the time of the European settlement around 1840 the local Maori were fearful of the tribes from the north, and reckoned the white settlers to be the lesser evil, even hoping for their protection. For their part, the Europeans came to the area that would later be Wellington in order to do business as **flax merchants, whalers or seal hunters**. At the end of 1840, over 2,500 new settlers had arrived in Wellington. The first group settled in the **Hutt Valley** at Petone and called their settlement »**Britannia**«. The marshy terrain, covered in thick scrub, created a lot of problems. Floods and an earthquake added to their troubles, soon making them move on southwest to what is today Thorndon. A prefabricated house at today's **Lambton Quay**, brought over from England to be set up as a school, for several years doubled up as courthouse, ballroom and even as the seat of provincial government. It was around this building that the town of Wellington grew up as the first and most successful settlement of the Company, taking its name from the **Duke of Wellington**, the hero of Waterloo, who was a strong supporter of Wakefield's plans.

? Files overboard

MARCO POLO INSIGHT

During the government's move from Auckland to Wellington the steamer White Swan, laden with civil servants and government documents, went down. Everybody aboard was saved, but most of the files were lost.

In 1865, the South's complaints about the isolation and inaccessibility of the capital Auckland were finally heeded. **Auckland lost its status** and Wellington became New Zealand's **third capital** after Russell/Okiato and Auckland. Thanks to the diplomats, banks, commercial headquarters and shipping agencies, as well as the foundation of Victoria University, it was soon to experience a boom. Hutt Valley was covered with housing developments and industrial installations all the way to the Rimutaka Mountains, with the city spreading out across the hills to the western coast.

THORNDON

Government quarter: Old Government Building The **most imposing building** in the parliamentary and government quarter is the Old Government Building (1876) at the northern end of Lambton Quay. Like the other buildings here it stands on land **reclaimed from the ocean** during the major earthquake of 1855.

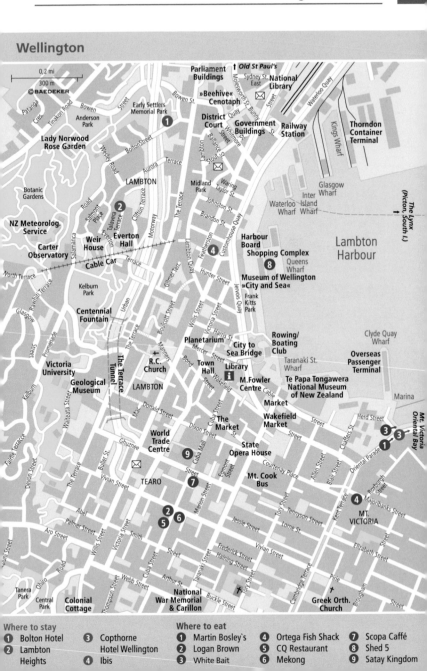

Wellington

0,2 mi
300 m
©BAEDEKER

Parliament Buildings
Old St Paul's
Sydney St. East
National Library
»Beehive«
Cenotaph
District Court
Government Buildings
Railway Station
Early Settlers Memorial Park
Bowen St.
Molesworth St.
Bunny St.
Whitmore St.
Ballance St.
Stout St.
Waterloo Quay
Kings Wharf
Thorndon Container Terminal
Lady Norwood Rose Garden
Anderson Park
Paranga Cres.
Tinakori Road
Bowen St.
Wesley Road
Bolton Street
Aurora Terrace
LAMBTON
Midland Park
Waring Taylor St.
Johnston St.
Brandon St.
Featherston St.
Customhouse Quay
Lambton Quay
Botanic Gardens
NZ Meteorolog. Service
Carter Observatory
Weir House
Everton Hall
Cable Car
Salamanca Road
Talavera Terrace
Clifton Terrace
Motorway
The Terrace
Gilmer Terr.
Hunter Street
Glasgow Wharf
Inter Island Wharf
Waterloo Wharf
Lambton Harbour
The Lynx (Picton, South I.)
Harbour Board Shopping Complex
Queens Wharf
Museum of Wellington »City and Sea«
Frank Kitts Park
Kelburn Park
North Terrace
Rawhiti Terrace
Centennial Fountain
Victoria University
Geological Museum
The Terrace
Urban
Boulcott St.
Willis Street
Victoria St.
Harris St.
Mercer St.
Bond Street
Wakefield Street
Planetarium
City to Sea Bridge
Library
Rowing/ Boating Club
Clyde Quay Wharf
Overseas Passenger Terminal
Taranaki St. Wharf
R.C. Church
Town Hall
M.Fowler Centre
Market
Te Papa Tongawera National Museum of New Zealand
Marina
LAMBTON
The Terrace Tunnel
Mac...
Donald Street
Dixon Street
The Market
Wakefield Market
Herd Street
Mt. Victoria Oriental Bay
World Trade Centre
Cuba Mall
Cuba Street
State Opera House
Mt. Cook Bus
Ghuznee Street
Vivian Street
TEARO
Martin Street
Egmont St.
Courtenay Place
Tory Street
Tennyson Street
Lorne St.
Kent Terrace
Blair St.
Allen St.
Oriental Parade
Elizabeth Street
MT. VICTORIA
Roxburgh Street
Majoribanks Street
Abel
Palmer Street
Aro Street
Willis St.
Victoria Street
Smith Street
Jessie Street
Frederick Street
Vivian Street
Haining Street
Devon St.
Fairlie Terrace
Bullet St.
Ohiro
Tanera Park
Central Park
Colonial Cottage
National War Memorial & Carillon
Arthur St.
Webb Street
Buckle Street
Cambridge Terrace
Pirie Street
Greek Orth. Church

Whilst the massive four-storey edifice (9,400 sq m/101,180 sq ft) in the Italian Renaissance style appears to be solid stone, it is in fact made entirely of wood – making it the **second-largest wooden building on earth**. Architect W H Clayton, used kauri, rimu and matai woods, in the process overrunning costs by so much that the government decided to forego an official inauguration party. The **22 chimneys** that originally adorned the structure were removed for constituting an earthquake risk. In front of the Government Building a monument honours Labour leader and Prime Minister (1940–1949) Peter Fraser. It is fitting that the law faculty of Victoria University is now housed in this historic building. There is a small exhibit on the building's history open to visitors..

Parliament Buildings (Beehive) North of the Government Building, look out for the »Beehive«, which is indeed a **round, beehive-like construction** housing ministerial offices, including those of the Prime Minister, and the cabinet room. Built in stages between 1964 and 1981, the design by London architect Basil Spence remains controversial to this day. Next to the

In this beehive-like building parliamentarians and officials work like busy bees

Beehive, **Parliament House** was built in 1922 from granite and taka-ka marble from South Island. This is where New Zealand's parliament convenes in a large chamber closely resembling that of the British parliament in London. On weekdays there are guided tours. The debating chamber of the Upper House, abolished in 1952, now serves as the setting for the ceremonial opening of parliament. Another part of the complex of parliamentary and government buildings is the **General Assembly Library Building** (1897), a neo-Gothic two-storey structure. The **statues in the park** honour Richard John Seddon, Prime Minister from 1893 to 1906, and John Ballance, Seddon's predecessor both as leader of the Liberals and as prime minister.

❶ Tours: daily 10am – 4pm, free admission, www.beehive.govt.nz

*National Library

Further north in Molesworth Street, past more government and court buildings, stands the National Library. The building, opened in 1987, incorporates the **Alexander Turnbull Library**, previously housed in Turnbull's former residence near the Beehive in Bowen Street, and which forms the basis of today's library. Among the more than 250,000 volumes is an extremely valuable and near-complete **collection of travels and discoveries in the southern Pacific**. The reading room, with a mural by Maori artist **Cliff Whiting** representing the separation of Mother Earth and Father Sky is worth seeing.

National Archives

Further north, the National Archives building exhibits important historical documents, including letters from James Cook, collected signatures for the petition leading to **female suffrage**, as well as the original Waitangi Treaty. Another institution housed here is the **National Portrait Gallery**.

*Old St Paul's

The next building along is the Anglican Old St Paul's church (1866), possibly the most beautiful of the so-called **Selwyn Churches**, designed by Frederick Thatcher on the order of Bishop Selwyn. Whilst the outside appears to be a simple white wooden structure in the English neo-Gothic style, the interior exerts its charm through the way the wood has been worked and the **effects of the light**. Formerly the church of Thorndon parish, Old St Paul's then served as the cathedral of Wellington until 1972, when the current cathedral, opposite the National Library, took over following its elaborate renovation. Bridal couples like to exchange vows in the historic church, which was built of New Zealand woods.

Birthplace of Katherine Mansfield

Visitors interested in **Katherine Mansfield** should make a detour from the northern end of Mulgrave Street along the adjoining Murphy Street, first to the **Katherine Mansfield Memorial Park**, given to the city by her father, and then across the urban motorway to Tina-

Room in the house where New Zealand's most famous author, Katherine Mansfield, was born

kori Road. It was on this street, at no. 25, a simple wooden house built wholly in the style of vintage Thorndon, that the **short story writer** was born in 1888. The house that was built in the year she was born has been restored to its original state and today serves as a museum exhibiting manuscripts, historical photographs and other memorabilia connected with the writer.

❶ Tue – Sun 10am – 4pm, admission: NZ$ 8, www.katherinemansfield.com

FROM LAMBTON QUAY TO CUBA STREET

Shopping and business mile

Starting at the station and running south, **Lambton Quay** (and its continuation, **Willis Street**) is the busy **main artery of Wellington**. The name »Quay« points to the fact that the shoreline once ran along here – all the land today lying east of it was lifted from the sea in 1885. There are few older buildings, apart from the District Courts (1879) and the Public Trust Building (1908).

Antrim House

Visitors looking for another attractive old building should go up Boulcott Street from Willis Street to Antrim House (63 Boulcott Street), a pretty **kauri-wood house dating from 1904**, today squashed between highrises. Designed by Thomas Turnbull for the shoe manufacturer **Robert Hannah**, it is open to the public. Otherwise, the city is dominated by the modern glass and steel façades of department stores, shopping malls and shops selling luxury goods – with the **Bank of New Zealand** at the southern end of Lambton Quay towering above them all.

❶ Mon – Fri 9am – 5pm, free admission

Situated near the waterfront, the Civic Centre comprises the old **Town Hall**, the elegant **Wellington City Library**, designed by Ian Athfield, and the **Michael Fowler Centre**. The former Public Library today houses the city's art collection, the **City Art Gallery**. The collection of modern art has changing exhibitions and short film screenings.

City Art Gallery: daily 10am – 5pm, free admission, http://citygallery.org.nz/

Civic Centre

Branching off at the Michael Fowler Centre, the **pedestrian area** of Cuba Street is flanked by **colourful boutiques and restaurants**. Here the atmosphere is a bit cosier, and more conducive to taking a seat at one of the numerous restaurants, than Willis Street, which does tend to be somewhat pricey, or Lambton Quay.

Cuba Street

✳ WATERFRONT

Wellington's **waterfront** is architecturally pleasing. Both Queens Wharf and **Frank Kitts Park** are framed by interesting groups of buildings. Look out for the impressive **Civic Centre**, reached by the

Wellington's showcase

Highlights Wellington

▶ **Museum of New Zealand Te Papa Tongarewa**
Information on the short but fascinating history of the country using a variety of interactive media
▶page 300

▶ **Mount Victoria**
From the summit of the mountain east of the city centre there are spectacular panoramic views across the city and the harbour.
▶page 302

▶ **Museum of Wellington City & Sea**
Excellent exhibition on the history of the city and its seafaring heritage
▶page 300

▶ **City Marine Drive**
This 40km/25-mile circular route allows plenty of opportunities to sunbathe on Wellington's most beautiful beaches.
▶page 302

hyper-modern **City to Sea Bridge**, and the new National Museum, opened in 1998. The activities on the water can be observed from the park. Here stands a mast of the Wahine ferry, which in 1968 sank in the harbour in a storm with 51 passengers aboard, as well as a bronze representation of the two boats used by **Abel Tasman** on his 1642 voyage when he discovered New Zealand.

*Museum of Wellington City & Sea	The well-endowed museum on Queens Wharf not only looks at the **economic, social and cultural history** of the New Zealand capital, but also at the significance of the Wellington port and the **history of seafaring**. Alongside model ships, a model of the harbour has been set up (opening times: daily 10am – 5pm). ❶ Daily 10am – 5pm, free admission, www.museumswellington.org.nz
**Museum of New Zealand Te Papa Tongarewa	The museum stands at the centre of pulsating life. A popular meeting point, the **Queens Wharf Retail & Event Centre** has pretty boutiques and restaurants. The most recent attraction of the New Zealand capital is the national museum »Te Papa« (Maori expression for »Our Homeland«), which opened in 1998 on the harbour's southern side. Here, visitors can use interactive multimedia to acquaint themselves with the **history of New Zealand and its inhabitants**. »Mountains to Sea« tells the story of New Zealand's creation in time-lapse. »Awesome Forces« is a multimedia show on earthquakes, and »On the Sheep's Back« looks at the economic role played by sheep-rearing. »The Time Warp« is an **exciting high-tech trip** through space and time. The heart of the museum is formed by Te Marae, a modern **Maori sanctuary**. Fascinating too are the Maori meeting point of Te Wharenui and a huge dug-out canoe used by the Maori as a warship. The new museum complex also houses the **collections of the national gallery**, with works by New Zealand, Australian and European artists of the 19th and 20th centuries. Some works by **Rembrandt** are also exhibited here. ❶ Daily 10am – 6pm, thu until 9pm, free admission, www.tepapa.govt.nz
Circa Theatre	On the square in front of the museum, the Circa Theatre, one of the most renowned of its kind in the whole of New Zealand, has recently been renovated.

FURTHER SIGHTS

*Botanical Garden, funicular railway	The Botanical Garden, 26ha/64 acres in size and situated in the heart of Wellington on the hills of Kelburn, forms the city's **green lung**. Getting there is an experience in itself, undertaken by **funicular railway**. This funicular railway, opened in 1902 and modernised some time ago, ascends from Lambton Quay opposite Grey Street, and

The funicular railway is a comfortable way to get to the Botanical Garden and enjoy the wonderful view

travels a distance of 610m/2,000ft to its terminal at an altitude of 122m/400ft. Once up here, visitors are rewarded with **wonderful views** across Wellington, before starting their walk through the Botanical Garden. The park was laid out in 1869. Right at the entrance, the recently refurbished **Carter Observatory** and a number of other university natural science institutes can be found. Highlights of the garden are the **Lady Norwood Rose Garden** with over 500 varieties of rose, Begonia House, the herb garden, the beds of Maori medicinal herbs and an environmental education garden. Finally, the northern exit on Glenmore Street features cast-iron gates and the old guardhouse, both fully retaining their Victorian style.

Bolton Street Memorial Park

From here, it is not far to the Bolton Street (Early Settlers) Memorial Park, where tombstones of significant figures can be found next to the restored old **Sexton's Cottage**, amongst them the last resting place of the British politician Edward Gibbon Wakefield and the former New Zealand prime minister Richard Seddon.

Victoria University

Stretching south of the cable car terminal, the buildings of Victoria University include the Hunter Building, which houses a deeply fascinating **geological museum**. East of the university, at the end of Waiapu Road, is the Visitor Centre of **Karori Wildlife Sanctuary**, where university staff look after a nearly extinct species of lizard, the **tuatara**.

Visitor Centre: daily 10am – 5pm

**Mount Victoria

At a height of 196m/643ft, east of the city centre is Wellington's **most famous viewpoint**. A small road winds its way up from Oriental Bay to the Byrd Memorial below the viewing platform. The terrace at the summit affords a **unique panoramic view** across the sprawling city, the harbour, Cook Strait, Hutt Valley and Kelburn Park with the university buildings. The **Byrd Memorial** commemorates the American aviator Rear Admiral Richard Evelyn Byrd, who in 1929 undertook the first flight over the South Pole, using New Zealand as an expedition base. Two camera men documented the successful undertaking in the film *With Byrd at the South Pole*.

AROUND WELLINGTON

**City Marine Drive

The 40km/25-mile City Marine Drive – which can also be done by bike – involves rounding the **Miramar Peninsula** east of Wellington, hugging the coast nearly all the way and giving the opportunity to explore some beautiful beaches. The tour is one of the most beautiful excursions in the city and goes to the pretty Oriental Bay, among other places.

Oriental Bay

Oriental Bay, these days an **affluent suburb** with charming wooden houses stretching up from the shore to Mount Victoria, used to be the place where **whales were gutted**. The promenade is perfectly suited to strolling, swimming and enjoying the view. To the right, the large building up above is the former St Gerard monastery dating from 1905, whilst the Freyberg Swimming Pool to the left was named after **Lord Freyberg**, a highly decorated First World War soldier born in Great Britain, first-in-command of the New Zealand troops in Europe and North Africa during World War II, and seventh Governor General of New Zealand. Following on, the route leads around **Point Jermingham** into Evans Bay, from where the Miramar Peninsula can be seen.

*View from the Massey Memorial

Past the airport on the raised sand bank connecting Miramar with the mainland, the route leads to the western shores of the peninsula. Its northern tip, Point Halswell, is home to the Massey Memorial, which commemorates **Prime Minister William Ferguson Massey** on the site of a former Maori pa. The strenuous climb is rewarded with a **fine view** of Wellington and Port Nicholson.

Point Gordon

Next up are **Mahanga Bay** and Point Gordon, a fortification built in the 1880s following the opening of the port at Vladivostok, when

Wellington • Surroundings

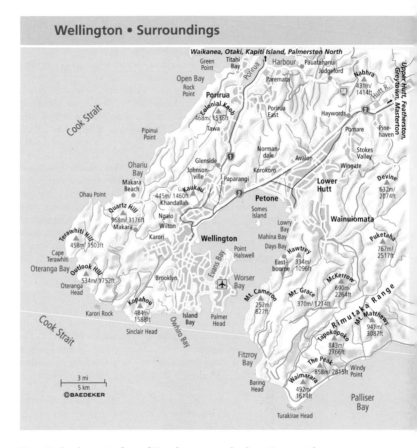

New Zealand was in fear of **Russian expansionism**. Fortunately, even the Czar of Russia did not try to advance as far as New Zealand.

Scorching Bay leads on to Worser Bay, both with pretty **beaches**. Port pilots used to have their base at Worser Bay. Travelling further south via Breaker Bay and along the southern end of the airport takes visitors to Lyall Bay, a beach very popular with **surfers** and giving views all the way to the mountains of South Island. Leading past rocky outcrops, the coast road carries on to Houghton Bay and Island Bay (surfing beach) to Owhiro Bay, where the road ends. From here, a two-hour **hike** in a westerly direction leads to the **Red Rocks**, a **volcanic formation** between the hiking trail and the sea. In winter-time, at Sinclair Head, a good 3km/1.8 miles further west, a **seal**

Lyall Bay
Worser Bay

colony may be observed. The drive back into the city leads inland from Owhiro Bay, via Happy Valley Road, Brooklyn Road and Nairn Street – with house no. 68, an **old cottage dating back to 1858**, to-day operating as a museum – and eventually reaching Willis Street.

Eastbourne Along the eastern side of the port, the Eastern Bay Drive leads, via Petone, to Eastbourne, the site of more beautiful beaches. Starting at Eastbourne, a waymarked trail offers hikers the opportunity to walk through natural woodland into the lovely **valley of Butterfly Creek**, where a pond ideal for a dip awaits.

Pencarrow Head A different walk leads from Eastbourne to Pencarrow Head (16km/10 miles there and back) on the eastern entrance to the harbour, where, in 1859, **New Zealand's first lighthouse** was erected. There are also great views across the bay of **Port Nicholson** from here.

Otari Museum of Native Plants Amateur botanists will enjoy the Otari Museum of Native Plants, which is not in fact a museum but a **very pretty garden** grouping together all the plants native to New Zealand and the Chatham Islands. The museum can be reached taking Wilton Road in the direction of Karori, to the west of the city.
❶ Daily from sunrise to sunset

*Kapiti Coast Stretching along the Kapiti Coast from Paekakariki via Raumati to Waikanae, there are a number of very pretty beaches, complemented by three **interesting museums**. The coast gets its name from Kapiti Island off the coast.

Tramway Museum The Tramway Museum at Elizabeth Park, on Highway 1 at Paekaka-riki, approx. 45km/28 miles north of the city on the Kapiti Coast, is a popular destination for day trippers. At weekends, visitors can board old trams that used to run at Lambton Quay for **nostalgic rides** to the Memorial Gates at McKays Crossing. The **Memorial Gates** commemorate the 2nd US Marine Division, who were stationed here during World War II.
❶ Sat, Sun and school holidays 11 – 4.30pm, tram ride: NZ$ 10, www.wellingtontrams.org.nz

Engine Shed In Paekakariki itself, the so-called Engine Shed relives the past glory of the railway age by stoking up **old steam locomotives**.
❶ Opening times on request, tel. 06 3 64 89 86, admission: donation requested, www.wellingtonnz.com

Southward Car Museum Admirers of nostalgic cars should stop at the Southward Car Museum, the »largest private collection of cars in the southern hemisphere«. Not far from the Tramway Museum, it displays numerous **vintage cars**, amongst them a Cadillac that used to belong to Marlene Dietrich and one that was used by Al Capone, as well as the **first two cars** (both Mercedes Benz) to run on the dusty roads of New Zealand in 1898. The museum lies approx. 50km/31 miles north of the city, 3km/1.8 miles south of Waikanae.

❶ Daily 9am – 4.30pm, admission: NZ$ 17, www.southwardcarmuseum.co.nz

Some 15km/9 miles northeast of Wellington, on the lower reaches of the Hutt River and enclosed by steep hills, the suburb of Lower Hutt (pop 100,000), was named after a former director of the New Zealand Company. Not far from there, **Petone** was where the first settlers arrived in 1840. However, the frequent **flooding** of the Hutt River soon led them to move further south. After the settlers had come to an agreement with the Maori on land sales in the area where Lower Hutt is today, **forests were cut down and gardens laid out** in their place. Gradually the settlement of Wellington pushed into the lower reaches of the Hutt River, turning Lower Hutt into a **residential suburb**. Several nursery gardens had to make way for new industrial enterprises. Today, research institutes and TV stations have also been established here.

Lower Hutt

The Dowse Art Museum is highly recommended (Laings Rd.), boasting a collection of New Zealand art, with a carved **Maori storage house** and the **glass art collection** the highlights.

❶ Daily 10am – 5pm, free admission, http://dowse.org.nz

Dowse Art Museum

Home to the **oldest Christian community in the Wellington area** (Eastern Hutt Rd), Christ Church was built of wood in 1854 and has been well restored following a 1989 fire.

Christ Church

In the suburb of Petone with its pulsating Jackson Street, the Settlers Museum (**The Esplanade**), telling the story of European settlement, is worth visiting. The museum also has an extensive archive, which primarily attracts many **genealogists**. They find information here about immigrants from Europe, Great Britain and Australia between 1839 and 1897.

❶ Wed – Sun 10am – 4pm, admission: donation requested, www.petonesettlers.org.nz

Petone, Settlers Museum

On Thursdays and Sundays, two markets – **Settlers Market** on Jackson Street and **Station Village Market** on the corner of Hutt Road/Railway Avenue – attract many visitors.

Markets

Southeast, the road leads further on to Wainuiomata Valley, covering the 20km/12.5 miles to the sea, where the bare rocks show graphi-

Wainuiomata Valley

cally the land elevations triggered by various **earthquakes**. The most recent spectacular **lifting of the ocean floor** happened during the devastating earthquake of 1855. The uppermost section of the beach was elevated some 6,500 years ago.

Rimutaka Forest Park

Just under 10km/6.2 miles south of Wainuiomata, Catchpool Valley offers good access to Rimutaka Forest Park with its campsites and **picnic areas**. Among the park's most **attractive hiking trails** are the »Five Mile Track« to the Orongorongo River (walking time approx. 4 hrs), the Middle Ridge Track (walking time approx. 2 hrs) and the Butcher Track (difficult climbing tour, approx. 1 hr), which gives a great **view of Wellington Harbour**.

Otaki

About 75km/46 miles north of Wellington, the small town of Otaki (pop 6,500) lies on the South Taranaki Bight. In former times, this area was settled by many Maori, and in the early 19th century was controlled by chief Te Rauparaha from nearby Kapiti Island. Today, Otaki is at the centre of a large vegetable-growing area. It was in Otaki that the **first Maori university** (University of Rauwaka) was established. This educational institution sees itself as the natural progression from Maori pre-school education and Maori school projects. From 1839 onwards the British missionary and later Bishop of Wellington, **Octavius Hadfield** (1814–1904), was active in Otaki. He showed the Maori the possibilities of agriculture. The clergyman strove for a good relationship between the white immigrants and the Maori, also stopping Maori chief Te Rauparaha from attacking Wellington. However, his freely given opinions on the land wars made him **unpopular in government circles**.

Rangiatea Maori Church

Otaki's main sight used to be the Rangiatea Maori Church, but unfortunately it burned down in 1995. The most beautiful Maori church in New Zealand has been rebuilt meanwhile and opened again in 2006. Nearby stands the **tomb** of Te Rauparaha; according to legend, his body was taken to Kapiti Island. One kilometre/0.6 miles further on look out for a Catholic Maori mission station established here in 1844. The mission church was added in 1857.

Upper Hutt

Situated some 30km/18.5 miles northeast of Wellington, the **dormitory town** of Upper Hutt in the Hutt River valley has 38,000 inhabitants, many of them commuters working in Wellington. However, there are also some larger companies and institutions that have their base here, such as the New Zealand Central Institute of Technology.

Kapiti Island

Covering 1,760ha/4,349 acres, this elongated island lies off the west coast some 70km/44 miles north of Wellington. Today, the little island enjoys **protected status**. Visiting is only possible with official authorisation from the Department of Conservation in Wellington, and there is no accommodation. On the mainland side the island displays gentle, forested slopes, but towards the west sheer cliffs up to 500m/1650ft high face the Tasman Sea.

Counting some 20,000 inhabitants and dominated by **agriculture**, this central town in the western foothills of the Tararua Range lies just under 100km/62 miles northeast of Wellington. From here the city is supplied with vegetables, milk and meat. The settlement of Levin was only founded in 1889 as a **railway workers camp**, receiving the name of a director of the railway company. — *Levin*

West of Levin, Lake Horowhenua is a popular destination for day trips. The Maori raised up **artificial islands** and established fortified villages here. The area around neighbouring dune lake **Lake Papai-** — *Lake Horowhenua*

Glitters by the sea: Wellington at night

tonga to the south saw bloody conflicts between the followers of Maori leader Te Rauparaha and local tribes.

Bathing beaches Approx. 8km/5 miles northwest of Levin the famous **Waitarera Beach** awaits. Off the coast look out for the wreck of **HMS Hyderabad**, which ran aground here in 1878. More charming sections of coastline can be found further south at Hokio Beach and further north on the estuary of the Manawatu River. On the beach there are attempts to strengthen the dunes through reforestation, in order to prevent the sand from blowing across and covering the fertile fields behind them.

Foxton Just under 20km/12.5 miles north of Levin, the village of Foxton (pop 3,000) in the Manawatu area was already a **European settlement** long before Levin was established. Founded in 1855, the village was later named after prime minister William Fox. Flax and wood were bought and sold at this **trading post** near the river estuary. However, when the railway was built away from the village, Foxton's development came to a halt. The main street has a number of **historic buildings**, amongst them the former courthouse, today home to a local history museum (open on Sun). The old »Tram Station« of the former horseracing track is another reminder of past times. The **Foxton Beach settlement** has many holiday and retirement homes.

** Whanganui National Park

Se–Sf 130

Region: Wanganui
Surface area: 740 sq km/285 sq miles

Stretching south of Taumarunui, this nature reserve is a huge area of bushland, like a jungle in parts, which has very few inhabitants and even fewer roads and paths. Winding its way through the park, the emerald-green Whanganui River, a paradise for paddlers, flows through largely mountainous and densely forested landscapes. From Pipiriki inwards the river is still tame, but the upper reaches feature rapids and narrow gorges.

Settlement history Before the European settlement the river was an important **canoe route** from the western coast to the interior of North Island. Nineteenth century settlers and tourists also used the river, navigable as far as Taumarunui, to reach ▶Rotorua for example. From 1843 onwards, a whole string of **Anglican mission stations** were established along the river, and in 1883 the French nun Marie Aubert founded a

The Bridge to Nowhere near Whanganui is a popular destination for excursions

Catholic **mission** named »Jerusalem«. Around the turn of the century, work started to convert the valley into **farmland**. On the lower reaches of the river around Wanganui, and on the upper reaches around Taumarunui this was not difficult, but the middle section – above Pipiriki – presented serious problems. The white settlers, amongst them many war veterans, and even the Maori displaced here, struggled with the **lush vegetation**, poor soils and heavy erosion.

It was impossible to persuade people to stay, not even with the bridge at Mangapurua, completed in 1936 but soon ridiculed as the **»Bridge to Nowhere«**. Something that did remain very popular well into the 20th century was to take pleasureboat trips on the river, overnighting in Pipiriki's elegant hotel, which has since burned down however.

The most beautiful sections of the river can only be accessed on foot.   Hikes
Some hiking trails, such as the **Matamateaonga Track**, open up particularly charming viewpoints on the river.

*Whanganui River Road The winding Whanganui River Road, leading upriver from Wanganui to Pipiriki, was completed in 1934. Some 11km/7 miles north of Wanganui, the sights of **Upokongaro** include St Mary's Anglican Church (1877) and the remains of a Maori pa. Atene (Athens; 35km/22 miles) has a small meeting house dating from 1886, which makes a good starting point for a hike of several hours on the »**Atene Skyline Walk«**. The once fairly large Maori settlement of Koriniti (48km/30 miles) boasts two carved meeting houses.

North of Koriniti, Operiki Pa (49km/30.5 miles) is an imposing **Maori fortification** with high walls. The grain mill in Kawana (56km/35 miles) was erected in 1854 and still functioned until 1913.

The former **Catholic mission station** of Ranana (61km/38 miles) lies near Moutoa Island, a river island also the site of a large Maori fortification in former times.

Hiruharama (67km/41 miles) occupies a quite idyllic position on a river bend, where the French nun Marie Aubert established a mission in 1883. However, the settlement really became famous through the commune where **poet James K Baxter** (1926–1972) spent the last years of his life. Religious revival movements influenced his work as much as his commitment to the poor did.

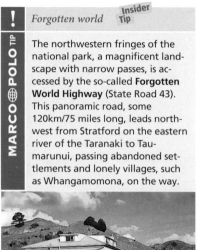

Pipiriki Pipiriki (79km/49 miles) was once home to an elegant hotel, which burned down in 1959. On the river a meadow is set aside for campers (albeit with no washing facilities). During the land wars, the town was an important **centre of the Hauhau movement**. The headquarters of Whanganui National Park are located in Pipiriki, with an information centre and museum.

Boat trips Today there are once more boat trips **on the Whanganui**. The journey from Taumarunui to Wanganui usually takes five days. The main travel season is the southern summer. Wanganui, Pipiriki and Tau-

Whanganui National Park

INFORMATION
Department of Conservation
Wanganui Conservancy Office
Ingestre Chambers
74 Ingestre St, Wanganui
Tel. 06 3 48 84 75
www.doc.govt.nz

Visit Ruapehu
54 Clyde St,
Ohakune
Tel. 06 385 8687
www.visitruapehu.com

marunui serve as starting points for **jet boat** trips. There is also the option, in summer, of paddling the 232km/144 miles downriver by **canoe** from Taumarunui to the point where the river joins the sea at ▶Wanganui.

Whangarei

✳ Se 126

Region: Northland
Altitude: 0–404m/1,325ft
Population: 82,000

The modern industrial city with a petroleum refinery and a factory producing cement, fertiliser and glass spreads out along a natural harbour on Northland's east coast, its many bays reaching far inland, and dominated by the five summits of Mount Manaia, which rise up to 404m/1,325ft above sea level. The climate is sub-tropical.

The **largest and most important settlement** north of ▶Auckland made up for its late development with very rapid growth. The deepwater port at Marsden Point can handle large tanker ships. Whilst European immigrants founded a settlement here as early as 1839, constant conflict with the local Maori impeded any further development. In 1845, when the war with Hone Heke was raging, most white settlers fled to Auckland. The woefully **inadequate infrastructure** at the time further hindered the development of the north. It was only in the mid-1930s that an all-weather road was built to Auckland. The big **breakthrough** for the town came in the 1960s, when a petroleum refinery and oil-fired power station were built. Whilst Whangarei displays all the negative attributes of an industrial town, it does have a more attractive core. Yachts animate the scene at the **Town Basin**, with nice shops and cosy eateries clustering around it.

Location and history

Everyone here enjoys fishing and angling. Whangarei also became famous as the birthplace of the Dutch-German-New Zealand solo sailor Laura Dekker, who sailed alone around the world at the age of 14 in a much-publicized feat that she completed in January 2012.

WHAT TO SEE IN AND AROUND WHANGAREI

Clapham Clock Museum

Several hundred old **timepieces**, the oldest dating back to the 17th century, vintage musicboxes and much more can be admired in the museum on Dent Street (near Quayside Town Basin) that was founded by Archibald Clapham in 1940.

❶ Daily 9am – 5pm, admission: NZ$ 10, www.claphamsclocks.com

Cafler Park, Whangarei Art Museum

Various types of fern thrive in this **oasis of tranquility**, lovingly laid out in the heart of the city. Part of the park is also a larger greenhouse, where a number of rare plants thrive. A few steps further ahead, the city's art museum is worth a visit; it shows an extensive collection of historical and contemporary works by local artists.

❶ Daily 10am – 4pm, admission: donation requested,
www.nzmuseums.co.nz

Mount Parahaki

A trip to the summit of the 242m/794-ft **Mount Parahaki** is recommended, not least because of the **splendid views**. The »pa« Maori fortification that once stood here has now been replaced by a large **war memorial**. The summit can be reached on foot, starting from Mair Park (approx. 1 hr), or by car via Memorial Drive.

*Whangarei Museum

A few miles further west, in the suburb of Maunu (on the road leading to ▶Dargaville), the Whangarei Museum not only shows splendid

Whangarei

INFORMATION
Whangarei Info
Tarewa Park,
92 Otaiki Road
Tel. 09 4 38 10 79
www.whangareinz.com/i-site

WHERE TO STAY
Lodge Bordeaux ££–£££
361 Western Hills Drive
Tel. 09 4 38 04 04
www.lodgebordeaux.co.nz

Award-winning motel with simple elegance. Generous rooms, some with own terrace.

Cheviot Park Motor Lodge ££
Corner Western Hills Drive & Cheviot Street
Tel. 05 08 24 38 46
www.cheviotpark.co.nz
Very quiet accommodation with rooms on groundfloor level, guarded parking lot and friendly service

Maori »feather cloaks«, but also memorabilia from the time of the very first immigrants from Europe. »**Clarke Homestead**«, erected in 1885, is also open to visitors. Another part of this museum complex is a **kiwi house**, where a few of these nocturnal animals may be observed.

● Daily 10am –4pm, admission: NZ$ 15, www.kiwinorth.co.nz

Smashed Pipi Insider Tip

MARCO POLO TIP

... is the name of a great combination of café, pub and craft gallery on Mangawhai Harbour southeast of Waipu. The enjoyment of (mostly) modern art is complemented by delicious snacks and excellent coffee. And to top it all, a splendid beach stretches out in front of the café.

About five kilometers (three miles) outside of the city centre, on the road to Tutukaka, **New Zealand's probably most often photographed waterfall** plunges 26m/85ft over basalt and lava stone into the deep. A round hiking trail runs through the park to the foot of the falls; or the natural spectacle can be observed from one of three platforms above the falls.

Situated 24km/15 miles east of Tutukaka these islands are a real **treasure trove for divers**. Whangarei is a base for **boat trips** and **fishing expeditions**.

Poor Knights Islands

Just under 40km/25 miles south of Whangarei, Waipu, with its 2,000 inhabitants, is situated in a picturesque location where a **river** flows into Bream Bay. The town was founded in the mid-19th century by Scottish immigrants who had already tried their luck in Canada and Australia, and the centre boasts a memorial to the founders complete with Scottish lion. The **Waipu House of Memories** remembers the Scottish pioneers.

Waipu

Bream Bay has some magnificent **beaches**, for instance the romantic Waipu Cove and Langs Beach, 10km/6.2 miles further south. Pretty day **trip destinations** in the area surrounding Whangarei include Tutukaka, Ngunguru, Matapouri, Wolley Bay and Sandy Bay, as well as Hikurangi (round trip approx. 80km/50 miles); furthermore there is Parua Bay and the beautiful beaches of Pataua (round trip approx. 90km/56 miles).

Beaches on Bream Bay and further day trip destinations

SOUTH ISLAND

Surface area: 150,437 sq km/ 58,084 sq miles
Population: 1 million
Population density: 7 inh./sq km/ 39 inh./sq miles

** Abel Tasman National Park

Sc–Sd 131

Region: Nelson
Surface area: 225.5 sq km/87 sq miles
Altitude: 0 – 1,163m/3,815ft

With its charming bays, bizarre chalk cliffs and tiny islets, Abel Tasman National Park is a prime destination for holidaymakers, hikers and water sports aficionados. Many of the brilliant beaches with turquoise water here are only accessible by boat or on foot. The vegetation has recovered well from its earlier over-exploitation by loggers.

Abel Tasman National Park is situated in the very north of South Island on the promontory dividing Tasman Bay from Golden Bay. The Department of Conservation (DOC) runs **visitor centres** in Motueka and Takaka, as well as **ranger stations** at the Totaranui and Marahau campsites. The visitor centres stock extensive information and maps, as well as **booking overnight stays** in the park (in a hut or own tent).

DOC stations

The very popular National Park is accessible all year round, with **high season** in December and January. The campsites and hut accommodation get booked up months in advance at these times.

Season

The **national park** was established in 1942, to commemorate the 300th anniversary of the discovery of the country by **Abel Tasman** in 1642 and named after him. At the time, Tasman was anchored near the Tata Islands in today's **Golden Bay**, when aggressive local Maori with their canoes attacked one of his boats, slaying several of his men. Following the incident, Tasman refused to set foot on land, and named the place »**Murderers Bay**«.

History

Milford Sound with Mitre Peak is one of the best known photo subjects in New Zealand.

Abel Tasman National Park

INFORMATION

Motueka Visitor Centre
Wallace Street Motueka
Tel. 03 528 6543
www.motuekaisite.co.nz

Abel Tasman Coast Track Help Desk
DOC Visitor Centre
79 Trafalgar Street, Nelson
Tel. 03 546 9339
www.doc.govt.nz

WHERE TO STAY

Kimi Ora Spa Resort ££ – £££
99 Martin Farm Road Kaiteriteri, RD2
Motueka 7197
Tel. 03 527 8027
www.kimiora.com
This extensive complex near Kaiteriteri village offers pure relaxation and spa treatment in a dream-like landscape. The resort owners place a high value on sustainability and environmental protection.

Caves

In the southwest of the national park, visitors in the know can still find parts of some **unexplored cave systems**. The most famous cave is **Harwood's Hole**, 300m/984ft deep. (Be careful! Due to the brittle rock, exploring caves in this area can be dangerous!).

Worthwhile hikes

Starting at the Takaka–Totaranui road, the **Wainui Falls Walk** (approx. 2 hrs there and back) leads to this 21 m/69-ft waterfall. The same road gives access to Lookout Rock (just under 2 hrs there and back), offering pretty views out to Golden Bay. Further north, at a height of 400m/1,312-ft, **Gibbs Hill** commands even better panoramic views. This latter hike, taking the aforementioned road as its starting point, requires half a day.

From Totaranui, **Pukatea Walk** leads along the northern side of the bay. Hiking south along the beach from Totaranui leads to Skinner Point, Goat Bay and Waiharakeke Bay (just under 4 hrs there and back). Heading north from Totaranui leads hikers to Anapai Bay, Mutton Cove and Separation Point (approx. 5 hrs there and back), the **northernmost tip** of the promontory.

Torrent Bay is the starting point for hiking trails leading to **Cleopatra's Pool** (a pool at the base of the waterfall, where swimming is possible) into the **Falls River Valley**, and to Cascade Falls (each approx. 2 hrs there and back). A hike north along the beach from Marahau takes in some pretty bays.

**Coastal Track

Hiking the eminently scenic Coastal Track takes **three days**. The starting point of the trail is at the limits of the park at Marahau in the south, leading along the coast to Separation Point on the northern tip, and further west to Wainui Inlet in the northwest corner of the park. Some bays have huts for **overnighting** (advanced reservations essential!). As some watercourses and lagoons may only be crossed at low tide, it is advisable to keep an eye on the **tides**. The most difficult place to cross the mouth of the creek is probably **Awaroa**.

AROUND TASMAN NATIONAL PARK

Founded in 1842 on the northwestern edge of the national park, the small town of Takaka (Nelson/Marlborough region; pop 1,300) lies at the foot of **Marble Mountain**, its marble adorning the parliamentary building in ▶Wellington and the cathedral in ▶Nelson. The small **Takaka Museum** and the »**Golden Bay Work Centre & Artisan Shop**« (a craft centre) are worth a look here. Around Takaka, the pretty beaches of **Golden Bay** (Pohara, Tata, Patons Rock and Tukurua) attract many bathers. Takaka

Approx. 5km/3 miles away, the **Te Waikoropupu Springs**, or »**Pupu Springs**«, are also of interest, primarily for the incredible volume of water they discharge. Most of the water feeding the springs is drawn from the Takaka River, which in dry summers disappears underground completely. In the 19th century, there was much digging for **gold** around the springs.

Situated just under 30km/18.5 miles northwest of Takaka, the village of Collingwood makes a good starting point for interesting hikes and day trips. Situated some 8km/5 miles southwest of **Collingwood**, the karst **caves of Te Anaroa** are worth visiting. Near the caves, look out for some bizarre rock formations. Just under 30km/18.5 north of Collingwood, the road reaches **Cape Farewell**, the northern tip of South Island. Pushing out eastwards from the Cape is the seemingly desert-

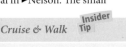

MARCO POLO TIP

Cruise & Walk   Insider Tip

Consider going on one of the very popular and exciting organised hikes and boat trips in the Abel Tasman National Park area, offered by a Motueka-based company. Information: Wilsons Abel Tasman National Park, P.O. Box 351, Motueka, Nelson, Tel. 03 5 28 20 27, www.abeltasman.co.nz

like **Farewell Spit**, a sandbank just under 30km/18.5 miles long, appears like a desert. The majority of the spit is a **sanctuary for seals and seabirds** and may only be visited as part of an organised coach tour. West of the Cape, both the fantastic **Wharaiki Beach** and the **Whanganui Inlet** (Westhaven) await discovery.

**Heaphy Track

Bainham (approx. 30km/18.5 miles south of Collingwood) marks the start of the famous **hiking trail** named after the explorer Charles Heaphy. Extending to just under 80km/50 miles overall, the trail demands 4 to 5 days' walking and leads through the dense primeval forests of **North West Nelson Forest Park** and along the western coast. On the coast in particular, the trail offers up **magnificent views**. Finishing at Karamea on the west coast, the Heaphy Track **follows an ancient Maori path** to the coastal jade deposits, later used by the gold prospectors too. Today, hiking is made easier by the **swing bridges** leading across ferny gorges and watercourses, as well as the huts for staying overnight. The return journey is best tackled by calling the **»Heaphy Air Taxi«**. Information and documents such as hut passes can be picked up from the DOC offices in Takaka and Nelson. **All-weather gear and boots** are a must. The trail as such is not too difficult though it does rise up to an altitude of 900m/2,953ft.

Motueka

Around 25km/15.5 south of Abel Tasman National Park, the small port of Motueka (pop 5,000) lies on Tasman Bay. In the town's fertile hinterland, **extensive specialized crops** (such as berries, kiwifruit, apples, hops and tobacco) have been established. Before the arrival of the white settlers the area had a strong Maori population. For a long time, the only way to get here was by boat. Worth seeing is the **Te Ahurewa Maori church**, erected in 1897 at the behest of Frederick Bennett, who in 1928 was the first **Maori to be made bishop**.

Cross swaying planks to go into the jungle

*Kaiteriteri Beach, Marahau Beach

The splendid beach of Kaiteriteri unfolds 14km/8.5 miles north of Motueka. Just under 10km/6 miles further north, the road reaches the pretty **beach** of Marahau, the start and finish point of the **coastal hiking trail** through the Abel Tasman National Park.

Extending west of Motueka across 400,000 ha/nearly 990,000 acres, is **Kahurangi National Park**. The core of this natural space, comprising a major part of the wild Tasman Mountains, which rise up to 1,700m/5,580ft, is formed by the **longest and deepest cave system known in the southern hemisphere**: the sandstone, marble and karst caves of Kahurangi. The national park now boasts nearly **600km/370 miles of marked hiking trails**. Particular favourites with walkers are the **Heaphy Track** and the **Wangapeka Track**.

Alexandra

✴ Rk 136

Region: Otago
Altitude: 180m/590ft
Population: 4800
❶ Alexandra Visitor Centre, 22 Centennial Avenue
Alexandra, Tel. 03 4 48 95 15, www.alexandra.co.nz

The largest town in Central Otago, situated 200km/124 miles northwest of ▶Dunedin (100km/62miles southeast of ▶ Queenstown) on the raging Clutha River, was established during the time of the 1860s gold rush. Today, there is not much left in Alexandra to recall the time of the gold prospectors. Instead, reservoirs and irrigation canals have been laid out, allowing a lucrative economy based on fruit plantations. The lush green crops in the valley form a stark contrast to the dry, bare mountain slopes.

This »shaky« bridge was built in 1879. Before that a punt had to be used to cross the river. Only pedestrians are allowed across the wobbly structure these days, but for many locals the picturesque bridge is the **symbol** of Alexandra.

Shaky Bridge

The new museum on Centennial Avenue focuses on the gold prospecting days, but also on the beginnings of winegrowing and the first sheep farmers in the region. The Art Gallery exhibits works by regional artists.
❶ Daily 9am – 5pm, free admission, donation requested.

Central Stories Museum & Art Gallery

Tucker Hill Lookout

Tucker Hill, rising up towards the northeast, might look fairly bare, but it commands good views of the small town situated amidst green fruit trees, as well as of the confluence of Clutha River and the serpentine Manuherikia River. Occasionally the tops of the **Remarkables** near ▶Queenstown are visible in the distance.

AROUND ALEXANDRA

Old gold prospector settlements

Alexandra serves as a base for visiting old gold mining settlements, first taking Highway 85 north to Omakau (pop approx. 200), and further northwest reaching the settlement of **Matakanui** at the foot of the Dunstan Mountains, these days effectively a **ghost town**. The road carries on to **Drybread**, the derelict gold prospector's village of **St Bathans**, to **Hills Creek** and from there back through the Ida Valley to the former goldmining village of **Oturehua**, which has now been settled by a few farmers. Parts of the old extraction equipment of Golden Progress and Hayes Engineering Works still survive here. Driving past the Idaburn reservoir, the road leads to **Ophir**, where gold finds in 1863 attracted thousands of fortune seekers. Ophir still has its historic **courthouse** and **post office**. Crossing the Manuherikia River on a suspension bridge brings drivers back to Alexandra.

Clyde

Roughly 10km/6 miles northwest of Alexandra (Hwy 8), the village of Clyde (pop 1,000) lies surrounded by hills on the Clutha River. In 1862, the discovery of gold in the river was followed by the establishment of a settlement south of Cromwell Gorge, formerly known as »Dunstan«, for around **4,000 gold prospectors**, complete with banks and hotels. Some of the buildings from the time of the gold boom are still standing. Visitors to the village cannot miss the **gold prospectors monument**. The courthouse dating from 1864 houses the local museum (opening times: Tue to Sun 2–4pm). Further **buildings of note** are the »Athenaeum« (1874), which used to put on theatre plays and concerts, the former town hall (1869; today a hotel), the former Hartley Arms Hotel (1865) and Dunstan House (1900). Other buildings still standing include the old post office, St Michael's Anglican Church (1877), St Dunstan's Catholic Church (1906) and St Mungo's Union Church (1894).

Museum: Tue –Sun 2pm – 4pm, admission: NZ$ 3, www.clyde.co.nz

? *Spectacular gold robbery*

MARCO ⊕ POLO INSIGHT

In the 1870s Clyde saw a spectacular gold robbery. Gold stored overnight in the supposedly safe prison disappeared as if by magic. The Clyde Museum keeps the memory of this puzzling event alive.

Clutha Hydro Electric Scheme

Since 1977, despite **massive protests** by conservationists and the **latent risk of earthquakes**, the individual building stages of the

Clutha Hydro Electric Scheme are being completed. North of Clyde, a dam (59m/193ft high) was finished in 1992, damming the 26km/16-mile long **Lake Dunstan**. Today, the lake has flooded Cromwell Gorge and with it the old village of Cromwell. The reservoir feeds a large hydroelectric power station, whilst its waters are used to irrigate the surrounding fruit plantations.

Lying some 30km/18 miles north-west of Alexandra, the small town of **Cromwell** (pop 3,000) on the confluence of the Clutha River (coming from Lake Wanaka and Lake Hawea) and Kawarau River (flowing out of Lake Wakatipu) was established from scratch after the damming of Lake Dunstan. The old settlement was situated at the entrance to Cromwell Gorge, which today is flooded. A few **historic buildings** from the gold prospectors settlement founded in the 1860s have been transplanted to Melmore Terrace and called **»Old Cromwell Historic Village«**. Cromwell Museum tells the interesting story of the town's history and the **building of the dam**.

! MARCO POLO TIP

Kawarau Challenge   Insider Tip

Adrenaline-seeking wildwater enthusiasts get more than their money's worth on the Kawarau River. Rafting excursions on rubber dinghies run twice daily down the raging river. Passing the Dog Leg Rapids is an unforgettable experience. Information: Challenge Rafting, Queenstown, Tel. 03 4 42 73 18, www.raft.co.nz

Old Cromwell Historic Village: daily 9am – 6pm, winter until 5pm, free admission, donation requested, http://cromwellheritageprecinct.co.nz

Approx. 8km/5 miles west of Cromwell, Highway 6 reaches the Kawarau Gorge Mining Centre, which is part of the Otago Goldfields Park and demonstrates the laborious task of gold extraction (shows: daily midday and 3pm).
❶ Tours by appointment, NZ$ 20 – 25, tel. 03 4 45 10 38, www.gold-fieldsmining.co.nz

*Kawarau Gorge Mining Centre

Balclutha · Catlins Forest
—————————————— ✳ Rk 137

Region: Otago
Altitude: 30m/98ft
Population: 4,000

Balclutha forms the centre of a wealthy sheep-grazing area. The town serves as a base for visiting Catlins Forest Park further south, a scenic if isolated and somewhat marshy landscape of rolling hills, extensive forests, roaring waterfalls and a coast battered by violent waves.

Balclutha   Counting 4,000 inhabitants, this little town lies on Highway 1, some 80km/50 miles southwest of ►Dunedin on the lower reaches of the voluminous Clutha River. The river divides into two estuaries here, forming the fertile **Inchclutha Island**. The town's name refers to the **Scottish heritage** of its inhabitants, »Balclutha« in Gaelic meaning »Town on the Clyde River«.

Clutha River   In the past, the raging Clutha River, pouring down from the mountains of South Island's interior, became notorious for its frequent **catastrophic flooding**. The **Clutha Valley Scheme** is intended to gradually tame the destructive forces of the river. A whole flight of barrages and attendant hydroelectric power plants were built. In the past, large quantities of **gold** were found in the sediments of the Clutha River and many of its tributaries. **Huge rubble mounds** serve as a reminder of the work of some 200 diggers ploughing up the riverbed at the beginning of the 20th century. Today, the search for the precious metal still goes on at numerous spots in the catchment area of the Clutha River.

> **!** **MARCO POLO TIP**
>
> *Yellow-eyed penguins*   **Insider Tip**
>
> At the beginning of the surprisingly unspoilt Catlins Coast – at Nugget Point in particular – visitors can watch yellow-eyed penguins waddle along the beach in the evening dusk. However, penguin-watching cannot be rushed. Sometimes it might take hours, and darkness to fall, before any of these cute creatures show up.

*Catlins Forest Park   This heavily forested landscape gained its name from a whaler who around 1840 purchased large swathes of land here off the Maori. The forest initially attracted many **lumberjacks**, with several sawmills starting up in business and shipping the wood from Hinahina. The only settlement remaining from the time of the logging boom is **Owaka** (pop approx. 400) at the entrance to Catlins Forest Park. A number of **pretty bays** adorn the coastline here. The name **»Cannibal Bay«** is a reminder of the attacks and carnage of the 1830s, when the feared Maori leader Te Rauparaha advanced far down into South Island.

Highway 92, Owaka   The main access road into the scenic southeastern corner of New Zealand's South Island is Highway 92, which from Balclutha leads through Catlins Forest Park and via Owaka to ►Invercargill. In Owaka, the park administration has established a small **visitor centre** giving information on the landscape, plants and animals of this area. Along the coast, the heavy swell has sculpted **bizarre rock formations, grottoes and caves** out of the layered rock. Particularly imposing is **Cathedral Cave**, reached by a narrow, steep little road forking off Highway 92. In some places the deserted coastline still harbours seal colonies.

Blenheim

⧫ Sd 132

Region: Nelson/Marlborough
Altitude: 0 – 30m/98ft
Population: 30,000

Lying in the sun-kissed Wairau Plain on the northernmost point of South Island, the friendly town of Blenheim boasts 2,600 hours of sun per year, lending it the reputation of being New Zealand's sunniest town. So it's not surprising that the city is called »The Sunshine Capital«. It is also not surprising then that conditions here are favourable for winegrowing.

Today, the former **government buildings** on High Street house the police. The **cannon** standing at the corner of High St/Seymour St was claimed, by Captain Blenkinsopp, to have been used to purchase the Wairau land off Te Rauparaha in 1831.
Old **agricultural equipment** as well as a **reconstructed immigrants' settlement** can be seen in Brayshaw Museum Park on New Renwick Road.

Brayshaw Museum Park

At Tuamarina on Highway 1 between Blenheim and ►Picton, the Wairau Affray Memorial commemorates the victims of the clash between white settlers and Maori in 1843.

Wairau Affray Memorial

About 4km/2.5 miles south from Blenheim, Highway 1 reaches a restored clay and straw hut, a remnant of the early European settlement. The lovingly restored Riverlands Cob Cottage belongs to the Marlborough Museum in Brayshaw Park (26 Arthur Baker Place, corner of New Renwick Road), which displays historical photographs, films and memorabilia.

Riverlands Cob Cottage

❶ Daily 10am – 4pm, admission: NZ$ 10, http://marlboroughmuseum.org.nz

Spreading out just about 40km/24 miles south (Highway 1) is Lake Grassmere, boasting **New Zealand's only saline extraction plant**. Seawater is pumped into the main lake, covering nearly 700ha/1,730 acres, to then evaporate in small basins. On average, 50,000t of sea salt are extracted here per year. The luminous white salt pyramids can be seen from afar.

> **?**
>
> *Blindheim on the Danube*
>
> Blenheim is named after the legendary 1704 battle at the small town of Blindheim on the banks of the Danube. Here, the Duke of Marlborough achieved a major victory over the French and Bavarian forces in the Spanish War of Succession.
>
> MARCO ⏺ POLO INSIGHT

Blenheim

INFORMATION
Blenheim Visitor Centre
Railway Station Sinclair Street
Tel. 03 577 8080 www.cityofblenheim.co.nz

WHERE TO EAT
Hans Herzog Estate ££££
81 Jeffries Road
Tel. 03 5 72 87 70
www.herzog.co.nz
The restaurant on the vineyard belonging to the Swiss family Herzog is considered to be one of the best in the country. But the compositions of Mediterranean, New Zealand and Swiss ingredients have their price!

Wairau River Winery ££ *Insider Tip*
264 Rapaura Road, Tel. 03 5 72 79 50
www.wairauriverwines.com
This family-owned vineyard, which is located about 15km/9mi ourside of town, serves fresh regional products, in the summer on the veranda, in the winter in front of the fireplace.

WHERE TO STAY
Old St Mary's Convent ££££
Rapaura Road, Tel. 03 570 5700
www.convent.co.nz
Former convent built in 1901 in an idyllic setting amidst vineyards and olive groves, with luxurious suites.

Radfield House ££
126 Maxwell Road
Tel. 03 5 78 86 71
www.radfieldhouse.co.nz
The rooms in this historical building with a beautiful garden are furnished with antiques; breakfast is excellent and the atmosphere is relaxed and friendly. Anyone who has been here once loves to come back.

*Marlborough Wine Trail

The area around Blenheim has ideal conditions for the ripening of grapes, resulting in **some of the best wines in New Zealand** being made here. The region is New Zealand's major winegrowing region. Typical of Marlborough wines is their fresh and fruity character. There are regular organised **excursions to the vineyards and wineries**. The »Marlborough Wine Trail«, with Blenheim as its starting point, gives some particularly good insights into New Zealand viniculture. The trail takes in vineyards whose names are common currency with lovers of good wine: »Montana«, »Te Whare Ra«, »Cellier le Brun« and the world-famous »Cloudy Bay«.

Kaikoura

Driving south on the coastal road from Blenheim takes visitors to the small town of **Kaikoura** at the foot of the Seaward Kaikoura Range. The rocks at the tip of the Kaikoura Peninsula boast a **colony** of **several hundred seals**, with some yellow-eyed penguins in amongst them too. These animals show very little fear of humans, and visitors taking a **pleasure boat** out to sea may observe – from the requisite distance of course – not only seals, but **black dolphins**, **Hector's dolphins**, **sperm whales** and **albatrosses** with a wingspan of over three metres/nearly ten feet.

Chatham Islands
✦ Ad 134/135

Region: Chatham Islands
Surface area: Surface area: 97 sq km/38 sq miles
Altitude: 0 – 283m/928ft
Population: 600
❶ Chatham Islands Council, P.O. Box 124, Council Office Building Chatham, Tel. 03 3 05 00 33, www.cic.govt.nz

Approx. 800km/500 miles east of ▶Christchurch, the Chatham Islands comprise the three main islands of Chatham, Pitt and South East Island. Most island-dwellers live off fishing and agriculture.

There are several scheduled flights each week from ▶Christchurch and ▶Wellington to the main island of Chatham. Travellers wanting to visit these islands must book at least one night's **accommodation**. The first inhabitants of the Chatham Islands, the »Moriori«, came from **Polynesia** and developed in complete isolation from the inhabitants of New Zealand's main islands. They were faced with one major limitation in the **lack of any large trees** they could have used to build houses and canoes. Their dwellings therefore were rather basic. First contacts with the white man were made in 1791, when **Lieutenant Broughton**, on an expedition led by the famous English captain George Vancouver, saw land that was not yet marked on any map. Broughton's boat was called Chatham, which came to be used as the name for the newly-discovered islands. In the 19th century, the islands would regularly be visited by European **sealers and whalers**. Up to the end of World War II, the Chatham Islands remained in a state of sleepy seclusion. A stormy if temporary change was brought about by the **rock lobster fishing boom**, which lasted from 1968 to

Getting there, land and people

Chatham Island

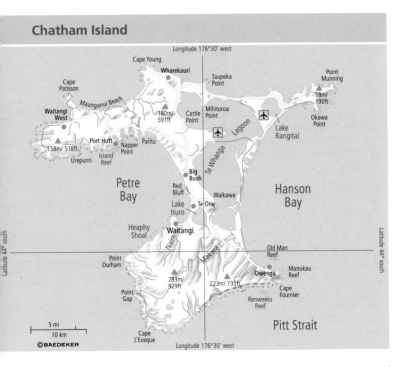

Longitude 176°30' west

Cape Young
Wharekauri
Taupeka Point
Point Munning
Cape Patisson
Maunganui Beach
180m/ 591ft
Cattle Point
Mihitoroa Point
58m/ 190ft
Waitangi West
Okawa Point
158m/ 518ft
Port Hutt
Napper Point
Paritu
Lake Rangitai
Te Whanga Lagoon
Urepuriri
Island Reef
Big Bush
Petre Bay
Red Bluff
Waikawa
Hanson Bay
Lake Huro
Te One
Heaphy Shoal
Waitangi
Old Man Reef
Point Durham
Manukau Reef
283m/ 929ft
223m/ 732ft
Owenga
Cape Fournier
Point Gap
Renweeks Reef
Pitt Strait
5 mi
10 km
©BAEDEKER
Cape L'Eveque
Longitude 176°30' west

Latitude 44° south

1972. Even after this ended, fishing was to remain a major source of income for the people living on the islands.

Main island Chatham

On the 900 sq km/nearly 350 sq-mile main island of Chatham, most of the inhabitants make a living from fishing or farming. Its 18,000 ha/nearly 44,500-acre central **lagoon** catches the eye. There are also a few shallow lakes on the island, which on the whole appears pretty flat. From Chatham, local fishing boats can take visitors to the other islands, most of them **bird sanctuaries**. The choice of accommodation options is modest: there is one tourist lodge, a basic hotel, a few private rooms, no restaurant, no bakery, and only two general grocery stores. The island capital of **Waitangi** has around 300 inhabitants. A small local museum holds Moriori cultural artefacts, as well as documenting the arrival of the white settlers and the Taranaki Maori. There is extensive material on Te Kooti too. On several chalk rocks on the main island – particularly on the western shore of the central lagoon and the east coast – **rock and tree carvings** are visible, nearly all showing seal-like figures. The Moriori also carved **human figures** into the bark of living trees.

A treat: freshly caught lobster

** Christchurch

——————————————— ✦ Sc 134

Region: Canterbury
Altitude: 0 – 448m/1,470ft
Population: 353,000

The largest town on South Island, forming its economic and cultural centre, spreads across a near-treeless plain bordered towards the southeast and the harbour by mountains ranging in height from 350m/nearly 1,150ft to 500m/1,640ft. Its austere architecture and particular flair have made Christchurch, named after the world-famous college in Oxford, England, renowned as »the most English« town in New Zealand. In recent times sever earthquakes have caused extensive damage to the city.

Christchurch

INFORMATION
Christchurch i-Site Visitor Centre
Botanic Gardens
Rolleston Avenue (near Canterbury Museum)
Tel. 03 379 9629
www.christchurchnz.com

SIGHTSEEING TOUR OF THE CITY
A large part of the city centre has been declared a »red zone« for the time being due to the earthquake damage; it is not open to the public. Only Cathedral Square is accessible. More and more of the city centre will be opened for visitors as the reconstruction progresses.

SHOPPING
The series of earthquakes from 2010 to 2011 has also affected the business world in the city centre. While there are some malls and supermarkets open, the number of visitors to the centre has been modest. The project Re:START is unique: a collection of dozens of shops and boutiques mostly housed in containers on the Cashel Mall property on Cashel Street.

WHERE TO EAT
As far as eating and drinking is concerned the selection in the city centre will remain limited for the time being. But the farther away from the centre the better the chances of finding good places to dine.

❶ *Brigittes Restaurant & Bar* £££
209 Papanui Road, Merivale
Tel. 03 3 55 61 50
www.brigittes.co.nz
This restaurant has been an institution for more than three decades. It serves breakfast, lunch and dinner. The kitchen uses fresh regional products.

❷ *Edesia* £££
12 Show Place, Addington
Tel. 03 9 82 54 71
Even though it is not easy to find this restaurant has established itself as a gourmet temple in the short time it has been open.

❸ *Untouched World's Native Garden Cafe* £££
155 Roydvale Avenue, Harewood
Tel. 03 3 57 93 99
www.untouchedworld.com
This popular eatery with a garden terrace is one of the best addresses in New Zealand as far as »organic cuisine«

Insider Tip

goes; they set great store by fresh, sustainably produced regional products.

❹ *The Ferry Speight's Ale House* ££

2A Waterman Place
Tel. 03 3 76 40 71
Hearty food is served here – from lamb chops to burgers – and lots of chilled beer to go with it.

WHERE TO STAY
The city's hotels were also severely damaged by the earthquakes in 2010 and 2011. But many purveyors have reconstructed their accommodation and are awaiting guests.

❶ *Charlotte Jane Boutique Hotel* ££££

110 Papanui Road
Tel. 03 355 1028
www.charlotte-jane.co.nz
At the edge of the city centre, only a few minutes' walk from Hagley Park, this small but fine boutique hotel welcomes guests to its Victorian ambience.

❷ *Chateau on the Park* £££

189 Deans Avenue, Riccarton
Tel. 03 2 48 89 99
www.chateau-park.co.nz
Located just a few minutes from the city centre in a pretty and quiet park, this hotel was reconstructed after the earthquake with its modern rooms and suites. Its Garden Court Brasserie is also very popular.

❸ *Best Western Camelot Motor Lodge* ££££
28 Rapanui Road

Tel. 03 3 55 91 24
www.camelot.co.nz
This modern, castle-style inn has 34 rooms , studios and apartments with the best of conveniences. It is currently one of the best accommodations on South Island.

❹ *The Heartland Hotel Cotswold* £££

88–96 Papanui Road
Tel. 03 355 3535
www.scenic-circle.co.nz
Email: cotswold@scenic-circle.co.nz
Feel like the Earl of Sussex in this elegant Tudor-style hotel on the edge of the city centre. Good shopping within walking distance.

Town planners used Christchurch's favourable position on a wide plain to implement a **generous street layout** of right angles and broad arteries. Only the winding course of the Avon River and the diagonal lines of High Street and Victoria Street break the **geometric city plan**. Its extensive parks, many sports facilities and well-kept gardens have earned Christchurch the nickname »Garden City«.

»Garden City«

Every year on 16 December, the »Canterbury Pilgrims & Settlers Association« celebrates with a religious service in the local cathedral to commemorate the **arrival of the first settlers** in 1850. In addition, on the Sunday closest to 16 December, a **»Memorial Walk«** leads from Christchurch via the Port Hills to the natural harbour of Lyttelton on the ▶Banks Peninsula, where the first English settlers set foot on the islands at the time. Christchurch was born of a very different **concept of colonialisation** to the one on North Island for example or even ▶Nelson, where the New Zealand Company facilitated the settlement of landless emigrants. **John Robert Godley**, scion of an English family of landed gentry and the founder of Christchurch, wanted to sell the land at a high price to wealthy gentlemen and have farm workers or craftspeople work on estates, following the English example. Class distinctions would thereby be enshrined here. Initially, circumstances allowed this concept to be realised. However, following the drought in Australia of 1850/1851, rich **sheep farmers** came to the Christchurch area, establishing huge »runs« for their animals. In 1855 all available land was spoken for. The »Canterbury Association« co-founded by Godley, which had brought several thousand settlers – Anglicans from England, Scottish Presbyterians, Irish Catholics and German Lutherans – into the Christchurch area, was dissolved.

Colonialisation

HISTORY

1850	The first white settlers land south of today's Christchurch
19th century	A model Anglican society is established
from 1852 onwards	Huge sheep farms are founded
1855	All estates around Christchurch are »sold«
1856	The small settlement of Christchurch is declared a town
19th/ 20th centuries	The town grows to be a commercial centre for the surrounding agricultural area
04.09.2010	A 7.1 magnitude earthquake damages many houses
22.02.2011	A 6.3 magnitude earthquake causes more damage and claims 185 lives

Pure nostalgia: the old Christchurch City Tram

Modelled on
England

The **English influence** on the city's founders is visible in the city centre. The settlers planted **trees from back home**, principally oak and willow. The architecture of the second half of the 19th century is also strongly reminiscent of the English model. Clubs practicing **»English« sports** such as cricket and tennis soon sprang up too. During a visit in the town's early years, the Anglican bishop Selwyn was critical of the settlement for doing too little for churches, parishes and schools. More durable, imposing **churches** were built from 1855 onwards, with neo-Gothic becoming the style of choice of the Anglican faith.

Architect
Mountfort

The city's physical aspect was much influenced by architect **Benjamin Mountfort**, who designed important buildings such as the Provincial Council Buildings, Canterbury Museum and the university's Great Hall (today's »Arts Centre«).

Earthquakes
in 2010 and
2011
(▸MARCO
POLO Insight
p. 334)

In 2010 and 2011 the region of Christchurch was shaken by a series of earthquakes. The Darfield earthquake on September 4, 2010 was the strongest with a magnitude of 7.1 while the **Christchurch earthquake** on February 22, 2011 measured 6.3 points. While the city of Christchurch suffered relatively little damage in 2010, the **results of the 2011 quake** were disastrous. The epicentre of the quake was a only a few kilometres away from the city centre and caused extensive **damage** there as well as in the parts of the city to the east, like Port Hill and Lyttelton. More than 180 people were killed, of which more than 100 died when the Canterbury Television building collapsed. Almost 6000 people were injured. The city's landmarks like Christchurch Cathedral, the Cathedral of the Blessed Sacrament and the Canterbury Provincial Council Buildings were destroyed. In Lyttelton Timeball Station collapsed. Up to 10,000 buildings had to be torn down, about 100,000 apartment blocks suffered extensive damage. Within a few days about one fifth of the residents left the city. The New Zealand government estimated the total damage at a value of 14 bil. euros.

WHAT TO SEE IN CHRISTCHURCH

*Cathedral
Square

The **pulsating heart** of Christchurch and the pride and joy of its long-term residents was until the earthquake the large open square right in the city centre, dominated now by the ruins of the stately Anglican **cathedral**. Clustered around the square are several historic buildings that were also severely damaged by the earthquake, such as the **Old Chief Post Office** dating from 1879, the former **Government Building** erected in the same year, the neo-Gothic **Press Building** and last not least the **Regent Theatre**, which only

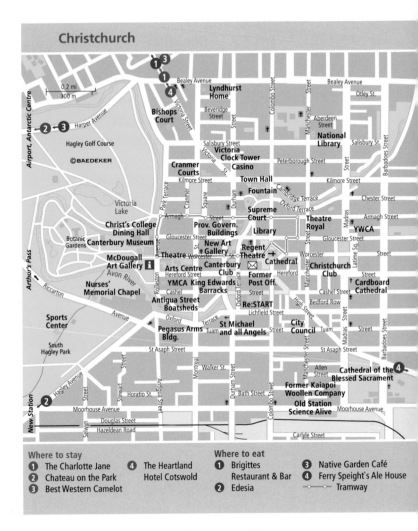

Christchurch

Where to stay

1. The Charlotte Jane
2. Chateau on the Park
3. Best Western Camelot
4. The Heartland Hotel Cotswold

Where to eat

1. Brigittes Restaurant & Bar
2. Edesia
3. Native Garden Café
4. Ferry Speight's Ale House
- Tramway

joined the ensemble in 1905. On the square itself a **monument honours John Robert Godley**, the founder of the city of Christchurch.

The **former landmark** of the city, Christchurch Cathedral, was severely damaged by the earthquake in 2011. The 65m/213-ft-high tower collapsed and the famous rosette on the front of the building

Christchurch
Cathedral

The Earth is Quaking

New Zealand is on the border of the Australian and Pacific plates. The plate border runs through North Island and South Island, which were separated about 85 mil. years ago. New Zealand is also located on the circum-Pacific Ring of Fire, a belt around the edge of the Pacific Ocean with many volcanoes.

▶ **The most severe earthquakes in New Zealand since 1900**
Earthquakes are measured by various means. The moment magnitude scale (MMS) measures the magnitude of the earthquake. The Modified Mercalli scale (MM) indicates the effects on humans and structures:

I	not felt	**VII**	very strong	● affected locations
II	very weak	**VIII**	severe	⟋ plate boundaries
III	weak	**IX**	violent	movements of plates
IV	light	**X**	extreme	The edges move about
V	moderate	**XI**	catastrophic	4.7cm/1.9in alongside each
VI	strong	**XII**	very catastrophic	other every year.

The map shows earthquakes from Level VIII.

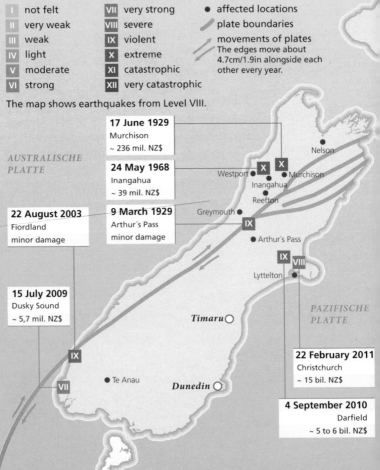

Aukland

17 June 1929
Murchison
~ 236 mil. NZ$

24 May 1968
Inangahua
~ 39 mil. NZ$

22 August 2003
Fiordland
minor damage

9 March 1929
Arthur's Pass
minor damage

15 July 2009
Dusky Sound
~ 5,7 mil. NZ$

22 February 2011
Christchurch
~ 15 bil. NZ$

4 September 2010
Darfield
~ 5 to 6 bil. NZ$

AUSTRALISCHE
PLATTE

PAZIFISCHE
PLATTE

Nelson
Westport
Murchison
Inangahua
Reefton
Greymouth
Arthur's Pass
Lyttelton
Timaru
Te Anau
Dunedin

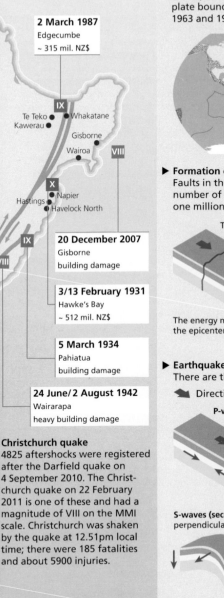

2 March 1987
Edgecumbe
~ 315 mil. NZ$

Te Teko ● ● Whakatane
Kawerau ●

Gisborne

Wairoa

IX

VIII

X

Hastings ● Napier
● Havelock North

IX

VIII

20 December 2007
Gisborne
building damage

3/13 February 1931
Hawke's Bay
~ 512 mil. NZ$

5 March 1934
Pahiatua
building damage

24 June/2 August 1942
Wairarapa
heavy building damage

Christchurch quake
4825 aftershocks were registered after the Darfield quake on 4 September 2010. The Christchurch quake on 22 February 2011 is one of these and had a magnitude of VIII on the MMI scale. Christchurch was shaken by the quake at 12.51pm local time; there were 185 fatalities and about 5900 injuries.

▶ **Earthquake regions around the world**
Earthquakes occur especially frequently along plate boundaries. The map shows events between 1963 and 1998.

▶ **Formation of earthquakes**
Faults in the earth's crust are responsible. The annual number of earthquake occurrences is estimated at one million.

The plates move toward each other. Friction is transformed into kinetic energy. Pressure causes the rocks to burst.

The energy moves out from the epicenter in circular tremors.

▶ **Earthquake waves**
There are three kinds of seismic waves:

 Direction of waves 　↘ waves

P-waves (primary waves)
They are longitudinal and propagate twice as fast as S-waves.

L-waves (Love-waves, named after the British mathematician A.E.H. Love) They are close to the surface and can cause the most severe damage.

S-waves (secondary waves)
perpendicular waves

was destroyed. It is presently not clear whether or not the cathedral will be rebuilt. The foundation stone was laid in 1864. It was designed by famous London architect **George Gilbert Scott**. But just a year later building work had to be halted for lack of funds and was only taken up again in 1873. At the time, architect Mountfort was handed the task of supervising the construction, changing Scott's design by adding **crenellations, turrets and small balconies** to the ecclesiastical structure. However, completion of the cathedral took until 1904, six years after Mountfort's death and 40 years after the start of the building work. The interior of the monumental church is a visual representation of the story of the Anglican Church.

Next to the cathedral stands the sculpture MThe Chalice (also called Millenium Cone). The 18m/59ft-high sculpture made of steel and aluminium by Neil Dawson was unveiled in 2001 during the city's 150th anniversary. It shows 42 leaves from native plants.

Trinity Centre
At the rear of the cathedral and dating from 1874 and also damaged by the earthquake, Trinity Centre – also designed by architect Mountfort – was **originally a church** but was later used for talks and meetings

Re:START
South of Cathedral Square, on Hereford Street and next to the city's former shopping mall, this unique **shopping and entertainment centre** developed in recent years. Shopping, tasty dining or just drinking a good coffee is possible – but in old building containers. The multi-media exhibit **Quake City**, also located here, is worth looking at as it shows the consequences of the sever earthquakes of 2010 and 2011.

❶ Daily 10am – 5pm, free admission, www.restart.org.nz

Old Chief Post Office
On the southwestern side of Cathedral Square stands the city's former main post office, which was also damaged by the earthquake. Designed by P F M Burrows in the **Italian neo-Renaissance style**, the building was originally built in 1879.

Regent Theatre
This cinema has been around since 1930, though it also suffered earthquake damage in 2011. The »Royal Exchange Building«, built in 1905 in the so-called Edwardian Style, was converted **from the stock exchange to a theatre**.

Press Building
The quake-damaged building on the northeastern side of Cathedral Square was built by the architects Collins & Harman in 1909 as a **printing and publishing house** for the city's oldest newspaper, founded back in 1861. The four-storey building, constructed in the English late Gothic style, boasts **distinctive window designs** which are different on each floor.

Dating from 1861, this impressive wooden structure east of the cathedral was built following a design by Mountfort in the style of **the Italian Renaissance**. It was also severely damaged by the earthquake in 2011. This is where the **»wool barons«**, the owners of the huge sheep herds, used to meet. The writer Samuel Butler also often spent time here, despite the fact that conversation was somewhat restricted to money and sheep, as he observed.

Christchurch Club

This nearby **gallery** (formerly the Canterbury Society of Arts Gallery), also on Gloucester Street, shows mainly contemporary and modern art. It was also heavily damaged by the Canterbury earthquakes and re-opened after refurbishment in February 2016 under the name Toi Moroki | Centre of Contemporary Art to reflect New Zealand's philosophy of using Te Reo Maori in all aspects of public life.

Centre of Contemporary Art

❶ www.coca.org.nz

Not far to the southeast, at 234 Hereford Street, 24m/79ft-high excentric sacred building by the Japanese architect Shigeru Ban catches the eye. It has served as the temporary Anglican cathedral since 2013. It is built from 96 earthquake-proof cardboard tubes and wooden beams. The façade consists of polycarbonate elements; the lower construction from abandoned containers.

M Cardboard Cathedral

❶ daily 9am – 7pm, winter only until 5pm, admission: donation requested, www.cardboardcathedral.org.nz

This **wooden Anglican church**, west of Christ Church Cathedral on Oxford Terrace, was built in 1872 following designs by W F Crisp. The precious interior furnishings and stained-glass windows attract many visitors. The freestanding bell tower was designed in 1861 by Mountfort. Despite some earthquake damage the church is still accessible.

St Michael's & All Angels Anglican Church

The **neo-Gothic buildings** erected for the provincial government between 1859 and 1865 northeast of the cathedral and beyond the River Avon were especially beautiful architectural monuments. Now they are **heavily damaged** and not accessible. Wooden structures were initially built around a courtyard, and later joined by a stone building topped by a tower. The jewel in the crown of the ensemble designed by Mountfort is the ornate **neo-Gothic debating chamber** with stained glass windows and a richly adorned barrel vault. In 1924, an extension was added on Armagh Street.

Provincial Council Buildings

Situated further south on the Avon River, Christchurch's former **City Council Chambers** was the city's visitor centre until the earthquake in 2011. Built in 1887 in the **Queen Anne style**, the redbrick build-

Former Visitor Centre

ing occupies the site where the »Canterbury Association« had its Land Office in 1851. The **Women Memorial** was unveiled in 1993 behind the Visitor Centre. The bronze monument was created to mark the centenary of **women's suffrage** in New Zealand. Opposite the Visitor Centre, the **Scott Memorial**, also heavily damaged in the 2011 earthquake, commemorates **Robert Falcon Scott**, who started out from Christchurch in 1912 on his Antarctic expedition. He became the second person to reach the South Pole after Roald Amundsen, but together with his team, later froze to death in a snowstorm. The memorial was created by his widow, sculptor Kathleen Lady Kennett, in 1917. Further south, the Avon was spanned in 1923 by the **Bridge of Remembrance**, serving as a war memorial to the New Zealand soldiers killed in the First World War.

Botanic
Gardens,
* Canterbury
Museum

Laid out in a park formed by a **bend in the River Avon**, Christchurch's Botanic Gardens (Rolleston Ave.) are well-tended and rich in species. Here the diverse Variety of New Zealand's flora can be studied. A specially marked **Historic Tree Walk** leads to magnificent old trees that were planted here in the 19th cent. already. There are **conservatories** with tropical plants, ferns and desert plants.

The eastern edge of the park is worth exploring for the stately **Canterbury Museum** museum, designed by Mountfort in 1870, which holds collections from the **colonial past**, as well as beautiful Maori carvings and objects made from nephrite (greenstone). The Antarctic Gallery is renowned for its collection dedicated to **Antarctic research** from its beginnings to the modern day. The first director of the museum and one of its most important collectors was the geologist **Julius von Haast**, who undertook extensive field trips on South Island. Working with other museums, von Haast used his extensive collection of **moa bones** to establish the local museum. Behind Canterbury Museum, take a look inside the McDougall Art Gallery, which focuses on work by New Zealand and British artists, alongside paintings, sculptures and ceramics.

Botanic Garden: daily 7am – 6.30pm, free admission, www.ccc.govt.nz/cityleisure/parkswalkways/christchurchbotanicgardens/visitorinformation/
Canterbury Museum: daily 9am – 5pm, admission: donation requested (min. NZ$ 2), www.canterburymuseum.com

** Christchurch Art
Gallery Te
Puna O
Waiwhetu

This art gallery, which was opened in 2003 on the banks of the Avon River, is an eye-catcher. It replaces the former McDougall Art Gallery. The impressive **glass front** of the **wave-shaped** cultural building shines day and night; it was designed by the architectural firm Buchan Group. The building shows mainly works by New Zealand and British artists, including pictures, sculptures and ceramics. In front of the gallery sculpture **»Reason for Voyaging«** by Graham Bennett is the first to impress visitors. Incidentally: the Maori name of the gallery refers to an **artesian well** on the grounds, which the Maori called »fountain whose waters reflect the stars«. The gallery is only partially open due to continuing repairs after the earthquake in 2011. There are regular special exhibits however.

❶ Daily 10am – 4pm, admission: donations requested, http://christchurchart-gallery.org.nz

*Arts Centre

Also designed by the architect Mountfort, near the museum the neo-Gothic buildings formerly housing **Canterbury University** were turned into an arts centre in the 1970s. At the time, the university's institutes moved to Ilam, a part of town further west. The construction of the building, originally divided by sciences, was begun in 1876.

The **architectural highlights** of the ensemble are the central Clock Tower (1877) with the main entrance and the Great Hall (1882). The room where the future Nobel Prize winner **Rutherford** (▶Famous People) carried out early physical experiments lies in the western corner of the main quadrangle. The famous philosopher **Karl Popper** (1902–1994) taught here from 1937 to 1945. The Arts Centre had theatrical and ballet troupes before the earthquake, as well as live music, and there were high-class arts performances on a near daily basis. The Arts Center will probably be closed until 2019 when restoration and reconstruction after the earthquake are to be finished.

❶ www.artscentre.org.nz

Crafts and food

Around the centre, a colourful if slightly sprawling arts-and-crafts operation has become established, with various **shops, galleries, crafts stalls and eateries**. The earthquakes of 2010 and 2011 only temporarily stopped the bustle. On Worcester Boulevard things get busy especially on weekends. Wares include beautiful crafts, valuable jewellery and tasty food.

Hagley Park

The trees of the 180ha/445-acre city park, which stands on former Maori land, stretching out behind the Arts Centre and Canterbury Museum were **imported from Europe**. Alongside various sports facilities (including the Cricket Oval), a golf course and a riding track have been established here.

Mona Vale

Northwest of Hagley Park, on the banks of the river Avon, the Mona Vale **stately home** boasts a 4ha/nearly 10-acre park with old trees. The mansion dates from 1905. Most of the gorunds are currently inaccessible because of the heavy earthquake damage.

❶ www.monavale.co.nz

Christ's College

The college on the northern side of Canterbury Museum was established as a **higher boys school** in the tradition of the English gram-

?

Rien ne va plus

Until a few years ago, gambling was strictly controlled in New Zealand. Only recently have casinos begun opening, with the first in New Zealand started up northwest of Town Hall in Christchurch.

mar schools soon after the settlement was founded. The first buildings on this site date back to 1857. Designed by Superintendent Fitzgerald, the **»Big School«** from 1863 is the country's oldest school building still in use today. The »New Classrooms« from 1886 were designed by the architect Mountfort, while between 1915 and 1925 Cecil Wood drew up the plans for the »Dining Hall« on the street side, »Hare Library« with the clock, and »Jacob's House« Since the 2010/2011 earthquake Christ's College is being used as the seat of the bishop of Canterbury until further notice and it is closed to the public.

❶ www.christscollege.com.

*Town Hall

Northeast of the Provincial Buildings, the modern Town Hall, erected in 1972 on Victoria Square, caughtt the eye until the earthquake in 2011. This imposing building was designed by the local architects' practice **Warren & Mahoney**. The Town Hall comprises a conference room and large auditorium, as well as further meeting and banquet rooms. The Town Hall is expected to re-open in June 2016 after extensive reconstruction.

Victoria Square

On Victoria Square, a **bronze statue in patina green** dating from 1903 commemorates Queen Victoria, while another, dating from 1932, depicts James Cook (▶Famous People). The **clock tower** standing on Victoria Street northwest of Town Hall since 1930, was originally planned as a decoration for the Provincial Government Buildings. Turning out to be too heavy for the lightweight roof construction, it now occupies a massive stone plinth.

Cathedral of the Blessed Sacrament

The Catholic cathedral – considered the country's **finest church in the Neo-Renaissance style** – was erected between 1901 and 1905 to the southeast of the city centre on Barbados Street. The cathedral, with a high dome above the crossing designed by architect F W Petre. It was severely damaged by the earthquakes in 2010 and 2011. whether or not it will be rebuilt has not been decided.

Ferrymead Historic Park

At Mount Pleasant in southeastern Christchurch, Ferrymead Historic Park is an **open-air museum** with a reconstructed pioneer settlement, an old tram and railway. This is where the country's **first railway** ran in 1863.

❶ Sat and Sun 10am – 4.30pm, admission: NZ$ 15.50, www.ferrymead.org.nz

PORT HILLS · LYTTELTON HARBOUR

South of Christchurch, between the city and Lyttelton Harbour, the **Port Hills** rise up to 446m/1,463ft above sea level. Like the offshore **Banks Peninsula** to the south, the Port Hills are of volcanic origin. These were the mountains that the first white settlers had to conquer in the mid-19th century in order to transport their worldly goods inland from the natural harbour of Lyttelton on the steep **»Bridle Path«**. Today, drivers can cruise across the Port Hills on Summit Road; it might be bendy but it does offer many fine vistas. This **panoramic road** was built in the first half of the 20th century at the behest of politician Harry Ell, who also had several roadhouses established along the route. The Port Hills were given a thorough shaking during the 2010/2011 earthquakes. Many houses were severely damaged and numerous ones had to be torn down.

*From Bridle Path to Summit Road

A further highlight south of Christchurch is Mount Cavendish, its lofty heights ascended by cable car, which is functioning again after post-earthquake repairs. The **panoramic views** over the city, the coast and the wide plain all the way to the Southern Alps are unique.

MARCO POLO TIP

! *Sign of Takahe* Insider Tip

Standing on Summit Road, still in the suburb of Cashmere, this famous roadhouse bears a name that has many associations – »Sign of Takahe«. Looking like a small castle, it housed one of South Island's top gourmet restaurants until the 2011 earthquake. It is expected to be re-opened in July 2016 by its former tenant. (Info: http://www.futurechristchurch.co.nz)Magnificent views can still be enjoyed from up here.

A little further on, the road reaches the **natural port** of Lyttelton, which also owes its creation to volcanic activity. Named after Lord Lyttelton, a notable member of the Canterbury Association, in the 19th century this port was the **gateway to New Zealand** for thousands of Europeans. It was also the first landing point in 1850 for those pious immigrants who moved on north with their possessions across the difficult »Bridle Path« to found the city of Christchurch. Since 1867 there has been a railway tunnel and since 1964 even a road tunnel to Christchurch – alongside the aforementioned Summit Road. The **epicentre of the February 2011 earthquake** lay close to Lyttelton and the city received heavy damages. More buildings collapsed in an aftershick on June 13, 2011. The most interesting places in the town, which today counts some 3,000 inhabitants, are connected by a **historical trail**. Information can be picked up from the **Lyttelton Historical Museum** (Gladstone Quay).

*Lyttelton

Lyttelton Historical Museum: temporarily closed, further info: www.lytteltonmuseum.co.nz

Idyllic location: Akaroa natural harbour

Timeball Station

Built in 1875, the **Timeball Station** functioned up to 1935, with the falling of the balloon showing the time. Constructed by prisoners, the edifice on Reserve Terrace had to be torn down after irreparable earthquake damage in 2011.

The nearby Anglican **Holy Trinity Church** (built in 1860) and the Catholic **St Joseph's Church** (1865) were also irreparably damage.

Ripapa Island

A long time ago, tiny Ripapa island in the harbour of Lyttelton had a Maori pa fortification. In 1885, a fort was erected here out of fear of Russian attack. For a while the island served as a quarantine station and prison, temporarily housing the First World War German marine officer who rose to international fame as the »Sea Devil«, **Felix Graf von Luckner** (1881–1966) as the highest ranking prisoner of war in New Zealand's history.

BANKS PENINSULA

Made by volcanos

Protruding into the South Pacific just below Lyttelton, Banks Peninsula is another result of fierce volcanic activity in the recent geological past. Bordered by the **deep natural harbours** of Lyttelton (northwest) and Akaroa (southeast), the peninsula has a **very favourable climate**, even allowing the cultivation of the frost-sensitive kumara sweet potatoes.

Lying in the southeast of the peninsula, the **natural harbour** which the Maori call »Akaroa« is today inhabited by approx. 800 people. The main attraction are the around 300 Hector's dolphins (the smallest species of dolphin in the world), who live in a nature reserve so that they will not become entangled and injured in fishing nets. Look out for the Catholic **parish church of St Patrick's**, dating from 1864. This is the third church of the missions established in 1840 by Bishop Pompallier.

Furnished in the style of the period, **Maison Langlois-Eteveneaux** in Rue Lavaud was built in 1845 by A Langlois and housed the Eteveneaux family between 1858 and 1906. The museum tells the story of this brief French episode. The Anglican **St Peter's Church** on Rue Balguerie was built in 1863 in the neo-Gothic style. The old Customs house, dating from 1852, is a remarkable work of carpentry. On the hill with the modern **lighthouse** (1980) called »L'Aube«, look out for the cemetery established by French settlers. About 5km/3 miles south of Akaroa, a small **Maori church** dates from 1878.

*Akaroa

Maison Langlois-Eteveneaux: tel. 03 3 04 10 13, admission: NZ$ 5, www. akaroamuseum.org.nz

In Okains Bay, the **Maori & Colonial Museum** (opening times: daily 10am–5pm) is worth visiting. The museum exhibits objects from the area, as well as from the Chatham Islands; look out for an impressive carved Maori meeting house and **old pioneer dwellings**.

Okains Bay

❶ Daily 10am – 5pm, admission: NZ$ 10, www.okainsbaymuseum.co.nz

Magnificent hiking trails, such as the **Mount Herbert Walk** and the **Summit Road Scenic Walk** lead across the mountainous peninsula. Hiking the highly scenic **Banks Peninsula Track** takes four days. The best-known of them is the **Bridle Path** between Lyttelton and Christchurch – the same trail that Christchurch's first settlers had to brave to get there.

*Hikes

From Akaroa, drivers can take the twisting Summit Road to return to Christchurch. Leading across what used to be the **rim of the volcano**, Summit Road offers fine vistas along the way and rejoins Highway 75 at Hilltop.

*Summit Road

WESTERN OUTSKIRTS OF CHRISTCHURCH

In parkland a fair way west of Hagley Park stands the former residence of the Dean family (1856); it also was heavily damaged by the 2010/2011 earthquakes. This family were already living here when

Riccarton House (Deans Cottage)

the Canterbury pilgrims arrived. The little cottage nearby, built in 1843, has been turned into a small museum.

Tours: daily 2pm, admission: NZ$ 18, www.riccartonhouse.co.nz

Air Force Museum
Further southwest, on the old Wigram **Airfield** (approx. 9km/5.5 miles west of the city centre), the Royal New Zealand Air Force has its **aviation museum**, displaying several old military planes alongside various aeronautical tools and equipment. The museum also shows interesting (war) films.

❶ Daily 10am – 5pm, free admission, www.airforcemuseum.co.nz

Yaldhurst Transport Museum
Some 12km/7.5 miles west of the city, many visitors come to the Yaldhurst Transport Museum to see its fleet of **vintage cars**.

❶ Daily 10am – 5pm, admission: NZ$ 20, www.yaldhurstmuseum.co.nz

Orana Park Wildlife Reserve
Spread out near the airport, Christchurch's extensive Zoological Gardens boast very **natural open-air enclosures** and an extremely popular **Kiwi House**.

❶ Daily 9am – 4.30pm, admission: NZ$ 29.50, www.oranawildlifepark.co.nz

*International Antarctic Centre
On Orchard Drive, just a short walk from the airport terminal, the International Antarctic Centre is well worth a visit. In the »Snow & Ice Experience«, an **artificial polar landscape**, complete with wind chill machine, gives visitors an idea of the adverse climatic conditions faced by researchers working in the Antarctic. In addition, the centre fully illustrates the **significance of Antarctica** for the entire globe, with educational multi-media shows amongst other things.

❶ Nov – Mar daily 9am – 7pm, April – Oct 9am – 5.30pm, admission: NZ$ 59, www.iceberg.co.nz

NORTHERN AND EASTERN OUTSKIRTS OF CHRISTCHURCH

Te Whatu Manawa
Decorated with beautiful carvings, this **meeting house** used by the local Maori was built around 1906 and is situated on the Rehua marae meeting area on Springfield Road.

Queen Elizabeth II Park
The spaciously designed **sports facilities and green spaces** in the northeast of the city were laid out for the 1974 Commonwealth Games. Special attractions include a **giant water slide** and a large maze. The new **meeting area** on Pages Road in the eastern suburb of Aranui is not for the exclusive use of the Maori. Look out for the carved entrance gate and the meeting house in the modern style with carvings in the tradition of various tribes.

About an hour's drive north of Christchurch lies **New Zealand's youngest wine-growing area**, the **Waipara region**. The first vineyards were only planted here in the 1980s, but it quickly became apparent that practically **all common grapes** could be cultivated. Whilst wine-growing has no real economic or cultural tradition here, a few vineyards have already managed to win **major awards** with their products.

MARCO POLO TIP

! *Red and white* Insider Tip

One of the pioneers of the Waipara wine region is Bruce Moore, who grows grapes for delicious red and white wines such as Pinot Noir, Cabernet Sauvignon, Riesling and Gewürztraminer. Sample the results in his cosy winebar. Information: tel. 03 314 - 67 77, www. waiparasprings.co.nz

Today, a very broad selection of red and white wines is made here, including Pinot Noir, Cabernet Sauvignon, Chardonnay, Sauvignon Blanc, Riesling and even the more unusual Gewürztraminer. Some vineyards offer **visits with wine tastings**. Coming from Highway 1, most of the wineries are accessible via side roads and cul-de-sacs.

❶ www.waiparawine.co.nz.

** Dunedin

────────────────────────── ✦ Sa 136

Region: Otago
Altitude: 0 – 390m/1,279ft
Population: 125,000

───────────────────────────────────────

When asked with city is the most beautiful in New Zealand many of its fans will say »Dunedin«. Once the richest city in the country, it not only offers a well preserved historic city centre but also an active cultural life. It also has New Zealand's only castle.

»Dun Edin« is the old Scots word for Edinburgh – a reminder of the fact that it was **Scottish immigrants** who settled here and founded a city in the southeast of New Zealand's South Island. Originally, Dunedin's intended name was probably »New Edinburgh«.

»New Edinburgh«

Before the white settlers arrived, a **sizeable Maori population** lived on the Otago peninsula. However, as time went on the Maori were decimated by a combination of bitter tribal feuds and brutal European seal hunters and whalers bringing diseases with them. In 1817 there was a **bloody conflict** between the Maori and the crew of a seal hunter by the name of Kelly. Seventy Maori were slain, and their village of **Otakau** razed to the ground. This Maori settlement gave its name to the natural harbour, the peninsula and eventually to the entire region: **»Otago«**. In 1848, the first colonists came ashore at the natural harbour of Otakau.

History

The news of gold found in central Otago (1861) attracted many new settlers, and Dunedin was soon larger than ▸Auckland, becoming **New Zealand's richest settlement**. Trade and commerce flourished too. The streets had lighting as early as 1863, and from 1879 onwards San Francisco-style **»cable tramways«** were established. Following the turn of the century, when the gold rush had died down, many younger people moved north to seek better ways of making a living. It is only in recent times that this trend has been reversed, with Dunedin not only home to **New Zealand's oldest university**, but also other colleges and institutes of higher education. At the moment, there are about **23,000 students** living in the city.

Wealth through gold

MARCO ⊕ POLO INSIGHT

? *First frozen meat*

It was at Dunedin that the world's first frozen meat factory was established. The first refrigerated ship with meat sailed from Port Chalmers for England in 1882. At that time the crossing took 98 days to cover 20,000km/12,000mi; today's ships take less than 30 days.

Dunedin, the economic and cultural centre of the south, lies at the end of the natural **Otago Harbour**, which reaches far inland and is framed by mountains and hills. Its city centre is well-preserved. Dunedin's 19th-cent. **townhouses** have to be seen: terraced houses with pillars, bays and balconies built for the town's wealthy citizens. They come from the time when Dunedin was very wealthy; in other parts of the country people were still building wooden cabins. Particularly beautiful examples can be found on Stuart Street and High Street. Bear the city there are **fabulous beaches** and – unusual for a large city – many **rare animals living in the wild**.

Urban landscape

The former Trinity Methodist Church (1869) at the corner of Moray Place/Stuart Street houses the first-night performances of the »Fortune« ensemble. The small »Globe Theatre« (104 London Street) mainly shows **avant-garde plays**, whilst the »Regent Theatre« on the Octagon offers more wholesome, traditional fare.

Theatre

The heart of the city is an octagonal square, where in 1887 a monument to the Scottish poet Robert Burns was unveiled. Every Friday, a popular and colourful **market** takes place on the **Octagon**.

Standing on the western side of the square, the **neo-Gothic St Paul's Anglican Cathedral** was completed relatively late, in 1915. It was designed by the London architects practice of Sedding & Wheatley.

St Paul's Anglican Cathedral

An impressive monument to neo-Gothic architecture:
St Paul's Cathedral

*Town Hall Catching the eye next to St Paul's is the imposing building of the Town Hall, with its frontage reminiscent of the **Italian Renaissance** style and a fine clock tower. The building was erected in 1880 following designs by the young Melbourne architect R A Lawson.

Civic Centre Its neighbour to the south is the Civic Centre with the **Public Libraries** and the **Visitor Centre**. The library has whole endowments and collections of manuscripts from the town's early days. **Genealogists** in particular will find what they are looking for here. Dunedin's oldest Christian church is the former **Congregationalist church** built in 1864 west of the Octagon at the corner of Moray Place/View Street following designs by David Ross. The building escaped demolition when it was purchased by the Adventist Church

R.C. Cathedral Even further west, on Rattray Street, look out for Dunedin's Catholic **St Joseph's Cathedral**, built between 1878 and 1886 following designs by **F. W. Petre**. The architect, who also designed major churches in Oamaru, Timaru, Invercargill, Wellington and Christchurch, was probably inspired by the Gothic cathedrals of Amiens and Reims. Alongside the Scottish-born Lawson, who had come to New Zealand via Australia, Petre was the most important architect working in Dunedin. However, his design for a tower above the crossing (the intersection of nave and transept) was too costly and his ambitious plans were only partially realised.

> **MARCO POLO TIP**
>
> *A sweet smell* **Insider Tip**
>
> On certain days, tourists strolling around Dunedin's city centre can catch a whiff of sweets and cocoa, emanating from Cadbury's chocolate factory on Cumberland Street (no. 280). Visitors with a sweet tooth can go on a guided tour, complete of course with a tasting session afterwards (opening times: daily 9am–3.15pm, admission: NZ$ 22, www.cadburyworld.co.nz).

Stuart Street From the Octagon, Stuart Street leads southeast. At its lower end look out for the two most impressive architectural examples of Dunedin's late **Victorian heyday**: the **court** and the **main railway station**.

Law Courts, Police Station The court buildings were completed in 1902 following designs by the government architect John Campbell. The **royal coat-of-arms** can be seen above the main entrance. Adjacent to the courthouse, the police station – a brick building dating from 1896 – was originally intended as a prison.

*Railway Station Diagonally opposite, on Anzac Avenue, the mighty castle-like main railway station dominates the surroundings. This functional building was erected between 1904 and 1906 following designs by George Troup in the **Flemish Renaissance style**. At the time, the architect

Dunedin

INFORMATION
Dunedin Visitor Centre
20 Princess Street
Tel. 03 474 3300
www.visitedunedin.co.nz

EVENTS
One week in mid-February is given over to the »Dunedin Festival«, with exhibitions, concerts and sports competitions. The bagpipe concerts, folklore and sporting demonstrations of »Scottish Week« at the end of March honour Scottish traditions. Important film festivals take place every year in April/May, and at the end of July.

WHERE TO EAT
❶ Bistro Two Chefs £££
121 Stuart Street
Tel. 03 477 2993
www.twochefsbistro.com
A better bistro with Parisian flair, elegant ambience with dark wood and antique mirrors. French bistro classics as well as contemporary New zealand cooking is served.

❷ Nova Café £££
29 The Octagon
Tel. 03 4 79 08 08
http://novadunedin.co.nz
Relaxed café right on the Octagon, the city centre. Excellent food to suitable prices for breakfast, lunch and dinner.

WHERE TO STAY
❶ Southern Cross Hotel £££
Cnr Princess & High Street
PO Box 96
Dunedin
Tel. 03 477 0752
www.scenic-circle.co.nz
The recently elaborately renovated best place to stay in town was in 1883 already.

❷ Leisure Lodge ££
Duke Street
Tel. 03 477 5360
www.accorhotels.com
Extremely well run hotel, situated amidst beautiful gardens in a good location between the busy city centre and Botanic Gardens

was ridiculed for his »gingerbread« house, but this did not stop the king from giving him a knighthood. The station houses a splendid interior, with colonnades, balustrades and mosaic floors. The platform is one kilometre long, the longest on New Zealand. Today it is only used for a tourist train.

South of the railway station, the **Otago Settlers Museum** is well worth a visit, displaying many interesting artefacts from the early days of the Scottish foundation of the town, amongst them numerous portraits of Scottish immigrants' families. The town's **technical achievements**, such as street lighting, tram and railway are also given their due.

*Early Settlers Museum

❶ April – Sept. daily 10am – 4pm, Oct – Mar daily 10am – 5pm, Thu until 8pm, free admission, www.toituosm.com

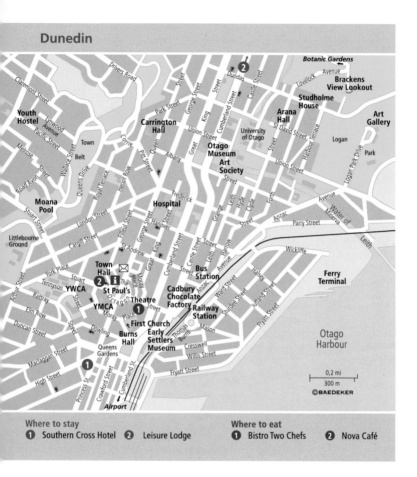

Dunedin

Where to stay
1 Southern Cross Hotel   2 Leisure Lodge

Where to eat
1 Bistro Two Chefs   2 Nova Café

*First Church Southeast of the Octagon, the First Church stands on Moray Place (Burlington Street). Complete with a remarkable tower, the church was built between 1868 and 1873 following plans by the architect Lawson. The foundation stone for the church, designed in the **Norman Gothic style**, was actually laid by the founder of the town, Thomas Burns.

Princess Street From the Octagon, Princess Street runs south, with a few chic-looking buildings lining the avenue. Further southwest, at the corner of Princess Street/High Street, the **Southern Cross Hotel**, built in 1883, has kept its splendour. Close by is the eye-catching frontage of the luxury »Wain's Hotel« (now Mercure Dunedin), opened in 1878. Look out for the grotesques on the ground floor windows. The **Bank of New Zealand** was built between 1879 and 1883 following designs by William Armson in the ornate style of the **neo-Renaissance**. The service hall has an **impressively designed ceiling**.

A few minutes' walk northeast of the Octagon, the Otago Museum is housed in an exceptionally imposing building designed in 1876 by David Ross. However, these days the building is rather squashed between the two lanes of Highway 1 (Great King/Cumberland Streets). The collections here document the **wealth** and **enthusiasm for learning** of the Victorian bourgeoisie which donated its art treasures. The museum is divided into **five sections**: Pacific cultures, archaeology, New Zealand's natural history, ancient and classic cultures, the maritime world, technological development and natural sciences (with a special **Discovery World Tropical Forest** exhibition) and the new Southern Land, Southern People gallery. Look out for the numerous artefacts made from **nephrite** (greenstone), amongst them axes and amulets. Many of these tools would have been made by the Maori on the Otago Peninsula. The impressive **Maori meeting house** was carved between 1872 and 1875 in Whakatane on the ▶Bay of Plenty on North Island.

*Otago Museum

MARCO ⊕ POLO TIP

Don't miss   *Insider Tip*

- Collection of crafted items made of nephrite
- Natural science section with Discovery World
- Collection »People of the World«

❶ Daily 10am – 5pm, free admission, Discovery World Tropical Forest: NZ$ 10, http://otagomuseum.nz

Close by, the former post office building houses the **gallery** of the Otago Art Society, showing works by artists from the region.

Otago Art Society Museum

❶ Daily 10am – 4pm, free admission, donation requested

Upon its foundation back in 1869, the University of Otago was **the first of its kind in New Zealand**. The Scottish clergyman Thomas Burns, the founding father of Dunedin town, was its first chancellor. The imposing buildings were erected from 1878 onwards north of the town centre on the Leith River and modelled on the University of Glasgow. The buildings were designed by Maxwell Bury in the magnificent style of **Scottish neo-Gothic**. Particularly imposing are the beautiful clock tower, the main entrance gate and the staircase. Numerous new institute buildings have sprung up around the venerable old ones, such as the Dental School, the only one of its kind in New Zealand. Keep an eye out as well for the **professors' houses** dating

*University of Otago

Spiral-shaped Maori jewellery made of green jade (nephrite)

from 1879, also designed by Maxwell Bury as semi-detached red-bricks, their gable arches offset by a white trim.

The Hocken Library in the Chinese Garden was bequeathed to the town of Dunedin by a **bibliophile doctor** in 1910. The collection comprises prints, maps, paintings and manuscripts dealing mainly with New Zealand and the South Pacific.

❶ Mon to Fri 9.30am – 5pm, Sat 9am – midday

Situated east of the university in Logan Park, this gallery displays rich treasures of New Zealand and European art both old and modern. Look out for works by the Dunedin-born painter **Frances Hodgkins**, who only rose to fame very late in life in London. **Colin McCahon**'s oeuvre is also well represented.

❶ Daily 10am – 5pm, free admission, http://dunedin.art.museum

*Bracken's Lookout

Bracken's Lookout northwest of the Dunedin Art Gallery commands a splendid view of the town. Thomas Bracken (1843–1898) was a poet and politician, penning the text of New Zealand's **national anthem** *God Defend New Zealand*. Close to the viewpoint (to the northwest), the **Botanic Gardens**, laid out in 1863, attract many visitors. Old indigenous and European trees provide shade here, and the broad cross-section of New Zealand's flora is well signposted. The 30ha/74-acre gardens are at their best when the **azaleas and rhododendrons** are in full bloom (August to October).

*Olveston

The estate situated on the so-called **Town Belt** (green belt) west of the Otago Museum boasts a **spectacular mansion**, erected in 1906 following designs by the English architect Ernest George. The house used to belong to a businessman and art collector born in Olveston near Bristol in England. Its turn-of-the-century furnishings are worth seeing, as are the many **paintings** illustrating various aspects of **colonial times** in New Zealand.

AROUND DUNEDIN

The summit of the 393m/1,289-ft **Signal Hill** north of the city gives **superb views** across Otago Harbour and Dunedin. In 1940, to commemorate the centenary of the signing of the Waitangi Treaty, a **memorial** was unveiled here. A piece of rock from Edinburgh Castle was given by the Scottish as an **anniversary present**, while bronze figures symbolise the past and the future. Another great view can be had from **Mount Cargill**, rising 676m/2,217ft a few miles further north.

Signal Hill

Named after Dr Chalmers, a co-founder of the »Free Church of Scotland«, and counting 3,000 inhabitants, the **port city** 12km/7.5 miles north of Dunedin hugs the banks of Otago Harbour. It was from here that in 1882 lamb meat was sent by refrigerated ship to England for the first time, and that the **South Pole explorers** Scott, Shackleton and Byrd set off for their expeditions. When container shipping became the norm in the 1970s, it breathed new life into Port Chalmers. The **Port Chalmers Flagstaff** on **Aurora Terrace Lookout** used to be a signal station to monitor shipping in the broad Otago estuary. **Churches** worth seeing include **Iona Church** (1883) with its 50m/164-ft tower, the **Anglican Church of the Holy Trinity** (1874) and the Catholic **St Mary's Star of the Sea Church**, built in the same year. The **Maritime Museum** of Port Chalmers is housed in the former Post Office (1877; designed by W H Clayton). Here, various exhibits tell the story of the port and New Zealand seafaring.

Port Chalmers

❶ Museum: Mon – Fri 10am – 3pm, Sat, Sun 1pm – 4pm, admission NZ$ 3, http://portmuseum.org.nz

A half-hour drive northwest of Dunedin takes visitors to the **wild, romantic gorge** of the Taieri River, which can be explored either by jet boat or in more leisurely fashion for 77km/46mi on the **Taieri Gorge Railway**.

Taieri Gorge

OTAGO PENINSULA

Approx. 20km/12.5 miles east of Dunedin, until recently it gave the chance to see (nearly) all the marine life that makes its home in New Zealand's waters. A new building is being planned.

Portobello Aquarium

❶ http://www.otago.ac.nz/marine-studies/aquarium/index.html

This **extravagant castle**, built from 1871 onwards for the wealthy banker and politician William J M Larnach as a present for his first wife Eliza, is a tourist attraction these days. The supervision of the works lay with the architect R A Lawson. Not completed until 1887, the mansion, with its 250sq m/2,690sq-ft ballroom, **cost a fortune**.

*Larnach's Castle

Following Larnach's suicide, his estate saw **chequered fortunes**: the surrounding lands were sold off piecemeal, and the government bought the castle with 14ha/34 acres of land to set up a psychiatric clinic. Later, it was turned into tourist accommodation with a nightclub. Renovated a few years ago, the castle and famous park, which was designed by the owner Margaret Barker herself, can now be visited.

i Daily 9am – 5pm, admission NZ$ 29, www.larnachcastle.co.nz

Otakau Maori Site

In 1940, at the exact spot where the Maori had an important settlement on the peninsula long before the arrival of the Europeans, the **Otakau Maori Site** was inaugurated to commemorate the centenary of the signing of the Waitangi Treaty.

*Taiaroa Head, Albatross Centre

The northern point of the Otago Peninsula, called **Taiaroa Head**, is famous as a breeding site for the **Royal Albatross**. The **Albatross Centre** has information on the identifying features of these giant birds. Nearby, yellow-eyed penguins, seals and sea lions may be observed too. From Dunedin, **boat trips** are organised to the cliffs of Taiaroa. Pretty beaches can be found south of Dunedin at **St Kilda**

New Zealand has romantic castles too: Larnach Castle

and **St Clair**. This sandbank connects the Otago Peninsula with the mainland. From St Kilda, home to many sports clubs, the **John Wilson Ocean Drive** runs right along the beachfront.

✱✱ Fiordland National Park
✧ Rh 135/136

Region: Southland
Surface area: 12,523 sq km/4,835 sq miles
Altitude: 0 – 2,502m/8,208ft
❶ Destination Fiordland, Lakefront Drive, Te Anau,
Tel. 03 2 49 79 59, www.fiordland.org.nz

By far the largest of New Zealand's national parks, and almost entirely devoid of humans, Fiordland National Park comprises the wilderness area of the southwest of South Island, the loneliest part of the country. A maze of deep fjords on the western coast and an intricate system of lakes in the interior characterize the landscape as much as the jagged mountain areas and dense evergreen southern beech forests.

To the north, the national park is bordered by the **Darran Mountains** with Mount Tutoko rising up 2,700m/8,858ft. To the east, large lakes mark the transition to the fertile plains of the drier Southland. To the west, the mountains plunge down steeply to the Tasman Sea, lashed relentlessly by the **»Roaring Forties«**. In the higher elevations and summit regions, long beard lichens and various types of moss thrive. Extremely high levels of precipitation – up to 6,000mm/236in per year – result in a great deal of **erosion**, as evidenced by the numerous waterfalls and sometimes **catastrophic avalanches in winter**.

Location

The largest fjords are Preservation Inlet, Dusky Sound, Doubtful Sound, George Sound and ▶Milford Sound. The latter is the best known and most easily accessible. The deep bays are commonly known as »sounds«, but they are in fact valleys **carved by Ice Age glaciers drowned in the sea**. At the eastern edge of the mountain range which crosses the entire South Island, glaciers have created **long gullies**, which today are filled by ▶Lake Te Anau, ▶Lake Manapouri, Lake Monowai, Lake Hauroko and Lake Poteriteri.

Fjords and lakes

SCENIC HIGHLIGHTS

New Zealand's largest fjord, the wonderfully scenic Dusky Sound, is 44km/27 miles long and studded with many forested islets. The

*Dusky Sound

?

Maori cemetery

In 1967, a 300-year old Maori cemetery was discovered in a cave on Mary Island in Lake Hauroko. Today, the »tapu«, which is one of the best preserved and oldest in New Zealand, is protected by a steel fence.

fjord takes its name from the travels of **James Cook**, who passed here on a dusky evening in 1770 during his first voyage around the world. Three years later, on his second round-the-world trip, he entered the fjord in order to overhaul his ship, the Resolution, and to stock up with provisions. There he met Maori who had retreated to the remote mountains, probably fleeing more aggressive tribes. Georg Forster has left vivid descriptions of these meetings and also of the plagues of local **sandflies**. Today, the area is practically devoid of people, and it's just the sandflies that remain. The once plentiful **seals** in the fjord, which Cook reported in his notes, have **nearly all been lost to hunting**.

Special tip — Overland the fjord is only accessible via **strenuous trails** starting from the access road at Doubtful Sound, or in the south starting from Lake Hauroko.

*Lake Hauroko — Some 100km/62 miles northwest of ▸Invercargill, the expanse of Lake Hauroko is framed by steep, densely forested slopes. Wind and storms from both north and south arrive here unchecked, which can occasionally make life dangerous for **boaters** and ehich should not be underestimated. There is a campsite approx. 6km/3.7 miles east of the lake, at the border of the national park.

Doubtful Sound — ▸Lake Te Anau · Lake Manapouri

HIKES IN FIORDLAND NATIONAL PARK

Important tips — The **magnificent scenery** attracts many nature-loving mountaineers. **Trekking tours lasting several days** (and fairly strenuous in parts) explore beautiful mountain forests, deep fjords and tranquil lakes. For detailed information on hiking trails, accommodation options and exact route descriptions, contact the **DOC information offices** in Te Anau and Tuatapere. Due to limited space in the huts, dates have to be booked early. Apart from on the organised tours, hikers need to bring all their own food and equipment. Changing weather and extensive rainfall tend to be the rule rather than the exception. Wet-weather gear, solid footwear and insect repellent are essential.

Milford Track — The famous Milford Track leads from ▸Lake Te Anau to ▸Milford Sound. It takes 4 days to conquer this quite **magnificent alpine trail.

Sleeping spaces in the huts need to be booked in advance. **Accompanied tours** are available.

This hiking trail crosses Hollyford Valley in the north of the national park, then follows Lake McKerow and eventually leads to the coast at Martins Bay. At least **4 to 5 days** should be allowed for this **long-distance trail**. Here too accompanied tours are available.

*Hollyford Track

The road to ▶Milford Sound marks the starting point of the Routeburn Track, which over 3 days leads across the 1,279m/4,196-ft **Harris Saddle** to the northern tip of Lake Wakatipu at Kinloch. This trail is a popular continuation of the Milford Track (see above). For views of **magnificent mountain scenery**, consider the Kepler Track, which provides a most exciting hike from the very popular ▶Lake Te Anau across to Lake Manapouri. This tour takes four days.

Routeburn Track, *Kepler Track

One of the most beautiful routes in Fiordland National Park is the Kepler Track

Lookout Bluff Track, Boundary Track   Lake Hauroko marks the starting point for **several fine hikes** through Fiordland national park. Both the Lookout Bluff Track and the Boundary Track are recommended trails. A 4-day tour leads from the northern tip of the lake (Hauroko Burn) to **Supper Cove** on Dusky Sound.

> **!**   *Scenic flights or boat trips*   **Insider Tip**
>
> Wonderful scenic flights, available from Te Anau and Milford, show the beauty of Fiordland National Park in its entirety. Or how about a 6-day scenic cruise aboard the Milford Wanderer motor sailboat on the trail of Captain Cook? The Fiordland Visitor Centre has all the information.

MARCO ⊕ POLO TIP

In the autumn of 2001, a new 53km/33-mile circular hiking trail was opened at the southeastern edge of Fiordland National Park, the ** **Tuatapere Hump Ridge Track**. The start and finish point is Blue Cliffs Beach on Te Wae Wae Bay (south coast). The track's sections follow the trail of the Maori and the loggers up to Hump Ridge, with its alpine flair, and then back down to the sea.

** Fox Glacier · Franz Josef Glacier

✦ Sa 134

Region: West Coast
Altitude: 300m/984ft – 3,085m/10,121ft

A visit to the »Ice Twins« must rank among the highlights of any trip to New Zealand. »Fox and Franz«, the Fox Glacier and its neighbour, the Franz Josef Glacier, flow from the perpetual ice of some of the highest summits of the New Zealand Alps in ▸Westland National Park down to 300m/984ft above sea level, where, surrounded by dense green forests, the tips of their icy tongues melt.

Glacier view   The two glaciers are at their most impressive at **sunset**. Extremely high annual levels of precipitation (sometimes up to 7,500mm/295in!) result in dense rainforest, and unfortunately also in many rainy days. Winter sees more **stable weather**, when the giant snow-covered mountains can often be clearly seen in the background.

Glacier tongues   Both the Fox Glacier, 13km/8 miles long, and the Franz Josef Glacier, 10km/6.2 miles long, negotiate a **significant drop in altitude** across a relatively short distance. Their steepness leads to a relatively fast flow down from the glacier head, which explains why the two glaciers reach this far down into the valley.

Fox Glacier · Franz Josef Glacier

INFORMATION
Franz Josef Visitor Centre
13 State Highway 6, Franz Josef Glacier
Tel. 03 752 0796
www.doc.govt.nz

WHERE TO EAT
Cook Saddle Café
£ – ££
19 State Highway 6, Fox Glacier
Tel. 03 7 51 07 00
Friendly restaurant in splendid surroundings

WHERE TO STAY
Franz Josef Glacier Country Retreat £££££
State Highway 6, Franz Josef
Tel. 03 752 0012
www.glacier-retreat.co.nz

The 12 residential units of this luxury accommodation on Lake Mapourika were only opened a few years ago.

Franz Josef Glacier
££££
36 Main Road, Franz Josef
Tel. 03 752 0729
www.scenichotels.co.nz
Traditional, comfortable mountain hotel with views of the Franz Josef Glacier

Glacier Country Hotel
£££
State Highway 6, Fox Glacier
Tel. 03 751 0847
www.heartlandhotels.co.nz
This cosy mountain hotel occupies a beautiful location between Fox Glacier and Lake Matheson.

FOX GLACIER

The Fox Glacier's snout is accessible via a 7km/4.3-mile road and then a footpath. Visitors with good footwear will not find **walking across the glacier tongue** difficult, but it can only be done as **part of the guided tours**, which run twice daily.

Glacier snout

The eponymous village has an **informative visitor centre**, which tells the story of the glacier's creation and describes the characteristics of the local rainforest. The centre also organises **nature hikes and excursions**.

Fox Glacier Visitor Centre

In good weather, the Peak Indicator viewpoint, situated 9km/5.5 miles further west, commands absolutely **magnificent views of the mountain summits and Fox Glacier's ice stream**. Sunrise or sunset are prime viewing times.

*Peak Indicator

Hidden away a few miles west of the Fox Glacier settlement, Lake Matheson is the most beautiful and **most photographed mountain lake in New Zealand**. Early in the morning, the lake shows the re-

Lake Matheson

flections of the summits of Mount Tasman and Mount Cook. There is a trail around the 600m/2000ft long and 200m/660ft wide lake.

FRANZ JOSEF GLACIER

Ice stream

Over the past 200 years, the relatively steep Franz Josef Glacier has pushed forward and pulled back again. Overall however, it has visibly retreated. The **meltwater** streaming from the glacier snout goes on to form the **Waiko River**.

Namesake

Franz Josef Glacier was discovered in 1865 by the German geologist and scientific explorer Julius von Haast, who named it after the Austrian emperor Franz Josef I.

*Waiko Valley, glacier snout

A narrow 6km/3.7-mile road leads along the southern side of Waiko Valley to the car park in front of the glacier snout. Along the way, short detours leading to **Peter's Pool** and **Sentinel Rock** are worthwhile, as are those to various **glacier viewpoints**. A hike through the wide riverbed and across rocks polished by the ice leads to the viewpoint at the glacier snout (walking time approx. 2 hrs there and back). Before exploring the **Franz Josef Glacier Valley Walk** alone, it is best to get information from the Visitor Centre about the condition of the trail and the weather. Visitors aiming to really explore the glacier should join one of the twice-daily **guided tours**.

> ! MARCO ◉ POLO TIP
>
> *White herons* Insider Tip
>
> Ornithologists get their money's worth in Okarito Lagoon, which, as New Zealand's only breeding site for white herons, enjoys strict environmental protection. Bird-watching hikes are organised between November and May.

Alex Knob

A **stunning view** of the Franz Josef Glacier can be enjoyed from the 1,295m/4,248-ft **Alex Knob**.

Franz Josef Glacier (village)

The very popular tourist village has a **Visitor Centre** which offers extensive information on the glacier, as well as on the geological history, flora and fauna. The centre also organises **nature hikes**.

*Lake Mapouraki

Highway 6 leads to the **very idyllic** Lake Mapouraki, some 8km/5 miles north of the village. Sometimes the majestic summits of the New Zealand Alps and the green forests nearby can be seen reflected in the lake. This is also a good place to spot **rare birds**.

Okarito

25km/15.5 miles north of Franz Josef village, Okarito is a small settlement established in the 1860s by gold prospectors. In good weather, the village offers **splendid views of the Alpine chain**.

* Greymouth

✴ **Sb 133**

Region: West Coast
Altitude: 0 – 300m/984ft
Population: 10,000

Named after Governor George Grey, this port town is the most important commercial centre on New Zealand's western coast. The town's economy was initially founded on gold mining, later to be replaced by coal extraction and the timber industry, and eventually complemented by a fairly successful pasture and dairy economy. Greymouth grew up on the site of the old Maori settlement of Mawhera.

The port town on the mouth of the Grey River is constantly threatened by flooding, whether from the interior or the wild Tasman Sea. In 1991, **massive flood barriers** were finally completed. Prolonged rainfalls are frequent, and feared as much as the **»Barber«**, a **cold, piercing wind** blowing in from the valley of the Grey River. These factors are partly responsible for the fact that the population has stagnated, or even decreased slightly, since the end of the 19th century.

Exposed to the elements

AROUND GREYMOUTH

Running some 11km/6.8 miles north of Greymouth, at Raparahoe, this **charming hiking trail** (approx. 4 hrs walking time) leads along the coast, through **dense primeval forest** with tree ferns and Nikau palms. Along the way, there are **pretty vistas** of the coast and the highest summits of the New Zealand Alps.

Point Elizabeth Walkway

All year round, tourists flock to the reconstructed gold prospectors settlement of **Shantytown**, some 11km/6.8 miles south of Greymouth. This **open-air museum** presents itself entirely in the style of the »wild« 1860s. Old buildings have been transplanted here from various parts of New Zealand: a church, Coronation Hall, General Store, stables and prison, alongside a hotel, hospital, a printers and workshops of various craftsmen. A steam train chugs through forest to an old saw mill. Shantytown also has old

*Shantytown

MARCO POLO TIP

! *The art of jade* **Insider Tip**

The Jade Boulder Gallery in Greymouth not only displays various types of New Zealand jade (»pounamu« in the Maori language), but also allows visitors to watch jade carvers at work. Particularly fascinating is the work executed by the internationally famous artist Ian Boustridge.

»claims«, where visitors can **have a go at gold panning**. Approx. 11km/6.8 miles east of Shantytown, the **Woods Creek Track** (about 1 hr) runs through an area that was »ploughed« by gold prospectors in the 1860s.

Open air museum: daily 8.30am – 5pm, admission: NZ$ 31.50, www.shantytown.co.nz

The old **gold prospector settlement** of Kumara (pop 300) lies 25km/15.5 miles south of Greymouth on the road that leads through Otira Gorge up to Arthur's Pass. In its heyday, the village counted up to 4,000 inhabitants. In the riverbed of the nearby **Taramakau River**, gold was still being extracted commercially as recently as 1982.

Kumara

The **coalfield** of Brunner, some 12km/7.5 miles east of Greymouth on Highway 7 encompasses the four once important coal mines of Dobson, Wallsend, Stillwater and Taylorville. The rich coal deposits on both banks of the Grey River were discovered by **naturalist Thomas Brunner** during his explorations of the western coast between 1846 and 1848. Coalmining was started as early as 1864.

Brunner

An old suspension bridge across the Grey River leads to the abandoned Brunner Mine, which now enjoys protected status as **New Zealand's first industrial monument**. Here, educational trails and films inform visitors about the history of coal mining on the west coast.

*Brunner Industrial Site

Approx. 32km/20 miles southeast of Greymouth, Lake Brunner lies in a highly scenic landscape and offers ideal conditions for anglers and paddlers. The **largest lake on the west coast** was created in a glacier tongue basin that was sealed off by an end moraine.

*Lake Brunner

Just under 50km/31 miles east of Greymouth, (taking a fork off Highway 7), the road reaches the lake named after the famous Austrian naturalist **Ferdinand von Hochstetter**. This unspoilt natural lake was expanded back in 1876 by the building of a dam. **Anglers** and **picnickers** in particular enjoy this place.

Lake Hochstetter

Some 70km/44 miles southeast of Greymouth, the **wild, romantic mountainscape** of Arthur's Pass awaits. As early as the 19th century, the first organised sightseeing tour led across the pass over to the west coast, and further on south to the Franz Josef or Fox Glaciers. As time went on, critics started warning that the unique flora in this part of the New Zealand Alps needed to be protected. In 1901, 70,000ha/nearly 173,000 acres were declared a **nature reserve**. In

**Arthur's Pass

Arthur's Pass connects the West Coast with Christchurch

Greymouth

INFORMATION
Visitor Information Centre
Cnr Herbert & Mackay Streets, Greymouth
Tel. 03 768 5101
www.greydistrict.co.nz

Arthur's Pass Information Centre
Main Road, Arthur's Pass
Tel. 03 318 9211
www.doc.govt.nz

WHERE TO STAY
Kingsgate Hotel Greymouth ££
32 Mawhera Quay
Tel. 03 768 5085
www.kingsgategreymouth.co.nz/
Originally built in 1906 this house is located near the city centre and has 98 modern and functionally furnished rooms as well as eateries (Alberts Restaurant, Albion Bar).

1929, extensions resulted in the creation of **Arthur's Pass National Park**. The protected landscape is extraordinarily rich in contrasts, covering both of the **fundamentally different sides of the Southern Alps**. The **altitude differences** are dramatic and range from 245m/some 800ft at the Tamarakau River to some 2,000m/over 6,500ft on the peaks of Mount Rolleston, Mount Murchison and Mount Franklin. Levels of precipitation vary between an annual 5,000mm/197in on the western side, and 1,700mm/67in on the drier eastern side. The national park on Arthur's Pass is accessible all year round, with visitor numbers peaking in the summer months of December and January. Amongst the most famous and beautiful **hikes** that can be undertaken from the Arthur's Pass settlement are the **Devil's Punchbowl Walk** (approx. 2 hrs), the **Bridal Veil Nature Walk** to the 130m/426-ft high Bridal Veil waterfall (approx. 2 hrs), the **Dobson Nature Walk** (approx. 4 hrs) and the **Bealey Valley Walk**, which also requires about four hours. All of the tours are worthwhile and offer unforgettable views of the beautiful landscape.

Big and little prospectors in Shantytown near Greymouth

* Hanmer Springs

✴ Sc 133

Region: Canterbury
Altitude: 366m/1,200ft
Population: 700
❶ Hanmer Springs/Hurunui Visitor Information Centre
40 Amuri Avenue West , P.O. Box 84 Hanmer Springs
Tel. 03 3 15 00 20, http://visithanmersprings.co.nz/

**In a protected basin just under 140km/87 miles north of
▶Christchurch, particularly powerful thermal springs erupt
from the rock. Their curative powers were known to the
Maori early on. The settlement has since developed into the
tranquil spa and holiday resort of Hanmer Springs, framed by
Hanmer Forest and the mountains of the Hanmer Range, popular in winter with skiers.**

ACTIVITIES IN AND AROUND HANMER SPRINGS

Spa guests can relax in the warm waters (up to 41°C/106°F) of the modern thermal spa, complemented by further **therapeutic facilities**.

Thermal spa

Adrenaline-seeking visitors get their money's worth on the nearby Waiau River. The river can be explored by **jet boat or on a wildwa-ter raft**, whilst the 31m/102-ft bridge across the river is used for bun-gee jumping.
❶ Daily 10am – 9pm, NZ$ 18

* Waiau River

This **huge forest area** comprises around 17,000ha/42,000 acres of southern beech forest, for the most part left in its natural state. The forest has several trails for strolling and hiking. Moutainbiking and riding on horseback are also possible. A 16km/10-mile Forest Drive gives access to some particularly charming spots (for a driving per-mit, contact the local Visitor Centre).

Hanmer Forest

In the summer, it is possible to take a four-wheel drive from Hanmer Springs over the highest pass (1437m/4742ft) to the remote **Moles-worth Station**. The former sheep farm with around 180,000ha/444,800 acres of pasture has been bought up by the state. In the past, the repeated burning off of the grass, overgrazing and a terrible plague of rabbits resulted in **heavy erosion damage**. Today, a part of the area has been recultivated and converted to organic farming, with cattle grazing instead of sheep. The remote Molesworth Station is New Zealand's **largest cattle farm**.

*Molesworth Station

✴ Hokitika

✴ Sa 133

Region: West Coast
Altitude: 0 – 50m/164ft
Population: 3,000

Lying on a particularly scenic section of the west coast, the small town of Hokitika once acquired a fair degree of wealth through its deposits of jade (nephrite) and gold. Timber processing has long since outstripped gold mining here.

St Mary's
The **symbol of the town** is the Catholic St Mary's Church, erected in 1914 in the neo-Romantic style to replace a previous building put up by Irish immigrants in 1865. It was heavily damaged in an earthquake in 2012.

Former
government
building
In the 19th century, Hokitika was the seat of the **provincial government** of Westland. The old government building is still standing. In front of it, look out for the impressive statue of **»King Dick«**, as the former prime minister Richard Seddon is called here. Seddon was the district's representative in parliament for 27 years.

Pretty to look at: Clock Tower of Hokitika

Clock Tower
On the crossroads of Sewell Street/Weld Street, a fine **clock tower** commemorates both the New Zealand soldiers killed in the Boer Wars, and the coronation of King Edward VII.

West Coast
Historical
Museum
Look out for the impressive **weapons and jewellery** made a long time ago of local nephrite by the Maori. The museum also documents the time of the gold rush.

Glow Worm
Dell
From the northern edge of town, a path leads to a **grotto** overgrown with ferns, where at night whole colonies of luminescent **glow worms** may be seen.

Surroundings
20km/12.5 miles south of Hokitika, the road reaches the idyllic

Hokitika

INFORMATION
Hokitika i-Site Visitor Centre
Carnegie Building
Hamilton St
Tel. 03 755 6166
www.hokitikainfo.co.nz

WHERE TO EAT
Stumper's Bar & Café ££
2 Weld Street
Tel. 03 755 6154
www.stumpers.co.nz

Popular meeting point in the heart of
town serving down-to-earth fare.

WHERE TO STAY
Jade Court Motor Lodge ££
85 Fitzherbert Street
Tel. 03 755 8855
www.jadecourt.co.nz
The spacious apartments of this colonial-
style motel are grouped around a lovingly maintained garden with many fragrant flowers.

Lake Kaniere and the impressive **Dorothy Falls**. Some 25km/15
miles south follows the **Hokitika River Gorge**, traversed by an old
suspension bridge.

About 30km/18 miles south of Hokitika lies the village of Ross, with   **Ross**
some 1,000 inhabitants. In the past, large quantities of gold were
found in the area. In 1907, for example, a **gold nugget weighing
nearly 3kg/half a stone** was unearthed – and handed over by New
Zealand's government as a coronation gift for King George V. After a
temporary decline in gold extraction, new deposits were discovered
in the 1980s, since exploited in open-cast mining. Worth seeing is a
restored gold prospectors cottage, today housing the local Visitor
Centre. From Ross, the **Water Race Walk** and the **Jones Flat Walk**
(hiking time 1 hr each) lead to the old gold fields.

Invercargill
—————————————— ✳ Rj 137

Region: Southland
Altitude: 0 – 47m/154ft
Population: 54,000

New Zealand's southernmost town was established from 1856
onwards on the New River estuary following designs by urban planner John T Thomson on a geometric grid plan. Invercargill was named after William Cargill, one of the founding
fathers of ▶Dunedin. The Gaelic prefix of »Inver« signifies a
river estuary.

Invercargill

INFORMATION
Visitor Information Centre
108 Gala Street in the
Southland Museum
PO Box 1012
Tel. 03 211 0895
www.invercargillnz.com

WHERE TO EAT
Paddington Arms ££
220 Bainfield Road
Tel. 03 215 8156
www.paddingtonarms.co.nz

This relaxed pub on the edge of town is in an historic building and serves down-to-earth cooking.

WHERE TO STAY
Queens Park Motels ££
85 Alice Street
Tel. 03 214 4504
www.queensparkmotels.co.nz
Holiday resort enjoying a beautiful and extraordinarily tranquil location in an immaculately kept park with golf course.

Economy For a long time, the interior's **lush pastures** ensured the town's wealth, with several large-scale abattoirs and frozen-meat factories producing goods for export. Sheepraising is still a major economic factor in this area.
Today, the large aluminium smelter in Bluff is one of the most important operations for many miles around.

Secular buildings The symmetrical **town hall** was completed in 1906 from a design by E R Wilson and is a reminder of the town's wealth at the time. In 1864 the **Kelvin Chambers** were built. For a short while, the building served as the seat of the independent provincial government of Southland which had seceded in 1861 from Otago only to return to the fold again in 1870.
Lennel House (102 Albert St), a mansion set in pretty gardens, was built in 1880 following designs by urban planner John T Thomson and is still in private hands.

Ecclesiastical buildings The most important churches in town – all made of brick – stand close to each other: **St John's Anglican Church** (1887), the Presbyterian **First Church**, erected in 1915 in the Byzantine style, and the Catholic **St Mary's** basilica. The latter was completed in 1905 following designs by F W Petre. The interior of this church is beautifully furnished in light-coloured Oamaru stone.

*Southland Museum & Art Gallery Invercargill's **main place of interest** is the Southland Museum & Art Gallery, showing important natural history exhibits (amongst them petrified wood from nearby Curio Bay), alongside rather impressive Maori artwork and memorabilia from the wild days when the whalers were in town. The art gallery is housed in a remarkable **pyramid-shaped building** at the entrance to Queens Park.

🛈 Mon – Fri 9am – 5pm, Sat, Sun 10am – 5pm, free admission, donation requested, http://southlandmuseum.com/

The 80ha/197-acre Queens Park with sports grounds and green spaces, a duck pond, wildlife park and playground is accessible from Queens Drive. The **Winter Gardens** are open daily.

Queens Park

AROUND INVERCARGILL

No other landscape in New Zealand is as spectacular as the region of Southland, at the base of South Island. Film lovers familiar with the epic *Lord of the Rings* trilogy know this already of course. Undulating mountains, marshy lowlands crisscrossed by rivers, lush green rainforests and snow-capped peaks dominate the area. The most difficult to access is the land of the southwest, carved by glaciers into deep valleys which, following the last Ice Age and rising sea levels, filled with water and became fjords. On the eastern side of the mountainous massif, the deep valleys created by the glaciers were sealed off by end moraines and dammed to form elongated lakes, such as Lake Te Anau, Lake Manapouri, Lake Monowai and Lake Hauroko. The **second largest settlement** of the Southland region has no more than 11,000 inhabitants. Gore is situated amidst fertile pastures at a major fork in the road northeast of Invercargill. Grain cultivation and horticulture are successful here as well. The town's **Country Music Festival**, which takes place every June, has made Gore famous beyond New Zealand's borders. South Island's annual sheep-shearing championships also take place in Gore.

Southland

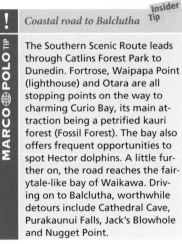

MARCO POLO TIP

Insider Tip

Coastal road to Balclutha

The Southern Scenic Route leads through Catlins Forest Park to Dunedin. Fortrose, Waipapa Point (lighthouse) and Otara are all stopping points on the way to charming Curio Bay, its main attraction being a petrified kauri forest (Fossil Forest). The bay also offers frequent opportunities to spot Hector dolphins. A little further on, the road reaches the fairytale-like bay of Waikawa. Driving on to Balclutha, worthwhile detours include Cathedral Cave, Purakaunui Falls, Jack's Blowhole and Nugget Point.

The entrepreneur **Robert Anderson** once resided in a stately mansion 7km/just over 4 miles north of Invercargill. The entire estate, including its well-kept park, was subsequently gifted to the town, and today houses a sizeable art collection with beautiful Maori portraits, early vistas of Bluff and a few fine examples of modern New

*Anderson Park & Art Gallery

New Zealand's southernmost harbour is in Bluff

Zealand art. The park also boasts a beautifully carved Maori meeting house.

❶ Closed temporarily; info: www.andersonparkgallery.co.nz

Bluff Established on a headland jutting out into Foveaux Strait, the port is dwarfed by the 265m/869-ft **Old Man Bluff (good views!)**. In the past, the port of Bluff was used to export large quantities of lamb meat. Today, it is also used by a small fishing fleet, **oysters and lobsters** from Foveaux Strait being much sought after. The local maritime museum tells the history of the port and oyster fishing.

New Zealand's only aluminium smelter On the opposite side of the harbour, at **Tiwai Point**, New Zealand's only aluminium smelter has been in operation as a New Zealand-Australian-Japanese joint venture since 1971. Since the discovery of the bauxite deposits of Weipa on the Cape York Peninsula in Queensland, Australia, aluminium oxide has been shipped from there to the southern point of New Zealand's South Island to be smelted. The smelter's huge demand for electric power is mainly covered by the **hydroelectric power station** on ▶Lake Manapouri. Large quantities of the material produced in the Tiwai Point Aluminium Smelter are exported to Japan.

❶ www.nzas.co.nz

Day trip to Stewart Island From Invercargill, **day trips** across Foveaux Strait to ▶Stewart Island can be made by plane or by ferry to **Halfmoon Bay**.

** Lake Te Anau · Lake Manapouri

———————————— ✴ **Rh 136**

Region: Southland
Altitude: 185m/610ft

Covering 344 sq km/133 sq miles, Lake Te Anau in the northeast of ▶Fiordland National Park is the largest lake on South Island, extending its arms – South Fiord, Middle Fiord and North Fiord – deep into the densely rainforested mountainous landscape of the national park.

Lake Te Anau · Lake Manapouri

INFORMATION
Destination Fiordland
P O Box 1 Lakefront Drive, Te Anau
Tel. 03 249 8900
www.fiordland.org.nz

WHERE TO EAT
The Bluestone ££
20 Lakefront Drive, Te Anau
Tel. 03 249 7421
Lobster, lamb and game feature on the menu, which is strong on local specialities. The restaurant commands beautiful views of the snow-capped summits of the Southern Alps.

The Moose ££
Te Anau Terrace
Tel. 03 249 7100
Good solid New Zealand fare is served in this popular restaurant, which at weekends also offers live entertainment.

WHERE TO STAY
Explorer Motor Lodge ££
6 Cleddau Street, Te Anau
Tel. 03 249 7156

www.explorerlodge.co.nz
Friendly hotel in a pretty park near the lake

Lakefront Lodge
££ – £££
58 Lakefront Drive, Te Anau
Tel. 03 249 7728
www.lakefrontlodge.co.nz
Attractive residential complex on the lake shore with spacious and very well furnished rooms

Kingsgate Hotel Te Anau ££
20 Lakefront Drive, Te Anau
Tel. 03 249 7421
www.qualityteanau.co.nz
Friendly hotel with contemporary design in well-kept gardens on Lake Te Anau

Fiordland Hotel ££
1 Burnby Dr, Te Anau
Tel. 03 249 7511
www.fiordlandhotel.co.nz
Quiet hotel with pleasant rooms and a wonderful view of the mountains in a well-tended park

»Cave of the Swirling Water«	It is thought the name of the lake refers to the »Te Ana-au« (meaning »Cave of the Swirling Water«, see below) **cave system**, which was probably known to the Maori in the past, but fell into obscurity because it was difficult to access.
Water level, harnessing hydroelectric energy	The surface of the lake is approx. 200m/656ft above sea level; however, with a depth of 417m/1,368, the lake reaches **far below sea level**. Lake Te Anau is connected with Lake Manapouri, making it an important part of the **Manapouri hydroelectric energy project**.
Te Anau (settlement)	On the southeastern point of the lake, the **lively tourist town** of Te Anau (pop 3,000) has grown tremendously over the last few decades, and now offers numerous accommodation options. Te Anau is also an **excellent base** for exploring Fiordland National Park and New Zealand's Southern Alps.
Murchison Range	In the remote Murchison Range on the western shore of Lake Te Anau, several of the supposedly long extinct **takahe birds** were discovered in 1948. Visitors interested in these **flightless feathered creatures** can also see them in Te Anau's Wildlife Park.
**Te Ana-au Caves	Also in this area, around the same time – and after much searching – the **unique glow worm caves**, the Te Ana-au Caves, were also rediscovered. These are only accessible from the lake. In geological terms, these caves are still fairly young. Whilst few stalactites and stalagmites have formed yet, they are very impressive. After a half-hour boat trip across the lake from Te Anau, and prepared by a good introduction, visitors penetrate the interior through a low cave entrance. The boat then goes on to a **subterranean waterfall**, where a second boat does the next leg to the wonderful grotto where the glow worms await. **Boat trips:** from NZ$ 75, www.realjourneys.co.n

? MARCO ⬤ POLO INSIGHT

Glow worms

The glow worms in the Te Ana au Caves are in reality insect larvae which lure their prey with their luminous filaments. It is dark and quiet inside the glow worm grotto, with only the filaments glowing like stars in the night sky.

**Milford Road	Te Anau marks the starting point for a highly **enjoyable drive** through the enchanting mountain scenery of the ▶Fiordland National Park to ▶Milford Sound. Milford Road leads along the eastern shores of the lake and through the Homer Tunnel down to the

Te Ana-au Caves: not everything that glows is a glow worm

Unique Animal World

Before the Polynesians settled here there were only three kinds of animals on the entire islands, all of them bats. Mammals rule the ecological system in other regions of the world, but in the niche called New Zealand all kinds of birds were able to develop. In the past they had almost no natural enemies here.

The first Polynesian settlers already changed the animal world drastically, even though there are not many of them and their interaction with nature tended to be harmless. But in only a few decades they still managed to completely eradicate the population of the giant moa bird.

Survival of the Fittest

One of the fundamentals of ecology is that each new species in an ecosystem is at first competition for the other species. In New Zealand imported dogs and cats are a threat to the national bird, the kiwi. Wasps accidentally brought in from Europe compete with local kaka parrots for their nourishment, honeydew. Rabbits, rats and opossums are multiplying without hindrance, a threat both to agriculture and to many indigenous plants and animals. Protection programmes have been initiated by the Department of conservation to secure the survival of endangered species.

Rare Birds

Wild kiwis are rarely seen in New Zealand. Not only is the heraldic animal endangered but the grey-brown bird is also nocturnal and extremely shy. In one of the many parks in New Zealand that work to save the kiwi it is possible to take a nocturnal tour with a relatively good chance of seeing the birds. It will be just as impossible to see a takahe bird in the wild. This rare species of bird, the size of a goose, was thought to be extinct until a small population was discovered in Fiordland in 1948. Meanwhile there are just about 300 of them living in New Zealand parks, where they are carefully tended and protected. The kakapo is also a rare bird. Since these flightless had no natural enemies before the settlement of New Zealand they have no reflex to flee. They remain where they are when rats, cats, dogs, martens or mink approach. As a protection all known specimens, meanwhile around 130, were moved to two islands where there are no predatory animals. Other rare birds can thankfully still be observed in the wild: there are gannet colonies near Muriwai and in Hawke's Bay; royal albatrosses live on Otago Peninsula. The rare yellow-eyed penguin can be seen here occasionally as well.

Insects and Reptiles

Tuataras have lived in New Zealand for 220 million years. They also have had to be evacuated to rat-free islands. Some have been released in Karori Wildlife Sanctuary near Wellington. The world's largest varieties of the grasshopper-like weta can only be found in New Zealand. The 90mm/4in-long shy nocturnal insects are rarely seen. But for anyone who does encounter one of these hoppers: please leave these both harmless and infrequent bugs alone – posterity will thank you! Hardly anyone will look for the katipo spider on pur-pose, one of the few poisonous animals on New Zealand. Anyone who does get bitten by the extremely uncommon black-and-red spider is not in any danger despite the unpleasant side effects. Normally the victim has up to three days' time to get an antidote from a doctor or hospital.

Adresses

The Karori Sanctuary Experience
end of Waiapu Road,
Karori, Wellington
tel. 04 920 92 00
daily 10am – 5pm;
Admission: NZ$ 17.50
www.visitzealandia.com
Tuataras and wetas, kiwis, takahes and many other rare New Zealand animals live behind a protective fence.

Pukaha Mount Bruce National Wildlife Centre
State Highway 2

between Masterton and Eketahuna
tel. O6 375 80 04
daily 9am – 4.30pm,
admission NZ$ 20,
www.pukaha.org.nz
Kiwi eggs are collected in the wild and brooded in a protected environment. In 2011 a snow-white female kiwi even hatched here.

Te Anau Wildlife Centre
Manapouri Road
Te Anau
free admission, donations requested
open from sunrise to sunset,
www.doc.govt.nz

Small native: the tuatara

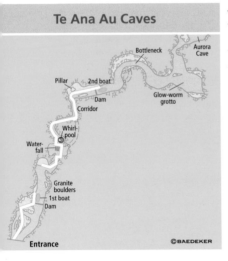

Te Ana Au Caves

world-famous fjord. Along the way, the road passes the magical **Mirror Lakes**, reflecting the majestic surrounding peaks in the early morning. Hikers also get their money's worth here, working up a sweat on the **Milford Track**, the most famous hiking trail in New Zealand. However, it's well worth it for the breathtaking scenery of the alps and fjords. The trail begins on the northern tip of Lake Te Anau at Glade House in the Clinton River valley. Te Anau is also the starting point for the 67km/40mi-long **Kepler Track**, allowing hikers to sample the magnificent mountainscapes between Lake Te Anau and Lake Manapouri.

LAKE MANAPOURI · MANAPOURI POWER PLANT

*One of New Zealand's most beautiful lakes

A good 30km/18 miles west of Te Anau (▶Lake Te Anau), one of the most beautiful lakes in New Zealand unfolds invitingly. The inland body of water covering 142 sq km/55 sq miles has **dozens of forested islets** and is surrounded by high mountains on all sides. It is only to the east, where the Waiau River flows through the lake, connecting it with Lake Te Anau, that the landscape is open. The lake's surface lies 178m/584ft above sea level, while at its **deepest point** it reaches 443m/1,555ft below sea level. In the 1960s, plans to lift the lake's water level by 12m/39ft in order to accommodate a hydroelectric energy project for the aluminium smelter resulted in fierce controversy, even contributing to a **change of government** in 1972. Meanwhile, a compromise has been found, leaving the water level of the lake unchanged: the power plant was installed in a cavern in the bedrock deep beneath the lake. However, in order to realise this **major prestige project**, a landing point for material and supply ships was built at Deep Cove in Doubtful Sound. The equipment needed to build the power station was then

> **!** MARCO ⊕ POLO TIP
>
> *Day trip to Doubtful Sound* **Insider Tip**
>
> A highly recommended day trip (run all year round by the Fiordland Travel operator) leads from Manapouri by boat and bus to Doubtful Sound, one of the very few fjords accessible to tourists. The trip includes a visit to the Manapouri power station, housed in a cavern. (Organized by Fiordland Travel, all year round)

driven by truck over a steep access road and across the 671m/2,201-ft Wilmot Pass to the construction site. Today, the road and landing are used for **tourism**. A steep spiral tunnel leads into the underground centre of the power plant where seven giant turbines are installed in a huge cavern. Every year, thousands of visitors admire this **masterpiece of engineering**, which is only accessible as part of an organised tour however.

Power plant centre: Oct. – April daily, 12.30pm, admission: NZ$ 77
www.realjourneys.co.nz

✳ Lake Wanaka

— ✳ Rk 135

Region: Otago
Altitude: 360m/1,181ft

This jewel in the crown of magnificent mountainscapes is at its most atmospheric in the autumn when the many deciduous trees brought over from Europe take on their seasonal colours. The most beautiful view across the fourth-largest lake of New Zealand can be enjoyed from the hamlet Glendhu Bay (14km/just under 9 miles west of Wanaka).

Situated at the southeastern end of the tranquil inland water, Wanaka (pop 3,000) is today the **most important settlement for miles around**. Whether it's summer or winter, Wanaka is always busy. In the warm season, the lake attracts holidaymakers, while in the cold season skiers and snowboarders get their money's worth in the surrounding area (Treble Cone is one of the peaks accessible by ski lift). The **Warbirds and Wheels Museum** at the aerodrome is very popular, as well as Stuart Landsborough's rather eccentric Puzzling World with its **maze** of colourful little houses, turrets, bridges, etc.

Warbirds and Wheels Museum: daily 9am – 4pm, admission: NZ$ 20
Puzzling World: daily 8.30am – 5.30pm, winter until 5pm, admission: NZ$ 12

*Wanaka (settlement)

From the funsport metropolis of ▶Queenstown, there is a choice of two routes to Lake Wanaka. The shorter one with its many bends – which does require **good driving skills** – is Cardrona Road (State Road 89), branching off Highway 6 at Arrow Junction and, after the pass summit, following the course of the Cardrona River. A **magical landscape** and a magnificent view makes up for the arduous drive.

*Cardrona Road

Travellers looking for a less strenuous driving experience can instead choose the option that is **50km/31 mile longer**: Highway 6 via Cromwell, and then up the broad Clutha River valley to Lake Wanaka.

Highway 6

Lake Wanaka

INFORMATION
Lake Wanaka Visitor i-Site
Information Centre
100 Ardmore Street, Wanaka
Tel. 03 443 1233
www.lakewanaka.co.nz

WHERE TO EAT
Capriccio ££ – £££
123 Ardmore Street
Tel. 03 443 8579
This popular restaurant serves up tasty
New Zealand and Italian dishes, accom-
panied by fine New Zealand wines.

Cardrona £
Crown Range Road
(15 mins. out of town)
Tel. 03 443 8153
Out here at the Crown Range it feels like
being back in the days of the gold rush.
The hearty fare includes lamb and game
specialities.

Lake Hawea Hotel £££
1 Capell Ave, Wanaka, Tel. 03 4 43 12 24
www.lakehawea.co.nz
Unsurpassable views matched by delicious specialities of a distinctly local flavour (game, lamb, fish, etc.) can be enjoyed here in the Grill Room.

Lake Hawea Lying about 15km/9 miles north of Wanaka town, the **smallest of
the three southern alpine lakes in Otago province** occupies a
surface area of around 140 sq km/54 sq miles and is some 30km/18
miles long. On the western shore of the lake, Highway 6 leads up to
the **Haast Pass**. At the site of the Lake Hawea settlement to the south
of the lake, a Maori village existed until 1836, when it was attacked
and destroyed. The **damming of the lake**, part of the Clutha River
Hydro Electric Scheme, raised the water level by 20m/65ft. In winter,
the dammed water is used as a reserve when the catchment area of
the Clutha River itself is iced over. Popular with **trout and salmon
anglers**, Lake Hawea reaches depths of between 64m/210ft and
410m/1,345ft below sea level!

Ski areas at New Zealand winter sports enthusiasts make the most of the nearby
Wanaka ski areas at **Cardrona** (southwest of Wanaka) and **Tremble Cone**
(southwest of Lake Wanaka).

*Haast Pass Named after the German naturalist Julius von Haast and only
564m/1,850ft up, this is the **lowest pass in the New Zealand Alps**.
However, it does connect the southern west coast region and the area
around Lake Wanaka, which is part of the Otago region. The road
follows an **ancient Maori trail leading to the nephrite deposits** in
the northwest of South Island. The modern road, only opened in
1965 after decades of construction work, leads through a **magnificent, jagged landscape**, albeit one which is frequently shrouded in

The turquoise blue Lake Wanaka looks quite placid in front of
majestic mountains

cloud. In wintertime, the pass suffers few closures due to snowfall, as
most precipitation here falls as rain. For the times when the rain
holds off, there are a few pretty picnic spots along the road too.

Mackenzie Country
—————————————— ✦ Rk–Sa 135

Region: Canterbury
Surface area: approx. 5,000 sq km/1,930 sq miles
Altitude: 460m/1,509ft – 2,623m/8,605ft
❶ Christchurch & Canterbury Tourism, Christchurch
Airport, 22 Durey Road Christchurch, Tel. 03 3 79 96 29
www.christchurchnz.com

Mackenzie Country unfurls in front of the mountains of the
Southern Alps and also encompasses the three major lakes:
Lake Tekapo, Lake Pukaki and Lake Ohau. A tough climate pre-
vails on this high plateau widely covered in tussock grass.
Winters are pretty cold up here, with a lot of snow, so it comes
as no surprise that it was mainly hardened shepherds from
the Scottish highlands who acclimatised best to this unique
landscape.

Access Coming from the east, there are two access roads into Mackenzie Country: the **Burke Pass** (Highway 8) or the little known **Mackenzie Pass** (a dirt road south of Burke Pass).

Economy The previously extensive **sheep pastures** are retreating. In recent times, game farms surrounded by high wire fences have sprung up in several places where sheep farms used to be. The tarmaced Highway 8 has opened up Mackenzie Country to tourism. Pretty **mountain lakes** attract visitors, along with the relatively recent **skiing areas**, while travellers wanting to explore ▶Mount Cook National Park usually come in through Mackenzie Country.

Upper Waitaki Power Development Scheme Mackenzie Country was much altered through the **hydroelectric power projects** of the Upper Waitaki Power Scheme (▶Waitaki). The centre of the action is **Twizel**, with its 1,000 or so inhabitants the largest settlement in the sparsely populated highlands.

MARCO ◉ POLO INSIGHT

With stolen sheep

Mackenzie Country was named after the Scottish shepherd and sheep rustler James McKenzie. In 1855, the infamous bandit – with his stolen sheep – crossed into the highlands, still unexplored at the time, via the pass he had discovered; he was caught later on in Lyttleton.

Situated on Highway 8, about an hour's drive northwest of the coastal town of ▶Timaru, **Fairlie** (pop 800) is the former administrative centre of Mackenzie Country. Until 1968, the village was the terminus for a railway line coming from Timaru. The old railway station today houses a **museum of regional history**, whilst a little further on, the Mabel Binney Cottage Museum is another visitor attraction.

Two Thumb Range Not far from Fairlie rise the mountains of the Two Thumb Range: Mount Dobson (in the direction of Tekapo, approx. 25km/12 miles) and Fox Peak (reached via Clayton, approx. 40km/25 miles), today established as **winter sports centres**.

Lindis Pass At a height of 970m/3,182ft, Lindis Pass connects the alpine part of Mackenzie Country, belonging to the Canterbury region, with the bare, dry heights of Central Otago.
This **old Maori track** through the mountains was rediscovered in 1857 by the land surveyor John T Thomson and soon used by many **gold prospectors**. The Lindis River valley still has several old farm buildings from the time of the early European settlers, chief amongst them the farm of Morven Hills Station, which was built by »Big Jock« McLeann in 1873. It had one of the largest sheep-shearing facilities in New Zealand. About 100,000 sheep lived here at that time.

✶✶ Marlborough Sounds Maritime Park

✳ Sd 132

Region: Nelson/Marlborough
Altitude: 0 – 1,203m/3,946ft
Surface area: 508 sq km/196 sq miles

Nowhere else in New Zealand does the sun shine as often as here in the Marlborough Sounds: over 2,000 hours per year. The heavily indented coastline with its many little islands and countless bays, mountains, beaches and a whole maze of waterways, creates a highly attractive setting which offers a great deal of variety to nature lovers, water sports enthusiasts and sailors.

The name »Marlborough Sounds« harks back to the Duke of Marlborough. Following the example of ▶Nelson and ▶Wellington, the name of a major **military hero was adopted**.

Namesake

Maori legends tell the following story: one day, the mythical heroes Kupe and Ngahue were fishing in Hawaiki and pursuing a huge squid, which was stealing their prey. On North Island's Wairarapa coast (at today's Castlepoint), Kupe nearly succeeded in catching the monster squid in a cave, but it wasn't until he reached the labyrinth of the Marlborough Sounds that he managed to kill it.

The Sounds
in Maori
mythology

Marlborough Sounds

INFORMATION
*Picton Visitor
Information Centre*
The Foreshore, Picton
Tel. 03 520 3113
http://destinationmarlborough.com

WHERE TO EAT
Escape to Picton
££-£££
33 Wellington Street, Picton
Tel. 03 572 9953
www.escapetopicton.com

This restaurant offers a successful mixture of nostalgia and modern design. The main focus of the food is quality, all of which has its price.

WHERE TO STAY
Lochmara Lodge
£ – £££
Lochmara Bay Queen Charlotte Sound
Tel. 03 573 4554
www.lochmaralodge.co.nz
Cosy lodge in an enchanting landscape, which can only reached by boat.

Havelock Around 40km/25 miles northwest of ▶Blenheim, in the northeastern corner of South Island, the village of **Havelock** (pop 500), named after a **British war hero**, occupies a position of unique beauty on the Marlborough Sounds. The settlement was founded on the site of an old Maori village, in order to supply the **gold prospectors** working 10km/just over 6 miles further west at Wakamarina. Today, Havelock's inhabitants predominantly make a living through aquaculture (primarily mussels) in the intricate network of the Marlborough Sounds estuaries. Havelock's claim to fame is as the place where nuclear physicist **Ernest Rutherford** (▶Famous People) and rocket scientist William Pickering went to school. The school today serves as a **youth hostel**, while the former Methodist church has established a memorial honouring Rutherford and Pickering.

Pelorus Bridge At Pelorus Bridge, just under 20km/12.5 miles west of Havelock, a **Scenic Reserve** on the river has attractive hiking trails. From Pelorus Bridge, a road leads into the romantic Maungatapu Valley.

A paradise for sailors and nature lovers: Marlborough Sounds

Several **pretty hiking tracks** lead through the Marlborough Sounds. One of them, the **Nydia Track**, begins at Mahau Sound, carries on across the Kaiuma Saddle to Nydia Bay and on to the Tennyson Inlet. The hike can be completed in 10 hours. Nydia Bay has camping facilities.

Starting from ▶Picton and Havelock, boat trips offer interesting excursions into the Marlborough Sounds, including the option of an exciting **sailing trip**. A variety of sea-going vessels, from basic dinghies to luxurious yachts and even large catamarans, can be chartered from several places. For further information contact the Marlborough Sounds Maritime Park Office on Auckland Street in Picton.

★★ Milford Sound

✳ Rh 135

Region: Southland
Altitude: Sea level
❶ Destination Fiordland, P. O. Box 1 Lakefront Drive, Te Anau, Tel. 03 2 49 79 49, www.fiordland.org.nz

This has got to be the most beautiful end of the world. Milford Sound lies on the southwestern coast of South Island and is an iconic symbol of New Zealand: lush green vegetation in the foreground, with the fjord lying resplendent, dominated by a steeply rising pyramid mountain resembling a bishop's mitre (Mitre Peak).

Arrival

By car or bus: from Te Anau (▶Lake Te Anau) on Highway 94 to Milford (120km/75 miles), by plane: from ▶Queenstown and Te Anau (▶Lake Te Anau) to Milford.

Bay landmarks

Amongst the first white people who encountered this magnificent scenery was **Captain Stoke** in 1851, who was taking his ship Acheron on a trip around the island for surveying purposes. Dropping anchor next to the roaring **Bowen Falls**, he baptised the 1,692m/5,551-ft symbol of this deep narrow bay **Mitre Peak**. Milford Sound, as this fjord is called, is 15 kilometres/9 miles long and has a narrow exit channel into the Tasman Sea. The steep mountains framing the fjord rise abruptly from the water to a great height. At up to 6,000mm/236in per year, precipitation levels are extremely high.

From Te anau to Milford Sound Spectacular in good weather, the 120km/75-mile **mountain road** of Te Anau (►Lake Te Anau), through the Eglinton Valley and the Homer Tunnel (named after the scientist Harry Homer), has turned Milford Sound into an easily accessible and very popular tourist attraction. However, visitors looking to attempt this trip should bear one thing in mind: There is **no petrol station along the way** nor on Milford Sound, meaning it is essential to **fill the tank up** in Te Anau. Anyone planning to stay the night on the only campsite on Milford Sound should reserve well in advance. In high season in particular, pitches here are highly sought-after, and there is a very real chance of not getting one. In winter, avalanches can sometimes make the road temporarily impassable.

The beautiful Mitre Peak is at the centre of Milford Sound

From Milford, **pleasure boats** explore Milford Sound, picturesque in good weather, in the direction of the Tasman Sea, giving passengers the welcome opportunity to see **Mitre Peak**, the fjord's symbol. Aboard the **MS Milford Wanderer**, visitors can undertake a cruise along the coast with its many beautiful fjords, including Doubtless Sound. In fact, the imposing landscape is best viewed from the water.

From Milford, it is only a short walk to the 160m/525-ft **Bowen Falls**, plunging down a »hanging« valley and named after a former governor.

Probably the best-known hiking trail in New Zealand, **Milford Track** is 54km/33 miles long and can be completed in 4 to 5 days. The starting point of the track is

Milford Sound

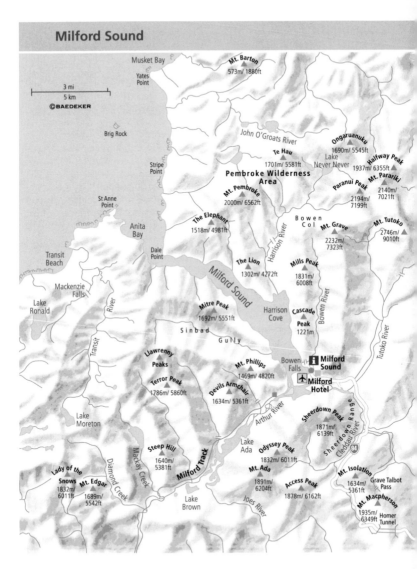

at Glade House on the northern tip of ►Lake Te Anau. The hiking trail initially follows the Clinton River, then continues through rainforest and a near-alpine landscape. Hikers climb the Mackinnon Pass, going by the romantic **Sutherland Falls** en route, and eventually descend into Arthur Valley. These wild waterfalls are really only accessible to those who decide to do the Milford Track, as unfortunately they are too remote for a day trip.

Please take note Milford Track, open between November and March, may only be attempted **in one direction**, i.e. from Glade House to Milford Sound. Hiking in the reverse direction is prohibited. Hikers going it alone have to register with the administration of Fiordland National Park before beginning the tour. Only **40 hikers per day** are allowed in. Tours led by a guide are also available. Following the usual Milford Sound boat trip, hikers are driven back to Te Anau by bus. Due to the **high levels of precipitation**, wet-weather gear is essential, as is insect repellent.

★★ Mount Aspiring National Park

✧ Rj–Rk 135

Regions: Otago, West Coast
Surface area: 3,555 sq km/ 1,372 sq miles
Altitude: 297m/974ft – 3,027m/9,931ft

A mighty pyramid-shaped rock, the 3,027m/9,931-ft Mount Aspiring is also known as the »Matterhorn of the South«. From a distance, this range of snowy peaks appears like a huge wall. Mount Aspiring is at the heart of New Zealand's second-largest national park, dominated by alpine scenery and bordering ►Fiordland National Park to the south. Together, and along with Westland and Mount Cook National Parks, they compose the Te Wahipounamu World Heritage Area and are part of the UNESCO world heritage.

Wealth of glacial formations The spectacular national park displays nearly the entire range of glacial formations, including finger lakes, ground moraines, lateral moraines and end moraines, drumlins, hanging valleys, glacial striations and glacier mills.

Haast Pass The national park's main access road is the Haast Pass road (HW 6). This **magnificent mountain road** leads along the eastern shore of Lake Wanaka and then heads for the north of this splendid alpine national park.

Mount Aspiring National Park

INFORMATION
Lake Wanaka i-Site Visitor Infor-
mation Centre
103 Ardmore Street, Wanaka
Tel. 03 443 1233
www.lakewanaka.co.nz

WHERE TO STAY
Edgewater Resort £££ – ££££
54 Sargood Drive,
PO Box 61, Lake Wanaka
Tel. 03 443 8311, www.edgewater.co.nz
This spaciously designed holiday hotel
on Lake Wanaka is a good base for ex-
ploring Mount Aspiring National Park.

HIKES IN MOUNT ASPIRING NATIONAL PARK

This beautiful hiking trail begins over in ▶Fiordland National Park
on the road to ▶Milford Sound, with the last section leading through
Mount Aspiring National Park to the northern Lake Wakatipu
(▶Queenstown). To complete this **splendid alpine tour** takes about
four days. Guided hikes are available, including just for sections of
the track.

**Routeburn Track

Following the course of the **Wilkin River**, it leads close to the eastern
boundary of the national park to the place where the Wilkin River
joins the Makarora River south of the Ranger station at Makarora
(Highway 6).

Wilkin Valley Track

** Mount Cook / Aoraki National Park

——————————— ✦ Sa 134

Region: Canterbury
Surface area: approx. 700 sq km/ 270 sq miles
Altitude: 650m/2,132ft – 3,754m/12,316ft

**Mount Cook National Park encompasses the heart of the New
Zealand Alps. Clustered around the two highest and most imposing peaks of the Southern Alps – Mount Cook (Aoraki),
3,754m/12,316ft high, and the 3,496m/11,470-ft Mount Tasman – are 15 more mountains reaching 3,000m/near 10,000ft,
plus about 200 lower peaks reaching at least 2,500m/8,200ft
in altitude. The national park is also traversed by the Tasman
Glacier, the largest of the Southern Alps.**

Aoraki/ Mt Cook Village   Mount Cook National Park, which merges in the west with Westland National Park, home to the **Franz Josef Glacier** and **Fox Glacier**, is easily accessible. From Twizel (or from Lake Pukaki), the paved State Highway 80 leads through an imposing alpine landscape to Aoraki/ Mount Cook Village (762m/2,500ft; pop 200). **Small planes** taking off from ►Christchurch and ► Queenstown also give access to the well-known tourist resort. Accommodation options include hotels, holiday apartments, a youth hostel and a campsite.

Visitor Centre   The **DOC Visitor Centre** on Bowen Drive has comprehensive material on the geology, flora and fauna of this alpine landscape, and also up-to-date information on the accessibility of climbing and glacier routes. A new attraction, which opened in 2008, is the interactive **Sir Edmund Hillary Alpine Centre** (at »The Hermitage« hotel) with museum, gallery, 3D cinema and planetarium; it honours the life and work of the man from New Zealand (►Famous People) who was the first to conquer Mount Everest and who trained for his expeditions at Mount Cook.

Overwhelming for every nature lover: 3764m/12421ft-high Mt Cook rises up behind Lake Tasman

Mount Cook/Aoraki National Park

INFORMATION
Aoraki/Mount Cook National Park Visitor Centre
Mount Cook Village
State Highway 80
Tel. 03 435 1186
www.doc.govt.nz

WHERE TO STAY
❶ *The Hermitage*
£££ – ££££
State Highway 80, Private Bay
Aoraki/Mount Cook Village
Tel. 03 435 1809
www.hermitage.co.nz
This comfortable mountain hotel

(212 rooms) has been sitting among splendid alpine scenery at the foot of Aoraki/Mount Cook since 1884. It has been modernised several times over the years, and was recently awarded the »Enviro Gold« mark for its environmental efforts.

❷ *Mainstay Heritage Gateway*
££
Main Road, Omarama
Tel. 03 438 9805
www.mainstay.co.nz
Comfortable establishment in Mackenzie Country, an ideal base for excursions into the national park

---

Today, the snowfields on Mount Cook are an extremely popular all-year-round ski area. Small planes and helicopters whisk skiers up the mountains, known as heli-skiing. Guided ski tours are also offered on Tasman Glacier. Murchinson, Darwin and Bonney Glaciers are more for experienced skiers. Nordic ski tours are also possible to Tasman and Kelmen Huts, but these are quite strenuous and so only recommended for experienced Nordic skiers.

All-year-round ski area

Due to the lack of natural predators, the deer released into the national park at the beginning of the 20th century, originally from Europe, multiplied so prolifically they became a pest. Many animals had to be culled, captured or rounded up in game farms.

Oh deer!

A worthwhile detour from Mount Cook village leads to the **»tip of the tongue«** of the Tasman Glacier, which today still measures 27km/16 miles in length and up to 3km/1.8 miles across. Like most glaciers the Tasman Glacier is receding. To reach it, drive approx. 8km/5 miles in the direction of Blue Lake and climb for about half an hour through scree to the Tasman Glacier Viewpoint, which commands a magnificent view of the **dramatic alpine backdrop**.

**Tasman Glacier Viewpoint

Arguably New Zealand's most beautiful, if also its **most demanding alpine mountain trail**, this track leads right across Mount Cook National Park and over into ▶Westland National Park. This involves conquering the 2,149m/7,050-ft **Copland Pass**, which reaches up

**Copland Track

Southern Alps Westland NP • Mount Cook NP

Whataroa, Hokitika, Greymouth

Tatare

Franz Josef

Tatare Stream

Omoeroa Hill
682m/
2238ft

3 mi
5 km
©BAEDEKER

Galway
Point

Gillespies
Point

Gillespies
Beach

Lake
Mueller

Lake
Gault

Lake
Matheson

Fox
Glacier

Fox River

Fox River

ook River

Waikukupa River

Ebenezer Peak
1333m/ 4374ft

Baird

Thelma Peak
2057m/ 6749ft

Fritz Range

Burster

Range

Drummond Peak
2515m/
8252ft

Franz Josef

Mt. Mitchell
1631m/
5351ft

Victoria
Range

Fritz Glacier

Agassiz
Glacier

Mt. Anderegg
2362m/ 7750ft

Glacier

Minarets

Victoria Glacier

Mt. Halcombe
2665m/
8744ft

3048m/
10000ft

Fox Range

Craig Peak
1914m/6280ft

Fox Glacier

Mt. Du Fresne
2251m/ 7386ft

Albert
Glacier

Mt. Haidinger
3066m/
10060ft

Glacier

WESTLAND

Balfour Glacier

Mt. Tasman
3498m/ 11477ft

Grand
Plateau

Malte Brun

Ryan Peak
1943m/ 6375ft

Balfour Range

NATIONAL PARK

La Perouse Glacier

La Perouse
3079m/
10102ft

Aoraki Mt. Cook
3754m/
12317ft

Mt. Myers
1699m/ 5574ft

Copland Range

Lyttle Peak
2251m/ 7386ft

Gulch Glacier

Mt. Copland
2345m/ 7694ft

Navigator Range

Strauchon Glacier

Pibrac

Novara Peak
2299m/
7543ft

Shiels Peak
2042m/ 6700ft

Price Peak
1913m/ 6277ft

Dilemma Peak
2619m/
8593ft

Misty Peak
1593m/
5227ft

Karangarua Range

Copland

River

Copland
Glacier

Lean Peak
2362m/ 7750ft

Mt. Cook Range

Turner Peak
2341m/
7681ft

Tasman

The Sierra Range

Mt. Gloin Peak
2073m/ 6802ft

Mt. Peculiar
1913m/ 6277ft

Karangarua River

Blizzard Peak
2408m/ 7901ft

Douglas
Neve

Douglas Glacier

Mt. Sefton
3157m/
10358ft

Mt. Wakefield
2050m/ 6726ft

The Nuns Veil
2736m/ 8972ft

Mountains

Bare Rocky Range

Mt. Thompson
2636m/ 8649ft

Brass Peak
2339m/ 7674ft

Mt. Howitt
1966m/ 6450ft

Mt. Ollivier
1917m/
6290ft

Mount
Cook

Jacobs River, Haast

Mt. Isabel
2545m/ 8350ft

Mueller Glacier

1

Mt. Townsend
2035m/
6677ft

Fettes Peak
2454m/
8052ft

Hooker River

Mt. Burns
2738m/ 8983ft

Fyfe Pass

Mt. Sealy
2637m/
8652ft

Tasman River

Burnett

Jollie River

Mt. Strachan
2545m/
8350ft

Landsborough

Arthur
Glacier

Mt. Hopkins
2682m/ 8800ft

Richardson
Glacier

Mt. Burnett
2035m/ 6677ft

Mount
Cook

Mt. Williams
2536m/ 8321ft

Mt. Brown
2179m/ 7149ft

2

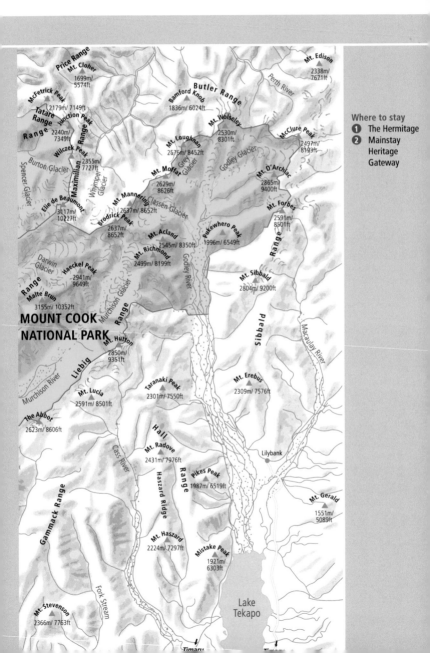

Where to stay
1. The Hermitage
2. Mainstay Heritage Gateway

MARCO POLO TIP

! *Scenic flights* Insider Tip

From Mount Cook, sightseeing flights are available over the summits and glaciers of the national park and its surroundings. Unforgettable panoramic flights by helicopter are another option. The helicopters are able to get closer to the summits than the planes. At Pukaki Airport near Twizel you can book your flight, including leather jacket, cap and goggles to wear on the flight in a well-maintained red Grumman Ag Cat bi-plane.
Tel. 03 4 35 00 77
www.redcat.co.nz
From NZ$ 195

among the firn fields of the majestic summits. Requiring at least four days, this walk is only suitable for **hikers and mountaineers with alpine experience**. Taking a local guide is highly recommended.

Mount Cook National Park has many waymarked **walking paths and hiking trails**, amongst them Bowen Track, Governor's Bush Walk, Kea Point Walk, Hooker Valley Walk, Red Tarns Track and, last but not least, Wakefield Track. There are points along these trails which give **breathtaking views**. Exact trail descriptions can be picked up from the Visitor Centre in Mount Cook village.

＊ **Nelson**

─────────────── ✳ **Sd 132**

Region: Nelson/Marlborough
Altitude: 0 – 458m/1,502ft
Population: 50,000

The wealthy port town of Nelson enjoys a very mild climate. Its urban landscape is dominated by many lovingly preserved old wooden buildings, ranging from mansions to cottages. The seafront and many parks and green spaces are also pleasing on the eye. In recent times, Nelson's charming location has attracted many artists and craftspeople. The country's three most popular national parks are nearby.

Sunshine town in the colonial style

This pretty, sunny town, with its colonial atmosphere, lies on the southeastern side of Tasman Bay in an area renowned for its very **mild climate** and many hours of sunshine. In the **fertile interior**, various types of fruit suitable for export are cultivated – particularly apples and pears – alongside grapes, hops and tobacco. A lucrative forestry economy has developed in the surrounding mountains. The timber is processed in the Nelson area and from there exported all over the world. Recently, the economic area of Nelson has experienced very dynamic growth, causing the population to increase by over 5% within a decade.

Nelson

INFORMATION
Visitor Information Centre
PO Box 194, Cnr Trafalgar & Halifax
Streets, Nelson
Tel. 03 548 2304
www.nelsonnz.com

WHERE TO EAT
The Boat Shed ££
350 Wakefield Quay
Tel. 03 546 9783
www.nelsonwaterfront.co.nz/
The interesting, Pacific-inspired culinary
creations are complemented by the finest New Zealand wines.

Broccoli Row
£ – ££
132 Collingwood St
Tel. 03 548 9621
Cosy restaurant in the town centre with
tasty vegetarian and fish dishes. On
weekdays only lunch, closed weekends

WHERE TO STAY
Rutherford Hotel
£££ – ££££
Trafalgar Square
PO Box 248, Nelson
Tel. 03 548 2299
www.rutherfordhotel.co.nz
Simply the best place in town, offering
all the comforts a traveller could desire.
The hotel has several restaurants and a
bar. The shopping area and the cathe-
dral are only a few minutes' walk away.

The Honest Lawyer £££ Insider Tip
1 Point Road, Monaco
Tel. 03 547 8850
www.honestlawyer.co.nz
Right on the waterfront, an old English
country pub has been recreated in a
modern design. The rooms have cosy
furnishings, and the bar and restaurant
are popular with foreigners and locals
alike.

History

In 1642, Dutchman Abel Tasman was the first European to lay down
anchor in the bay now named after him. However, as the local Maori attacked one of his boats, he did not come ashore. Before the arrival of the Europeans, Maori tribes would periodically come across
from North Island for the **rich fishing grounds and jade deposits**. In the late 1820s, the Maori leader Te Rauparaha and his allies
launched several attacks on the villages and fortifications of Tasman
Bay. When **William Wakefield** arrived in 1839, looking for land to
settle, he met just a few Maori. Only three years later, a larger group
of European immigrants settled here, establishing a prosperous agricultural centre. In 1858, Nelson became the first settlement in New
Zealand to be granted **city status** by Queen Victoria. The young
city, with just under 3,000 inhabitants at the time, also experienced
rapid economic growth, largely through **copper mining** in the Dun
Mountains, some 20km/12 miles away, and the **discovery of gold**
in the area. In 1871, **Ernest Rutherford** (▶Famous People) was
born in Nelson, and later in life was duly elevated to »Lord Rutherford of Nelson«.

WHAT TO SEE IN NELSON

Christ Church Cathedral
With its exposed position on Trafalgar Square, Christ Church Cathedral stands on the exact site of a pre-European **Maori fortification**. In 1842, the New Zealand Company established a settlement here. Following the »Wairau Affray«, the frightened settlers fortified the hill, naming it Fort Arthur after their slain leader Arthur Wakefield. The first church was erected up here in 1850, and construction of the cathedral started in 1925. However, many changes to the design, due to the **danger of earthquakes** amongst other things, delayed completion until 1967.

> **!** *Flea market*   Insider Tip
>
> **MARCO ⊕ POLO TIP**
>
> Every Saturday morning, a colourful and popular flea market takes place at the Montgomery Parking car park in Nelson. Access is via Trafalgar Street, Hardy Street or Bridge Street.

Trafalgar Street
The vibrant main artery of the town is Trafalgar Street, lined by many shops. Look out for **Melrose House**, a mansion erected around 1875 in the Italian style, today used by the town administration for ceremonial purposes. At the southern end of the street, the stately Fairfield House (1883), which was blessed by the Dalai Lama when he visited in 1996, continues to enchant visitors.

Milton Street
On **Milton Street**, both Fellworth House and Grove House are impressive buildings erected in the second half of the 19th century for rich merchants.

Botanical Hill
It might measure barely 150m/492ft, but Botanical Hill is considered to be the geographical **centre of New Zealand**. There are pretty views over the town from up here, and the beautiful gardens attract visitors all year round.

*Suter Art Gallery
Founded by Bishop Suter in 1889, this institution (between Bridge Street and Hardy Street) with a modern annex possesses an **excellent collection of paintings**, including works by Woollaston, Van der Velden, Hodgkins and Richmond.
❶ Daily 10.30am–4.30pm, admission: donation requested, www.thesuter.org.nz

Bishop's School
The school, erected in 1844 on Nile Street at the behest of Bishop Selwyn, is furnished in period style and today open to the public as a museum.

Nelson Haven
The port of Nelson, protected by a long jetty, has a **real buzz** to it. All kinds of New Zealand produce is shipped from here, primarily fruit,

wine, wood and timber. But watch out: the **tidal range** can cover 4m/13ft!

This museum, situated in **Isel Park** in the southwest of the city and telling the story of both the city and the region, is worth visiting. A fair amount of space is given over to the history of the local Maori, including extensive information on the only clash between the Maori and white settlers on South Island, which entered the history books as the »**Wairau Affray**«.

*Nelson Provincial Museum

❶ Mon – Fri 10am – 5pm, Sat, Sun 10 – 4.30pm, admission: NZ$ 6, www. museumnp.org.nz

The former manor house of the Marsden family, who emigrated from England, next to the museum, built in the 19th century and still furnished in the style of that period. The house is surrounded by a park with some of New Zealand's **oldest exotic trees** and some especially magnificent **rhododendrons**.

Isel House

❶ Oct. – May Tue – Sun 11am – 4pm, admission: donation requested, www.iselhouse.co.nz

Nelson't city centre with its many restaurants and boutiques is very pretty

How about a quiet evening walk along Tahunanui Beach?

AROUND NELSON

*Founders Park
Extending some 2km/1.2 miles north of the city, on Atwahai Drive, Founders Park is an **open-air museum** with various Victorian buildings, some of them reconstructed. Of particular interest is an old windmill as well as an exhibition on the history of Nelson (opening times: daily 9am–6pm).

❶ Daily 10am – 4.30pm, admission: NZ$ 7, www.founderspark.co.nz

Tahunanui Beach
At the end of Rocks Road lies the city's **most popular sandy beach**, Tahunanui Beach, with a campsite and many entertainment and leisure facilities. Swimmers and sunbathers will get their money's worth, just like joggers and windsurfers. Another beach popular with locals is **Rabbit Island**, which largely consists of sanddunes (25km/15.5 miles west).

*Day trip to Cable Bay and Croisilles Harbour
It might be hard work for the driver, but the journey north from Nelson to Cable Bay with its pretty bathing beach, and on via Rai Valley to the charming Croisilles Harbour, is **extremely scenic**. The more adventurous can continue on to **Admiralty Bay** and **French Pass**.

*Mount Richmond Forest Park
The highly scenic Mount Richmond Forest Park stretches south and east of Nelson across the mountains of the Richmond Range to the valley of the Wairau River. A popular hike in the park is the **»Wakamarina – Onamalutu Track«**, which follows in the footsteps of the gold prospectors. Requiring two days, the hike starts 20km/12.5 miles south of Canvastown.

Occupying 3,760 sq km/1,450 sq miles, the vast and mountainous forest area extends from Tasman Bay (Motueka Valley) across the Tasman Mountains to the west coast (Karamea Bay). Several hiking tracks lead through the primeval landscape with its lush local vegetation, the most famous tracks being the »Heaphy Track« (▶Abel Tasman National Park) and the »Wangapea Track«, each of which takes around four days.

*North West Nelson Forest Park

* Nelson Lakes National Park

✦ Sc 132/133

Region: Nelson/Marlborough
Surface area: 960 sq km/370 sq miles
Altitude: 600m/1,968ft – 2,338m/7,670ft
❶ St. Arnaud DOC Visitor Information Centre, View Road, Private Bag, St. Arnaud, Tel. 03 5 21 18 06, www.doc.govt.nz

The national park occupies large swathes of wild, mountainous country, crossed by the so-called Alpine Fault, a pronounced geological fault zone. The Alpine Fault causes the truly enormous differences in height between the mountains, their highest peaks covered in snow right into the summer. Thick honeydew beech forests stretch along the lakeshore in particular.

Two elongated lakes, **Lake Rotoiti**, lying at an altitude of 610m/2,000ft, and **Lake Rotoroa**, lying about 100m/330ft further down, fill the tongue basins carved out by Ice Age glaciers and sealed off by moraines. The lake further up is accessible via a dead end road and attracts mainly **watersports enthusiasts** and visitors looking for relaxation. The lake lying below is a paradise for **anglers**, being more difficult to access and therefore quieter.

Nelson Lakes National Park

WHERE TO STAY
Murchison Lodge ££
15 Grey St., Murchison
Tel. 03 5 23 91 96
Tel. 08 00 5 23 91 96
www.murchisonlodge.co.nz

This comfortable lodge is located west of the parks and a good starting point for great tours of the area, including a place in the woods where a natural fire burns constantly.

The beautiful mountain landscape around Nelson Lakes is now a popular trekking region

Hikes The national park has several waymarked hiking trails. Exact route descriptions are available from the Visitor Centre in St Arnaud and the Lake Rotoroa ranger station.

Winter sports For winter sports enthusiasts there is the ski area at **Mount Robert** south of Lake Rotoiti and one at **Rainbow** (c. 25km/15mi south of St Arnaud).

Otago

Region: Otago
Altitude: 0 – 3,027m/9,931ft
Population: 212,000

The Otago countryside, from the broad Waitaki River in the north to Catlins Forest Park in the south, comprises the green and often foggy coastal area with the main towns of ►Balclutha, ►Dunedin and Oamaru. The region's interior is fairly sparsely populated, with a near-continental climate. Summers are dry and hot, while winters can get very cold.

Sculpted by ice The landscape of central Otago consists of a high plateau ruptured into block mountains during the upthrust of the Southern Alps, with jagged breaks towards the west and softer slopes towards the east. The **Clutha River**, one of **New Zealand's most voluminous and fast-flowing rivers**, has dug **deep gorges** into the plateaus on its way

Otago

INFORMATION
Alexandra Visitor Centre
21 Centennial Avenue Alexandra,
Central Otago
Tel. 03 448 9515
www.centralotagonz.com

Oamaru Visitor Information Centre
1 Thames Street, Oamaru, Waitaki
District
Tel. 03 434 1656
www.visitoamaru.co.nz

west from the Alpine lakes, Lake Wanaka and Lake Hawea. During the Ice Ages, the landscape was reshaped. The mountains ground down by the glaciers display more rounded shapes and are covered in tussock grass, while glaciers and moraines created the elongated and deep fjord-like lakes. Otago's westernmost point forms part of the Southern Alps. The **region's highest elevations** are the 3,027m/9,931-ft Mount Aspiring, 1,816m/5,958-ft Mount Earnslaw and the near 2,500m/8,202ft-high Remarkables near Queenstown.

The name of the region stems from the former **Maori settlement of Otakau** on the Otago Peninsula northeast of ▶Dunedin. The name of the settlement was initially used for the whole peninsula and later on for the entire region.

Etymology of a landscape

The Otago region was initially settled by moa hunters, later by seal hunters and whalers, and from 1860 onwards by gold prospectors. Around this time, a tremendous **stream of immigrants** began pouring into the country's interior. In 1860 the whole region counted 12,000 inhabitants; this number multiplied to become 70,000 just 11 years later. Once the gold fields were cleared out, all that remained was to mine gold-bearing quartz seams and dig up the riverbeds. Some of the short-lived gold prospector settlements were able to expand their infrastructure and carry on as agricultural and logistical centres. Artificial irrigation created green **orchards and gardens** in the previously bare valleys. Following the gold rush, the export of frozen meat brought new prosperity, with markets for both the sheep's wool and meat. However, due to **rabbit plagues and erosion**, many of the large »runs« (extensive sheep pastures) began to make a loss. By order of the government, most of these were then divided into smaller parcels of land to be farmed more intensively. As time went on, people began to understand the full significance of the latent economic potential in the unbridled waters streaming down from the mountains in huge quantities. Massive dam projects were implemented for electricity generation, irrigation and anti-flood measures. In conjunction with this, a lot more roads were built. Cen-

History, economy

? *Stone baskets*

According to Maori tradition the Moeraki Boulders are those gourds and provision baskets which a long, long time ago were washed onto the shore from the ancestors canoe Arai-te-uru and turned to stone.

tral Otago's landscape has been much altered by the building works. It was the **infrastructure** set up for the dam projects which made modern auto tourism possible. Several former **gold prospectors settlements** – such as Queenstown – which had become sleepy backwaters, were revitalised. Today, many places bustle with the activity of holidaymakers seeking adventure, summer relaxation or the adrenaline rush of winter sports.

Oamaru The centre of northern Otago is Oamaru. The most important sights can be explored on the circular **Oamaru Historic Walk** beginning at the Boer War Memorial (Thames Street). Extracted from numerous local quarries, the white **Oamaru limestone** has been used to build many distinguished buildings in New Zealand and Australia.

Janet Frame House, penguin breeding station The author **Janet Frame** (1924 – 2004) grew up in Oamaru; she was nominated for the Nobel prize for literature in 2003. She achieved her breakthrough in Europe through the movie version of her autobiographical novel *An Angel at my Table*. Janet Frame grew up in the house at 56 Eden Street (**Janet Frame House**). The Oamaru coast boasts a breeding station for penguins, where just before sunset, **blue penguins and yellow-eyed penguins returning from the sea** may be observed up close. An **observation webcam** has been installed.
Janet Frame House: Nov. – April daily 2pm – 4pm, admission: NZ$ 6, www.janetframe.org.nz
Breeding station: 10am until the penguins return depending on the time of year 7pm – 11.30pm, tours: from NZ$ 15

*Totara Estate About 8km/5 miles south of Oamaru, Highway 1 reaches the Totara Estate, where **frozen meat** was produced in this area for the first time. The former slaughterhouses and processing facilities may be visited; guided daylong trips are also offered. Old trees shelter the **imposing manor house**, which dates from 1868, and on the nearby hill a monument honours Thomas Byrdone, founder of the local frozen-meat industry.
❶ Sept. – May 10am – 4pm, admission: NZ$ 10, www.heritage.org.nz

*Clark's Mill Approx. 4km/2.5 miles further south, the road reaches Clark's Mill, built in 1865, and the only mill still standing in this region. Today, the machinery is largely intact and the water-powered mill is a listed **technical monument**.
❶ Late Oct. – April Sun 1pm – 3pm, Feb. daily 10am – 4pm, admission: NZ$ 10, www.heritage.org.nz

Massive **spherical rocks**, some of them weighing several tons, with circumferences of up to 3m/nearly 10ft, lie scattered on the beach some 35km/22 miles south of Oamaru. Natural scientists explain that they were formed many millions of years ago on the ocean floor by chemical concretions (i.e. coalescing rock) around solid cores. Once the ocean floor had lifted, they were washed free onto the beach by the swell, but, being harder than the surrounding cliffs, remain in the place where they formed.

✲✲Moeraki Boulders

Some of these boulders are still sitting firmly in the ground. The eye-catching turtle-shell patterns are a result of the extrusion of yellow calcite. Whilst these boulders enjoy **strict protection as natural monuments**, unfortunately the number of the smaller, transportable specimens is decreasing. Anyone who wants to admire them has to hurry.

Huge round rocks on the beach: are these maybe the petrified calabashes of the Maori ancestral canoe?

✱✱ Paparoa National Park · Pancake Rocks

──────────── ✳ Sb 133

Region: West Coast
Surface area: 306 sq km/118 sq miles
Altitude: 0 – 1,455m/4,773ft

The absolute highlight of Paparoa National Park, established in 1987, are the world-famous Pancake Rocks. The warm ocean current passing this section of the coastline, and the high, protective limestone cliffs, have resulted in a favourable microclimate with rich, thriving subtropical vegetation. Even Nikau palms grow here.

✱✱Pancake Rocks   The **main attraction of the national park** are the so-called Pancake Rocks. Found right beside the sea, they are highly impressive lime-

Pancake Rocks in the craggy West Coast look like stacks of pancakes

Paparoa National Park · Pancake Rocks

INFORMATION
Paparoa National Park Visitor Centre
4294 Coast Road
Punakaiki
Tel. 03 731 1895
www.doc.govt.nz

WHERE TO STAY
Punakaiki Rocks Resort £££
State Highway 6, Punakaiki, West Coast
Tel. 03 731 1167
www.punakaiki-resort.co.nz
Modern hotel with quite comfortable rooms.

stone parcels looking like layered flat cakes or pancakes. At times of strong swell, the water pushed out through »blowholes« eroded from the rock sprays high into the air. The spectacular »pancakes« are accessible via a short **circular hiking trail** beginning at Dolomite Point. Secure platforms offer an unhindered view of the **roaring and gushing blow holes** that pierce these rocks. The viewing platforms also offer great views of the interior, with the **Southern Alps** visible in fine weather.

The national park's visitor centre can be found in the small village of Punakaiki, the starting point for exploring the national park. The centre not only tells the complex **story of the Pancake Rocks**, but also has much interesting information on the local flora and fauna. Many craftsmen also live in Punakaiki.

Punakaiki

A few hiking trails of varying length lead to interesting, sometimes **wild and romantic stretches of coast**. One of them is the **Truman Track**, leading through dense forest to the steep, rugged coast at Perpendicular Point. **Punakaiki Cavern Track** accesses a few impressive caves and waterfalls. Another hiking track leads to the »Ballroom Overhang«, where the limestone rocks show particularly spectacular erosion. Several arduous longer routes lead in to the still largely **unspoilt mountains** of the interior, or the truly enchanting rainforest landscape along the **Pororari River**. Particularly recommended trails are the Punakaiki – Pororari Loop Track (including a river crossing) and the 2km/1.2mi-long Upper Pororari Track.

Worthwhile hikes

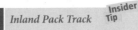

MARCO ⊕ POLO TIP ! **Inland Pack Track** *Insider Tip*

The Inland Pack Track (Razorback Road) can be pretty hard work, but it's one trail sure to leave a lasting impression. Taking about three days, the hike follows an old route from the 1870s through the wild mountain country. A word of warning however: several creeks and other watercourses have to be negotiated without assistance, where the bridges or other crossings are missing or have been swept away by floods.

Picton

⟶✴ **Se 132**

Region: Nelson/Marlborough
Altitude: 0 – 379m/1,243ft
Population: 3,000

Situated on the northeastern point of South Island and near the head of the picturesque Queen Charlotte Sound , it is from Picton that the ferries run between South Island and North Island (▶Wellington). The small seaside town, which has managed to hold on to its traditional character, is framed by steep mountain slopes inland.

History The settlement of Picton was founded in 1848 on the site of an abandoned Maori fortification. The name commemorates a general killed in the **battle of Waterloo**. For years, Picton was in fierce conflict with neighbouring ▶Blenheim over which town was to be the seat of the provincial government of Marlborough. In 1862, it was suggested that the two railway lines already in existence on the two main islands be connected by an effective steamboat service. In 1898, prime min-

Ferries heading for North Island depart from Picton harbour in its picturesque location on the northern point of South Island.

ister Richard Seddon supported the concept of a **rail ferry**, which was then quickly realised.

WHAT TO SEE IN AND AROUND PICTON

This interesting museum on London Quay is a reminder of the **whaling tradition** in the Picton area which lasted nearly 150 years. Whaling only stopped here in the 1960s.

Picton Museum

❶ Daily 10am – 4pm, admission: NZ$ 6, www.pictonmuseum-newzealand.com

At the port exit, look out for the freighter Echo, built in 1905, alongside the convict transport ship Edwin Fox, constructed back in 1853 in India from particularly resistant teak.

Museum ships

On the way to Waikawa Bay, situated to the northeast, the road reaches Victoria Domain Lookout, commanding **splendid views across Queen Charlotte Sound** and the port of Picton.

Victoria Domain Lookout

Extending north of Picton, the exceptionally scenic Queen Charlotte Sound boasts many **picturesque bays**. The best way to explore this magical coastal landscape is by pleasure boat. The most beautiful spots are Mistletoe Bay, the Bay of Many Coves, Endeavour Inlet,

**Queen Charlotte Sound

Picton

INFORMATION
Visitor Information Centre
The Foreshore, Picton
Tel. 03 520 3113
http://marlboroughnz.com

WHERE TO EAT
Spinnaker **££–£££**
Beach Raod Waikawa Marina
Tel. 03 5 73 91 52
www.spinnakerwaikawa.co.nz
Comfortable café restaurant with a view of the yacht harbour. The fish and seafood is especially good.

WHERE TO STAY
Punga Cove Resort **£ – ££££**
Endeavour Inlet, Queen Charlotte Sound, Marlborough Sounds
Tel. 03 579 8561, fax 03 579 8080
www.pungacove.co.nz
One hour by boat north of Picton, this supremely comfortable complex is hidden away in a picturesque bay of the Marlborough Sounds.

Beachcomber Inn AA
27 Waikawa Road, Picton
Tel. 03 573 8900, fax 03 573 8888
www.pictonhotel.com
This centrally located hotel is a good base for boat trips into Charlotte Sound.

! *Wreck diving* Insider Tip

Queen Charlotte Sound off Picton offers a very special experience: a dive to the wreck of the Mikhail Lermontov cruise liner, which was sailing under the Soviet flag when it sank in 1986 in the bay of Port Gore.

Resolution Bay and Ship Cove. Running from Anakiwa to Ship Cove, the **Queen Charlotte Walkway** is a beautiful hiking trail. There is also a road, Queen Charlotte Drive, on which to access this picture book landscape. Picton is the starting point for organised **boat excursions** and **fishing trips**, often leading into Ship Cove, visited several times by James Cook (▶Famous People), Queen Charlotte Sound or further out into the Marlborough Sounds.

M Robin Hood Bay   From Picton, it is worth considering a trip to the picturesque Robin Hood Bay a few miles further east. However, with its steep sections, this detour can be a **demanding drive**.

Cook Strait   At its narrowest point, the **storm-lashed strait** between New Zealand's two main islands measures just 23km/14 miles across. Starting from Picton, the ferries initially make their way through the picturesque Sounds before heading for the open sea and finally arriving at the wide open harbour bay of ▶Wellington on North Island.

** **Queenstown**

✦ Rj 136

Region: Otago
Altitude: 330m/1,082ft
Population: 11,000

Today, the former gold prospector settlement on the eastern shore of Lake Wakatipu is South Island's undisputed tourist hotspot and New Zealand's »Adventure Capital«. All year round it offers a wide variety of entertainment and leisure activities. The options range from bungee jumping, jet boating and white water rafting to paragliding and climbing – to name but a few.

Getting there   Travellers driving to Queenstown from the western coast or ▶Invercargill take State Highway 6, and from ▶Dunedin State Highway 8. Scheduled coaches and charter buses connect the town with all the important hubs on South Island. The airfield at Frankton, 6km/3.7 miles northeast of Queenstown, is used by international airlines from Australia. It is also one of New Zealand's **major heliports**.

Queenstown

INFORMATION
Queenstown Travel & Visitor Centre
P.O. Box 353, Queenstown
Tel. 03 442 4100
www.queenstown.co.nz

WHERE TO EAT

❶ Roaring Meg's
57 Shotover Street
Tel. 03 442 9676
www.roaringmegs.co.nz
This former 19th century gold prospectors cottage today serves cosy candle-lit dinners.

❷ The Bath House
Lakefront, 28 Marine Parade
Tel. 03 442 5625
Popular meeting point for a good lunch or dinner.

❸ Fishbone Bar & Grill ££
7 Beach Street
Tel. 03 4 42 67 68
www.fishbonequeenstown.co.nz
Bright, modern grill restaurant, where fish & chips, but also salmon and oysters, are served.

❹ Vknow ££
Fernhill Road/Richards Park Lane
Tel. 03 4 42 54 44
www.vknow.co.nz
Comfortable restaurant with wine bar, serves a mixture of Italian, French and Kiwi cooking. Especially delicious: gourmet pizzas.

❺ Ferburger £
42 Shotover Street
TTel. 03 4 41 13 32
www.ferburger.com
Fastfood restaurant that serves unbeatably tasty giant burgers

WHERE TO STAY

❶ Browns Boutique Hotel ££££
26 Isle Street
Tel. 03 4 41 20 50
www.brownshotel.co.nz
Nice quiet centrally located hotel. The rooms face either the lake or the mountains.

❷ Eichardt's ££££
Marine Parade
Tel. 03 441 0450
www.eichardtshotel.co.nz
These historic walls, in a prime location on the lakeshore, shelter one of the best small hotels in the world.

❷ Heartland Hotel Queenstown £££
27 Stanley Street
Tel. 03 442 7700
www.heartlandhotels.co.nz
With its central location and blessed with good views, this cosy hotel complex laid out following the Swiss model offers pleasant rooms.

The centre of this **bustling tourist town** occupies a charming position on a headland jutting out far to sea and is landscaped as **Queenstown Gardens**. The best starting point for a circular walk is the **Old Stone Library** (1877), which shares a roof with the court-

Walking tour around Queenstown

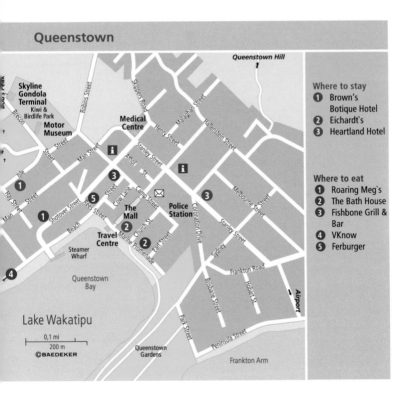

Queenstown

Skyline Gondola Terminal
Kiwi & Birdlife Park
Motor Museum
Medical Centre
Queenstown Hill
Robins Street
Skippers Road
Brecon Street
Isle Street
Hay Street
Main Street
Main Street
Beach Street
Shotover Street
Rees Street
Cow Lane
Camp Street
Stanley Street
Henry Street
Ballarat Street
Malaghan Street
Halfenstein Street
Arnot St.
The Mall
Police Station
Travel Centre
Church St.
Marine Promenade
Earl Street
Coronation Drive
Sydney
Melbourne Street
Stanley Street
Frankton Road
Brisbane Street
Hobart St.
Airport
Park Street
Peninsula Street
Queenstown Gardens
Frankton Arm
Steamer Wharf
Queenstown Bay
Lake Wakatipu

0,1 mi
200 m
©BAEDEKER

Where to stay
① Brown's Botique Hotel
② Eichardt's
③ Heartland Hotel

Where to eat
① Roaring Meg's
② The Bath House
③ Fishbone Grill & Bar
④ VKnow
⑤ Ferburger

house. Carry on walking beneath magnificent old trees towards Camp Street and **St Peter's Anglican Church** (1932), which looks a lot older than it really is. **Church Street** leads to the shores of the lake. Passing the **Lake Lodge of St Ophir** (1873), the walk leads to the Queenstown Gardens (see above). On the way back, at the end of the pedestrian zone, **the Mall**, look out for **Eichardt's Tavern**, which has been in business since 1871 and recently underwent a deluxe renovation. At the jetty, trout and eels, which normally live wild in the lake, can be observed being fed at the **Underwater World**. The veteran **steamer Earnslaw** docks at »Steamer Wharf«. The lakeshore esplanade leads to **St Omer Park** south of the jetty, which commands fine views of the lake and the centre of Queenstown. In the northwest of Queenstown, near the valley station of the **Skyline Gondola**, a few kiwi birds can be observed in a darkened enclosure of the **Kiwi Birdlife Park**.

❶ Kiwi Birdlife Park: Nov. – Mar. 9am – 6pm, otherwise less, admission: NZ$ 43, http://kiwibird.co.nz

The view from Bob's Peak over the tourist town Queenstown and Lake Wakatipu is wonderful.

Framed by high peaks, the z-shaped lake at Queenstown has a surface area of 293 sq km/113 sq miles, is approx. 80km/50 miles long, at its broadest point barely 5km/3.1 miles wide, and reaches a depth of up to 378m/1,240ft. Its water level rises and falls about 12cm/5in regularly. The lake was formed during the last ice age, 15,000 years ago, through massive glacial movement. The first Europeans arrived at Lake Wakatipu in 1853, and a few years later the lake was explored in its entirety. The Otago **gold rush** of the 1860s brought countless gold prospectors into the area. At the time, around three dozen passenger ferries in all operated on the lake.

*Lake Wakatipu

The **Skyline Gondola** takes visitors up to Bob's Peak (446m/1,463ft),

MARCO ⊕ POLO TIP

Steamboat, or steam train!   Insider Tip

A special tourist attraction plying Lake Wakatipu is the Earnslaw, a steamer built in 1912. The steam theme continues in the shape of the Kingston Flyer vintage steam train running at certain times between the settlement of Kingston, at the southeastern end of Lake Wakatipu, and the village of Fairlight. Information on these two steam-powered options can be picked up from the Visitor Centre.

with its **fantastic views** (see also page 405) of Queenstown lying below, Lake Wakatipu stretching out next to it, and the striking peaks of the Remarkables visible on the opposite side.

❶ Daily from 9am, tickets from NZ$ 30, www.skyline.co.nz

*Remarkab-
les

The beautiful mountain scenery of the Remarkables, rising up to 2,300m/7,546ft high, can be accessed by several hiking tracks, which have varying degrees of difficulty.

*Skippers
Canyon

The fearless might consider a drive in a converted bus through the wild Skippers Canyon, some 20km/12.5 miles long and quite forbidding in parts. Be warned though – anyone attempting this somewhat treacherous and hazardous route in their hire cars will be driving **without insurance**. Four-wheel-drive and jet boat tours of the canyon are available too.

Arrowtown is a living reminder of the wild times of the gold rush

Scenic flights over the alpine mountain landscape of the Southern Alps and Fiordland National Park (or Milford Sound) leave from the Queenstown airfield.

Scenic flights

❶ Flights by appt. from NZ$ 235 per person, tel. 03 4 4230 34, www.helicopter.co.nz

WHAT TO SEE IN THE SURROUNDING AREA

Just 20km/12.5 miles northeast of Queenstown, the **former gold prospectors settlement** of Arrowtown lies in the valley of the Arrow River at the feet of the Crown Range. Thanks to its captivating scenic position, the town has now become a **focal point for tourism**. Gold was first discovered here in 1862, but a year later gold mining operations suffered a serious setback when a number of gold prospectors perished in a devastating flood. In more recent times, many **old miners' houses** have been restored. The building erected for the Bank of New Zealand in 1875 today houses a branch of the **Lakes District Centennial Museum**, telling the story of the area surrounding Wakatipu Lake. The displays on gold mining are very informative (opening times: daily 9am–5pm). Down at the Arrow River, visitors can hire pans and try their luck **panning for gold**. One unusual feature is the **Chinatown** on the western edge of the settlement. In the late 1860s, numerous workers from South East Asia came here to hunt for gold in the deep gorges of Arrow River and Shotover River. Whilst the Chinese were very frugal and hard-working, there was frequent friction with their white neighbours, forcing the Chinese to settle outside the town. Their small stone cottages and mud brick huts have now been restored, as has the Chinese shop at Bush Creek.

*Arrowtown

Lake District Centennial Museum: daily 8.30am – 5pm, admission: NZ$ 8, www.museumqueenstown.com

ACTIVE HOLIDAYS IN THE QUEENSTOWN AREA

Queenstown's tourist information offers a great variety of tourist activities, ranging from **guided tours** to adrenaline-fuelled **bungee jumping**.

To this day, the gorge of **Shotover River** is considered the epitome of modern **adventure tourism**. Daredevil jet boat pilots fight the strong currents, while wildwater enthusiasts can hurtle down the river in a kayak or inflatable dinghy. Travellers can also zip around the **Kawarau River** on board a jet boat or take part in an exciting rafting tour.

*Whitewater adventure

*Bungee jumping on the Kawarau River	The old Kawarau Bridge offers adventure-seeking tourists from all over the world a special experience: an adrenaline-fuelled **jump into the gorge** of the creek, with an elastic bungee band slung around their ankles (▶MARCO POLO Insight p. 138).
Paragliding, ballooning etc.	For yet more thrills, book a place for the tandem skydiving, paragliding or ballooning. A trip in a hot-air balloon also provides **unforgettable impressions** of the beautiful landscape around Queenstown.
*Winter sports areas	Queenstown is probably New Zealand's **most-visited winter sports destination**. The season lasts from June to September or October. **Coronet Peak**, 15km/9 miles further north and rising up to 1,650m/5,413ft, is equipped with lifts and snow cannons. Just as easily accessible are the ski areas high up in the famous **Remarkable Mountains**. Access is via Highway 6 (in the direction of Kingston) and Tollgate (10km/just over 6 miles east of Queenstown). From there, it is another 14km/8.5 miles uphill to the ski stations. A shuttle bus operates here.
Highland horseback rides	**Western-style horseback rides** into the Queenstown highlands are becoming increasingly popular. Amongst the trips on offer are exciting rides to remote farms and abandoned goldfields.
Short hikes	The fantastic mountain scenery around Wakatipu Lake can be explored on a number of **hiking trails with great views**: to One Mile Creek, Queenstown Hill, Sunshine Bay, Frankton Arm, Lake Sylvan, and on to the summits of Ben Lomond and Big Hill.
**Routeburn Track	This trail leads from the valley of the Dart River across Harris Saddle to the Te Anau–Milford road, crossing the **sublime Fiordland mountain scenery**. With a little luck you can see an alpine kea parrot. While the route is only 32km/19mi long it is quite a challenge – the highest point of the trail is Harris Saddle at 1255m/753ft above sea level. Completing the Routeburn Track (closed in winter) requires three to four days. Tip: this hike may be combined with the **Milford, Greenstone or Caples Track**.
Greenstone – Caples Track	This **circular track** (hiking time approx. 4 days) leads through the valleys of the Greenstone River and Caples River, both flowing into Wakatipu Lake. The best starting point for the trail is Elfin Bay on the western shore of Lake Wakatipu.
Rees – Dart Track	This hiking trail, exploring the valleys of the **Rees and Dart rivers** and also conquering the 1,447m/4,747-ft **Mount Cunningham** Saddle, requires four days. The best starting point is at Paradise to the north of Lake Wakatipu or at the Invincible Mine.

✳ Stewart Island

✦ Rh 137/138

Region: Southland
Surface area: 1,746 sq km/674ft
Altitude: 0 – 978m/3,208ft
Population: 400

Visitors to Stewart Island, around 30km/18.5 miles off the southern coast of New Zealand's South Island can enjoy tranquility, a surprisingly mild climate and dreamy sunsets. Its multitude of bays gives Stewart Island a heavily indented aspect. Fairly mountainous and densely forested, the main island is surrounded by a plethora of small islands.

Mystical evening atmosphere on Stewart Island

Stewart Island

INFORMATION
Rakiura National Park Visitor Centre
Main Road, Halfmoon Bay
Stewart Island
Tel. 03 219 0002
www.doc.govt.nz

WHERE TO STAY
❶ Glendaruel B & B £££
38 Golden Bay
Tel. 03 219 1092

www.glendaruel.co.nz
This very cosy little hotel in a wonderfully scenic location commands great views of the Paterson Inlet.

❷ South Sea Hotel £
Elgin Terrace, Halfmoon Bay
Tel. 03 219 1059
Traditional hotel also popular with backpackers, with a restaurant serving up wonderful fish dishes

Getting there The **ferry** crossing from Bluff to Halfmoon Bay, the only real settlement on Stewart Island, takes approx. 1 hour. In the main travel season (December and January), the ferry runs daily. **Day trips aboard small planes are also available**, starting from ▶Invercargill.
ℹ NZ$ 75 one way, tel. 03 2 12 76 60, www.stewartisland.co.nz

Halfmoon Bay Stewart Bay's transport, logistical and **tourist centre** is Halfmoon Bay (Oban). This is also the only place to find accommodation (hotel, lodge, motel, hostel, and camping park with rental caravans), all of which fill up quickly in the high season, making early booking essential.

*Peaceful island paradise Total peace and tranquillity, a surprisingly mild climate and some **dream sunsets** are on offer 30km/18.5 miles from the southern coast of New Zealand's South Island. Cut off from the main island by the Foveaux Strait, this islet looks like a frayed triangle from the air. Stewart Island may only occupy a surface area of 1,746 sq km/674 sq miles, but its **coastline extends for over 1,600km/994 miles**. Its highest elevations are **Mount Anglem** (978m/3,208ft) to the north, together with **Mount Rakeahua** (676m/2,217ft) and **Mount Allen** (749m/2,457ft) in the centre of the island.

Nature reserve Stewart Island provides a sanctuary for numerous endangered animal species (the kiwi bird amongst them), which is why large areas now enjoy protected status or are designated as a **national park**. A warm ocean current in the west creates a surprisingly **mild climate** considering the latitude, with the relatively high mountains also protecting the island from the worst of the stormy winds.

Stewart Island

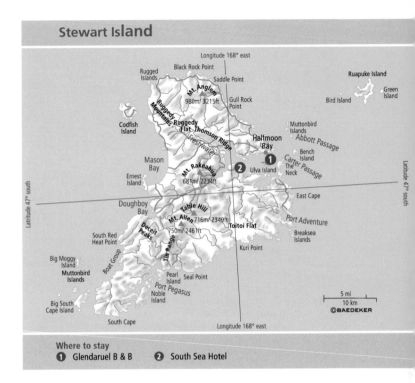

Where to stay
1 Glendaruel B & B   2 South Sea Hotel

The main sources of income here are fishing (cod and lobster in par- | **Economy**
ticular), aquaculture and tourism.

WHAT TO SEE ON STEWART ISLAND

The Rakiura Museum on the beach of Halfmoon Bay (Oban) gives | **Rakiura**
insights into the flora and fauna of the island and looks at the history | **Museum**
of seal hunting and whaling.

Lewis Acker, an American-born **whaler** whose house, constructed | **Acker House**
from stone, clay and shells, is still standing south of Halfmoon Bay,
lost his estate to the government. Acker's Point boasts the island's
only lighthouse.

The island offers unhurried hikes, with huts available for overnight- | **Hikes, boat**
ing. In the summertime, **guided tours** are available too. Pleasant | **trips**

boat trips lead to **Port Adventure Bay** in the east and to the beaches of the **Paterson Inlet** estuary, which reaches far into the island's interior.

✱ Timaru

✦ Sb 135

Region: Canterbury
Altitude: 0 – 96m/315ft
Population: 28,000

The east coast town on the southern edge of the extensive Canterbury Plains lies in a protected harbour bay. In 1859, British immigrants landed here and founded a European-style town. Victorian and Edwardian architecture characterise the city's appearance. Today, Timaru is a significant point of export (for frozen meat in particular) and provides an important economic and administrative centre for a large catchment area.

Timaru – a sporting town

Timaru has bred some **world-famous athletes**, amongst them boxer Bob »Ruby Robert« Fitzsimmons (1863–1917), who won the first of his three world championship titles back in 1891. World record-breaking runner John E Lovelock, who won Olympic gold in the 1,500m at the 1936 games in Berlin, also came from Timaru. And on four legs, one of the most famous racehorses in the history of sport, »Phar Lap«, was raised in Timaru and went on to win many big races on different continents in the 1920s and 1930s.

WHAT TO SEE IN TIMARU

*Caroline Bay, Maori Park

Where is the best place to meet in Timaru? In Caroline Bay of course, not far from the city centre, with its well-kept parks, a beautiful beach and **wide array of entertainment and leisure activities**. In the

Timaru

INFORMATION
Visitor Information Centre
2 George St, Timaru
Tel. 03 687 99 97
www.southisland.org.nz

EVENTS
Every year from 26 December (Boxing Day) onwards, Caroline Bay celebrates the »Timaru Christmas Carnival«, a popular fair that lasts just under two weeks and is unequalled for miles around.

warm season in particular, things get very busy here. Extending to the north of Caroline Bay, Maori Park features an eye-catching wooden **lighthouse** erected back in 1877.

This modern octagonal building on Perth Street gives a good insight into the natural and cultural history of the Timaru area. It honours the inventor and **pioneer of flight Richard William Pearse** (1877–1933), who completed several successful flights aboard home-made contraptions in the years 1902/1903

*South Canterbury Museum

❶ Tue – Fri 10am – 4.30pm, Sat, Sun 1.30pm – 4.30pm), admission: donation requested, https://museum.timaru.govt.nz/

The church next to the museum was built in 1886 in the Early English Gothic style, using local »**bluestone**«.

St Mary's Anglican Church

The Catholic basilica on Craigie Avenue, with its two towers and **copper-roofed dome** was completed in 1911, following designs by the renowned (at least in New Zealand) architect W F Petre.

Basilica of the Sacred Heart

The exhibition on Waiiti Road, which also shows some fine work by **New Zealand artists** is housed in an elegant building dating from 1905. There is also a sculpture garden. The name of the gallery (pronounced like »egg and tie«) comes from Gaelic and means »at home«.

Aigantighe Art Gallery

❶ Tue – Fri 10am – 4pm, Sat, Sun 12pm – 4pm, free admission

The name of the industrial area, extending to the north of the town, hints at its previous existence as a **place for washing sheep** before shearing. By appointment arranged through the Visitor Centre, some operations can be visited, including a brewery, a mill and a textile factory.

> **?** | *Protected place*
>
> MARCO ⊕ POLO INSIGHT
>
> The Maori place name »Te Maruin« means something along the lines of »protected place«. This name points to the fact that there was a settlement here before the arrival of the first European whalers in the 18th century.

AROUND TIMARU

With a population of just 130, the village of Cave, situated some 35km/22 miles west of Timaru on Highway 8, emerged in the 19th century as the **outpost of a huge sheep-shearing operation**. A gem, to be found approx. 2km/1.2 miles outside the village on a hill, is **St David's Presbyterian Memorial Church**, built to honour the pioneers of Mackenzie Country. The church, with its crenellated tower, was erected in the Norman style.

Cave

*Maori rock art In both the immediate and more distant surroundings of Timaru, rock paintings in **caves and on overhanging rocks** are evidence of the fact that this landscape was settled very early by the Maori or their predecessors. The most impressive paintings can be seen at **Dog Rock**, not far east of the town, and at Craigmore, approx. 30km/18.5 miles southwest of Cave.

Around Geraldine The agricultural centre of **Geraldine** (pop 2,000) lies some 35km/22 miles north of Timaru between the plains and the hill country. Early white settlers planted European trees here. In **Pleasant Valley**, running 17km/10.5 miles west of Geraldine, look out for St Anne's Anglican Church (1862), South Canterbury's **oldest church**. The old buildings belonging to **Orari Gorge Farm**, founded in the mid-19th century some 16km/10 miles northwest of Geraldine, are listed. Two wild and romantic places near Geraldine are **Waihi Gorge** (13km/8 miles northwest), and **Te Moana Gorge** (19km/12 miles west).

Extending a good 23km/14 miles north of Geraldine, **M Peel Forest Park** is a near- **primeval forest area** with romantic waterfalls and picnic spots. The old buildings of **Mount Peel Station** nearby belong to a sheep farm founded in the 1860s.

> **MARCO POLO TIP**
>
> *Fancy a local brew?* **Insider Tip**
>
> Then this is the place to visit! The DB Mainland Brewery on Timaru's Sheffield Street offers guided tours (Mon to Fri at 1pm on appt., admission: NZ$ 20, tel. 03 6 87 42 30). The brewery counts among the oldest in New Zealand and combines modern technology with traditional know-how.

Waimate Just under 50km/31 miles south of Timaru, the town of Waimate (pop 3,000) is an important focal point for this area dominated by agriculture. The main attraction is the listed »Te Waimate Station« **sheep farm**. The farm's first buildings were erected in 1854 from the wood of a single totara tree. Also look out for **St Augustine's Anglican Church**, built in 1872 from roughly cut wood and sporting a conspicuous spire above the crossing. The old courthouse of 1879 houses an interesting local history **museum**. **Seddon Square**, the well-kept village square, honours the farmer Michael Studholme, Maori chief Huruhuru and Dr Margaret Cruickshank, **New Zealand's first female doctor**. The latter attended to her local patients here until 1918. The summit of **Mount John**, 446 m/1,463-ft rising in the nearby Hunters Hills, commands a memorable view, capturing the vastness of the **Canterbury Plains**.

ℹ Tue – Fri 1pm – 4pm, Sat, Sun 1pm – 3pm

Just under 80km/50 miles north of Timaru, Ashburton town lies at the river of the same name amidst the Canterbury Plains, which are known as the **»granary of New Zealand«**. In this area archaeologists have discovered remains of hunting camps used by the ancient nomadic Archaic Maori. Some overhanging rocks still bear simple **rock paintings**. Today's town of Ashburton grew up around a river crossing that was very important for coach transport. In 1858, a **roadhouse** was set up as a stop-over point for the coachmen. It was only twenty years later that artificial irrigation of the naturally dry land started. Trees were planted and fields laid out. One of the first successes of artificial irrigation in Ashburton is **Domain Park**: the area where trees now provide shade was in centuries past covered in steppe vegetation. A few 19th-century **brick buildings**, as well as **five churches** are still standing.

Ashburton

Just under 50km/31 miles north of Ashburton, Rakaia Gorge attracts many day trippers, particularly in the summer months. In the winter, the **ski runs** at **Mount Hutt**, rising up approx. 50km/31 miles north-west, lure winter sports enthusiasts from all over New Zealand.

Rakaia Gorge

✴ **Waitaki River**

✴ Sa–Sb 135

Regions: Otago, Canterbury
Altitude: 0 – 548m/1,797ft

The broad, flowing expanse of the Waitaki, forming the border between the regions of Canterbury and Otago, is fed by the snowfields and glaciers of the Southern Alps. Its main tributaries come from the alpine lakes of Lake Tekapo, Lake Pukaki and Lake Ohau. Together with its numerous tributaries, the Waitaki has a catchment area of nearly 12,000 sq km/4,630 sq miles.

It is only in recent times that two **large-scale hydroelectric projects** have altered both the course of the river and the landscape. On the river's upper reaches at Twizel, the **Upper Waitaki hydroelectricity scheme** has been set up, whilst the central reaches boast three major hydroelectric stations: Benmore, Aviemore and Waitaki. Today, the Waikati valley is a **chain of lakes**. The water of the reservoirs is also used for various agricultural and horticultural irrigation projects in the dry plain on the lower reaches of the river.

Energy provider and life giver

The former **construction workers camp** of Twizel (pop 1,000), founded as part of the »Upper Waitaki Power Development Scheme«

Twizel

Waitaki River

INFORMATION
Dunedin Visitor Centre
20 Princess Street
Tel. 03 474 3000
www.visitedunedin.co.nz

WHERE TO STAY
Lake Tekapo Scenic Resort ££
Lakeside, Highway 8
Tel. 03 680 6808
www.laketekapo.com
Holiday hotel adapted to special needs
and set amidst magnificent alpine scenery

in Mackenzie Country, lies only a few miles south of ▶Lake Pukaki. Even after the completion of the dams and power stations, the little town has carried on expanding. Today, Twizel is one of the focal points of the new holiday and leisure landscape of **Mackenzie Hydro Lakes**, which came into being as a kind of side product of the dam being built. On many of the chain of natural and artificial lakes, visitors may **fish, paddle, or hire boats**. Today, there are also some nice picnic areas and various accommodation options. A relatively new addition are the **winter sports stations** for skiers and snowboarders. Thus, the landscape around the newly created Mackenzie Hydro Lakes has now developed into an **all-year-round holiday area**.

*Maori rock art
At Takiroa, near Duntroon (on the southern shore of Waitaki Lake), nomadic Maori tribes living here before the arrival of the Europeans left some highly **impressive rock art**, accessible from Highway 83.

*Lake Tekapo
With its milky-turquoise colouring and covering 88 sq km/34 sq miles, the largest of the three lakes created by **Ice Age glaciers** in the Mackenzie Highlands extends some 50km/31 miles northeast of Twizel in front of the summits of the Southern Alps, framed by **treeless, tussock-covered slopes**. At its southern point, a dam was constructed back in 1954 to regulate the water level of the lake, usually maintained between 704m/2,310ft and 710m/2,329ft. Three years earlier, »Tekapo A« was built here as the country's **first hydroelectric power plant**. In 1977, the 25km/15.5-mile canal from Lake Pukaki to Lake Tekapo was built and its waters used to power the Tekapo B power plant, built in the same year. Counting 400 inhabitants, the village of Tekapo, south of the eponymous lake, is famous for its **Church of the Good Shepherd**, built in 1935 for the many shepherds on the vast sheep pastures of Mackenzie Country. At the church, look out for a **bronze sculpture of a sheepdog**, created by the wife of a shepherd.

One of the most popular lakes on New Zealand's South Island:
picturesque Lake Tekapo

A good 16km/10 miles south of Tekapo, Highway 8 leads to the
»Irishman Creek« farm, the former residence of William Hamilton (
▶Famous People), the **inventor of the jet boat**. Today, a small mu-
seum honours his memory.

Irishman
Creek

Above Lake Tekapo to the southeast, the 671m/2,201-ft Burke Pass
(Hwy 8) leads from Mackenzie Country across to **Fairlie**. The crossing is named after **Michael John Burke**, who explored the area in
1855.

Burke Pass

Also a **milky turquoise-blue** in colour, Lake Pukaki lies some
13km/8 miles north of Twizel. Covering 81 sq km/31 sq miles, this is
the second largest of the former glacier lakes in the Canterbury Region. To the north, the powerful **Tasman River**, fed by large glaciers,
empties itself into the lake, which lies 500m/1,640ft above sea level.
Incidentally, the Pukaki Dam and Pukaki Canal were built in the late
1970s to link into the hydroelectric power project on the upper
reaches of the Waitaki River. **Pukaki High Dam** was erected at the
southern end of Lake Pukaki in order to regulate water levels. High-

Lake Pukaki

way 8 runs along its crown and the hydroelectric power plant is situated at the mouth of the Tekapo Canal. Another canal connects Lake Pukaki with **Lake Ohau**.

Coloured by rock flour
Lake Pukaki owes its milky blue colour to so-called rock flour. This rock sediment was rubbed off by glaciers and flushed by the Tasman River into the lake.

*Lake Ohau
Some 30km/18.5 miles west of Twizel, the road reaches a scenic gem: Lake Ohau, which is fed by the Hopkins and Dobson rivers. It is the smallest of the three lakes in the Mackenzie Basin. On a clear day, the **snow-capped peaks of New Zealand's Alps** are reflected in the 60 sq km/23 sq-mile lake on the border between Canterbury and Otago. A canal connects Lake Ohau with Lake Pukaki and Lake Tekapo. The three Southern Alps lakes are integrated into the hydropower project on the upper reaches of the Waitaki River. In the summer time, Lake Ohau is a **popular destination**, attracting holidaymakers to fish, paddle and camp up here. In the 1950s already **Lake Ohau Lodge** opened on the lake shore with all modern comforts. It is still a popular jumping off point for exploring and other activities in the area around Lake Ohau.

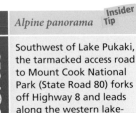

Alpine panorama Insider Tip

MARCO POLO TIP

Southwest of Lake Pukaki, the tarmacked access road to Mount Cook National Park (State Road 80) forks off Highway 8 and leads along the western lakeshore. In favourable weather, there are sublime views of the nature reserve's majestic peaks.

Winter sports
In recent winters, there has been an increase in predominantly younger visitors to Lake Ohau. They are attracted by the **pistes for downhill skiers and snowboarders**, which are prepared (snow permitting) high above the lake on **Mount Sutton**.

West Coast · Westland
✶ Sb 132/133

Region: West Coast
Altitude: 0 – 3,754m/12,316ft

The strip of land stretching out on South Island's rough western coast (up to 50km/31-miles wide) was explored first by seafarer Abel Tasman and then in the 18th century by James Cook (▶Famous People). Its interior boasts dense rainforests and high peaks, explored in the 19th century by Thomas Brunner and later by Julius von Haast, who found extensive coal deposits here.

The name West Coast, or Westland, is today used to designate the **sparsely populated coastal region** between Jackson Bay and Haast River in the south and Karamea in the north. As few as 35,000 people live here, and the number of inhabitants has been in continual decline for years. The most important **central settlements in the region** are ▶Greymouth, ▶Westport and ▶Hokitika. Many places are still pervaded with the pioneering spirit of the **loggers** and **gold prospectors**. To get an idea of the atmosphere of the western coast in the 19th century, head for the reconstructed gold prospectors settlement of **Shantytown** south of ▶Greymouth.

Sparsely populated

When the gold rush had abated, timber and coal became more important factors in the economy. North of Westport, and on the Grey River in particular, **coal mining** flourished for a while. Despite the existence of large deposits, mining operations have been in decline over recent decades, with many abandoned coal pits already overgrown with **lush rainforest vegetation**.

Coal

Empty beaches on the west coast of South Island

West Coast · Westland

**Lowland Rainforest
The high level of precipitation hitting the western coast has fostered the creation of a rainforest which is **unique on the planet**. This lowland rainforest has a **biodiversity** rarely seen anywhere else today. Whilst there are occasional attempts to harness the economic potential of the rainforest by the felling of trees, committed **conservation activists** from all over the globe are fighting against the logging of New Zealand's lowland rainforest.

Fishing and pastoral economy
These days, a fishing industry and pastoral economy have become important **sources of income**. In many places, fisheries and aquacultures (salmon and trout in particular) have been established, but large cattle and sheep farms have also been created. A fairly new addition is the **game farms**, with animals whose meat yields the highest export gains (for example, roe deer and fallow deer) being kept in large enclosures.

Tourism
The **long isolation** of the southern part of the west coast was ended by the opening of the road over the Haast Pass in 1965, which has done much to revive west coast tourism. The new pass meant that visitors were able to explore South Island on a **circular trip** – including the two imposing glacial streams of the ►Fox Glacier and the ►Franz Josef Glacier, both to be found in the area. In 1960, the **Westland Tai Poutini National Park** was established.

** WESTLAND TAI POUTINI NATIONAL PARK

Highlights of South Island
Established back in 1960 and considerably extended in 1982, Westland National Park today covers a surface area of around 1,200 sq

km/460 sq miles, from the western coast at Gillespies and Okarito (**sanctuary for white herons**) up to Mount Tasman, at 3,498m/11,476ft one of the highest summits of the New Zealand Alps.

The main attractions of the national park are the glaciers ►Fox Glacier and ►Franz Josef Glacier (described elsewhere) flowing down from the perpetual ice of the New Zealand Alps to approx. 300m/984ft above sea level, where **evergreen rainforest** with high tree ferns thrives. Together, Westland Tai Poutini National Park and ►Mount Cook National Park form the major »**Te Wahipounamu**« nature reserve. This huge area has been included in **UNESCO's World Natural Heritage list**, primarily for its unique rainforest. On the coast itself, the climate is relatively warm and less humid, with an annual level of 2,500mm/98in of precipitation measured down at sea level. However, the precipitation levels increase with height, rising to 5,000mm/196in per year in the outlying western mountains of the Southern Alps, and to **record amounts** over 7,600mm/300in per year in the high-alpine zone or summit region.

Westland National Park is a moutain hiker's paradise

In Westland National Park, long, frequently heavy **rain or snowfalls** must always be expected; without them of course there would be no snowfields, glaciers or rainforests.

The **main access road** to the national park is State Highway 6, allowing the discovery of all the well-known – and also many lesser known – natural sights.

State Highway 6

The Westland Tai Poutini National Park area has several waymarked hiking **tracks**. Hikers are strongly advised to obtain up-to-date information on the **condition and accessibility** of the trails from the Visitor Centre in Franz Josef (►Franz Josef Glacier) or the tourist village of ►Fox Glacier.

Hikes

✴ **Westport**

✦ Sb 132

Region: West Coast
Altitude: 0 – 55m/180ft
Population: 4,000

Situated at the point where the Buller River flows into the Tasman Sea, the second-largest town on the west coast grew out of a gold prospectors camp set up in the 19th century. The fairly isolated port town owes its economic development to its interior, which is rich in raw materials, huge coal deposits in particular.

Coal port on the north-western coast

The »black gold« continues to be transported from Westport, either abroad by ship or by train to ►Christchurch on the eastern coast of South Island. The area's rich resources of **coal, chalk and clay** have led to the establishment of a large-scale cement production site. Timber processing is another important factor in the local economy.

What to see

In the town centre, with its orderly layout, look out for the old brewery building in Queen Street housing the **Coaltown Museum**, which tells the history of coal mining in simply epic breadth (opening

Cute seals in Tauranga Bay at Westport

times: daily 8.30am–4.30pm). Other places of interest are the time-honoured **St John's Anglican Church** and the stately building housing the **Bank of New South Wales**.

❶ Coaltown Museum: April – Nov. daily 10am – 4pm, Dec. – Mar. daily 9am – 5pm, admission: NZ$ 15, http://buller.co.nz

AROUND WESTPORT

Protruding way out to sea, this rocky cape some 20km/12.5 miles west of Westport bears a **lighthouse visible from afar**. The first European to sail by here was Abel Tasman. He called the cape »Rocky Cape«. But it was James Cook who later gave the cape its name in 1770, having had to fight with adverse winds here.

Cape Foulwind

North of Westport, the »black gold« is still mined today at Waimangaroa and Denniston, at Granity, as well as at Stockton and Ngakawau.

Coal mining areas

The road from Westport to Punakaiki leads to a **gold mine** that was opened as far back as 1866. The 19th-century machines and tools are still used today, lending the place a **museum-like character**.

Mitchell's Gully Goldmine

Scenic hiking trails lead around Cape Foulwind, and also into the old gold and coal mining areas. More information, on the »**Britannia Track**« and »**Denniston Walkway**« in particular, can be picked up from the Visitor Information Centre at Westport.

Hikes

At Westport, the near-170km/105 mile long Buller River flows into Tasman Lake. Named after a director of the New Zealand Company,

Buller River

Westport

INFORMATION
Visitor Information Centre
123 Palmerstson Street Westport
Tel. 03 789 6658
www.westport.org.nz

WHERE TO EAT
The Town House **££**
Cobden Street/ Palmerston Street
Tel 03 7 89 71 33
www.thetownhouse.co

No matter if breakfast, lunch or dinner, here the food is always good and cheap.

WHERE TO STAY
Archer House **££**
75 Queen Street
Tel. 03 7 89 87 78
www.archerhouse.co.nz
The three guestrooms in this 1890 house, which was once owned by a wealthy grocery dealer, are tastefully decorated with antiques.

the **main river on South Island's west coast** flows out of Lake Ro-toiti in ▶Nelson Lakes National Park and runs west through densely forested high mountain country, forcing itself through deep gorges along the way. In the years 1929 and 1968, the Buller River area was shaken by strong seismic shocks, triggering **massive avalanches**.

Howard Junction
Highway 6 follows the winding course of the river to Howard Junc-tion. **Picnic areas** have been set up in a few nice spots. Particularly scenic sections include Upper Buller Gorge and Lower Buller Gorge – Sinclair Castle. Lying in the curve of a valley on the upper reaches of Buller River, the remote **gold prospectors settlement** of Mur-chison was created in the 1860s.

*Seal colony
A particularly popular destination, **Tauranga Bay** offers the oppor-tunity to observe or even photograph, from a suitable distance of course, the very sociable members of a large **colony of seals**.

Reefton
Situated in the valley of the Inanahua River with a current population of around 1,000, the village of **Reefton** became famous through the gold discovered here. Today, the once thriving gold mining centre, some 80km/50 miles southeast of ▶Westport in the mountainous interior of Victoria Forest Park, only serves to supply farmers, forest workers and coal miners. The fact that gold mining used to be paramount here is evi-dent in the place name, »Reef Town«. Around 1866, large quantities of gold were found in the area. The gold-bearing quartz veins were exploited from 1870 right up to the 20th century. When gold extraction stopped, coal mining took over; however, even this is now much reduced. Noteworthy architectural testimo-nies to the time of the gold rush are the **Sacred Heart Church** and **St Stephen's** church (both 1878), the courthouse (1872) and the School of Mines (1886) with its rich collection of minerals. Head out east for 2km/1.2 miles to discover the **Blacks Point Museum**, which does a good job of telling the history of gold mining in the Reefton area. In **Crushington**, 2km/1.2 miles further east, the two monster machines »Wealth of Nations« and »Globe Battery« are a reminder of the time when large quantities of gold-bearing quartz were smashed up here.

? MARCO ⊕ POLO INSIGHT

The Town of Light

The gold rush brought Reef-ton technological innova-tions. Reefton was the first town in the southern hemis-phere with electricity and electric street lights (1888), which is why it was also called »The Town of Light«.

❶ Blacks Point Museum: Oct. – April Wed – Fri, Sun 9am – 12pm, 1pm – 4pm, Sat 1pm – 4pm, admission: NZ$ 5, www.reefton.co.nz

*Victoria Forest Park
In Victoria Forest Park, covering 2,090sq km/807 sq miles north and east of Reefton, some former gold and coal mines may still be discov-

Better living: home on wheels near Reefton

ered. **A word of warning:** the old and often overgrown mines can easily turn into highly dangerous pitfalls. In the heart of the park, some 40km/25 miles south of Reefton, lies the ghost town of **Waiuta**, where gold was extracted until a few years after the Second World War.

PRACTICAL
INFORMATION

The best way to travel to New Zealand and to various attractions there and is explained in this chapter. Also why water flow anti-clockwise out of the bathtub, why shaking hands isn't always good and where the prettiest public restroom in the whole country is, maybe even in the whole world.

In the Antipodes everything is upside down

Of course we don't seriously mean that people in the **Antipodes** (from the Greek = »opposite« and »feet«) are standing on their heads. However, anyone who travels to New Zealand from the opposite side of the globe has to familiarise themselves with the »upside-down« world of the southern hemisphere. For example, if the European and North American experience is to associate the north with cooler weather and the south with warmth, in New Zealand the exact opposite holds true: the further south one travels, the colder it gets, and the further north, the warmer.

The position of the sun

This is to do with the position of the sun, which has its highest point above the equator, or in the corridor between the northern tropic (Tropic of Cancer) and the southern tropic (Tropic of Capricorn). Seen from Europe this lies to the south, but from New Zealand it's to the north. Naturally, the position of the sun has a bearing on the **seasons**: when it is summer in Europe or the US, for instance, it is winter in New Zealand; when in Europe or the US the days are gradually becoming longer, it is autumn in New Zealand, with the days becoming ever shorter. Even letting the water out of the bathtub can be a confusing experience: above the northern hemisphere, the **Coriolis force** makes the water swirl clockwise, whereas in the southern hemisphere the water rotates anti-clockwise.

Arrival · Before the Journey

GETTING THERE

By air

Depending on the route and airline, a flight from Europe or the US to New Zealand can take anything between **12** (for the US West Coast) **to 25** (London) hours. Together with their codeshare partners, several international airlines or alliances offer daily scheduled flights to New Zealand from the world's major airports, either »eastbound« via Hongkong, Bangkok, Singapore, Kuala Lumpur and Sydney, or »westbound« via London, Los Angeles, Vancouver and Honolulu. **Time-saving connections** are available from: Air New Zealand, British Airways, Emirates, Singapore Airlines, Qantas and Lufthansa. New Zealand's **most important international airport** is situated on the edge of the city of Auckland (North Island). Some international airlines also service the airports of Wellington (North Island) and Christ-church (South Island). Travellers are strongly advised to study the prices and routes, as well as the number of changeovers involved, and to start planning early. Given the prospect of spending up to 36 hours aboard a plane, another factor determining

INTERNATIONAL AIRLINES
Air New Zealand
Tel. 0800 128 4149 (UK)
Tel. 1800 551 447 (ROI)
Tel. 1800 262 1234 (US)
Tel. 1800 663 5494 (Canada)
Tel. 0800 557 778 (SA)
Tel. 13 24 76 (Australia)
Tel. 09 357 3000 (New Zealand)
www.airnewzealand.com

British Airways
Tel. 0844 493 0 787 (UK)
Tel. 1890 626 747 (ROI)
Tel. 1-800 247 9297 (US)
Tel. 1-800- AIRWAYS (Canada)
Tel. 011 441 8600 (SA)
Tel. 13 00 767 177 (Australia)
Tel. 09 966 9777 (New Zealand)
www.britishairways.com

Malaysia Airlines
Tel. 0871 423 9090 (UK)
Tel. 01 676 1561 (ROI)
Tel. 1800 552 9264 (US)
Tel. 021 419 8010 (SA)
Tel. 13 26 27 (Australia)
Tel. 0800 777 747 (New Zealand)
www.malaysiaairlines.com

Qantas
Tel. 0845 7 747 767 (UK)
Tel. 01 407 3278 (ROI)
Tel. 1 800 227 4500 (US/Canada)
Tel. 13 13 13 (OZ)
Tel. 011 441 8550 (SA)
Tel. 09 357 89 00 (New Zealand)
www.qantas.com.au

Singapore Airlines
Tel. 0844 800 2380 (UK)
Tel. 167 10 722 (ROI)
Tel. 800 742 3333 (US)
Tel. 1 800 227 4500 (US/Canada)
Tel. 13 10 11 (OZ)
Tel. 021 6 601 (SA)
Tel. 0800 808 909 (New Zealand)
www.singaporeair.com

INTERNATIONAL AIRPORTS
Auckland International Airport
Tel. 0800 AIRPORT or 0800 247 767
www.aucklandairport.co.nz
Location: 24km/15 miles south of the
city centre
Onward transport from the airport: Air-
bus, shuttle bus and taxi to the city centre

Wellington International Airport
Tel. 04 385 51 00
www.wellington-airport.co.nz
Location: 9km/5.5 miles southeast of the
city centre near Lyall Bay
Onward transport from the airport:
Stage Coach Flyer Express Bus, shuttle
bus and taxi to the city centre

Christchurch International Airport
Tel. 03 358 50 29
www.christchurchairport.co.nz
Location: 12km/7.5 miles northwest at
Harewood
Onward transport from the airport: public
bus, shuttle bus and taxi to the city centre

FREIGHT COMPANIES/BROKERS
Cruise People
88 York Street, London, W1
Tel. 020 723 24 50
www.cruisepeople.co.uk

Freighterworld
180 South Lake Avenue, Suite 340
Pasadena, CA, 91101-2655
Tel. 800 531 7774, www.freighterworld.com

Freighter Travel
248 Kennedy Road Napier
Tel. 0064 (0) 6 843 77 02
www.freightertrips.com

New Zealand's major airport is in Auckland

the choice of airline might be the level of comfort on offer. **Prices vary considerably**, depending on the season. Flights are cheapest (as is accommodation) in New Zealand's winter (April to September). In this period a London – Auckland ticket might be available **for under £1,000/$1,500**. In the **main tourist season** (October to March) however, a ticket could cost between €1,200 – €1,800 (US$1,600 – US$2,400 / £1,050 – £1,600, with flights around Christmas and New Year inevitably the most expensive.

Relax on a stopover As a direct flight from just about anywhere to New Zealand can be very tiring, some airlines offer the option of a **stopover** somewhere. In this way, on the journey to or from New Zealand, travellers can take in interesting cities such as Hong Kong or Los Angeles, or add in a relaxing **beach holiday in the South Seas**. In most cases, up to three stopovers are included in the one-way price, with any additional ones incurring an extra fee. Some major airlines offer detailed good-value stopover programmes.

By ship Many of the **cruise liners** operating in the Pacific Ocean also dock at interesting ports in New Zealand, most notably Auckland, Wellington and Wellington. Anyone travelling to Canterbury should disembark in Akaroa, which is only 83km/50mi from Christchurch. For more information, contact any good travel agent. There is also the option to travel to New Zealand aboard a **freighter ship**. They sail from ports such as Hamburg, Antwerp, Rotterdam and Genova in continental Europe, Tilbury in the UK, and Long Beach (California) and New York in the US, to Taurangi, Auckland and Napier in New Zealand. A sea trip such as this lasts about 6 weeks, and the price for the passage is between £1,300/US$2,000 and £3,500/US$5,400.

CUSTOMS REGULATIONS

The Customs regulations for entering New Zealand are constantly being updated, making it essential to get the most **up-to-date information** as close as possible to the date of travel (▶Information, diplomatic and consular representations). The following website is very useful: www.customs.govt.nz. Alongside items of personal use (clothing, cameras, camping gear, etc.), visitors over 17 years of age may import **duty-free**: 200 cigarettes or 250 g tobacco or 50 cigars (or a mixture of these tobacco products with a maximum weight of 250 g, 4.5 l wine or beer and max. 1.125ml of spirits, and presents up to a max. value of NZ$700.

Entering New Zealand

New Zealand has strict **regulations** on importing food, plants, animals and other objects. The following items may not be taken into the country or have to be declared on arrival: straw items, wooden items or carvings, animal skins, certains kinds of **seashells**, oriental medicines, fresh or dried plants, seeds. Moreover, no foods may be brought in, especially not **honey**. Exceptions can be made for baby food (in tins). All kinds of food and **equipment** used for camping, animals or other outdoor activities should be declared in the declaration form that is given to each passenger before arriving in New Zealand.

Strict regulations

Trying to export **plants or animals** without the required permit or the attempt to do such is against the law in New Zealand and **will be punished**. Violations are punished severely; in the case of »first offenders« as well prison sentences of several months are the rule, not rarely combined with a fine of several thousand dollars. The same applies to catching or inappropriate care of animals. This applies not only to **acutely endangered species** but to all that the Department of Conservation has listed as endangered. A list is available online at: doc.govt.nz/about-doc/role/international/endangered-species/cites/cites-species/nz-cites-listed-species/. These include **geckos**, birds (kaka, parakeet) and orchids. Catching animals or trying to take plants of any kind out of New Zealand is strongly advised against. New Zealand's customs officials are very meticulous with their checks and not afraid to issue **heavy fines**.

Insider

MARCO POLO TIP

Don't forget to clean your shoes!

In order to prevent contagions and diseases, the aircraft cabins – with passengers on board – are disinfected, as is the luggage. Shoes and other items must be clean to be allowed to enter the country.

There are currently **no limits on the import or export** of New Zealand or foreign currencies.

Foreign currency

Duty-free shopping	Duty-free shopping is possible in a few shops in Auckland, Wellington and Christchurch, as well as in designated shops at the international **airports**.

Returning to Europe	No duty has to be paid on items for personal use (see above) that were **already brought into New Zealand**, also 200 cigarettes or 100 cigarillos or 50 cigars or 250 g of tobacco, either 1 l of spirits or strong liqueurs over 22 vol. % of alcohol or 2 l of spirits under 22 vol. %, such as sparkling wine or port, furthermore 4 l of still wine and 16 l of beer. Tobacco products and alcoholic beverages only allowed to over 17-year-olds. Other goods and presents are duty-free up to a value totalling £390. For the **European Union**, no duty has to be paid on items for personal use (see above) that were already brought into New Zealand, also 200 cigarettes or 100 cigarillos or 50 cigars or 250 g of tobacco, 1 l of spirits with over 22 vol. % of alcohol or 2 l of spirits under 22 vol. %, 4 l of wine, 16 l of beer. Tobacco products and alcoholic beverages are only allowed to over 17-year-olds. Other goods and presents are duty-free up to a value totalling €415. For the **US**, the following quantities are exempt from duty: 200 cigarettes, a reasonable quantity of smoking tobacco and 100 cigars, plus 1 l of alcoholic beverage. The minimum age for these imports is 21. Souvenirs and presents may be imported duty-free up to a value of US$800. For **Canada**, the following quantities are exempt from duty: 200 cigarettes and 50 cigars and 200 g of tobacco, 1.14 l of liquor or 1.5 l of wine. Souvenirs and presents may be imported duty-free up to a value of CAN$750. For **South Africa**, the following quantities are exempt from duty: 200 cigarettes and 20 cigars and 250 g of tobacco, 2 l of wine and 1 l of other alcoholic beverages, 50 ml of perfumery and 250 ml of eau de toilette. Souvenirs and presents may be imported duty-free up to a value of ZAR3,000.

Personal documents	To enter New Zealand, British citizens and other British **passport** holders with the evidence of the right to live permanently in the UK may be granted a Visitor's Permit valid for 6 months on arrival. British citizens, as well as citizens of the ROI, US, Canada, and South Africa do not need a visa but do need to show a passport valid for at least three months after the return date(or children's passport with passport picture). Upon entering the country, both the **Passenger Arrival Card** and return ticket have to be presented. Often officials will also require proof of sufficient **financial means** (at least NZ$1,000 per person per month) for the duration of the stay in New Zealand.

Apply for visa	Visitors planning to stay for **over three months** must apply to the New Zealand embassy (▶diplomatic representation) in their home country for a visa. For all visa regulations consult the following website: www.nzembassy.com

Beautiful shopping deals: goods for up to £390 can be brought duty free into the UK

An overseas driver's licence can be used for up to 12 months, although if it was not issued in English, drivers must arrange for an **official translation**. The International Driving Licence is only valid in conjunction with a driving licence issued by the home country.

Driver's license

Apart from the aforementioned documents, visitors should also carry their immunization record booklet, telephone numbers of their travel health insurance and accident insurance, and other useful membership cards (e. g. automobile club, youth hostel membership card).

Visitors who lose their passport should immediately notify the police and the diplomatic representation of their home country. It is recommended to carry **photocopies** of these documents, making it much easier to arrange **replacement papers** for lost originals.

Loss of personal documents

Visitors leaving New Zealand by plane currently do not have to pay a departure tax at the airport from which they fly out.

No departure tax

TRAVEL INSURANCE

A hospital stay, or visit to the doctor or dentist, can become very expensive for the patient, as only accidents are covered by free treatment. Taking out a **private overseas health insurance** policy before starting a trip to New Zealand is strongly recommended.

Costs of illness

Beach Holidays

Uncrowded
beaches

New Zealand's beaches are still unspoilt by the concrete beach front-ages of hotels and holiday apartments or the culture of competing towels. Most beach areas are quite isolated and often framed by lush vegetation. There are still many **tranquil bays** which might rarely see two visitors in the same day. New Zealand's sandy beaches have a particularly broad range of col-ouring. In subtropical Northland, light-coloured and limestone sandy beaches dominate; sandy beach-es with a pink to reddish shimmer are typical for the Coromandel Peninsula; and on the west coast of North Island the beaches are pre-dominantly made up of dark sand due to their volcanic origin. **Gold-en-coloured sand** is more characteristic of the pretty beaches on the northern tip of New Zealand's South Island.

Swimming
season, water
temperatures

In New Zealand, the swimming season starts at the end of October and usually ends in early March. On the **beaches** to the north and east of North Island, swimmers can expect water temperatures of 20°C/68F° and above. On South Island's beaches the water is cooler. It is only at Marlborough Sound, Tasman Bay and Golden Bay, as well

Popular swimming beaches

NORTH ISLAND
Bay of Islands
over 150 little islands, mostly green and forested

Bay of Plenty
Good conditions for swimming, surfing and fishing

Hawke's Bay (near Napier)
Fertile fruit and vegetable garden coun-try, bordered to the southwest by Cape Kidnappers, where gannets may be seen close-up

Hot Water Beach and Hahei Beach
On the Coromandel Peninsula, hot ther-mal springs on the beach

Orewa Beach (near Auckland)
Recreation area for Aucklanders

Ninety Mile Beach (on the northern tip)
Over 100km/60 miles of uninterrupted sandy beach

SOUTH ISLAND
In the Abel Tasman National Park
Near Nelson or in the Marlborough Sounds

Banks Peninsula
Peninsula with a very favourable climate and many small bays

Beaches at the Moreaki Boulders
Close by is also the pretty fishing village of Moreaki

Sumner Beach and Taylor's Mistake Beach near Christchurch
Recreation area for Christchurch

as sometimes on the beaches near Christchurch, that visitors can expect **water temperatures** of 18–20 °C/64–68F°.

Nudism is still not really a part of New Zealand culture. There are no official nudist beaches. Even topless (sun)bathing is generally frowned upon.

On most beaches swimmers are left to their own devices, with only a few much-frequented beaches or those close to urban areas having **lifeguards**. A particular annoyance are the **sandflies** whose very painful bites can mar many a late afternoon and evening. Protective clothing and headgear, neck protection, a long-sleeved shirt, flip-flops/bathing shoes, plus sunscreen with a high protection factor, are highly recommended, due to the **strong sun rays** and the ozone hole issue (▶Health). Near larger settlements and industrial facilities, as well as at estuaries, the beaches and water itself may be polluted; it is perhaps better to refrain from swimming in these areas.

Dangers on the beach

Electricity

The New Zealand national grid runs on alternating current with a voltage of 230/240 and a frequency of 50 Hertz. All **UK and European electrical appliances** can run on this – the slightly higher tension unlikely to interfere with them – while visitors from North, Central and South America, plus the Caribbean, will need to bring a transformer. Many hotels provide 110 Volt sockets for electric razors. New Zealand has only three-way flat pinned plugs, so travellers from Europe (outside the UK and ROI) and other countries should bring a **multiple adapter** with flat pins and an option for increased voltage (so-called world travel adapter), or purchase one locally (called a powerplug adapter).

Bring an adapter

Emergencies

Ambulance, fire service, police	**Breakdown assistance**
Tel. 111	0800 AA HELP or 0800 22 43 57
	* 222 (from mobile/cell phone)

Environmental crime, injured animals
Tel. 0800 362 468

Damaged roads and facilities
Tel. 0800 999 005

Etiquette and Customs

Pretty relaxed

Tourists from all over the world praise the legendary **New Zealand hospitality** and helpfulness. Daily etiquette tends to be relaxed and easy-going, which probably harks back to the time of the whalers, lumberjacks, gold prospectors and pioneer settlers.

Greetings with the nose

An increasing number of New Zealanders consider **shaking hands** by way of greeting as superfluous. »Gidday« (Good Day) is the standard greeting; it is getting more and more rare now to hear »Sir« or »Madam«.

The common Maori form of greeting is sometimes perceived as an unusual kind of **»kiss«**. Instead of a handshake or an air-kiss, noses are rubbed together. In the language of the Maori this kind of greeting is called **hongi**.

Solo travellers

Women will face few problems exploring New Zealand on their own. However, there is always a risk if **hitchhiking** is the chosen form of transport.

Photography

Respectful photographers or visitors wanting to film should ask the people they want to capture for their **permission** first. This holds particularly true for taking pictures of local Maori.

Clothing

New Zealanders prefer relaxed clothing , and only a few top gourmet restaurants operate an obligatory tie policy. A **fancy wardrobe** is only required for special occasions.

Health

Medical care

New Zealand's public and private medical provision is of a **high standard**. Even in rural areas, any central settlement will have a doctor's surgery and a pharmacy. All hospitals maintain an emergency service. Larger hotels offer guests who fall ill the services of a contracted doctor. Since not prescription medication might not be available in New Zealand it is recommended that travellers bring enough

required medicines from home. Bear in mind for medication that contains narcotics that the appropriate prescription and the original package should be taken along (customs requirement). In case of illness it is usual to consult a general practitioner, GP first, who will then refer the patient on to a specialist.

New Zealand's **pharmacies** keep normal business hours. All larger settlements will have a 24-hour service on call. Prescription **drugs** require a doctor's prescription. Tourists needing to take a particular medication regularly should carry a prescription which can be confirmed or renewed by a New Zealand doctor, avoiding potential problems entering the country.

Getting medicine

These days, the **thinning ozone layer** above the southern hemisphere offers only limited protection from the sun's UV rays. Extended exposure to the sun is not a good idea, particularly when it's at its highest in the sky between 10am and 3pm. It is recommended to wear a hat with neck flaps, long-sleeved clothing and long trousers. Always apply a sun screen with a **very high solar protection factor** and wear a good pair of sunglasses.

Sun protection, ozone hole

While New Zealand might have no poisonous snakes or dangerous wild animals, other pests can make life difficult, especially the **sandflies**, whose bites result in a bad itch. It is a good idea to keep exposed parts of the body, hands and legs in particular, covered by long sleeves or long trousers. Large clouds of sandflies haunt the humid Westland and Fiordland.

Dangers in nature

Wasps are a nuisance in the northern and central regions of South Island. Travellers allergic to wasp stings should always carry suitable medication or antihistamines.

Many New Zealand inland waters are host to **parasites** of the giardia lamblia variety, spread by animal and human faeces. Usually ingested orally by humans, these result in heavy bouts of diarrhoea which have to be treated with medication.

Lurking in some stagnant bodies of waters, **microorganisms** can enter the human body through the nose or ears and can cause a potentially dangerous strain of meningitis. Visitors swimming in **freshwater lakes and ponds** should keep their heads above water at all times.

Drinking **tap water** is no problem in New Zealand. However, good quality table and mineral waters are available anywhere. **Water from springs**, brooks, rivers and lakes should always be boiled before drinking. The New Zealand health authorities have been warning for a while now of parasites that can occur in an increasing number of bodies of water.

Water

Information

Up-to-date information on individual sights can be picked up from local **tourist offices**. In this guide, their addresses are listed under the individual key words (▶Sights from A to Z). Signs with a green »i« (for information) on a white background point out **Visitor Information Network** offices, which have extensive local information.

TOURIST INFORMATION

Tourism New Zealand Manaakitanga Aotearoa
P.O. Box 91 893
Auckland Mail Centre Auckland
New Zealand
www.newzealand.com

Tourism New Zealand Manaakitanga Aotearoa (USA)
Suite 300
501 Santa Monica Boulevard
Santa Monica, CA 90401
Tel. (0) 310 395 74 80
www.newzealand.com

Tourism New Zealand Manaakitanga Aotearoa (Australia)
Level 12, 61 York Street
Sydney, NSW 1225
Tel. 02 82 99 48 00
www.newzealand.com
Under www.newzealand.com/travel/ International, visitors can find a wealth of information on the country and its people, and may order a free detailed New Zealand travel map.

i-SITE Network

Every tourist spot in New Zealand runs a Visitor Centre, to be found in the i-SITE Network of Tourism New Zealand. The individual addresses can be found under: www.newzealand.com

REPRESENTATIONS

New Zealand High Commission in the UK (also responsible for ROI)
New Zealand High Commission
New Zealand House, Haymarket
London SW1 Y4TQ
Tel. 020 7 839 930 84 22
www.nzembassy.com/uk

New Zealand Embassy in the US
New Zealand Embassy
37 Observatory Circle, NW
Washington DC 20008
Tel. 202 328 48 00
www.nzembassy.com/united-states-of-america

New Zealand High Commission in Canada
New Zealand High Commission Canada
99 Bank Street, Suite 727
Ottawa, Ontario
Tel. 613 238 59 91
www.nzembassy.com/canada

New Zealand High Commission in Australia
New Zealand High Commission
Commonwealth Avenue
Canberra, ACT 2600
Tel. 02 62 70 42 11
www.nzembassy.com/australia

New Zealand High Commission in South Africa
New Zealand High Commission

Pretoria, 125 Middel Street
New Muckleneuk 0181
Tel. 012 435 90 00
www.nzembassy.com/south-africa

British High Commission in New Zealand
British High Commission
44 Hill Steet
Wellington 6011
Tel. 04 924 28 88
http://www.ukinnewzealand.fco.gov.uk

British Consulate General in New Zealand
British Consulate General
Level 17, 151 Queen Street
Auckland 1010
Tel. 09 303 29 73
http://ukinnewzealand.fco.gov.uk/en

Irish Consulate in New Zealand
Consulate of Ireland in New Zealand
6th floor, 18 Shortland Street
Auckland 1001
Tel 09 977 22 52, www.ireland.co.nz

US Embassy in New Zealand
Embassy of the United States of America
29 Fitzherbert Terrace
Thorndon, Wellington
Tel. 04 462 60 00
http://newzealand.usembassy.gov

Canadian High Commission in New Zealand
High Commission of Canada in New Zealand/Haut-Commissariat du Canada en Nouvelle Zélande
Level 11, 125 The Terrace
Wellington 6011
Tel. 04 473 95 77
http://www.canadainternational. gc.ca/new_zealand-nouvelle_ zelande

Australian High Commission in New Zealand
Australian High Commission New Zealand
72-76 Hobson Street
Thorndon, Wellington
Tel. 04 473 64 11, www.australia.org.nz

South African Consulate in New Zealand
South Africa Consulate New Zealand
22 The Anchorage, Whitby
Wellington
Tel. 04 234 80 06

WEBSITES
www.newzealand.com
Official website of the New Zealand tourism organisation

www.doc.govt.nz
Website of the New Zealand department for nature conservation

www.i-site.org.nz
Website of the local New Zealand information points

Language

The national, and most commonly used, language is English. The Maori Language Act (1987) made the Polynesian language spoken by the Maori the country's **second official language**. Not many people

English and Maori

in New Zealand speak foreign languages, despite many schools teaching French, German, Japanese and various others.

New Zealand English   New Zealanders speak a fairly »broad« English, which can be quite easily understood, in contrast to some Australian English. However, there are a few **slang expressions** that cannot be found in any dictionary.

Maori   The Maori language is of Polynesian origin and related to those languages known from Hawaii and Tahiti. Many New Zealand schools have **compulsory basic Maori** classes for all pupils. Official statements are published in both English and Maori. Many localities, such as rivers and mountains, have Maori names. The prefix »wai« for instance, refers to water. As a language, Maori is very **soft and melodious**. Whilst it is a purely phonetical language, with the stress on the first syllable, the vowels, short or long, are pronounced in a similar way to English. The main exception is the long »e«, pronounced as in »fed«, short »o« as in »saw«, long »o« as in »sawn«, and long »u«, pronounced as in »food«. The causative prefix »wh« at the beginning of a word is pronounced »f«, and the stress falls on the third syllable.

Language guide

Colloquial Kiwi English expressions

awesome	breathtaking
beaut	very good, outstanding
billy	tea kettle
bloke	real man, mate
booze	beer, alcohol
buck	dollar bill
bush	forest
coupla	a few drinks
cracker	great guy, great thing
cuppa	cup of tea or coffee
dag	funny guy
dairy	corner store
deli	delicatessen shop
decent	good, nice
different kettle	another thing, story
domain	large public park
facilities	toilets/WC
fair go	chance, to give a chance
to fix one up	to make right, to pay
gidday!	good day, hello

good on ya!	excellent! Well done!
greasies	fish and chips
gumboots	wellington boots/wellies
had it	finished (also broken)
heavy going	tiring, strenuous
jersey	jumper
jug	beer mug, kettle
joker	mate
Kiwi	New Zealander; type of bird; fruit
keen	ambitious, smart
laid back	easy-going, relaxed
licenced	restaurant where alcohol is served
loo	toilet
loopies	tourists
mate	friend, comrade
megabucks	a million dollars or more
metal road	dirt road
my shout	my round
neat	perfect, excellent
no hassle	no problem
no worries	all OK
oncer, one off	unique piece, a one-off event
paddock	open field, pasture
peckish	a bit hungry
petrol	gas
piece of cake	easy
pissed	drunk
pissed off	very angry
to plug into	to join something
pushbike	bicycle
see ya!	see you later! Bye!
she	universal pronoun for more or less anything
she'll be right!	all OK! It'll sort itself out!
sheila	woman
station	sheepfarming operation
stuff like that	something similar
ta!	thanks!
tea	tea, dinner
telly	TV set
track	path, trail, platform
tramping	hiking
tucker	meal
wee	small
wop-wops	back of beyond

Dictionary for drivers

construction	building site
expressways	urban motorways/highways
gas stations	petrol stations
gravel highways	rough gravel track
highway	arterial road
king's highway	arterial road between urban centres
logging roads	roads used for timber transport
maximum 100	speed limit 62 mph/100 kph
ramp speed	speed on the ramp
secondary highway	provincial main road
tertiary roads	often gravel roads
truck	(often articulated) lorry

Maori words

a	of, belonging to
ahi	fire
Ahitereiria	Australia
ao	cloud
Aotearoa	Long white cloud, New Zealand
ara	path, street
ariki	chief, high priest
aroha	charity
ata	shadow
atua	deity, spiritual entity
awa	river, canal, valley
haere mai!	welcome!
haere ra!	farewell!
haka	warrior dance
hau	wind
Hawaiki	mythical home of the Maori
hei-tiki	necklace made from nephrite (greenstone)
hongi	traditional greeting (rubbing noses together)
hua	fruit, egg
ika	fish
iti	small
iwi	tribe
kai	food
kainga	unfortified settlement
karakia	incantations
kia ora!	hello! greeting
kino	bad
ko	ceremonial digging stick for planting

koru	loop pattern
kumarar	sweet potato
ma	white, clear
mana	standing, reputation
manga	tributary
manu	bird
marae	meeting place
mata	brimstone; also foothills
maunga	mountain
mauri	life force
moana	lake
moko	tattoo pattern
muri	end
mutu	finished
noa	common, not subject to »tapu«
nui	large, many
o	of, place of
one	beach, silt
pa	fortified settlement
pae	place of rest, horizon
pakeha	stranger, white (also foreign)
papa	surface with vegetation, meadow
patu	weapon, club
po	night
pounamu	nephrite (New Zealand jade)
puke	hillock
puna	source
rangatira	high-ranking person
rangi	sky
rau	a hundred, many
riki	small, few
roa	long, high
roto	lake
rua	cave
tah	one
tai	sea, coast, tides
tangi	mourning
tapu	divine prohibition, »taboo«
te	the (and many other meanings)
tea	transparent, light, white
Te Papa Atawhai	Department of Conservation
Te Puna Korero Whenua	Department of Survey and Land Information
tiki	first human, gable figure
tipua	demon

tohunga	priest, expert
tuahu	sacred place
umu	earthen oven
utu	vengeance
wai	water
wairua	soul, spirit
wainui	sea, ocean
waka	canoe
waka huia	small treasure chest
whanau	large family
whanga	bay, estuary
whare	house, flat
whare wananga	institution of higher education
whare whakairo	carved meeting house
whata	elevated space, food storage place
whenua	land

Literature and Film

Fiction **Armstrong, Adam:** *Song of the Sound*. Corgi, London, 2002. Wonderfully told novel about the fateful meeting of two people against the backdrop of one of the planet's last paradises

Mansfield, Katherine: *The Garden Party*. Penguin Classics, 2008. This work by the great New Zealand author and one of the founders of the English short story ranks among the classics of 20th century literature.

Coffee-table books **Potton, Craig:** *New Zealand North and South*. Craig Potton Publishing, Nelson, 2007

Apse, Andris: *New Zealand Landscapes*. Andris Apse, Whataroa, Westland.

Films **Niki Caro:** *Whale Rider* (2002) The winner of several awards, this film tells the story of a whale and a little girl on a small East Cape settlement.

Jane Campion: *The Piano* (1996) A 19th-century story of a deaf-mute Scotswoman coming to New Zealand with her daughter to marry a New Zealand man

Lee Tamahori: *Once Were Warriors* (1998) This very moving film about contemporary Maori life is based on the novel *Warriors* by Alan Duff

Peter Jackson: *Lord of the Rings* (2002) ▶Baedeker Special p. 78

Measurements and Weights

Nowadays, New Zealand has **changed** from imperial measurements and weights to the metric system. Temperatures are given in degrees Celsius (°C), liquids are measured in litres (l), hectolitres (hl) and millilitres (ml). Units of weight are the gram (g) and kilogram (kg). Lengths and distances are measured in kilometres (km), metres (m), centimetres (cm) and millimetres (mm). Speed is measured in kilometres per hour (km/h). Whilst New Zealand operates the metric system, many New Zealanders still use the old **Standard Imperial** System.

Metric system

MEASUREMENTS AND WEIGHTS	
Length units	***Liquids and weights***
1 inch (in) = 2.54 cm	1 pint (pt) = 0.568 l
1 foot (ft) = 30.48 cm	1 gallon (gal) = 4.546 l
1 yard (yd) = 91.44 cm	1 ounce (oz) = 28.35 g
1 mile (mi) = 1.61 km	1 pound (lb) = 453.59 g

Media

The main provider of television programmes is »Television New Zealand Ltd«, showing US films and series alongside reports and **documentaries** on New Zealand and its people.

Television

Programmes broadcast by the New Zealand private station »TV 3« as well as the »Sky TV« pay-TV station can also be received. In a few tourist centres, **local TV stations** introduce the sights of the region, accompanied by a lot of advertising.

The state-owned »Radio New Zealand« and »National Radio« broadcast nationally on medium-wave and ultra shortwave. Outside larger settlements however, **reception** is limited to a few medium-wave stations. Alongside those, local private stations sometimes have programmes of interest to tourists.

The programme broadcast by **»Tourist Information FM Radio«** is on air around the clock, with many inter-

MARCO ⊕ POLO INSIGHT   **?**

Radio Programmes

BBC World Service
Bush House, Strand
Tel. (0)20 708 372
Email: asia.pacific@bbc.co.uk,
www.bbc.co.uk/worldservice
Voice of America
330 Independence Avenue
SW Washington DC 20237
Tel. 202 203 49 59
Email: askvoa@voanews.com
www.voanews.com

esting New Zealand topics. The programme also offers a platform to local providers of tourist services, amongst them hotels and restaurants.

Programmes broadcast by the **BBC World Service** can be picked up in New Zealand through local radio stations or online. Radio New Zealand also broadcasts a selection of World Service programmes each week. Check the website, www.bbc.co.uk/worldservice for **current programme schedules** with frequencies. Voice of America also broadcasts on various frequencies (see website) and online.

Money

Currency The unit of currency is the **New Zealand dollar** (1 NZD/NZ$ = 100 cents). In circulation are notes in denominations of NZ$5, NZ$10, NZ$20, NZ$50 and NZ$100, and coins of 1, 2, 5, 10, 20 and 50 cents, as well as NZ$1 and NZ$2. Currently, the **import and export** of national and foreign currencies in the shape of banknotes, coins, travellers cheques or other means of payment is not subject to any restrictions. The arrivals halls of the major airports and seaports have **bureaux de change**. Due to the better rate of exchange, larger amounts should only be changed once in New Zealand. However, it is recommended to get hold of some NZ$ at home, in order to have some New Zealand change on arrival.

MARCO POLO INSIGHT

?

Exchange rates

NZ$1 = £0.45
£1 = NZ$2.20
NZ$1 = €0.59
€1 = NZ$1.67
NZ$1 = US$0.65
US$1 = NZ$1.54

Paying without cash **Credit cards** are an everyday means of payment in New Zealand, with the most common being Mastercard, Visa and American Express. They come in particularly handy for **car rental**, as this usually dispenses with the need for a security cash deposit. Banks, hotels, restaurants and many shops accept **travellers cheques** made out in NZ$. Some banks will also cash in travellers cheques make out in US$.

New Zealand banks have a **network of many branches**, which are usually open Monday to Friday (not on public holidays however) from 9.30am to 4.30pm. There is no shortage of **cash machines** (Automatic Teller Machines, ATM), particularly in commercial

MARCO POLO TIP

!

Lost card? Insider Tip

Before leaving for New Zealand, travellers are advised to make a note of the relevant emergency service number to ring to report immediately any loss of credit or debit card.

streets and centres, allowing travellers to take out money using credit and debit cards with the »Maestro« sign in conjunction with the
personal secret number (PIN). These transactions are **subject to a
charge**, so it is best to find out what terms apply to the relevant card
abroad with the issuing bank before travelling.

National Parks

Covering over 5 million hectares/12.3 million acres, New Zealand's 14
national parks and other nature reserves (forest parks and maritime
parks in particular) occupy around a **third of the country's surface**.
Their diverse scenery ranges from the mangrove coast of the north via
volcanoes in the centre of North Island to the glaciers and fjords of
South Island. The **most important national parks** and other nature
reserves are described in the main section of this guide (▶Sights from
A to Z), which also has the addresses of the visitor centres.

Protected
land

All nature reserves are open to the public. Responsibility for their
management, along with the maintenance of roads and hiking trails,
as well as other tourist facilities, lies with the **Department of Conservation (DoC)**. All national parks have bases or DoC visitor centres with information about the conditions on the ground.

Tourist
facilities

Taranaki Volcano (Mount Egmont) in Taranaki National Park is an
extraordinarily popular are for hiking

National Parks and Walking Areas

National parks

1 Bay of Islands
  Maritime and Historic Park
2 Northland Forest Park
3 Hauraki Gulf Maritime Park
4 Coromandel Forest Park
5 Kaimai-Mamaku Forest Park
6 Pirongia Forest Park
7 Raukumara Forest Park
8 Pureora Forest Park
9 Whirinaki Forest Park

10 Te Urewera National Park
11 Egmont National Park
12 Whanganui National Park
13 Tongariro National Park
14 Kaweka Forest Park
15 Kaimanawa Forest Park
16 Ruahine Forest Park
17 Rimutaka Forest Park
18 Haurangi Forest Park
19 Tararua Forest Park

20 Abel Tasman National Park
21 Marlborough Sounds
   Maritime Park
22 Kahurangi National Park
23 Mount Richmond Forest Park
24 Nelson Lakes National Park
25 Victoria Forest Park
26 Lewis Pass National Reserve
27 Paparoa National Park
28 Hanmer Forest Park
29 Lake Sumner Forest Park
30 Arthur's Pass National Park
31 Craigieburn Forest Park
32 Westland National Park
33 Mount Cook National Park
34 Mount Aspiring National Park
35 Otago Goldfields Park
36 Fiordland National Park
37 Catlins Forest Park
38 Stewart Island

Auckland

NORTH ISLAND
Te Ika a Maui

Wellington

SOUTH ISLAND
Te Waipounamu

Christchurch

Dunedin

©BAEDEKER

**Stewart
Island**

Walking areas

A Lake Waikaremoana
  (Te Urewera National Park)
B Tongariro Northern Circuit
  (Tongariro National Park)
C Abel Tasman Coast Track
  (Abel Tasman National Park)
D Heaphy Track
  (North-West Nelson Forest Park)
E Routeburn Track
  (Mount Aspiring & Fiordland
  National Parks)
F Milford Track
  (Fiordland National Park)
G Kepler Track
  (Fiordland National Park)
H Rakiura Track
  (Stewart Island)

DEPARTMENT OF CONSERVATION
DoC Headquarters
Whare Kaupapa Atawhai /
Conservation House
PO Box 10420
Wellington 6143, NZ
Tel. 04 471 07 26, www.doc.govt.nz

LONGER HIKES
Great Walks Booking Desk
Lake Front Drive, Te Anau, NZ
Tel. 03 249 85 14
www.doc.govt.nz/parks-and-recreation/
tracks-and-walks/great-walks/

The **national parks** offer a variety of activities, ranging from fishing and hunting through kayak, canoeing and mountainbiking to skiing, diving and hiking. However, the activities are strictly regulated at a local level. Visitors planning to go fishing, hunting, canoeing or on longer trekking tours should first contact the local DoC base and apply for the relevant **permit or licence**.

Regulated activities

The hiking trails and tracks maintained by the DoC are laid out in such a way that any potential visitor can get an idea of which track is suitable and which highlights they want to see. When there are **many visitors** (mostly during the main summer travel season), access to particularly popular tracks is limited.

Tracks, walks

The DoC maintains basic campsites and huts (cabins) where visitors can spend the night. **Reservations** can be made through the DoC bases.

Basic accommodation

Some of the attractive natural places have **hotels**, lodges, holiday parks and various leisure facilities such as golf courses, ski lifts, etc. However, the DoC does keep an eye on these commercial facilities, in order to stop them taking over. **Peak-season** visitors planning to stay the night in or near a national park are well advised to book early.

Commercial facilities

Post · Telecommunications

Since New Zealand postal service was **deregulated** letters and postcards can be delivered by various companies with varying reliability. Each of them maintains its own agencies and collection points, issues its own stamps and operates differently marked letterboxes. Visitors sending a letter or postcard should take care to check that the stamps and the letterbox belong to the same company. The post shops and letterboxes of **New Zealand Post** are the most reliable; their red colouring is easily recognizable. Their shops are usually in supermarkets or **stationery shops**, which is practical and convenient.

Postal service

DIALLING CODES
From UK, ROI, US, Canada,
South Africa to New Zealand
0064, followed by the local dialling code
omitting the 0

From New Zealand
to UK: 0044
to ROI: 00353
to US/Canada: 001
followed by the local dialling code
without the 0

Within New Zealand
Auckland/Northland: 09
Coromandel/Bay of Plenty/ Waikato/
Central: 07
East Coast/Taranaki/ Hawkes Bay/
Whanganui: 06

Wellington: 04
South Island: 03

SPECIAL TELEPHONE NUMBERS
Directory Enquiries Domestic
018

Directory Enquiries Overseas
01 72

Local Operator
010

International Operator
01 70

Toll Free Numbers
start with 0800

New Zealand Post Currently, the **postage** rate for a postcard or a standard letter sent worldwide via New Zealand Post stands at NZ$2.50. They usually take 6 to 10 days to arrive. New Zealand Post's **post offices** (or agencies offering postal services) usually operate the following opening hours: Mon – Fri 9am – 5pm, www.nzpost.co.nz.

Poste restante New Zealand Mail post offices keep poste restante mailings for **one month**. If they have not been claimed within that time they are returned to sender. Poste restante items to be sent to New Zealand have to be labelled as follows: name of recipient, c/o General Delivery, Main Post Office, town/city, four-digit post (ZIP) code (if known). Good to know: tourists may also have **post forwarded** to them. Most accommodation providers will also hang on to mail for a while; just ask for **poste restante service**.

Telephone Most public telephones operate with **phonecards** (Cardphones). Coin-operated phones (Payphones) have become rare. Phonecards for NZ$5, NZ$10, NZ$20 and NZ$50 and also rechargeable »Calling Cards« (e. g. »Yabba«, issued by NZ Telecom) are available from newspaper kiosks, petrol stations and in many dairies and **supermarkets**.

Mobile (cell) phones Mobile phones will automatically dial into the appropriate New Zealand provider via roaming. A locally-bought **prepaid card** can be cheaper than one brought in from abroad.

All larger towns and tourist centres have internet cafés, public librar-　Email and
ies and other institutions where visitors can pay a small fee to use an　online
Internet terminal and send and receive emails.　services

Prices and Discounts

Travelling by **train** is particularly good value with the »Best of New　Passes save
Zealand Pass«. Visitors planning one or more **domestic flights**　money
should ask the airlines about **»Air Passes«**. Air New Zealand, Qantas
New Zealand and Origin Pacific offer
particularly cheap air passes, but only in
conjunction with an international flight.

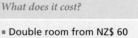

Restaurant prices are similar to those
in western countries. However, visitors
can save money by choosing BYO
(Bring Your Own) restaurants, which allow diners to bring their own drinks
(don't forget to buy them beforehand!).
One of the cheapest accommodation
options is the **backpacker hostels** which can be found all over the
country. Hostels are also a good place to pick up helpful tips for excursions or to find fellow travellers. Most hostels offer laundry facilities, cheap Internet access and sometimes even free tea or coffee.

MARCO⊕POLO INSIGHT	**?** *What does it cost?*
	▪ Double room from NZ$ 60
	▪ 3-course dinner from NZ$ 30
	▪ Simple meal from NZ$ 10
	▪ Cup of coffee from NZ$ 3
	▪ 0.5 l beer from NZ$ 5
	▪ Bus ticket Auckland–Wellington from NZ$ 30

Time

New Zealand lies **near the international date line** and is 12 hours　Regular time
ahead of Greenwich Mean Time (GMT). Time Zones see map p. 456

In New Zealand's cold season, which corresponds to the European　Summer time
and North American warm season (end of March to end of Oct), the
time difference between the UK or Ireland and New Zealand is 11
hours; during New Zealand's summer time (early/mid-Oct to end of
March) it is **13 hours** however.

Toilets

Using the bushes is taboo in New Zealand! In every town, near　Loos with
tourist attractions and even in the great wide open spaces there are　style

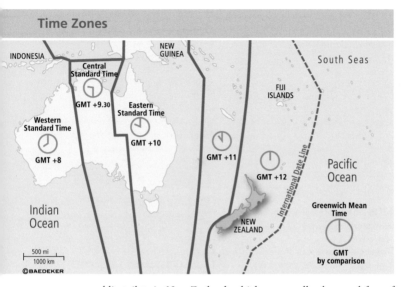

Time Zones

public toilets in New Zealand, which are usually clean and free of charge. They are not always separated into men's and women's areas. New Zealand's **most beautiful restrooms** are on North Island: **Friedensreich Hundertwasser** designed the public loos in Kawaka for his chosen homeland. The men's room in the Skytower in Auckland has urinales with a spectacular view.

Transport

Overland, on water and in the air

Public transport options are only really satisfactory in larger towns and their catchment areas. Longer distances are often covered by **plane**. Travelling by **train** is comfortable enough, but the trains usually only run once a day between two places. The rail network has also been thinned out in recent times. The most important means of public transport is the **overland bus** running between all the major towns and tourist centres. **Ferries** connect the two main islands, as well as serving the smaller offshore islands.

PLANE

Airports and airfields

All of New Zealand's major cities and important tourist centres can usually be reached via Auckland, Wellington or Christchurch. There

DOMESTIC AIRLINES
Air New Zealand
National
Tel. *0800 737 000
www.airnz.co.nz

Qantas New Zealand
Tel. *0800 808 767
www.qantas.com

Sounds Air
Tel. *0800 50 50 05
www.soundsair.com

RAIL INFORMATION
RailNewZealand
Tel. 03 9 68 96 19
www.railnewzealand.com
Regular rail, bus and ferry traffic

KiwiRail
Tel. 04 4 95 07 75
www.kiwirailscenic.co.nz
Tourist rail travel

IMPORTANT RAILWAY
STATIONS
Auckland
Britomart Railway Station
12 Queen Street, City Centre

Wellington
Wellington Railway Station
Bunny Street, City Centre

Christchurch
Christchurch Railway Station
Addington

BUS COMPANIES
InterCity
Tel. 09 5 83 57 80
www.intercitycoach.co.nz

Johnston's Coachlines
Tel. *08 00 66 22 66
www.johnstons.co.nz

Kiwi Experience
Tel. 09 3 36 42 86
www.kiwiexperience.com

Magic Bus
Tel. *08 00 08 20 01
www.magicbus.co.nz

Nakedbus
Tel. 09 00 6 25 33
http://nakedbus.com

Newmans
Coach Lines
Tel. 09 5 83 57 80
www.newmanscoach.co.nz

Tours & Travel
Tel. 03 379 52 11
www.toursandtravel.co.nz

Pacific Tourways
Tel. 03 359 91 33
www.pacifictourways.co.nz

Reesby Coachlines
Tel. 07 347 00 98
www.reesby-buses.co.nz

Thrifty Tours
Tel. 09 3 59 83 80
www.thriftytours.co.nz

FERRY NORTH ISLAND -
SOUTH ISLAND
Interislander
Wellington (North Island) -
Picton (South Island)
Tel. *08 00 80 28 02
www.interislander.co.nz

are regional airports on North Island at Hamilton, Rotorua and Palmerston North, and on South Island at Nelson, **Queenstown** and Dunedin. The following airports are also regularly served: Bay of Islands, Blenheim, Gisborne, Hokitika, Invercargill, Kaitaia, Milford Sound, Motueka, Mount Cook, Napier/Hastings, New Plymouth, Oamaru, **Stewart Island**, Takaka, Taupo, Tauranga, Te Anau, Timaru, Wanaka, Wanganui, Westport, Whakatane and Whangarei.

Discounts on domestic flights

Package tours often include discounted domestic flights. For more information, contact airlines serving New Zealand or any good travel agent. Air New Zealand, Qantas New Zealand and Origin Pacific offer good-value **air passes** (3–8 coupons). However, these are only valid in conjunction with an international ticket. Any passenger of 12 years of age or older has to pay a departure tax. The exact amount varies from airport to airport.

TRAIN

Currently few routes only

Unfortunately, the last two decades have seen a drastic thinning-out of the railway network. These days, passenger trains only do the commuter runs on lucrative routes in more **densely populated areas** such as Auckland and Wellington, while tourist trains only run on three routes of special interest. However, there are **signs of change**. Recently, the railway network passed back into state hands. The government's »Tourism Strategy 2015« is committed to the environment and climate protection, and includes the extension and **modernisation of rail travel**.

Schedules and prices

Detailed timetables and information on fares can be picked up from any railway station or tourist information office, along with most travel agencies. Senior citizens and students, plus holders of youth hostel membership cards, disability badges and specific tourist passes, can benefit from **generous discounts** on travel prices.

BUS

Bus passes

Most New Zealand bus companies offer tourists value-for-money passes with various offers and discounts, to be used during a specific time on a route network or parts thereof. Bus passes that are valid for several weeks on the **entire route network** are very popular. There are even special bus deals for **backpackers** and **bikers**.

Watch out, weekend!

During the week there are few problems in reaching even lesser known destinations by bus, but the timetables are much reduced on Sundays and public holidays. It is a good idea to **book a seat early**, particularly during the main tourist season (Dec–March). **»Nakedbus«** is one of the most interesting budget bus companies. Early bookers can get their tickets here at dumping prices (www.nakedbus.com). They also offer cheap accommodation at your destination (www.nakedsleep.com).

FERRIES

New Zealand's capital of Wellington is connected with the port of Picton on the **northern tip of South Island** by modern, conventional ferries, which run at least twice daily in the off season and up to five times a day in the main summer travel season. The ferry takes around 3.5 hours to negotiate the passage through the Cook Strait, one of the windiest and choppiest waterways in the world. The Lynx **fast ferry**, taking only half that time, runs three times a day. In either case, a timely reservation is strongly recommended.

Wellington–Picton

A regular ferry service is also available between Bluff in the south of South Island and Halfmoon Bay on the southern offshore Stewart Island. **Early booking** is advisable here too, at least in high season.

Bluff–Stewart Island

ROAD TRAFFIC

Following British tradition, cars in New Zealand drive on the left. However, a vehicle coming from the right has the **right of way**! Exercise special caution when making a right-hand turn. Before crossing any road pedestrians are well advised to look first right and then left. Up-to-date information for visitors about varying traffic regulations can be found in the Internet at http://www.nzta.govt.nz/assets/resources/whats-diff-driving-nz/docs/driving-in-nz.pdf.

Driving on the left

Multi-lane **motorway-style highways** are only found in the major conurbations, around Auckland, Wellington and Christchurch in particular. The (usually numbered) **highways** are tarmacked, well kept and signposted, albeit sometimes **rather twisty**. Drivers may still frequently encounter narrow bridges that can only be crossed **one car at a time, taking it in turns**.

Roads

One Lane Bridge

There are also still bridges that are used by both road traffic and the railway. In these situations the train always has the right of way!

On **South Island** in particular, drivers have to contend with sheep unexpectedly running onto the road. Careful driving is advisable here. Anyone injuring an animal by reckless driving can expect serious problems.

Sheep

Traffic Signs

Parking

Parking signs
apply Mon to Sat, 8am to 6pm

No parking

Warning Signs

Falling rocks

Building work

Detour

Danger of skidding

General
danger sign

Right lane
closed

End of asphalt
surface

School bus

Bends ahead

Railway crossing

Road narrows

Dip in road

Pedestrian crossing

Side winds, gusts

Roundabout

Bend

Instructions

Give way

Bottleneck!
Other direction has priority

Limited Speed Zone
(50 km/h when road is bad,
otherwise 100 km/h)

So far, the **volume of traffic** in New Zealand is perfectly manageable outside major towns and cities. Only in the larger urban areas, particularly Auckland and Wellington, but also Dunedin and Christ-church, has the phenomenon of the »rush hour« entered local parlance.

Traffic density

Road signs in New Zealand conform to international standards. Distances are given in **kilometres (km)** and speeds in km/h.

Road signs

In any car, putting on a **seatbelt** is compulsory. **Helmets** are required for cyclists as well as motorcyclists, and infractions can incur **heavy fines**. The current is 80mg of alcohol per 100ml of blood, for drivers under 20 years old it is 0mg.

Drink-drive limit

Signs and yellow markings to that effect should be heeded. Parking infringements can incur **stiff fines** and tow-away fees.

No parking!

A flashing red light and **wailing siren** announce police in action. If the police want to stop a driver their vehicle will **always pull up behind** them.

Police in action

The national driver's licences of English-speaking countries such as the UK, ROI, the US, Canada and South Africa are **recognized** for any stay not exceeding three months. It is a good idea to carry an **International Driving Permit** as well, to avoid potential misunderstandings. See www.nzta.govt.nz for details.

Driver's licence

! *Keep the rules!*   Insider Tip

MARCO ⊕ POLO TIP

Outside built-up areas: 60mph/100kmh. Within built-up areas: 30mph/50 km/h. From 100m/about 330ft before a railway crossing: 18mph/30km/h. While passing a stationary school bus: 12mph/20kmh. Keeping to the limits is advised!

New Zealand uses practically the same fuels for motor vehicles as in Europe. Prices are similar too. Only in more densely populated areas will drivers find a relatively comprehensive network of petrol stations, with plenty also available along the most important overland routes. However, in thinly populated areas there can be problems finding petrol. Therefore it is **best to top up in good time** or carry a full spare can, rather than running the tank down to the last drop. Bear in mind also that many rural petrol stations often **close** between noon on Saturday and Monday morning.

CAR HIRE

Booking a hire car in advance from home costs less than waiting until arrival in New Zealand. Drivers should ensure that the rental price

Important tips

CAR HIRE COMPANIES

Avis
Tel. 08445 810 147 (UK)
www.avis.co.uk
Tel. 021 428 1111 (ROI)
www.avis.ie
Tel. 1-800 331 1212 (US)
Tel. 1-800 879 2847 (toll-free) (CA)
Tel. 011 923 3660 (SA)
Tel. 612 9353 9000 / 136-333 (toll-free) (OZ)
Tel. 09 275 7239 (NZ)
www.avis.com

Mighty Cars & Campers
Tel. *0800 200 80 801 (NZ)
Tel. +800 200 80 801 (from abroad)
www.mightycampers.com

Britz New Zealand
Tel. *0800 831 900 (NZ)
Tel. +800 200 80 801 (from abroad)
www.britz.co.nz

Budget
Tel. *0800 283 438 (NZ)
Tel. +64 95 29 77 84 (from abroad)
www.budget.co.nz

Hertz
Tel. *0800 654 321 (NZ)
www.hertz.com

Maui
Tel. *0800 651 080 (NZ)
Tel. +64 92 55 39 19 (from abroad)
www.maui.co.nz

Wilderness Motorhomes
Tel. 09 2 82 36 06
http://wilderness.co.nz
Motorhome rental,
winner of the »Enviro Gold Award«.

AUTOMOBILE ASSOCIATION CENTRES
Auckland Central
PO Box 5 99 Albert Street
Tel. 09 966 8800

AA HOTLINE
Tel. *0800 500 222 (Road Service)
Tel. *0800 500 543 (Tourism Service)

AA ONLINE
www.aa.co.nz
www.aatravel.co.nz

includes **sufficient insurance cover**. In most cases, third-party insurance and fully comprehensive cover with a certain excess are included. On top of that, there are provincial taxes to be paid. Drivers wanting to drop off the vehicle at a different location are charged a substantial fee for the privilege. Usually, any car rental requires leaving a deposit. Most car rental companies **only accept credit cards**. Drivers have to be 21 years of age to hire a regular car. The minimum age for renting a **camper van** (motor home, RV = recreational vehicle) is 25. Anybody wanting to drive a hire car in New Zealand has to show their national or an internationally accepted driver's licence. The International Driving Permit however is only valid in combination with the national counterpart. Before leaving the compound of the rental car company, drivers should ensure they check the state of the vehicle. Any defects must be reported immediately to the company.

All major car rental companies maintain **toll-free hotlines**. These 0800 numbers can be used for information as well as to make a booking. These days, **online reservations** are equally easy. In New Zealand, the international car rental companies are joined by a large number of **local providers**, with some of them specialising in hiring out campervans and motorhomes, or even motorbikes.

Car rental companies

AUTOMOBILE CLUB

The New Zealand automobile club has branches in **all major towns** and cities. Members of a foreign automobile club (e. g. RAC, AA Ireland, AAA) can take advantage of six months **free membership** in the AA upon showing their membership card, and may pick up **good, free roadmaps** from their offices.

Automobile Association (AA)

TAXI (CAB)

Airports, the centres of all major cities, as well as all the important tourist centres, are served by a good number of taxis , which can also be pre-ordered over the telephone by day or night. However, taxi rides in New Zealand are **not cheap**, and the drivers do expect a generous tip on top of the regular fare. A **people carrier** or minibus (shuttle bus), which can transport a number of passengers plus luggage, can be a good value mode of transport. They run on much frequented routes such as between the airports and the city centres.

No shortage of taxis

Travelling with Disabilities

New Zealand law stipulates that every new and renovated building must have disabled access. Many hotels, motels, restaurants, cinemas, etc., as well as **numerous sights**, are now accessible to disabled visitors. If advised in good time with specifics on the disability, **airlines**, bus companies and other transport companies will do their best to accommodate disabled visitors. However, many **urban buses** are not yet adapted to disabled requirements.

Access to buildings

Travellers with a disability who possess the relevant documentation are entitled to a **special parking permit** for the duration of their stay in New Zealand. Many car parks have designated bays for the disabled. Information on **barrier free accommodation**, transport, organisations and addresses are available from New Zealand Disabilities Resource Centre in a list on www.nzdrc.govt.nz.

Parking permit

Climate

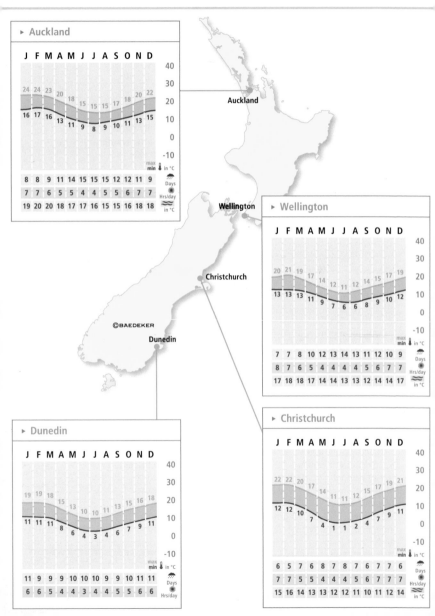

▸ Auckland

	J	F	M	A	M	J	J	A	S	O	N	D	
max	24	24	23	20	18	15	15	15	17	18	20	22	in °C
min	16	17	16	13	11	9	8	9	10	11	13	15	
Days	8	8	9	11	14	15	15	15	12	12	11	9	
Hrs/day	7	7	6	5	5	4	4	5	5	6	7	7	
in °C	19	20	20	18	17	17	16	15	15	16	18	18	

▸ Wellington

	J	F	M	A	M	J	J	A	S	O	N	D	
max	20	21	19	17	14	12	11	12	14	15	17	19	in °C
min	13	13	13	11	9	7	6	6	8	9	10	12	
Days	7	7	8	10	12	13	14	13	11	12	10	9	
Hrs/day	8	7	6	5	4	4	4	4	5	6	7	7	
in °C	17	18	18	17	14	14	13	13	12	14	14	17	

▸ Dunedin

	J	F	M	A	M	J	J	A	S	O	N	D	
max	19	19	18	15	13	10	10	11	13	15	16	18	in °C
min	11	11	11	8	6	4	3	4	6	7	9	11	
Days	11	9	9	9	10	10	10	9	9	10	11	11	
Hrs/day	6	6	5	4	3	4	4	5	5	6	6	6	

▸ Christchurch

	J	F	M	A	M	J	J	A	S	O	N	D	
max	22	22	20	17	14	11	11	12	15	17	19	21	in °C
min	12	12	10	7	4	1	1	2	4	7	9	11	
Days	6	5	7	6	8	7	8	7	6	7	6	7	
Hrs/day	7	7	5	5	4	4	4	5	6	7	7	7	
in °C	15	16	14	13	13	12	12	11	10	11	12	14	

©BAEDEKER

Auckland

Wellington

Christchurch

Dunedin

When to Go

Roughly speaking, North Island extends from the **subtropical** to the warm-moderate climate zone, while South Island stretches from the warm-moderate far into the **cool-moderate** climate zone. Due to the oceanic climate, with no extremes of either heat or cold, any season is suitable for a trip to New Zealand.

Climatic zones

New Zealand's seasons are the opposite to those of the northern hemisphere. Spring lasts from September to November, **summer from December** to February, autumn (fall) from March to May and winter from June to August. **Spring** has fairly pleasant temperatures. Everything is green and in blossom, with wintry conditions only reigning still in the high mountain regions of South Island. Exciting outdoor activities such as hikes and cycle tours are already possible. Alpine tours however are only recommended from mid-October onwards. **Wet-weather gear** and a warm jumper should always be packed, as heavy rainshowers may occur in the daytime, and in the evenings it can get pretty chilly.

Reversed seasons

As in western countries, **summer** in New Zealand is the most popular time to travel and, because of the school holidays, is also the main tourist season. Relatively high temperatures and long daylight hours allow full enjoyment of New Zealands' scenic delights. On North Island, summer is also the season with the **least precipitation**. Even then, travellers should carry rain protection and a warm jacket for cool evenings. In the summer high tourist season, beaches and mountainsides, campsites and mountain huts are very busy, making **early reservations** for accommodation, ferry passages, etc. essential.

Peak season for tourists

Autumn in New Zealand is known for its relatively **settled periods of fine weather**. Conditions allow beautiful hikes up to May, although they could be affected by the **first snow showers** in the mountains. Most high alpine trails are closed as early as mid-April. In terms of clothing, the same applies as in spring.

Beautiful hiking

In high mountain altitudes, New Zealand's **winter** is characterised by surprisingly low temperatures and frequent heavy snow. Places with a winter sports infrastructure have a proper **ski season**. Due to the markedly oceanic climate at lower altitudes, winter here is much milder than in similar parts of Europe or the US, for example. Nonetheless, warm waterproof clothing is still essential.

Index

List of Maps and Illustrations

Photo Credits

Publisher's Information

1st Edition 2017
Worldwide Distribution: Marco Polo
Travel Publishing Ltd
Pinewood, Chineham Business Park
Crockford Lane, Chineham
Basingstoke, Hampshire RG24 8AL,
United Kingdom.

Photos, illlustrations, maps::
167 photos, 40 maps and and illustra-
tions, one large map
Text:
Prof. Dr. Heinrich Lamping, Dr. Gerlinde
Lamping, Dr. Georg Bareth, Dr. Cornelia
Hermanns, Susanne and Martin Hagg,
Nora and Helmut Linde, Andrea Mecke,
Rotraut Schönleber, Claudia Walker,
Reinhard Zakrzewski
Editing:
Barbara Schmidt-Runkel, John Sykes,
Robert Taylor
Translation: David Andersen, Barbara
Schmidt-Runkel, John Sykes, Robert
Taylor
Cartography:
Christoph Gallus, Hohberg;
MAIRDUMONT Ostfildern (large map)
3D illustrations:
jangled nerves, Stuttgart
Infographics:
Golden Section Graphics GmbH, Berlin
Design:
independent Medien-Design, Munich

Editor-in-chief:
Rainer Eisenschmid, Mairdumont
Ostfildern

Printed in China

Despite all of our authors' thorough
research, errors can creep in. The pub-
lishers do not accept any liability for thi
Whether you want to praise, alert us to
errors or give us a personal tip Please
contact us by email or post:

MARCO POLO Travel Publishing Ltd
Pinewood, Chineham Business Park
Crockford Lane, Chineham
Basingstoke, Hampshire RG24 8AL
United Kingdom
Email: sales@marcopolouk.com

FSC
www.fsc.org
MIX
Paper from
responsible sources
FSC® C011918

MARCO POLO

HANDBOOKS

www.marco-polo.com

New Zealand Curious Facts

Happy Feet: The island nation helps lost penguins, turns WCs into works of art and even has a special day just for flip-flops.

►Shrek the sheep
New Zealand's most famous sheep was named Shrek. In 1998 it ran away from its herd and lived alone in a cave for years. When it was found in 2004 its wool weighed five times more than that of a sheep that is sheared regularly. Shrek then had a one-of-a-kind media career and lived to the ripe old sheep age of 17 years.

►What style!
In Kawakawa there is a public WC that was personally designed by the artist Friedensreich Hundertwasser. It can even be used!

►Hip and no flop!
Already in the 1950s, long before they flip-flops from Asia conquered the world, they were »in« in New Zealand. They were called jandals, short for Japanese sandals. They are celebrated on December 2, which is National Jandal Day.

►Clever keas
For a long time crows were considered to be the most intelligent birds. But in 2011 biologists at the University of Vienna found out that New Zealand keas were capable of the same feats as crows.

►Better than brakes!
Baldwin Street in Dunedin is considered to be the world's steepest street. Since asphalt would be too slippery it is paved with concrete slabs. Don't forget to use the handbrake if you park here.

►Do as the locals do!
Taumatawhakatangihangakoauauotamateaturipukakapikimaungahoronukupokaiwhenuakitanatahu is the Maori name of a hill south of Waipukurau in Hawke's Bay. With 85 letters it is the second longest place name in the world. Incidentally, the locals just call it »Taumata«.

►Happy ending for Happy Feet?
In 2011 an emperor penguin found its way to the beach at Peka Peka. After a detour of 3,000km/1,800mi veterinarians fed the exhausted resident of the Antarctic and released it at sea with a tracking device. The tracker was lost but hopefully Happy Feet found its way back home.